Blood on the Tracks

volume 4

Shuzo Oshimi

CHAPTER 25 Limit

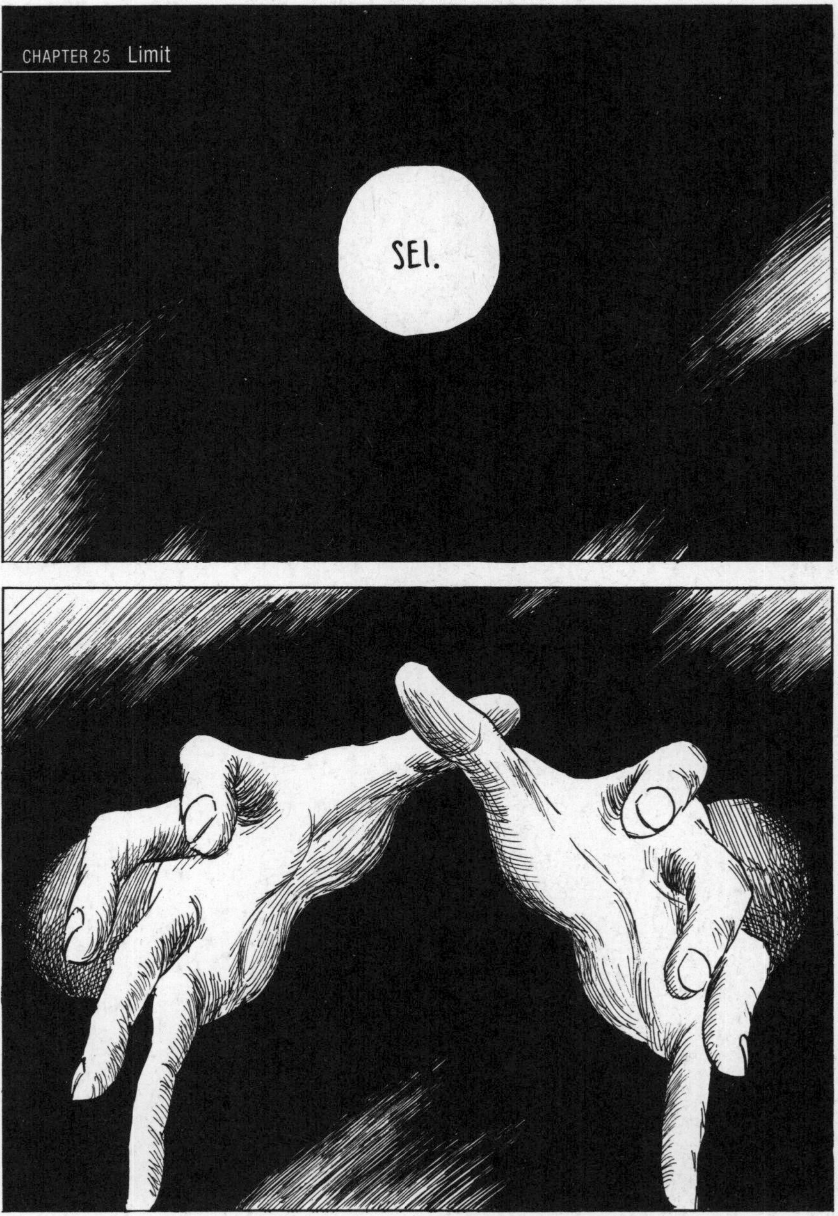
SEI.

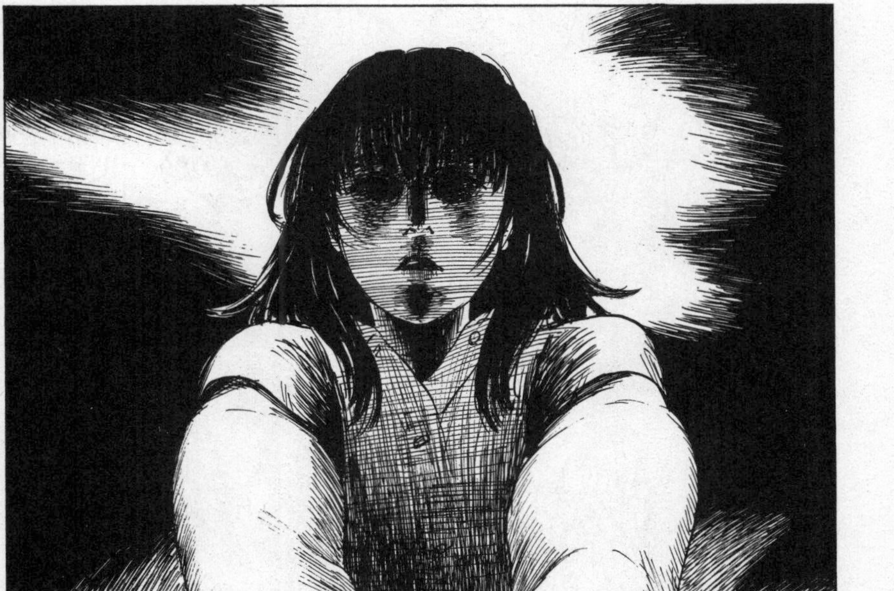

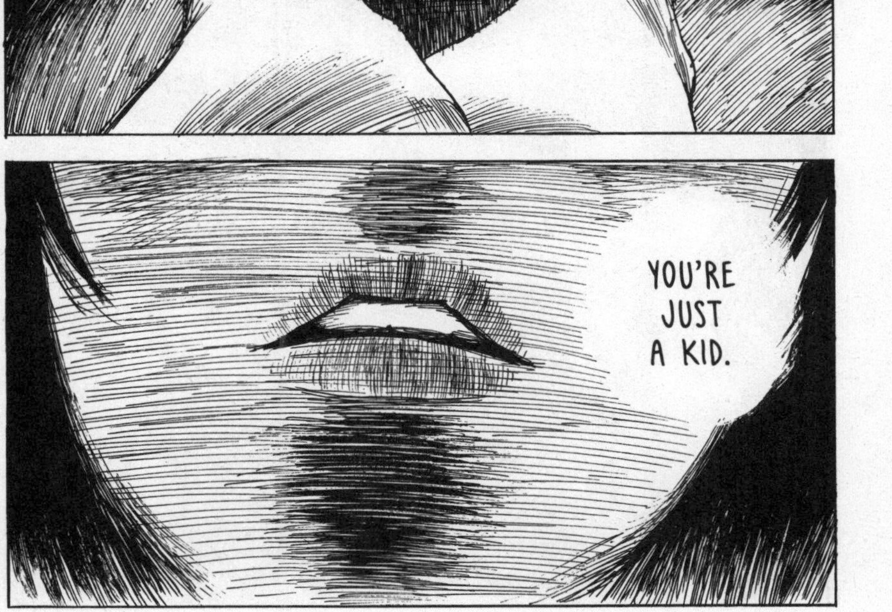
YOU'RE JUST A KID.

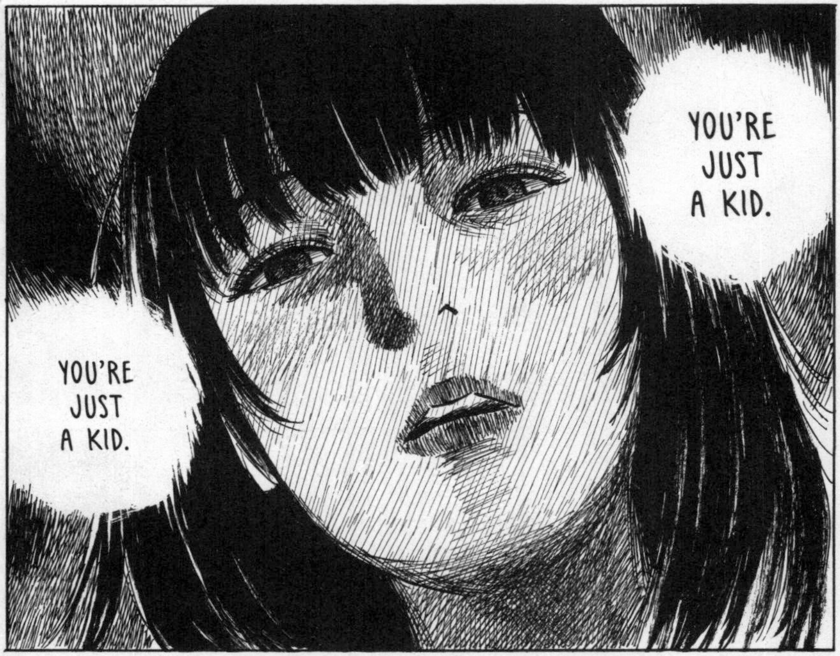
YOU'RE JUST A KID.
YOU'RE JUST A KID.

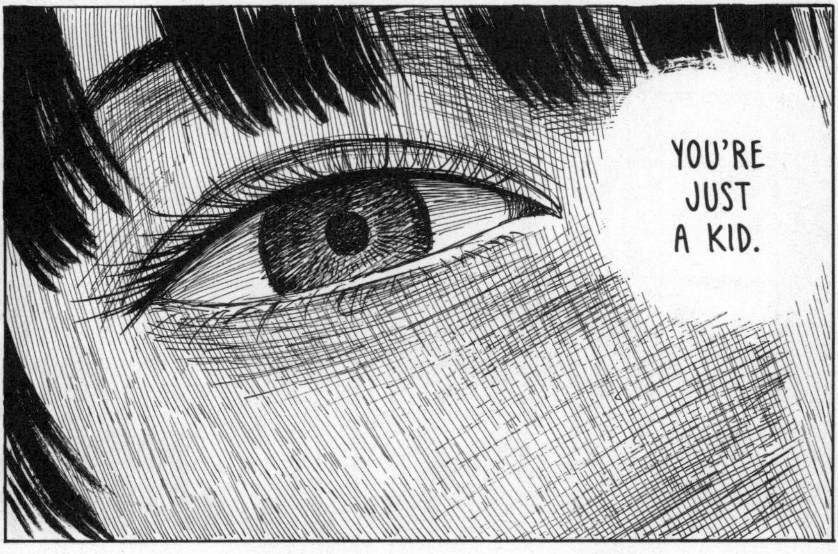
YOU'RE JUST A KID.

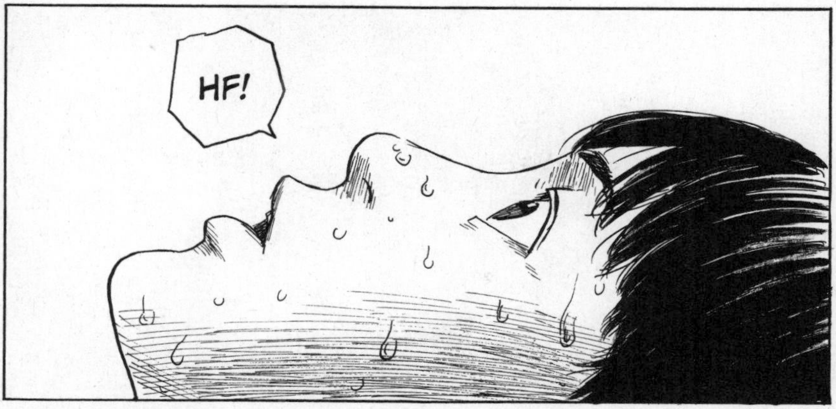
HF!
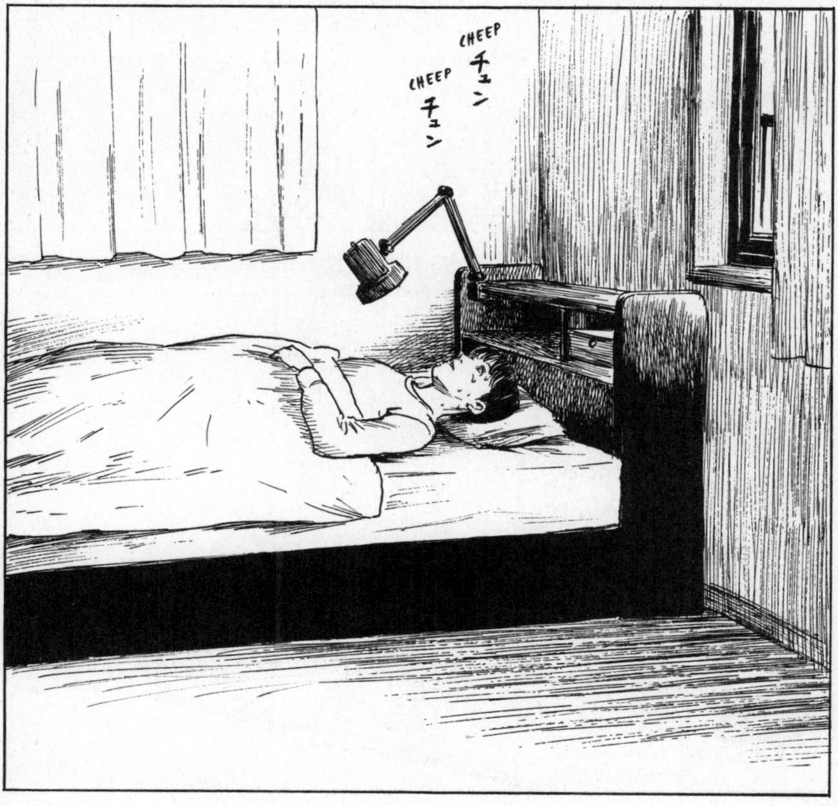
CHEEP
チュン
CHEEP
チュン

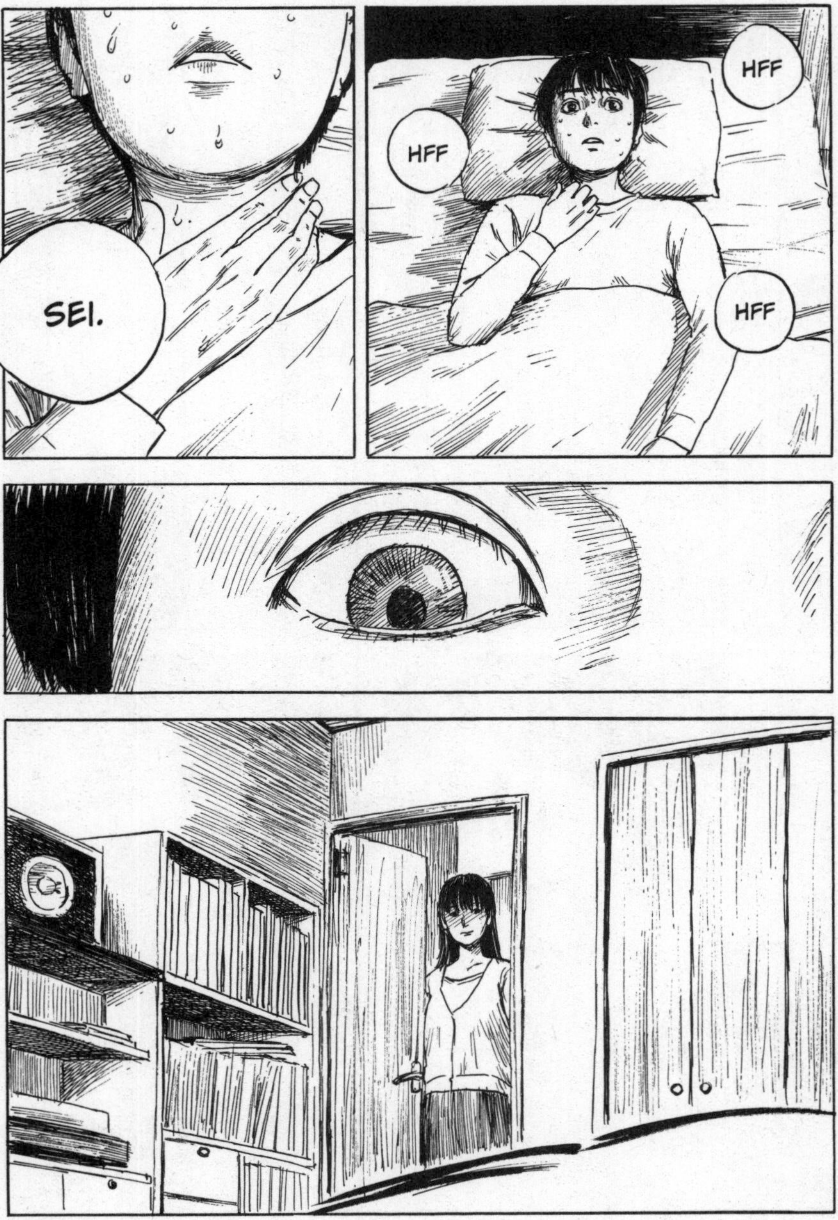
HFF
HFF
HFF
SEI.

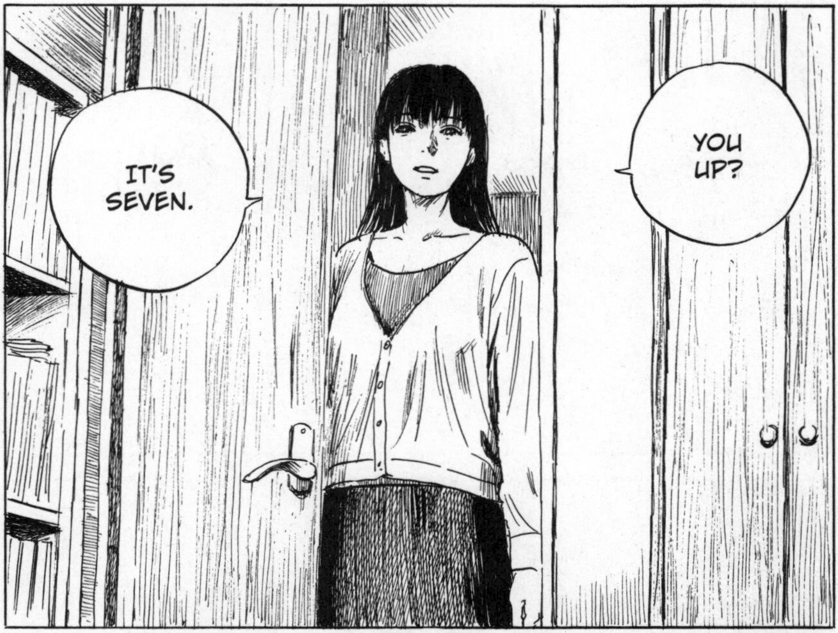
YOU UP?
IT'S SEVEN.
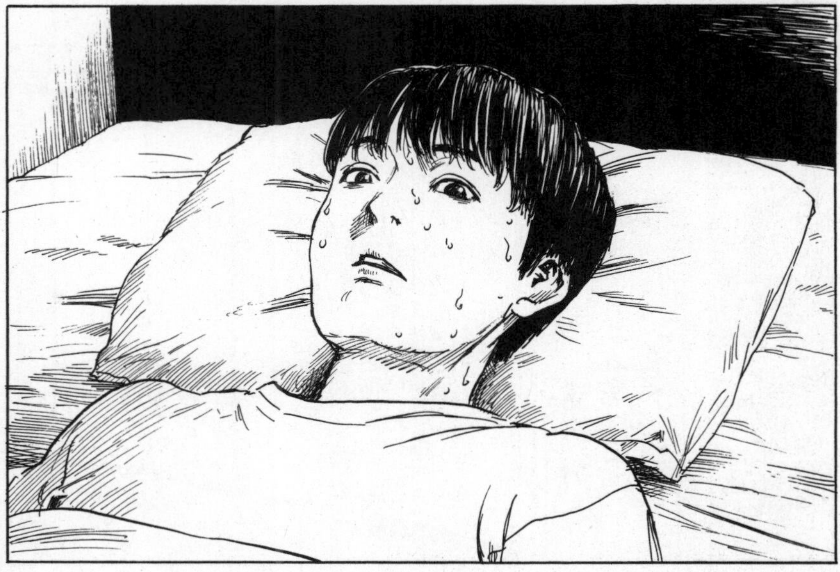

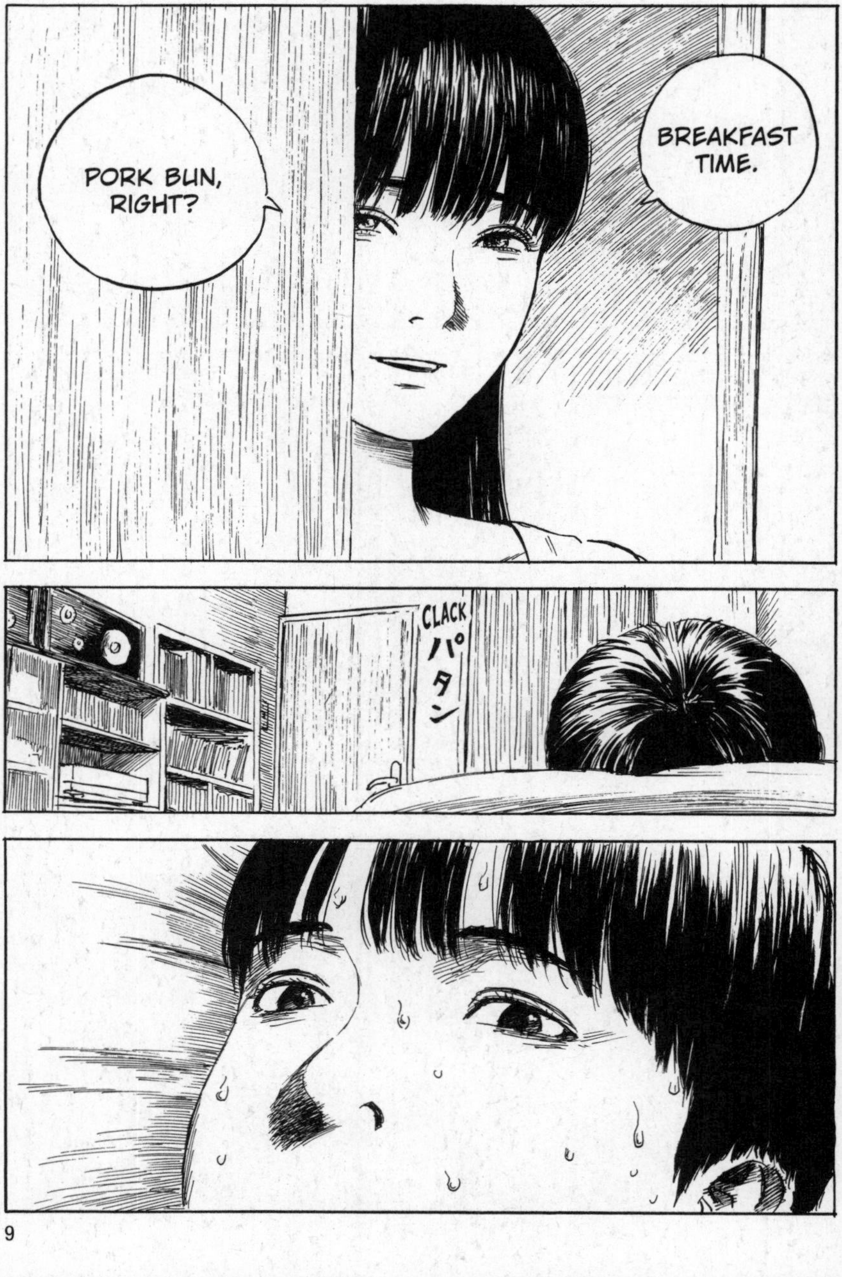
BREAKFAST TIME.
PORK BUN, RIGHT?
CLACK
パタン

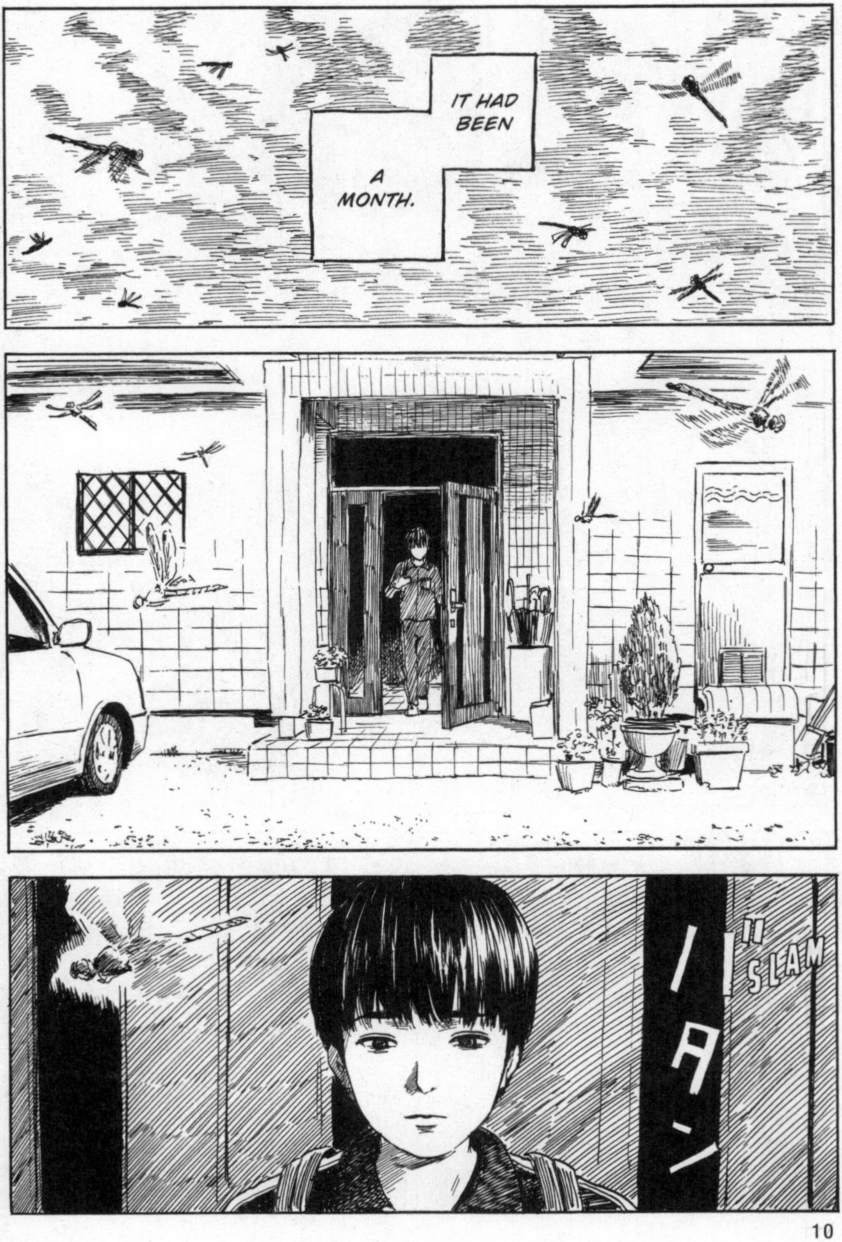
IT HAD BEEN
A MONTH.
バタン
SLAM

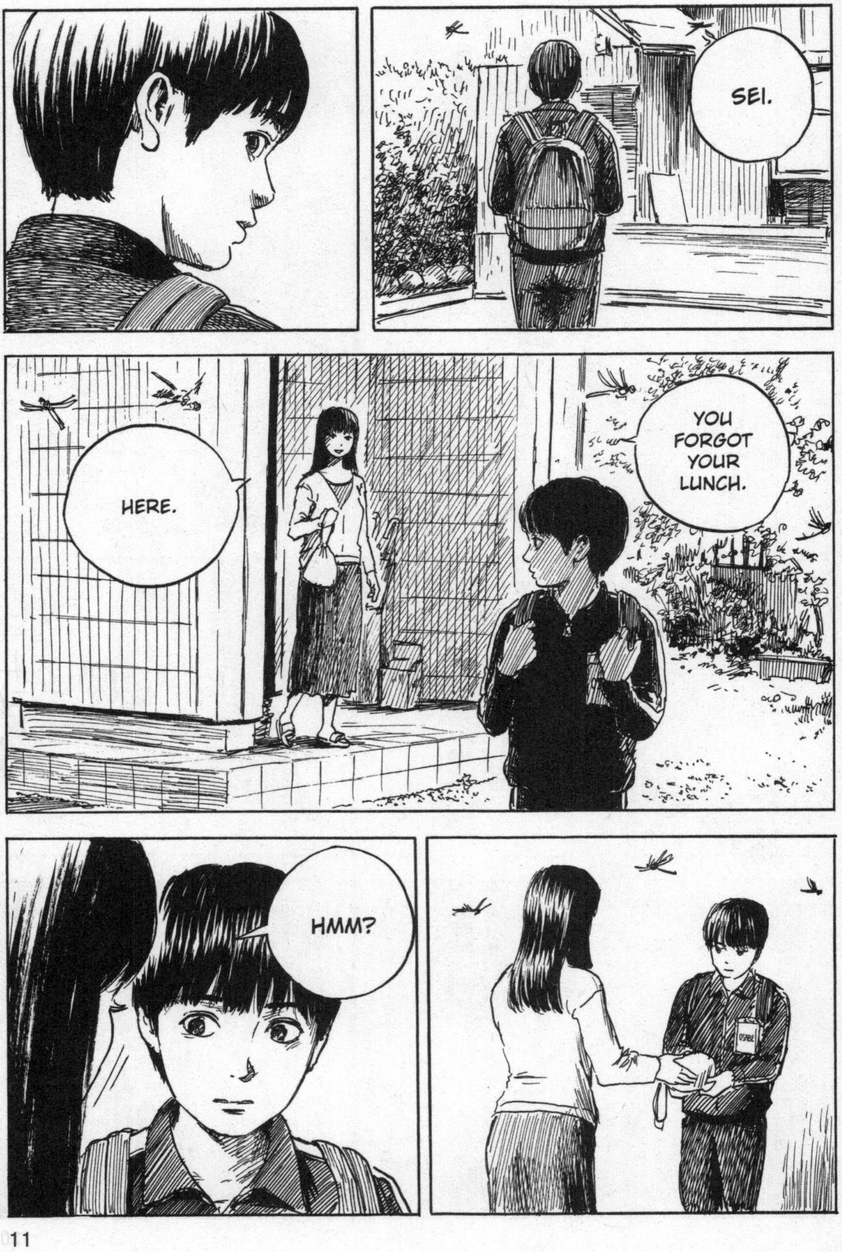
SEI.
YOU FORGOT YOUR LUNCH.
HERE.
HMM?

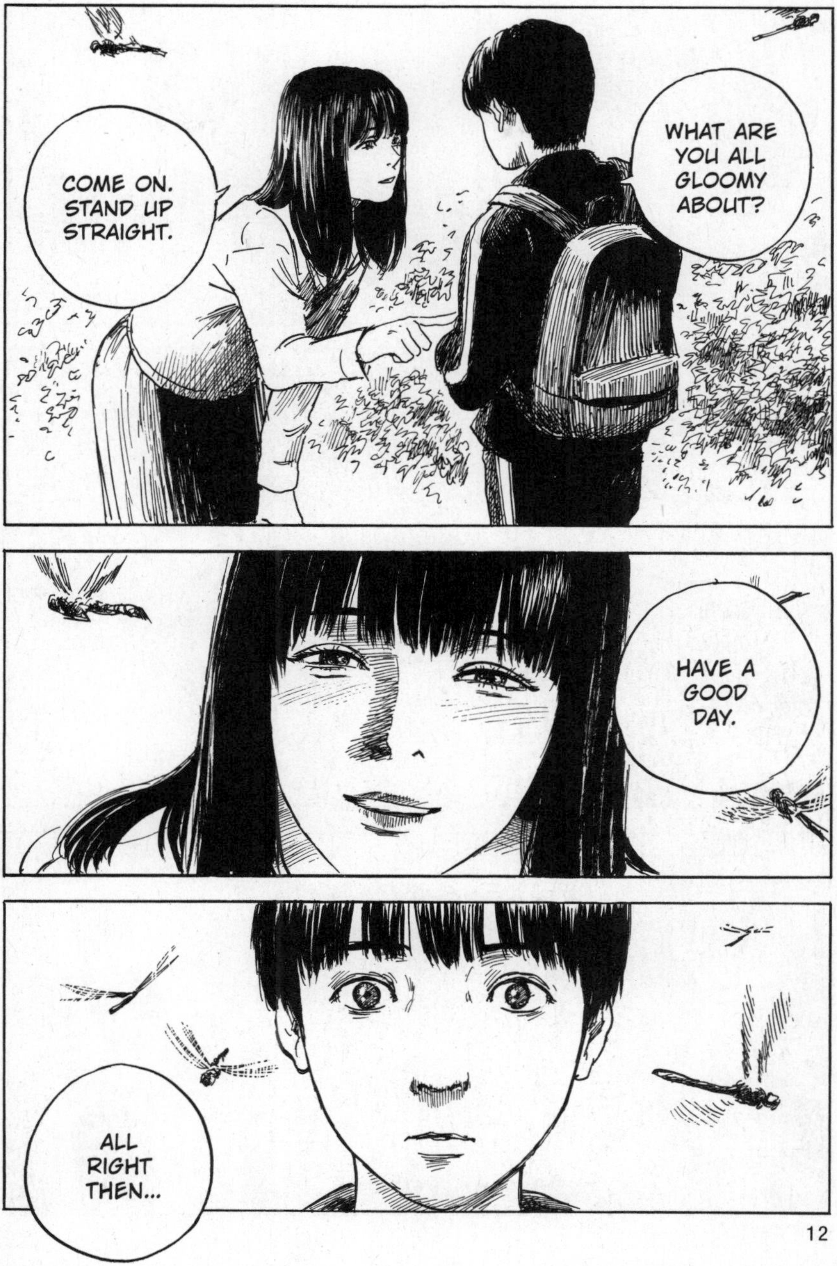
WHAT ARE YOU ALL GLOOMY ABOUT?
COME ON. STAND UP STRAIGHT.
HAVE A GOOD DAY.
ALL RIGHT THEN...

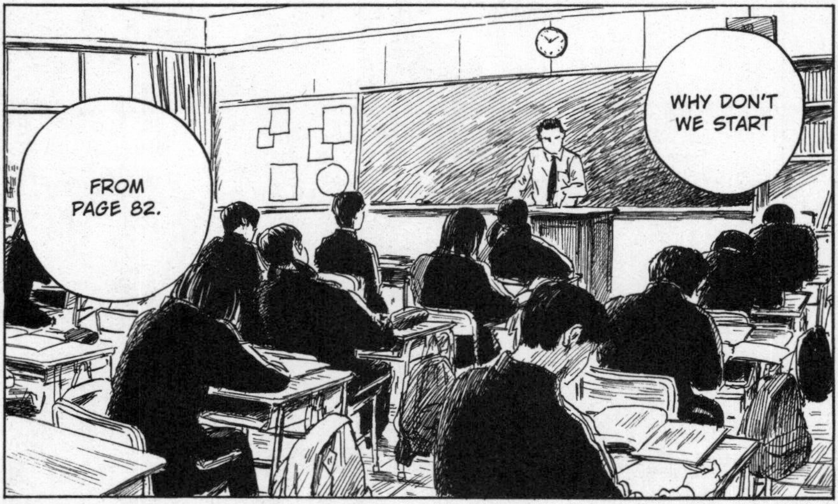
WHY DON'T WE START
FROM PAGE 82.

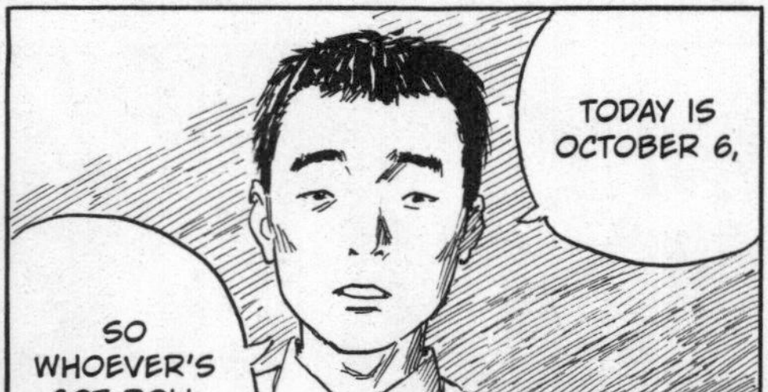
TODAY IS OCTOBER 6,
SO WHOEVER'S GOT ROLL NUMBER 6.

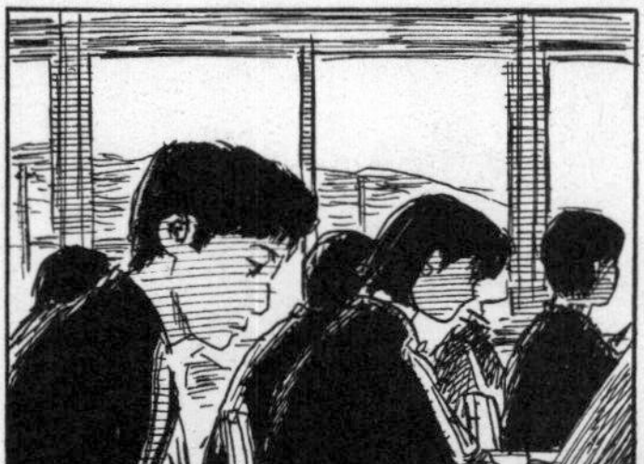

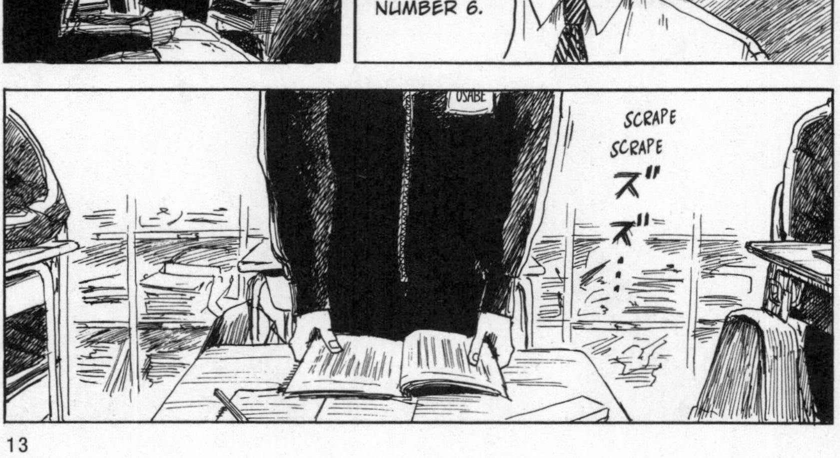
OSABE
SCRAPE
SCRAPE
ズ
ズ…

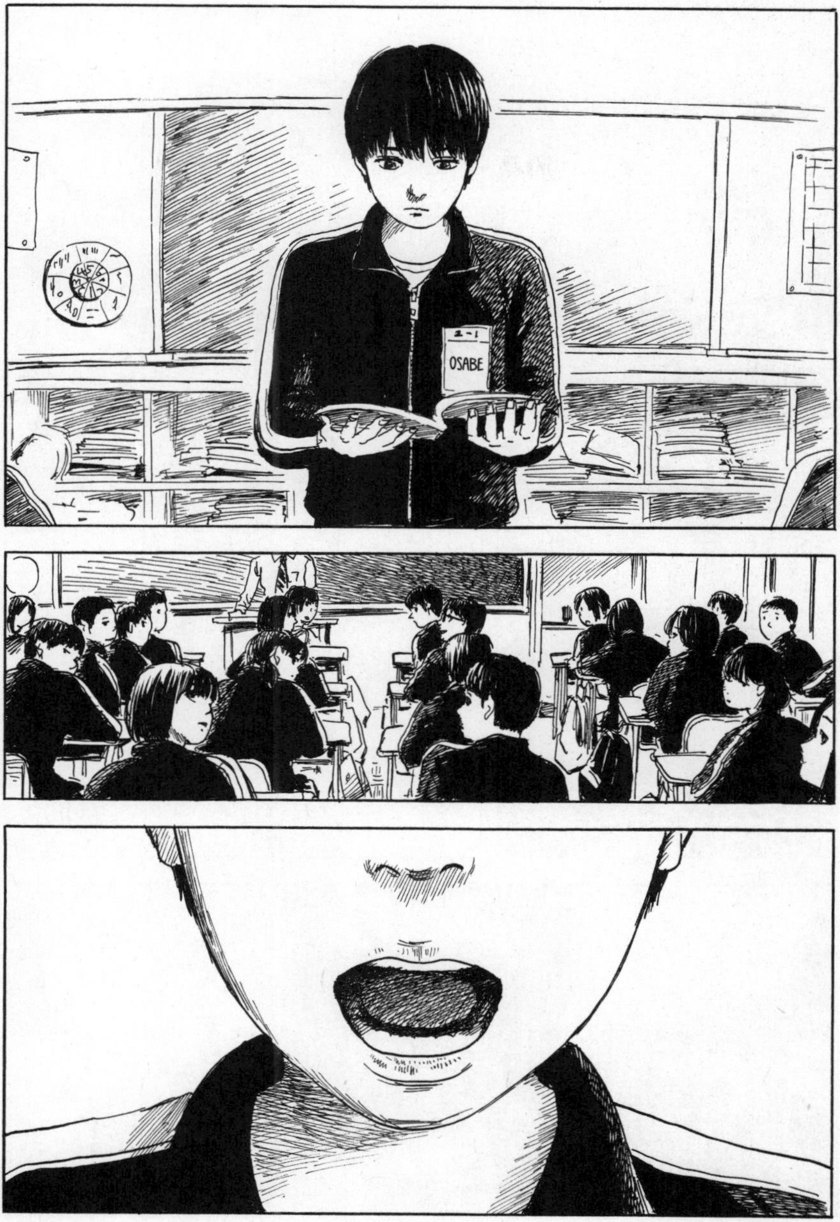
2-1
OSABE

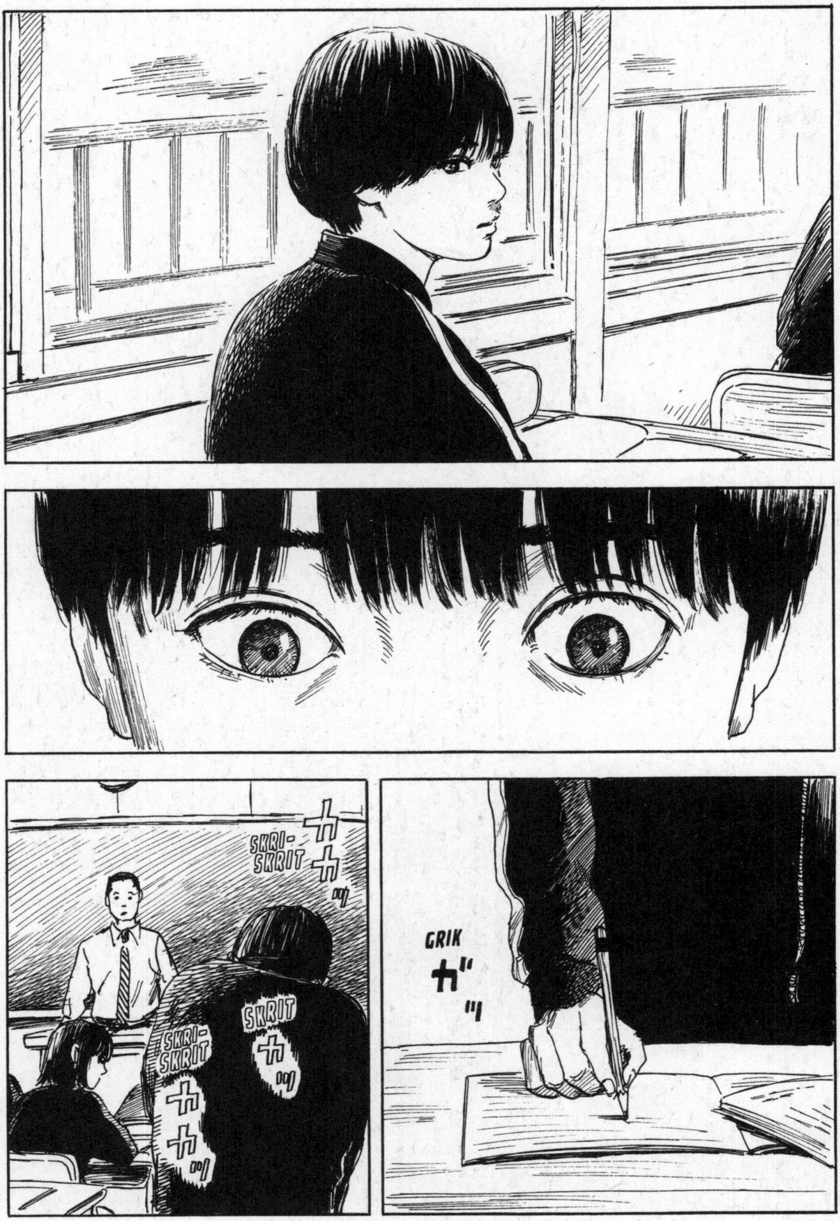
GRIK
ガッ
SKRI-SKRIT
カカッ
SKRIT
カッ
SKRI-SKRIT
カカッ

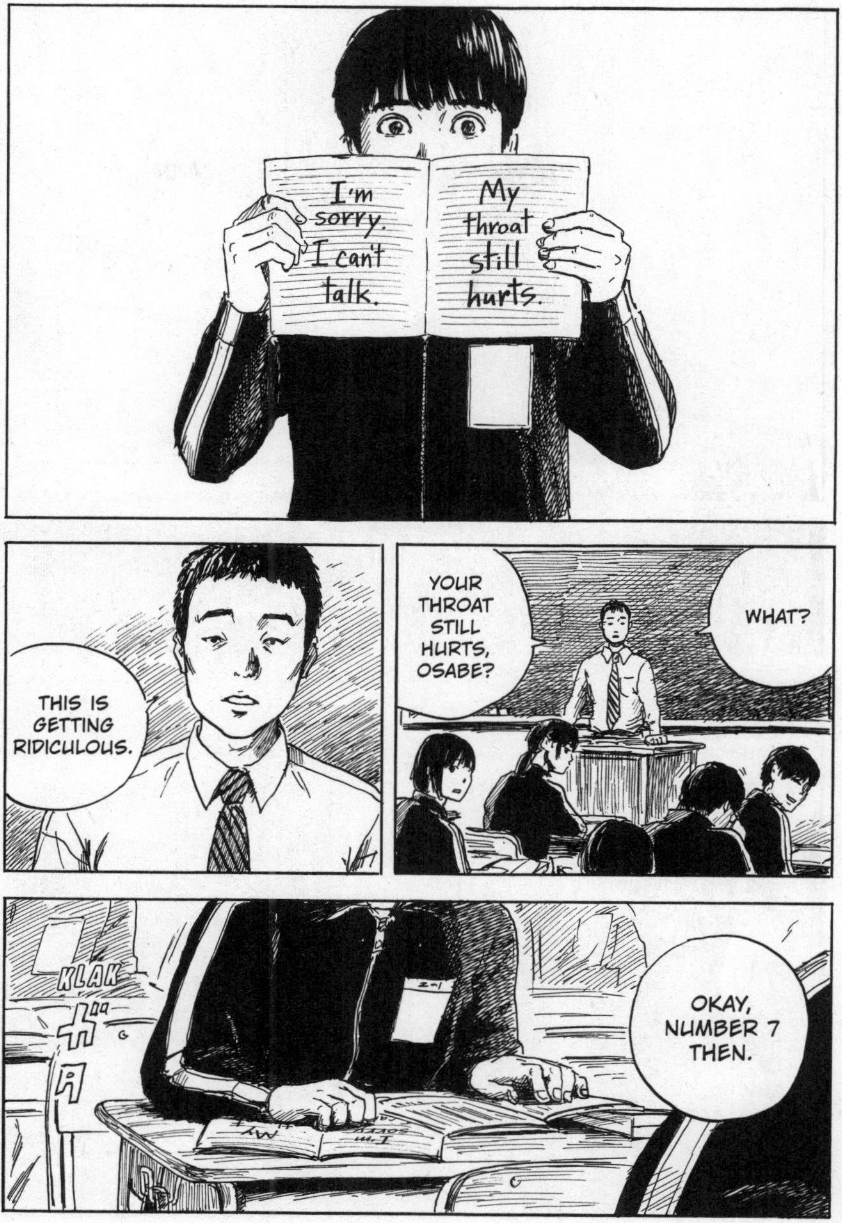
I'm sorry. I can't talk.
My throat still hurts.
WHAT?
YOUR THROAT STILL HURTS, OSABE?
THIS IS GETTING RIDICULOUS.
OKAY, NUMBER 7 THEN.
KLAK
ガタ

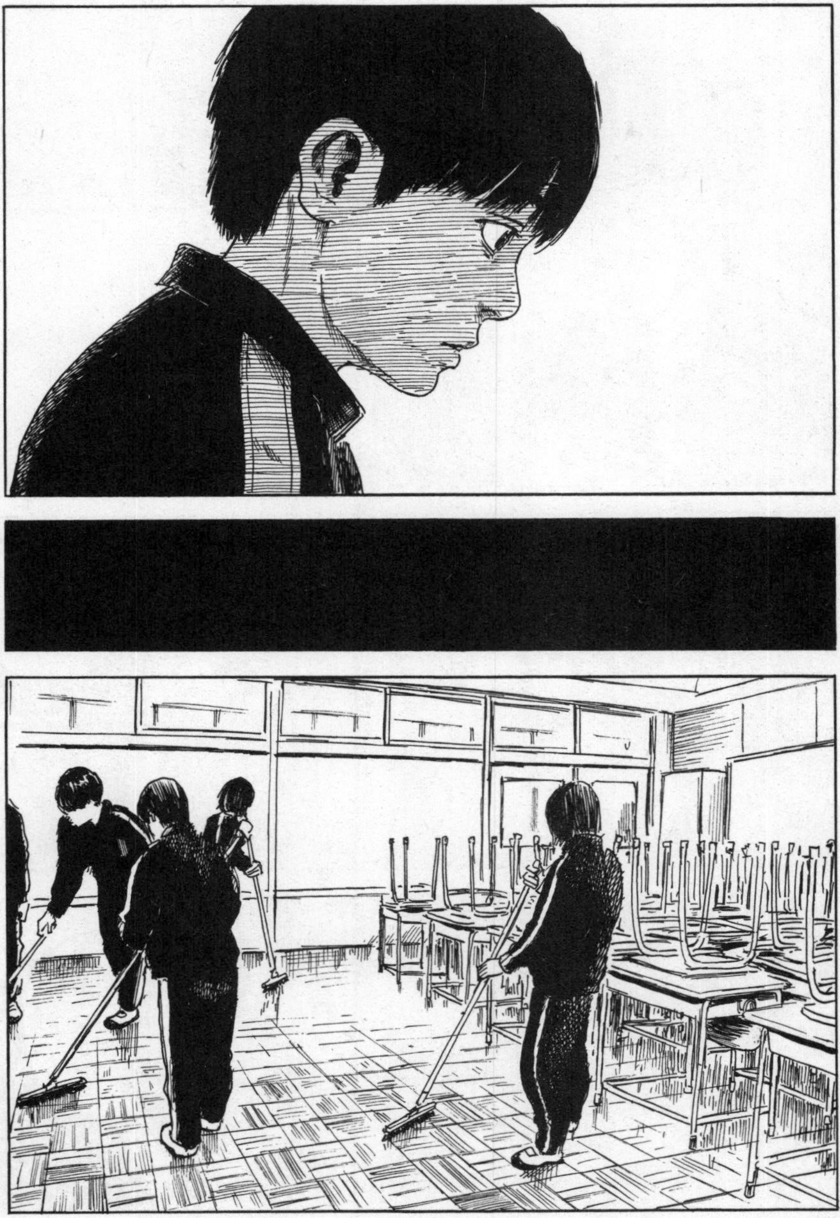

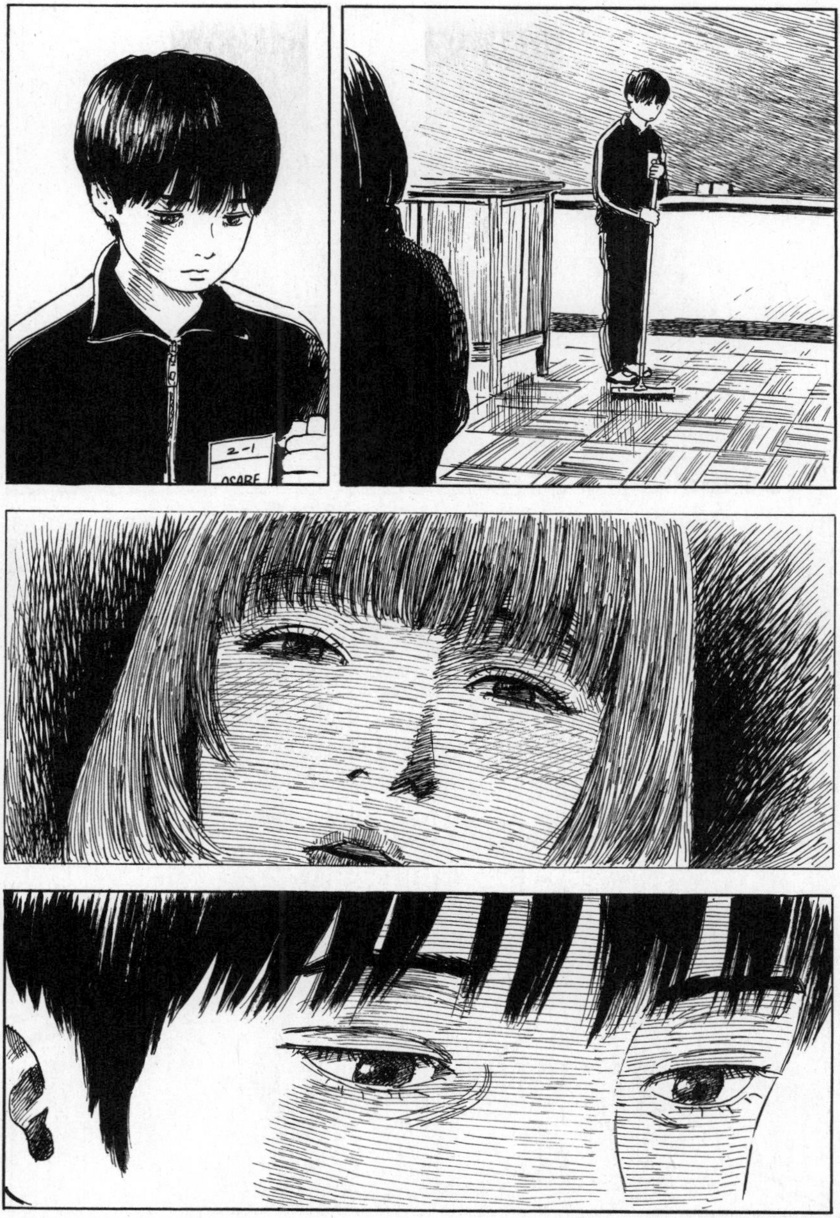
2-1

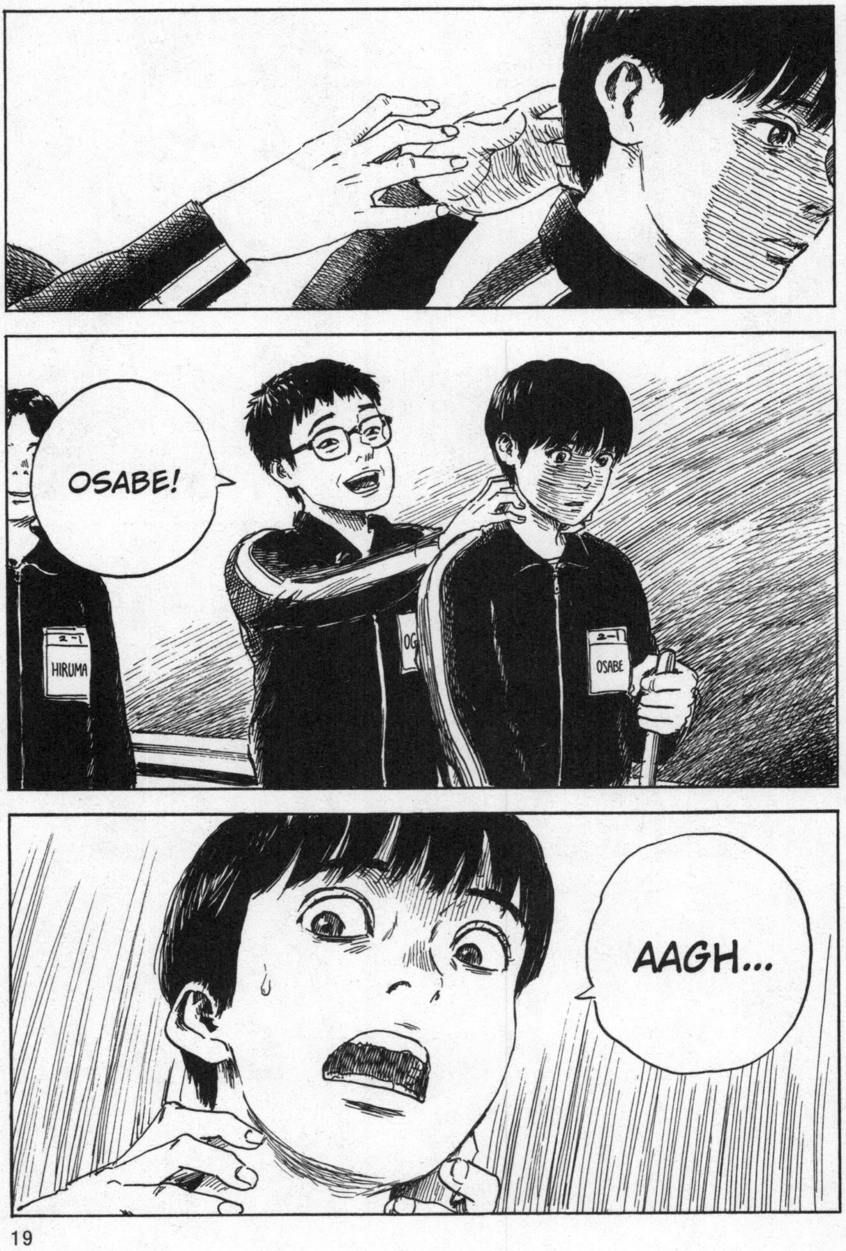
OSABE!
2-1
HIRUMA
OG
2-1
OSABE
AAGH...

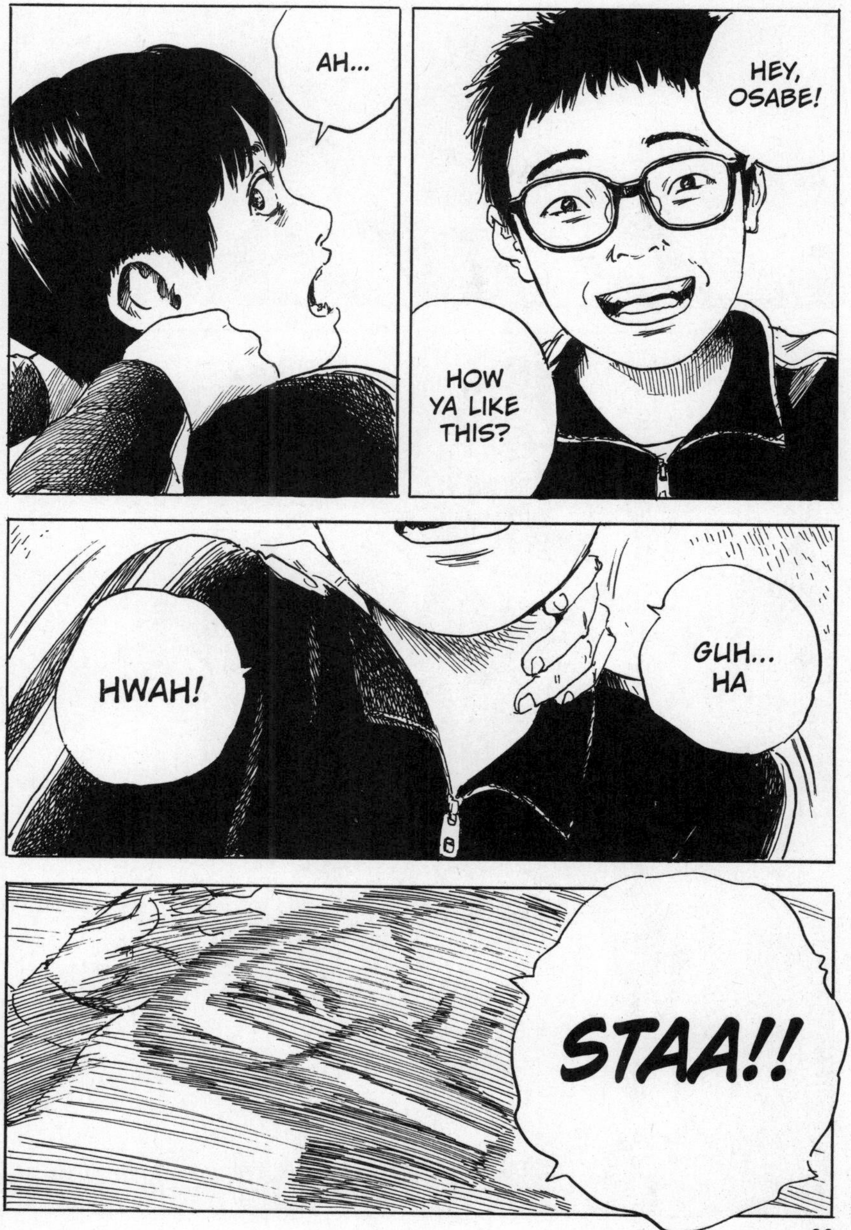
HEY, OSABE!
HOW YA LIKE THIS?
AH...
GUH... HA
HWAH!
STAA!!

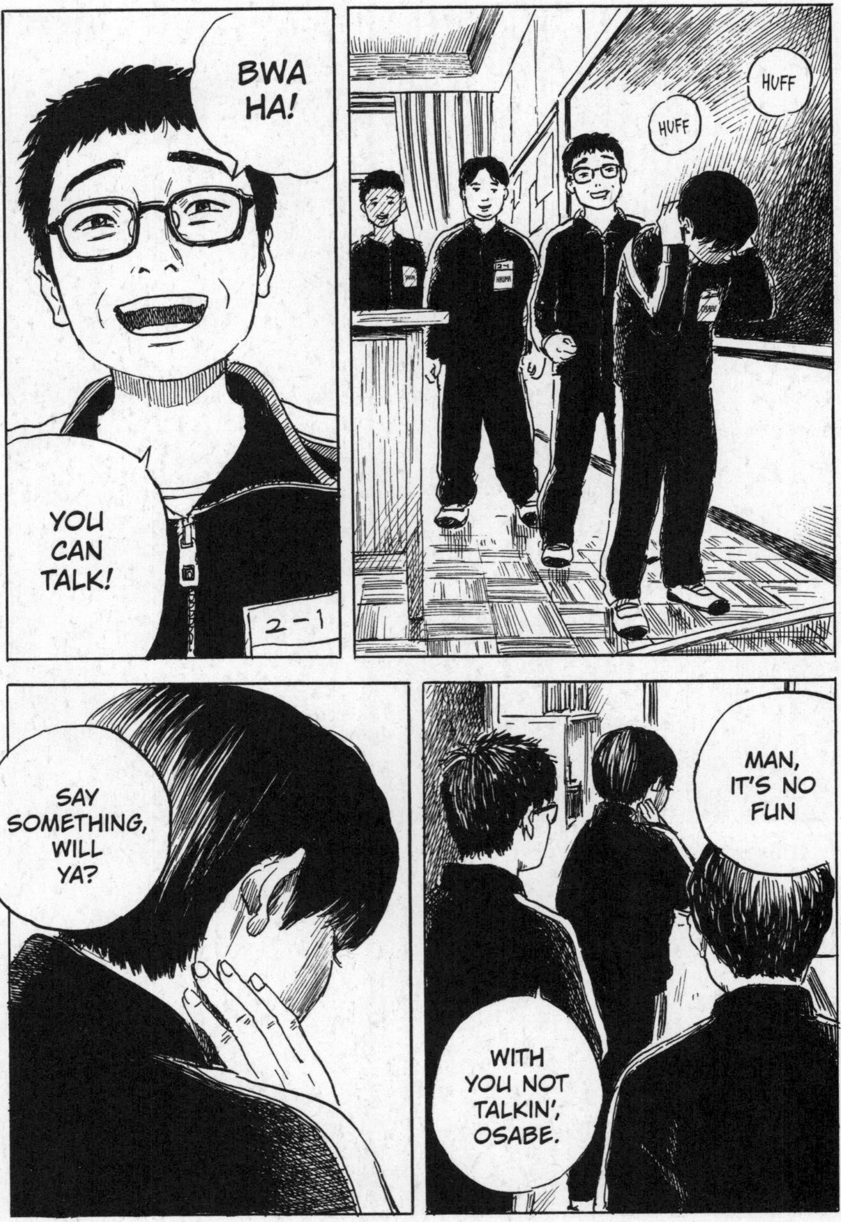
HUFF
HUFF
BWA HA!
YOU CAN TALK!
2-1
MAN, IT'S NO FUN
WITH YOU NOT TALKIN', OSABE.
SAY SOMETHING, WILL YA?

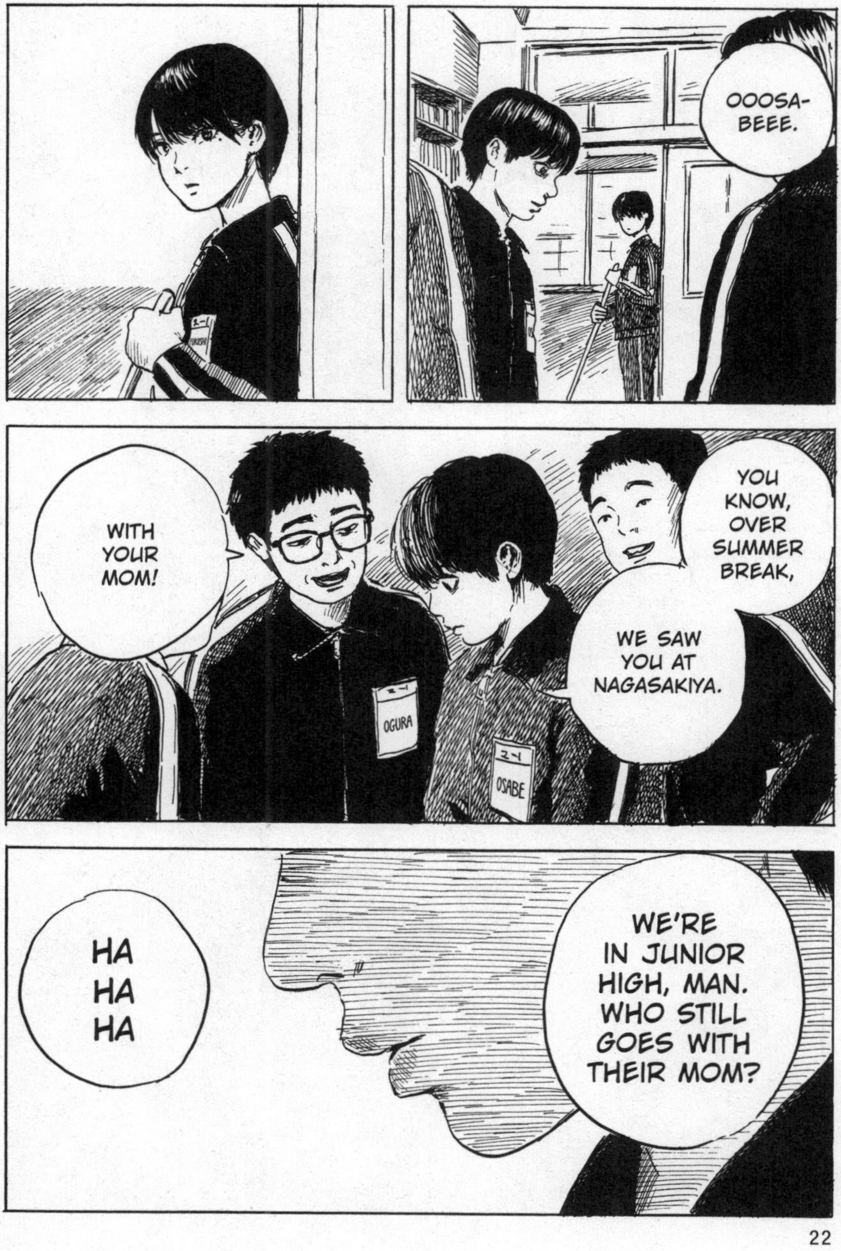
OOOSA-BEEE.
YOU KNOW, OVER SUMMER BREAK,
WE SAW YOU AT NAGASAKIYA.
WITH YOUR MOM!
OSABE
OGURA
WE'RE IN JUNIOR HIGH, MAN. WHO STILL GOES WITH THEIR MOM?
HA HA HA

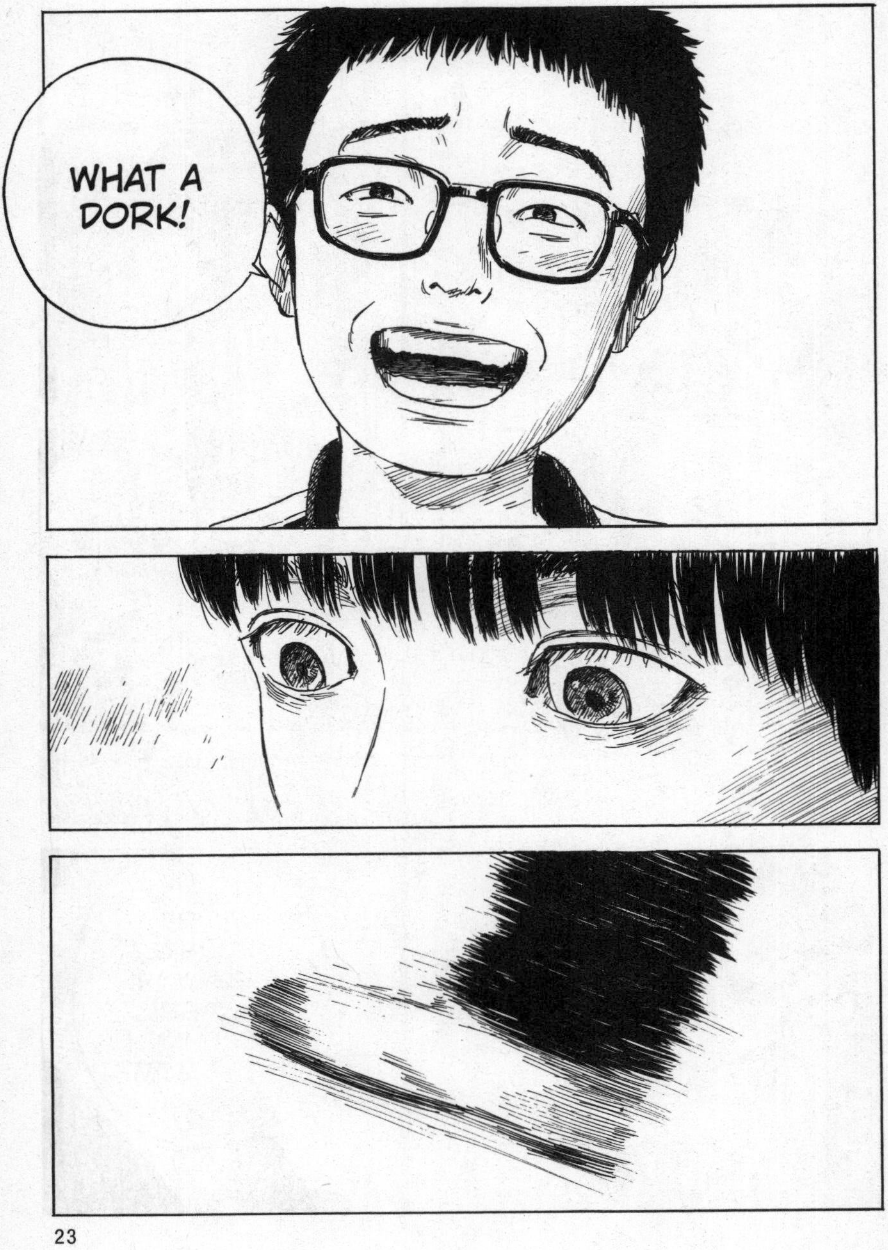
WHAT A DORK!

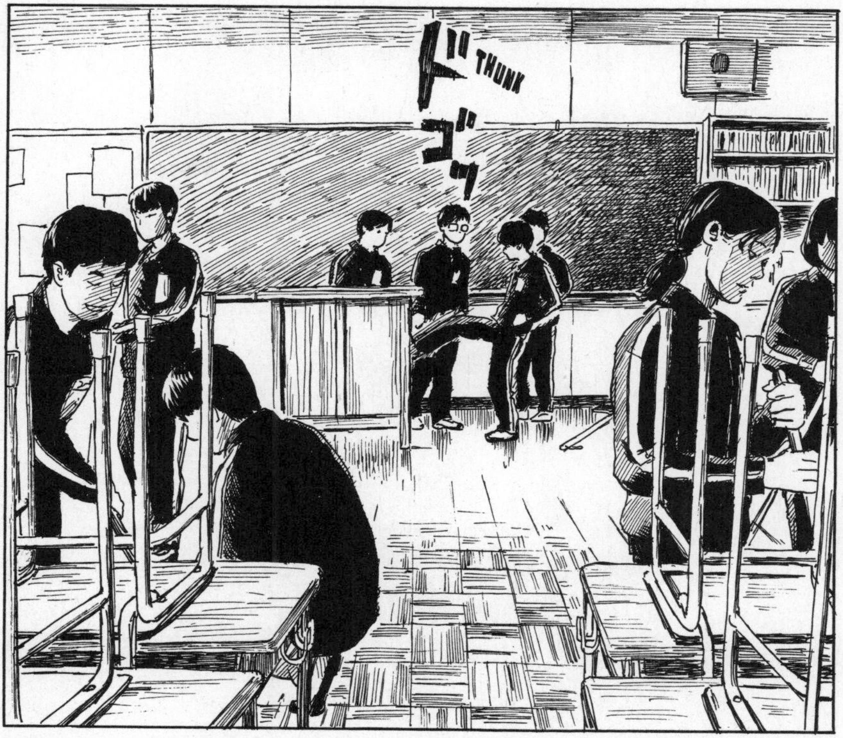
ド
THUNK
ゴッ

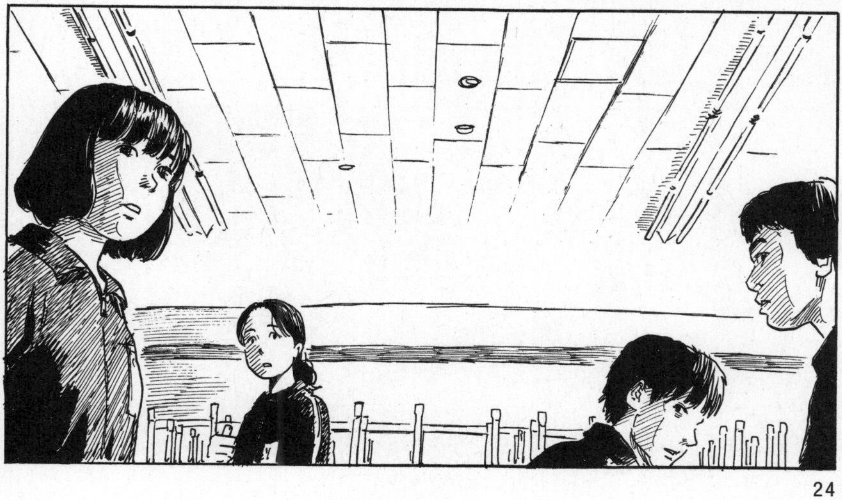

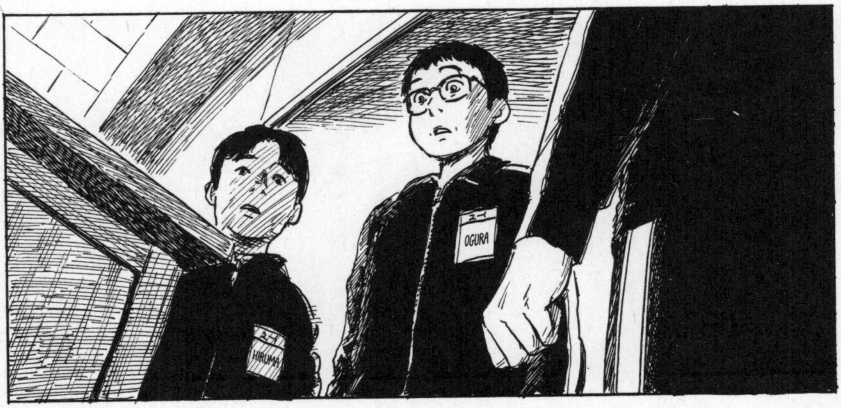
OGURA
HIRUMA

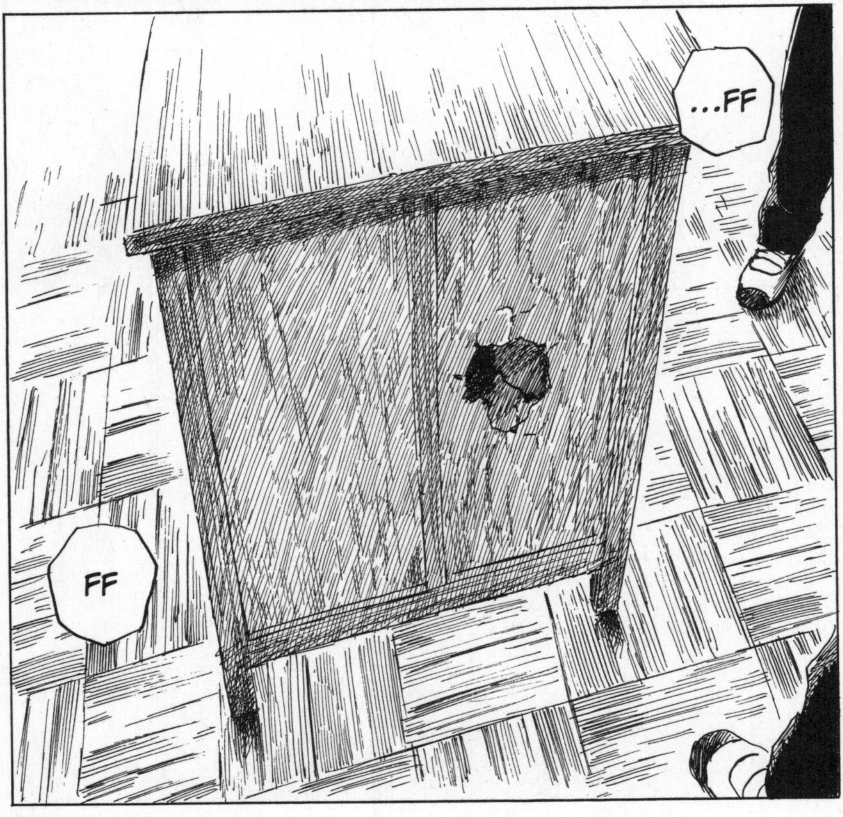
...FF
FF

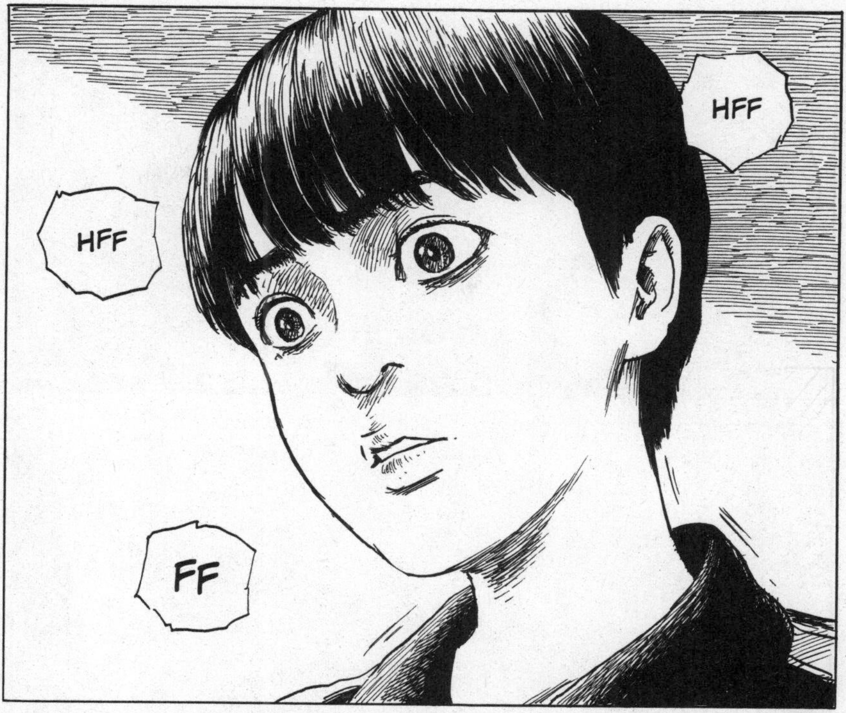
HFF
HFF
FF
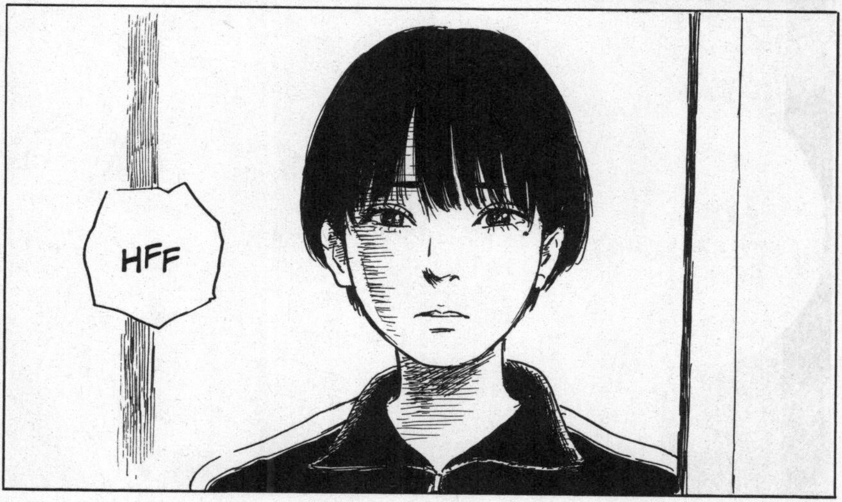
HFF

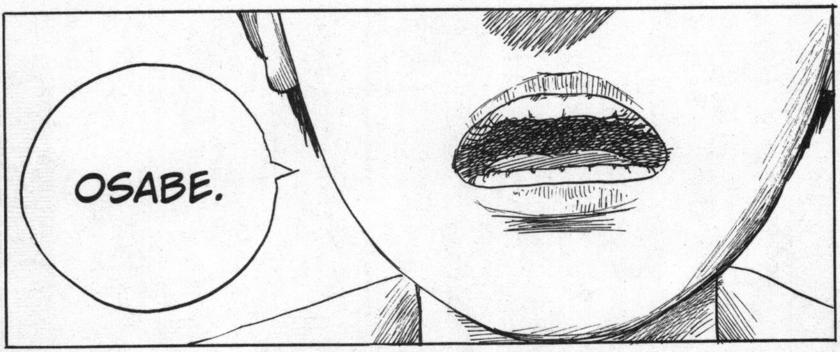
OSABE.

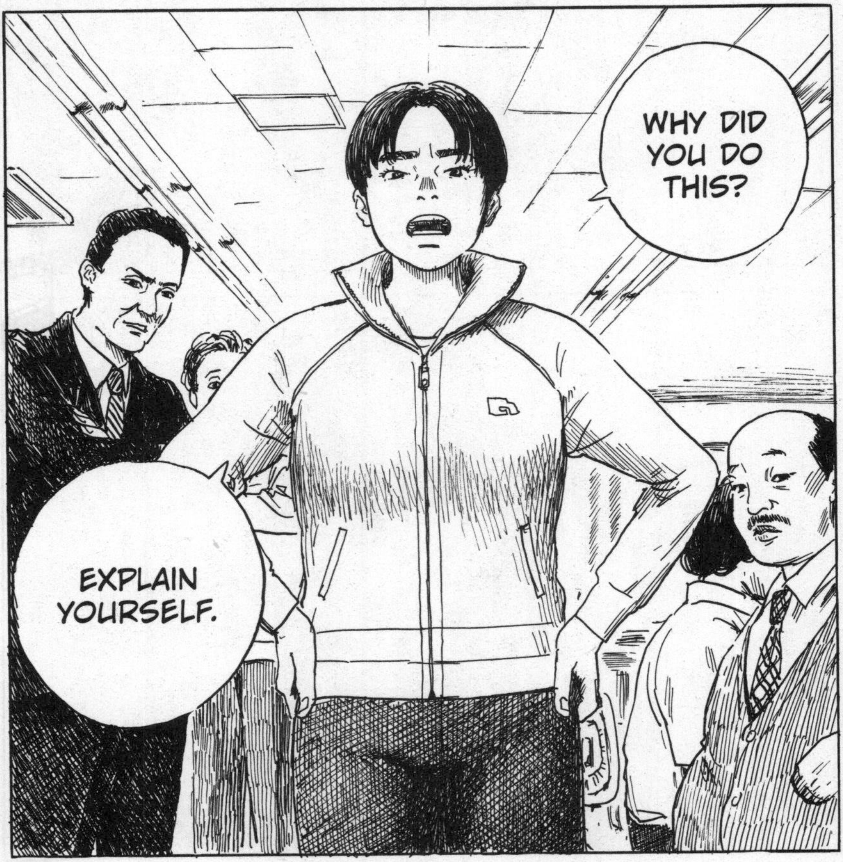
WHY DID YOU DO THIS?
EXPLAIN YOURSELF.

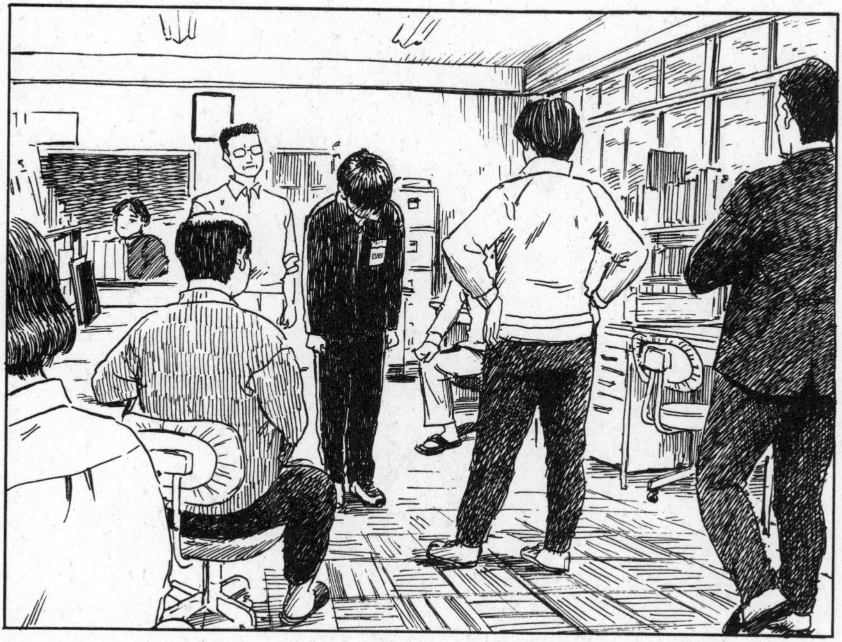

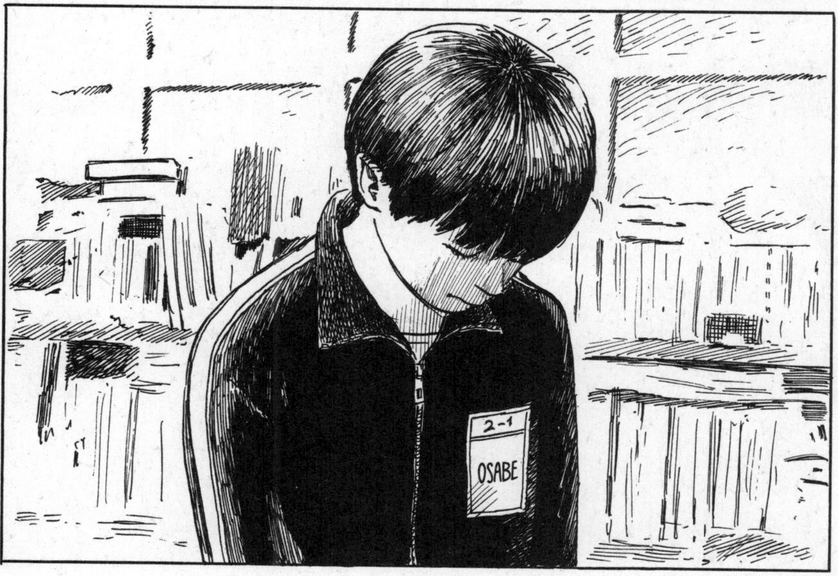
2-1
OSABE

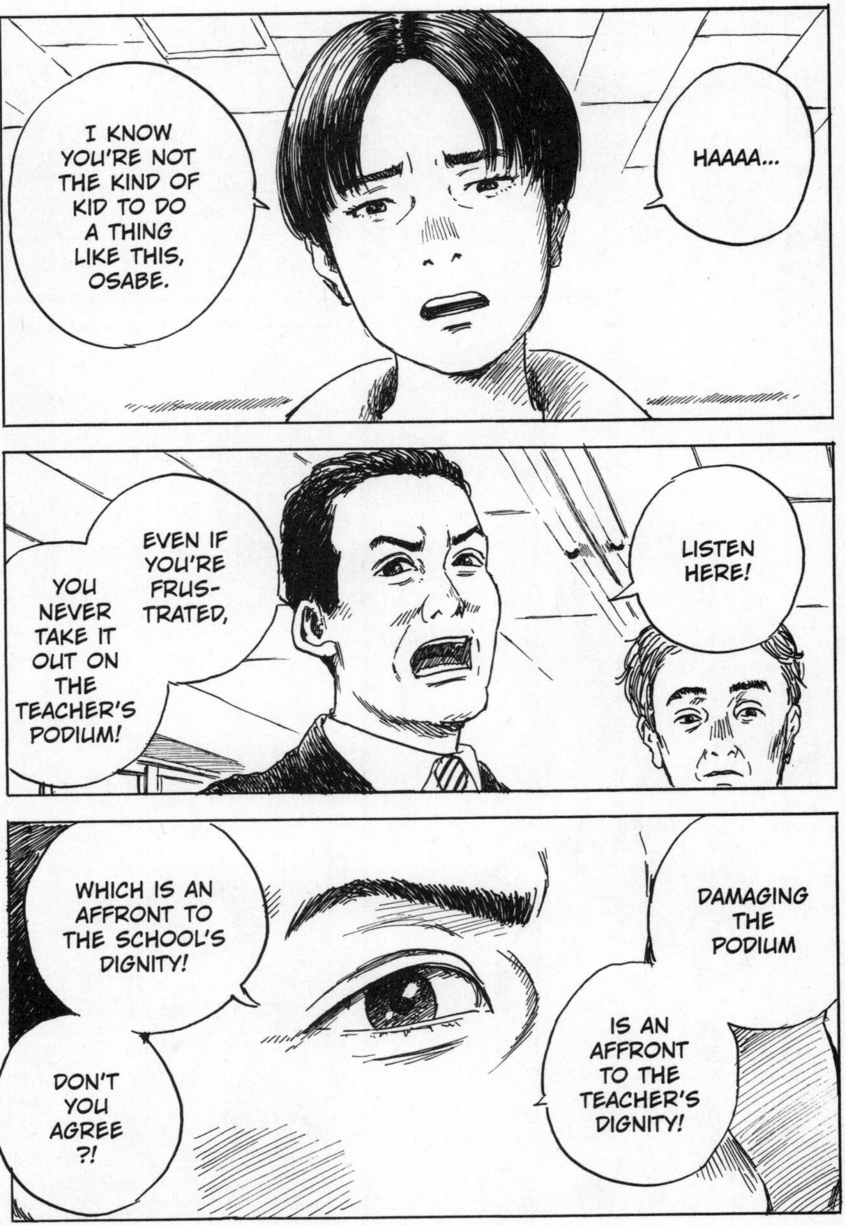
HAAAA...
I KNOW YOU'RE NOT THE KIND OF KID TO DO A THING LIKE THIS, OSABE.
LISTEN HERE!
EVEN IF YOU'RE FRUS-TRATED,
YOU NEVER TAKE IT OUT ON THE TEACHER'S PODIUM!
DAMAGING THE PODIUM
IS AN AFFRONT TO THE TEACHER'S DIGNITY!
WHICH IS AN AFFRONT TO THE SCHOOL'S DIGNITY!
DON'T YOU AGREE ?!

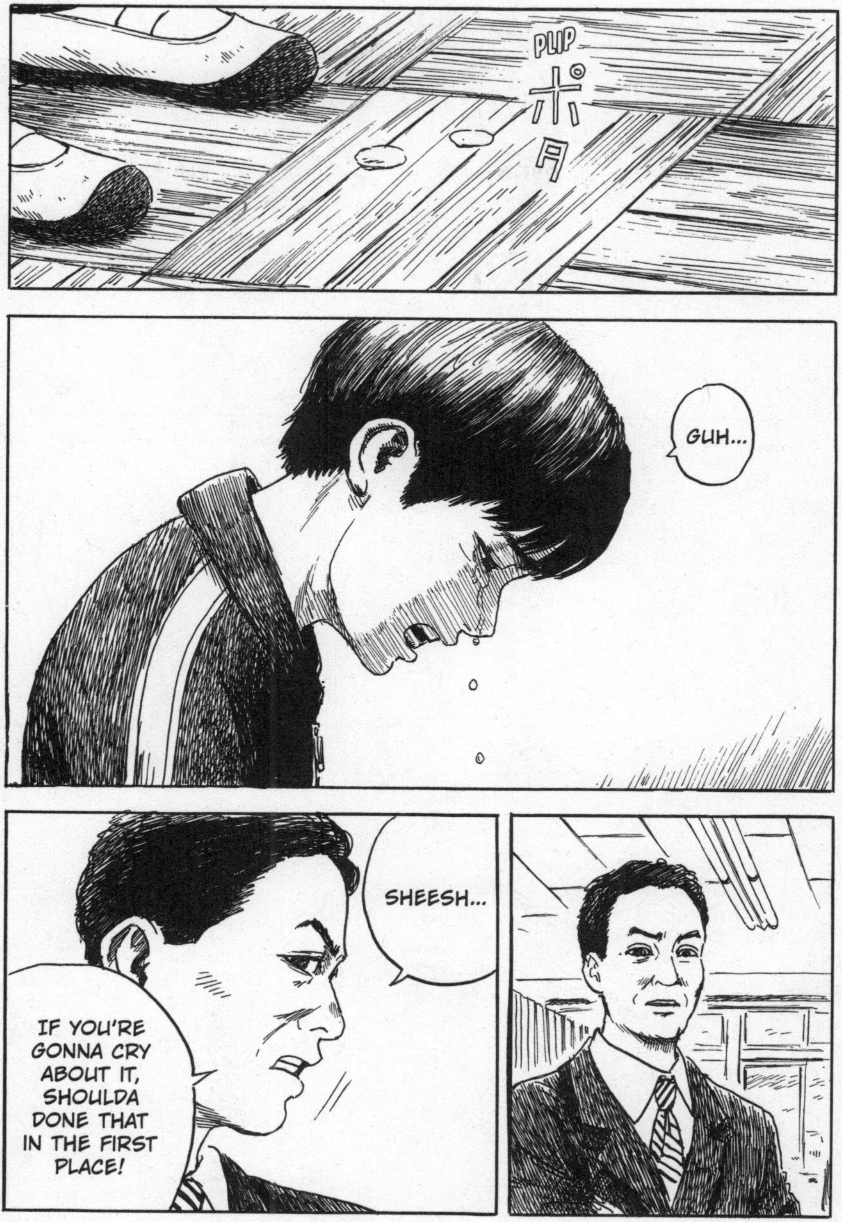
PLIP
ポタ
GUH...
SHEESH...
IF YOU'RE GONNA CRY ABOUT IT, SHOULDA DONE THAT IN THE FIRST PLACE!

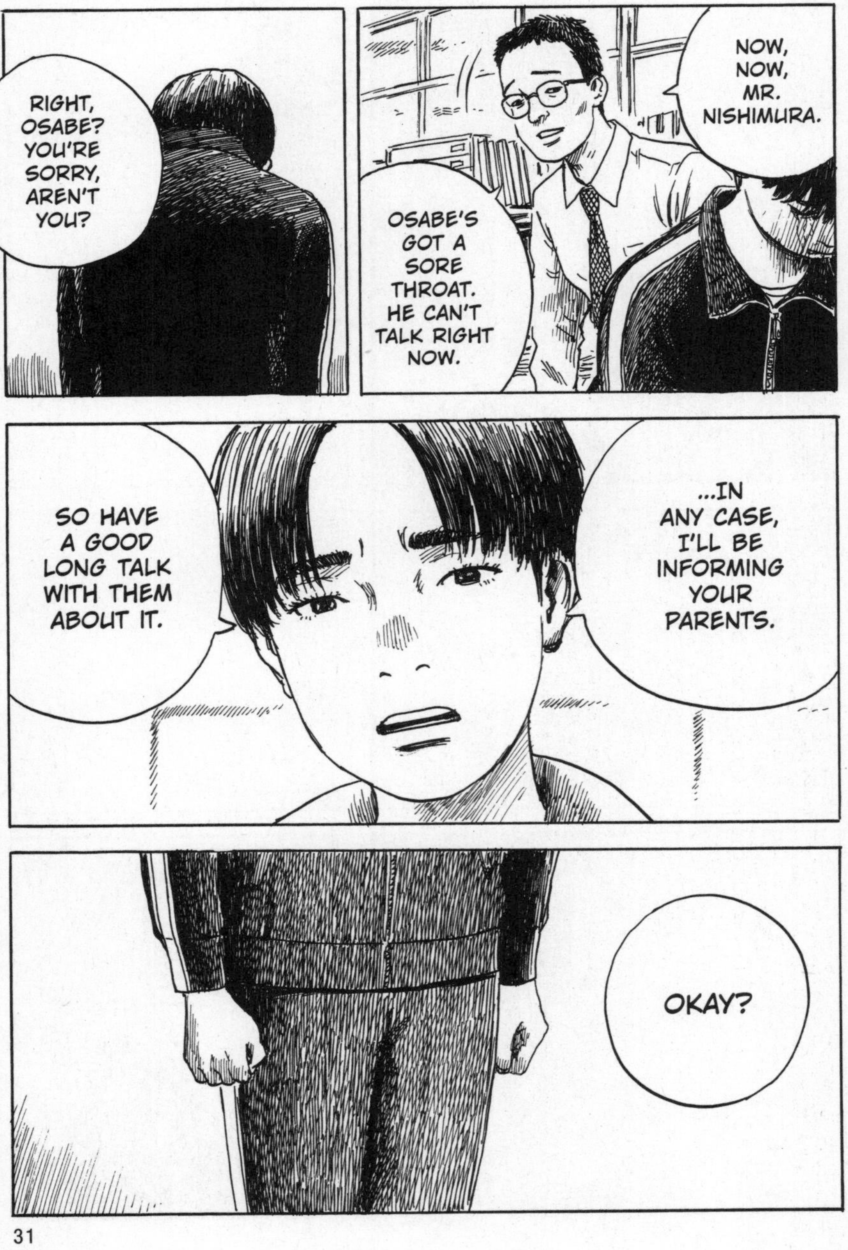
NOW, NOW, MR. NISHIMURA.
OSABE'S GOT A SORE THROAT. HE CAN'T TALK RIGHT NOW.
RIGHT, OSABE? YOU'RE SORRY, AREN'T YOU?
...IN ANY CASE, I'LL BE INFORMING YOUR PARENTS.
SO HAVE A GOOD LONG TALK WITH THEM ABOUT IT.
OKAY?

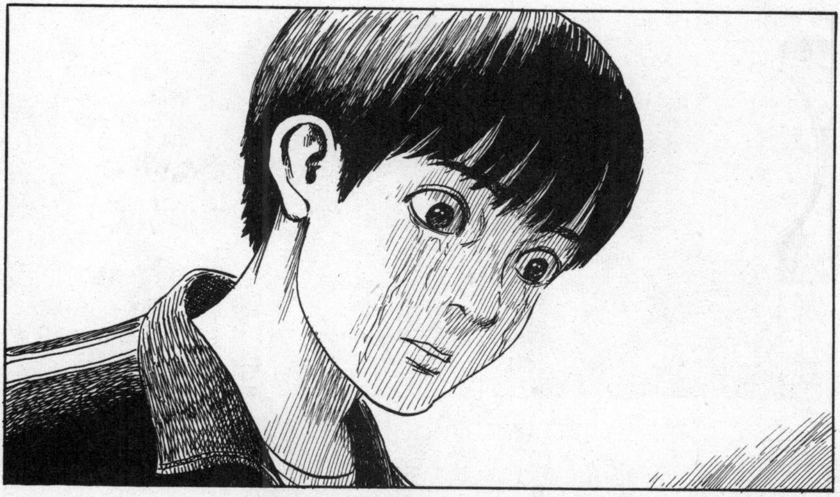
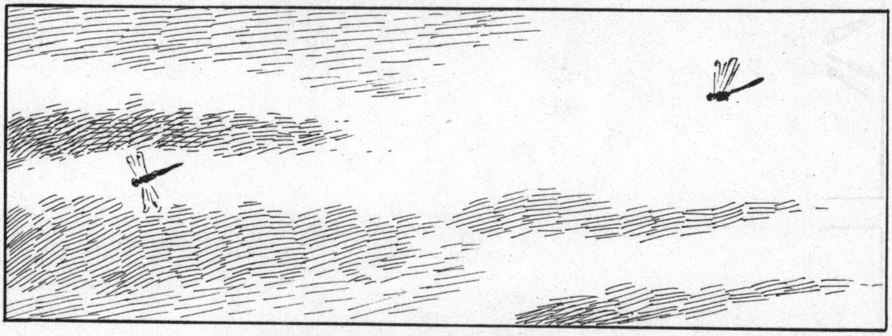
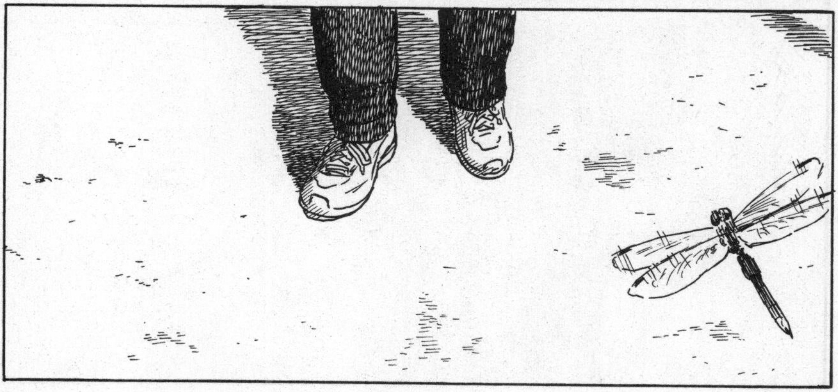

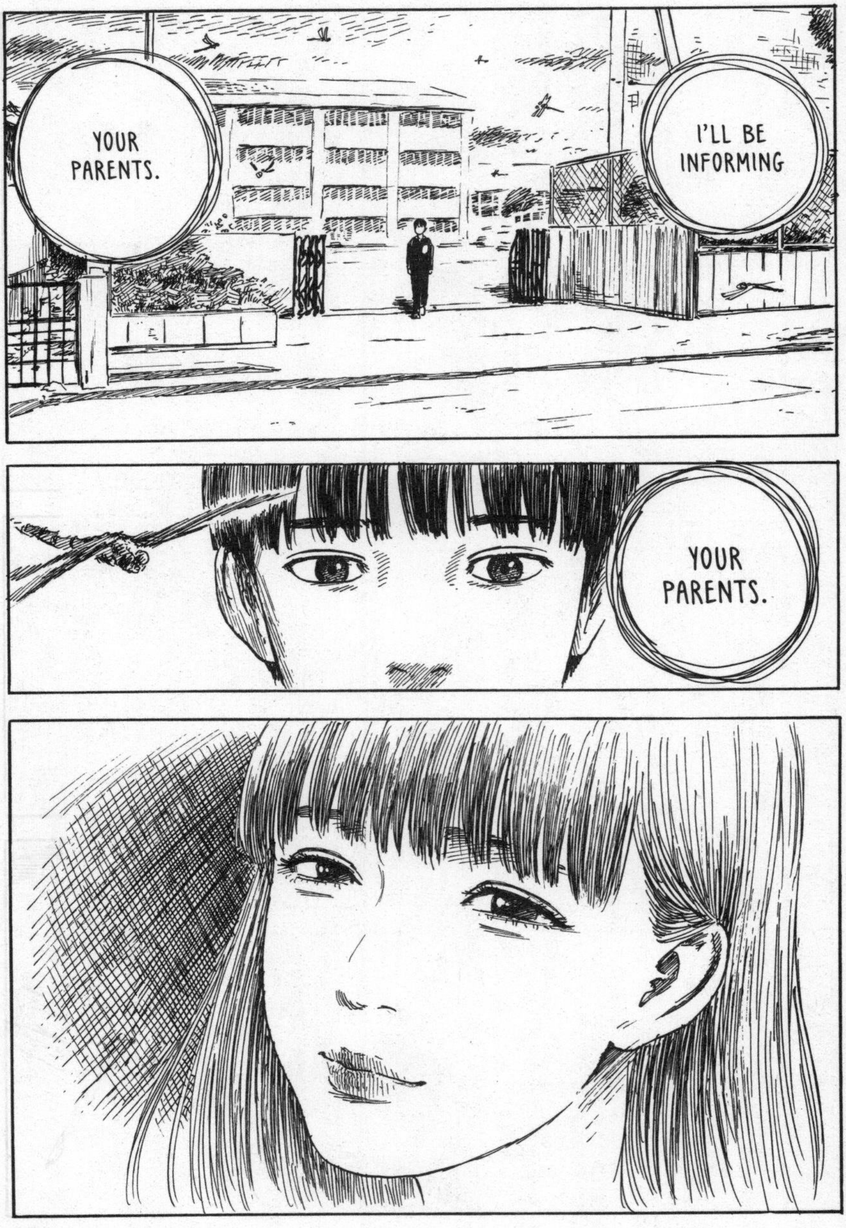
I'LL BE INFORMING
YOUR PARENTS.
YOUR PARENTS.

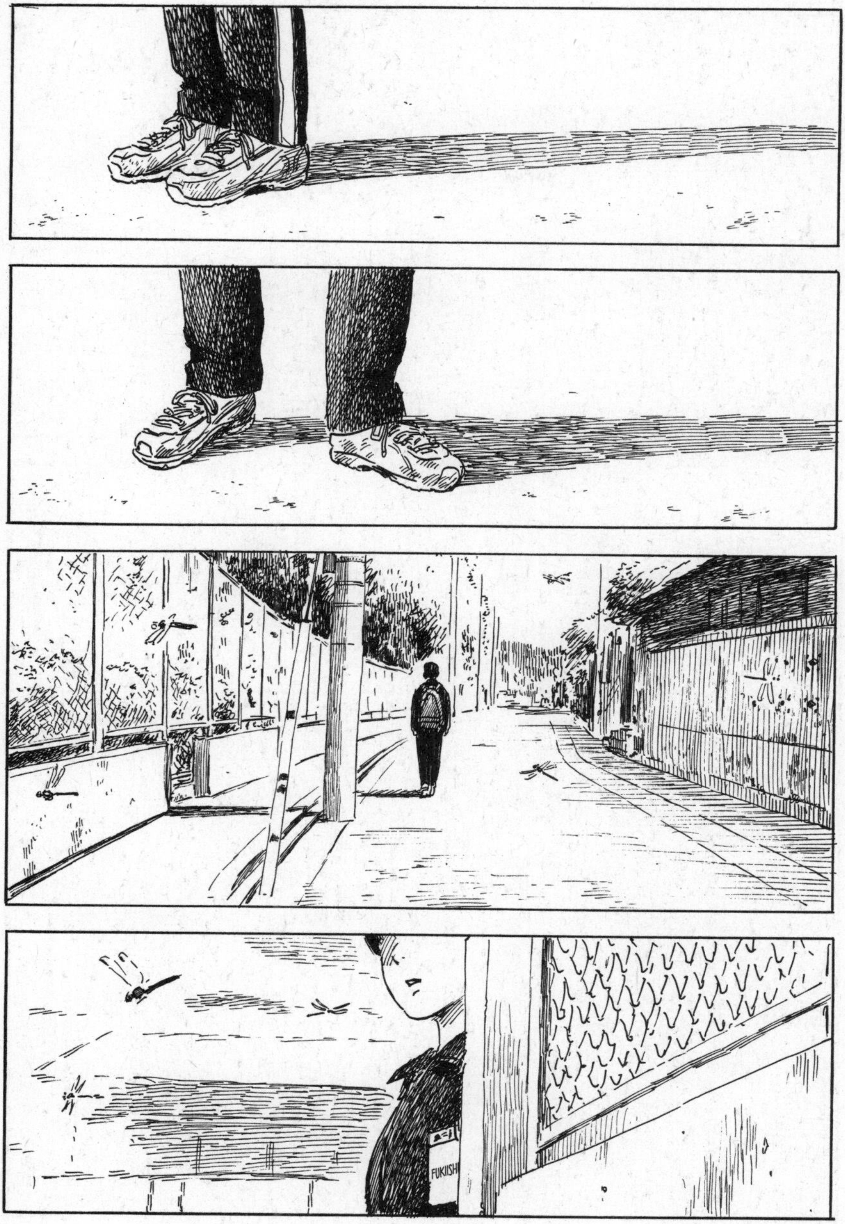
FUKIISH

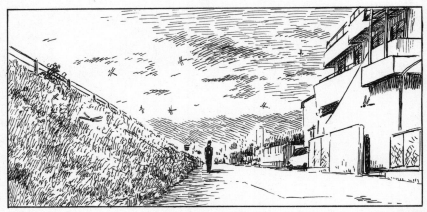

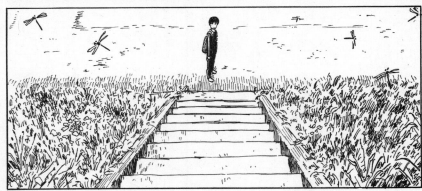

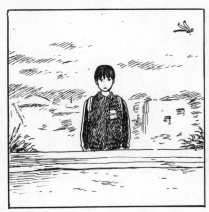

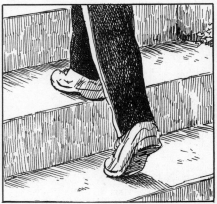

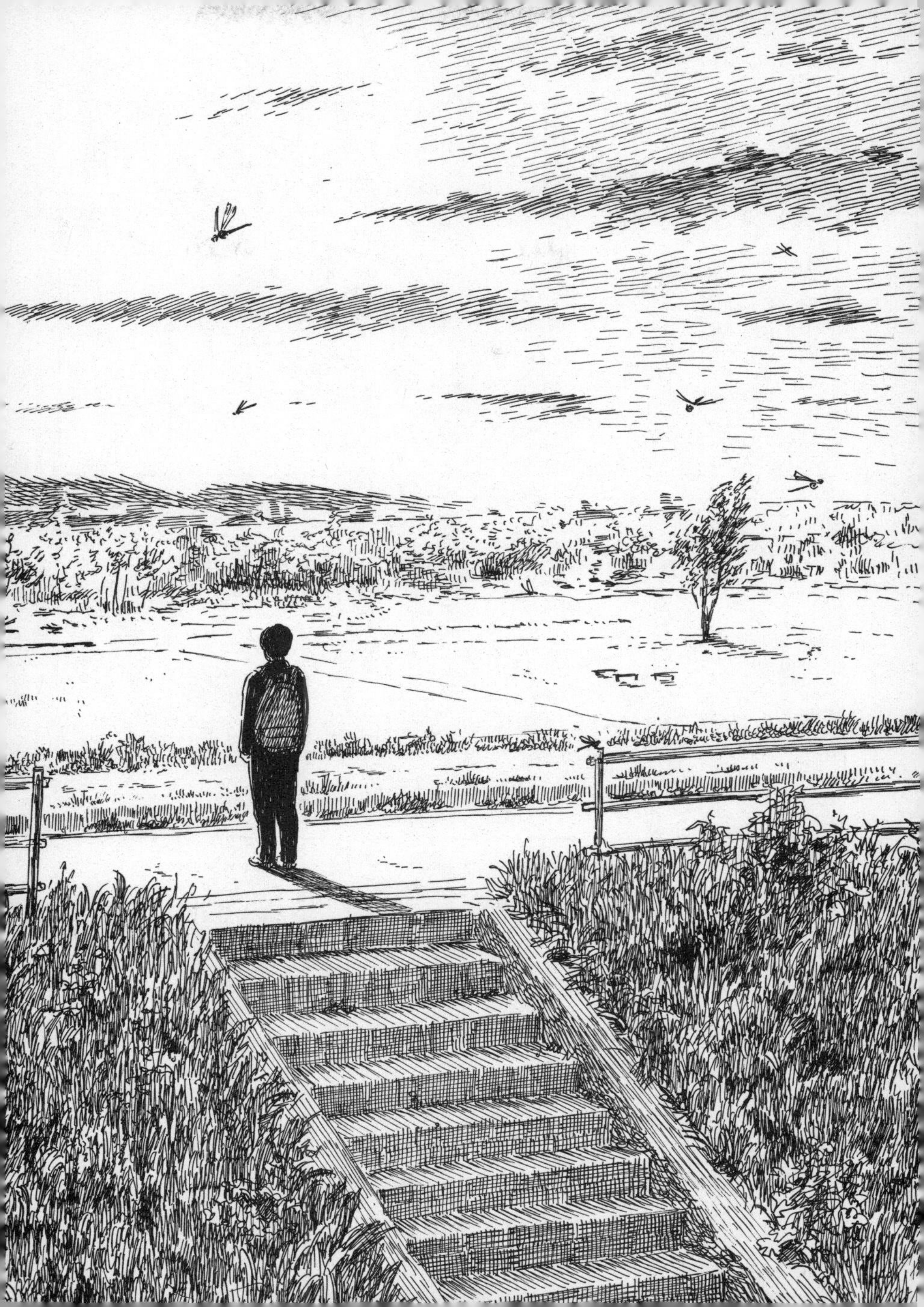

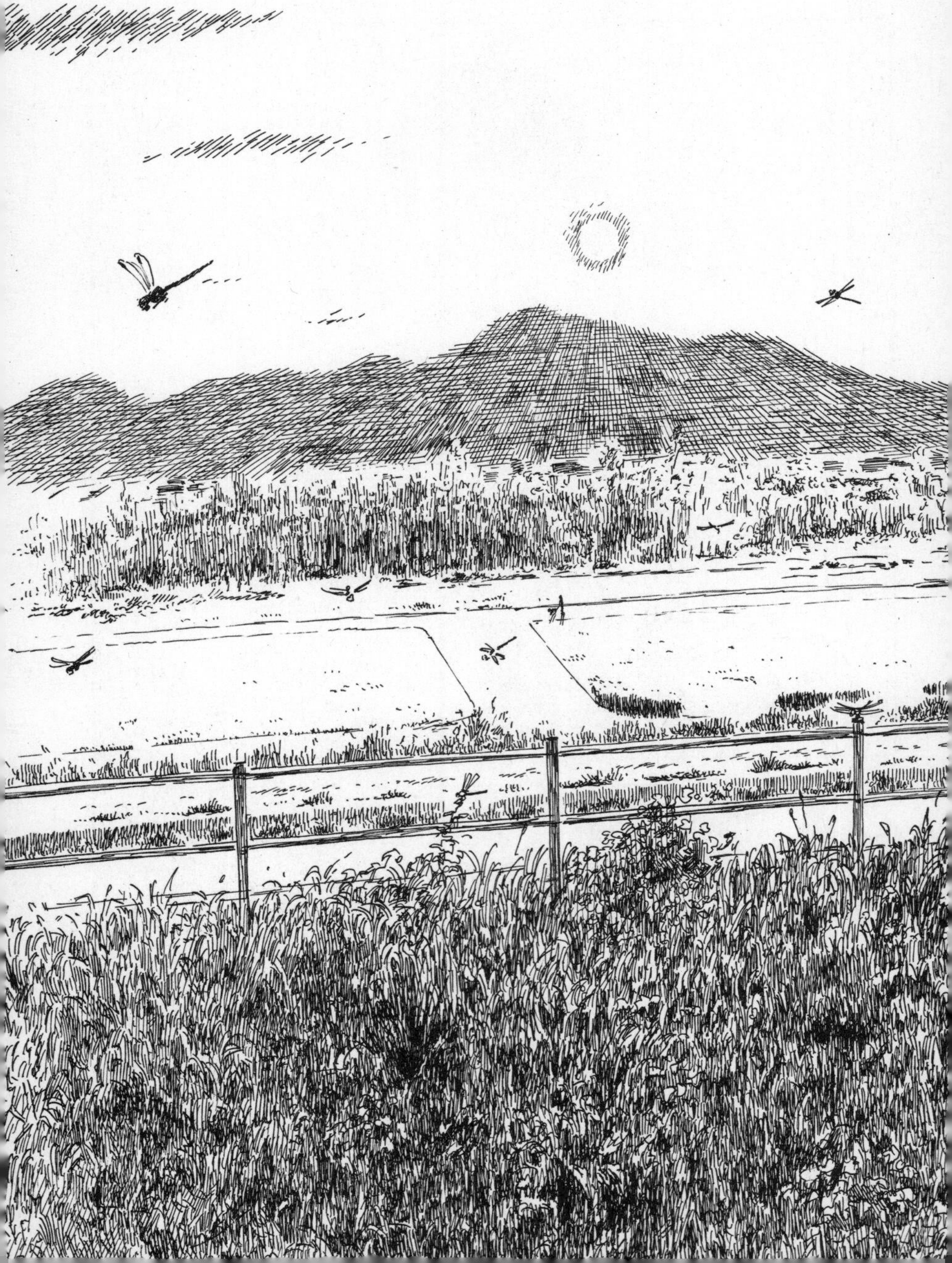

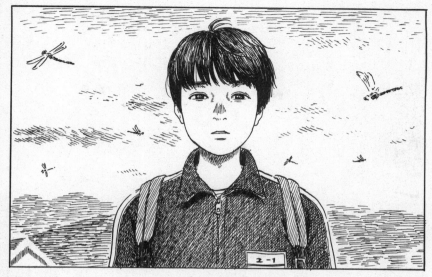

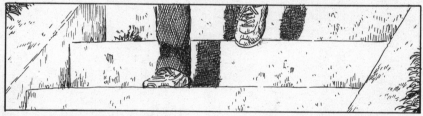

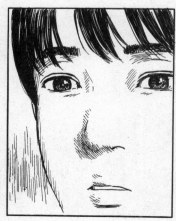

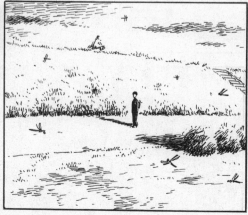

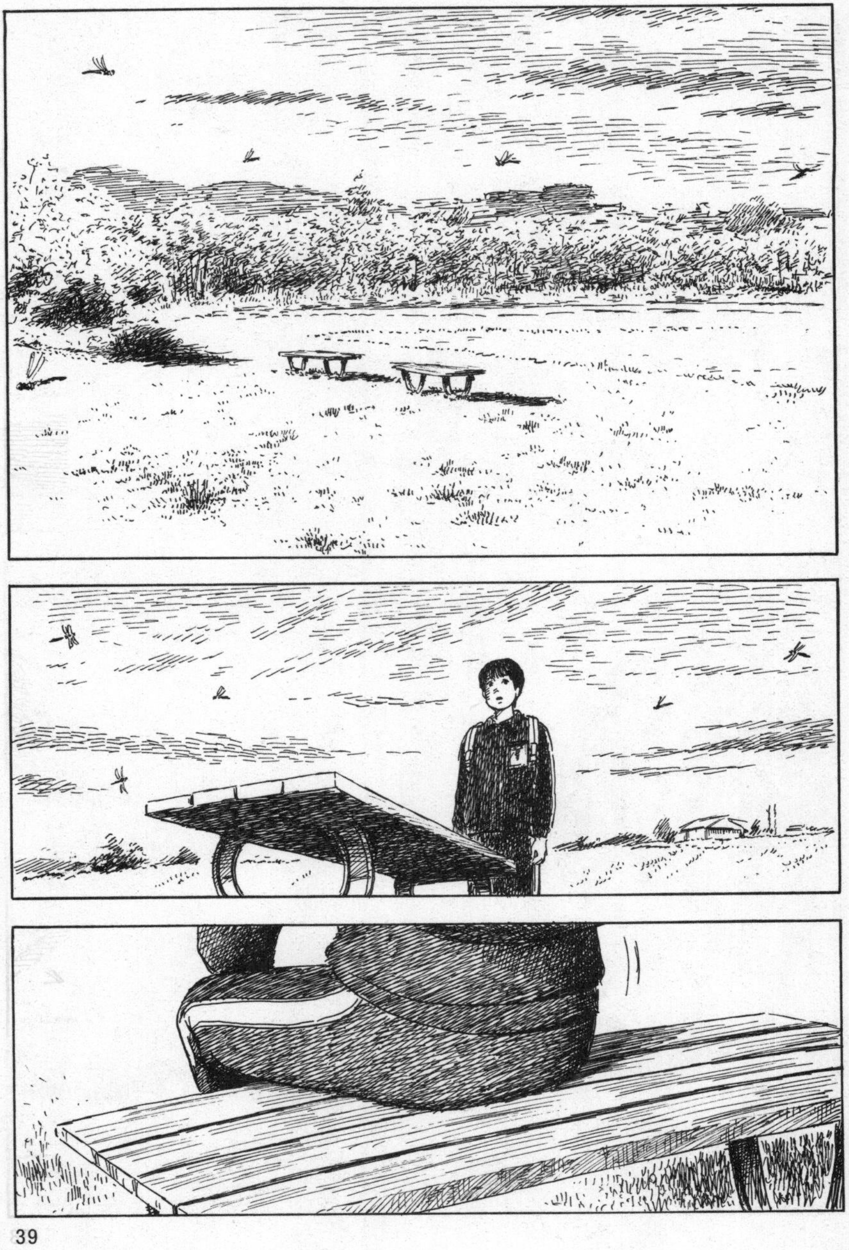

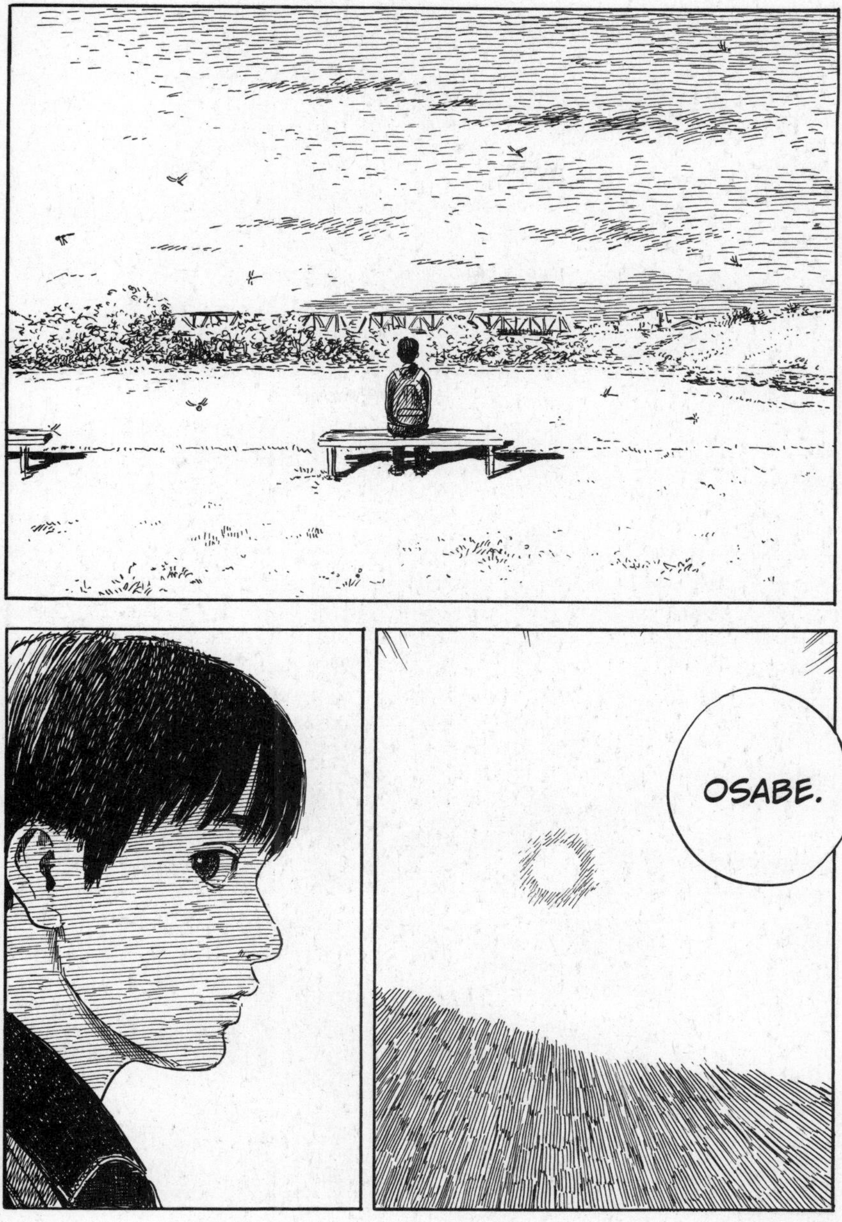
OSABE.

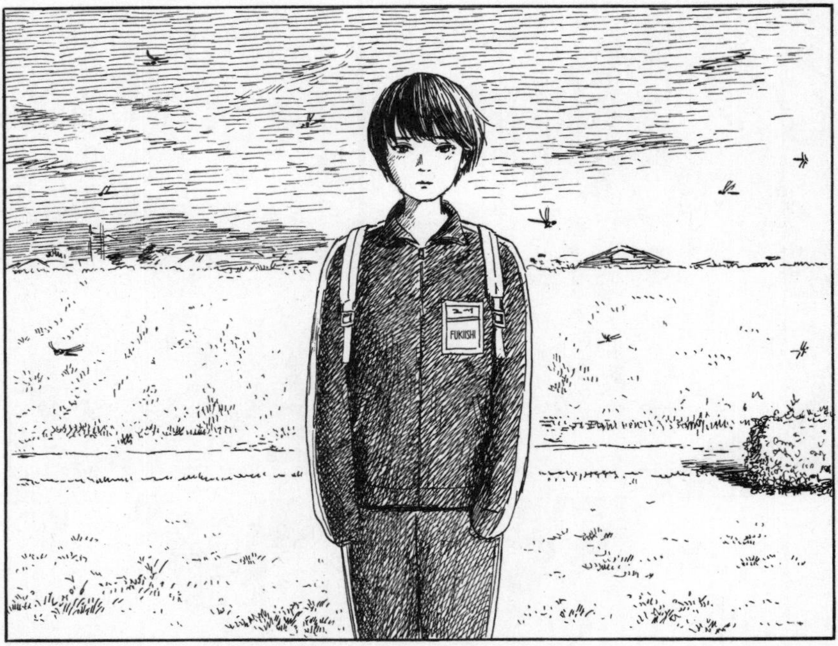
FUKIISHI

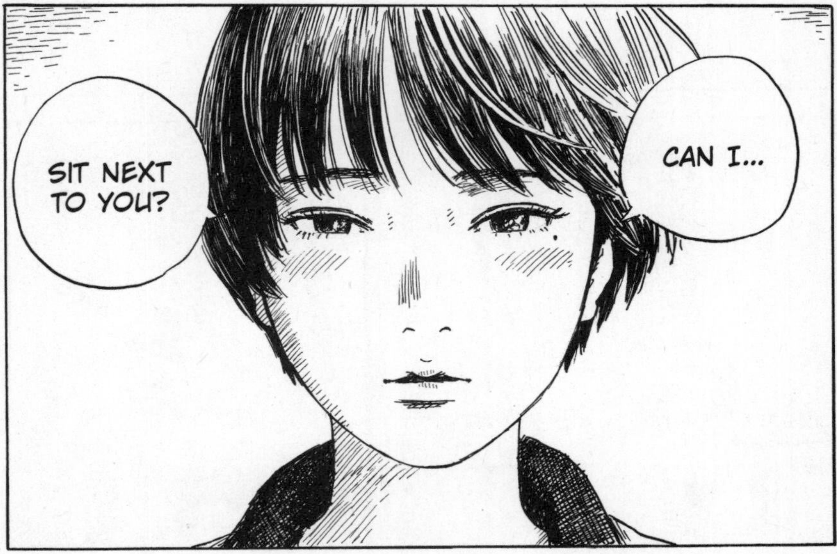
CAN I...
SIT NEXT TO YOU?

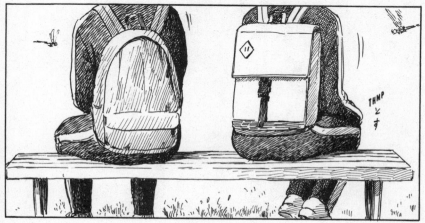

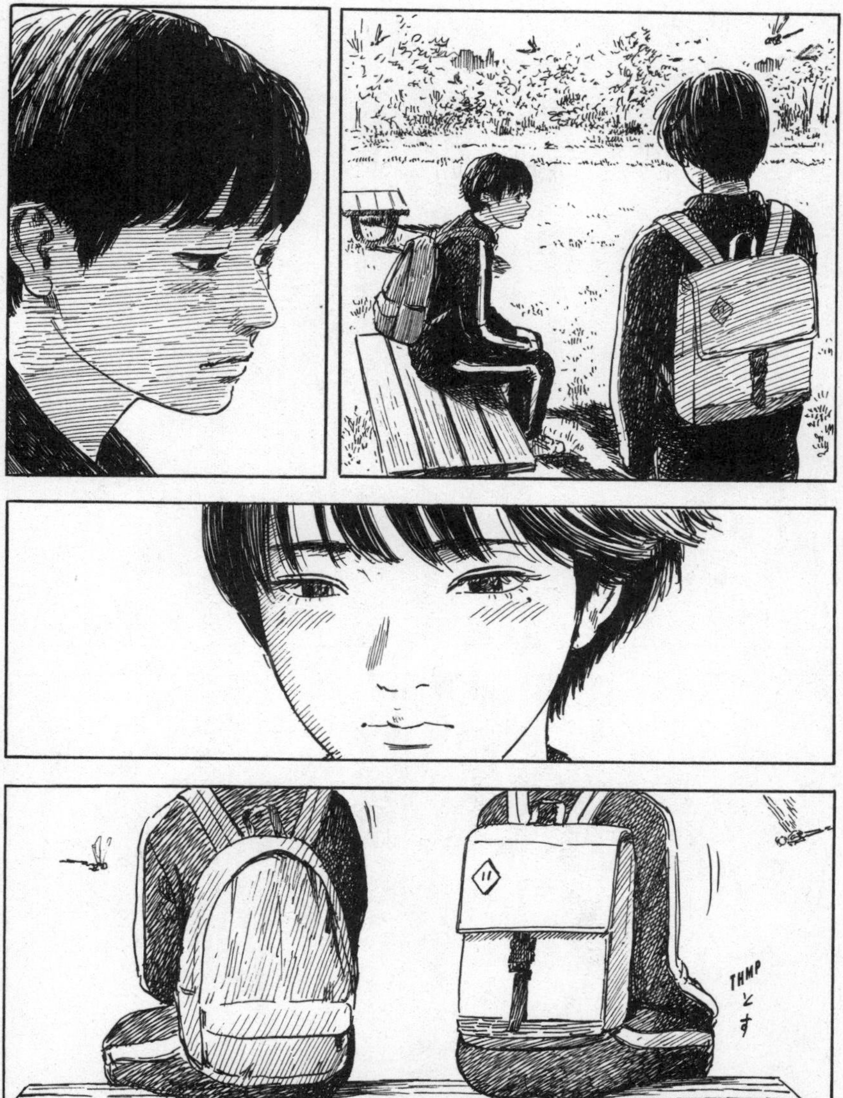
THMP
とす

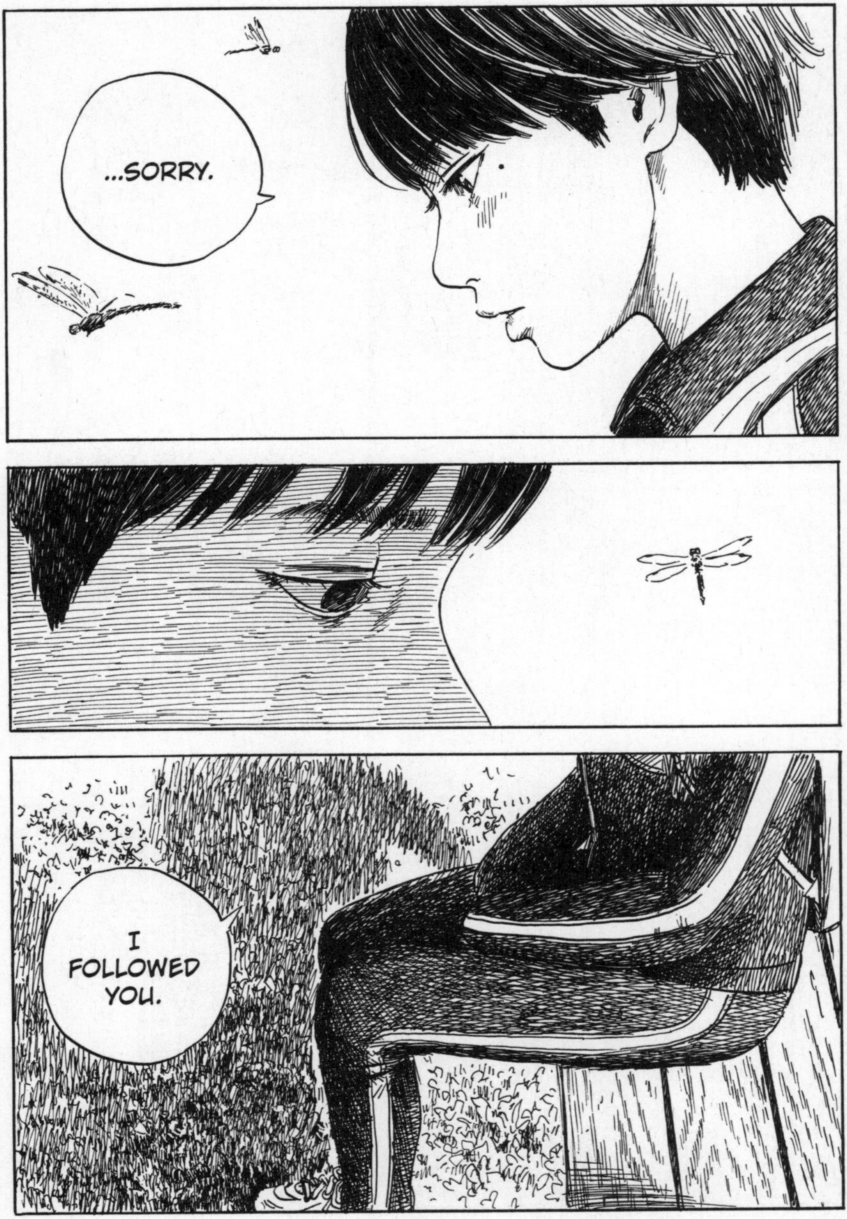
...SORRY.
I FOLLOWED YOU.

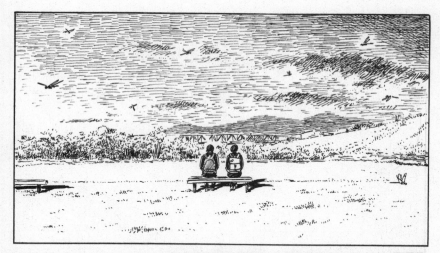

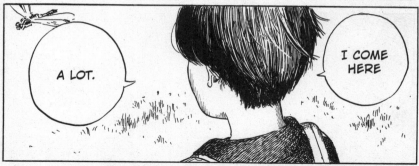

I COME
HERE

A LOT.

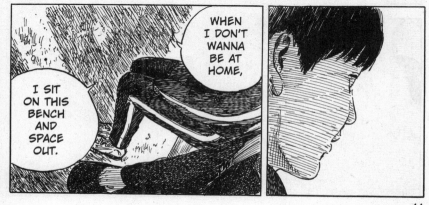

WHEN
I DON'T
WANNA
BE AT
HOME,

I SIT
ON THIS
BENCH
AND
SPACE
OUT.

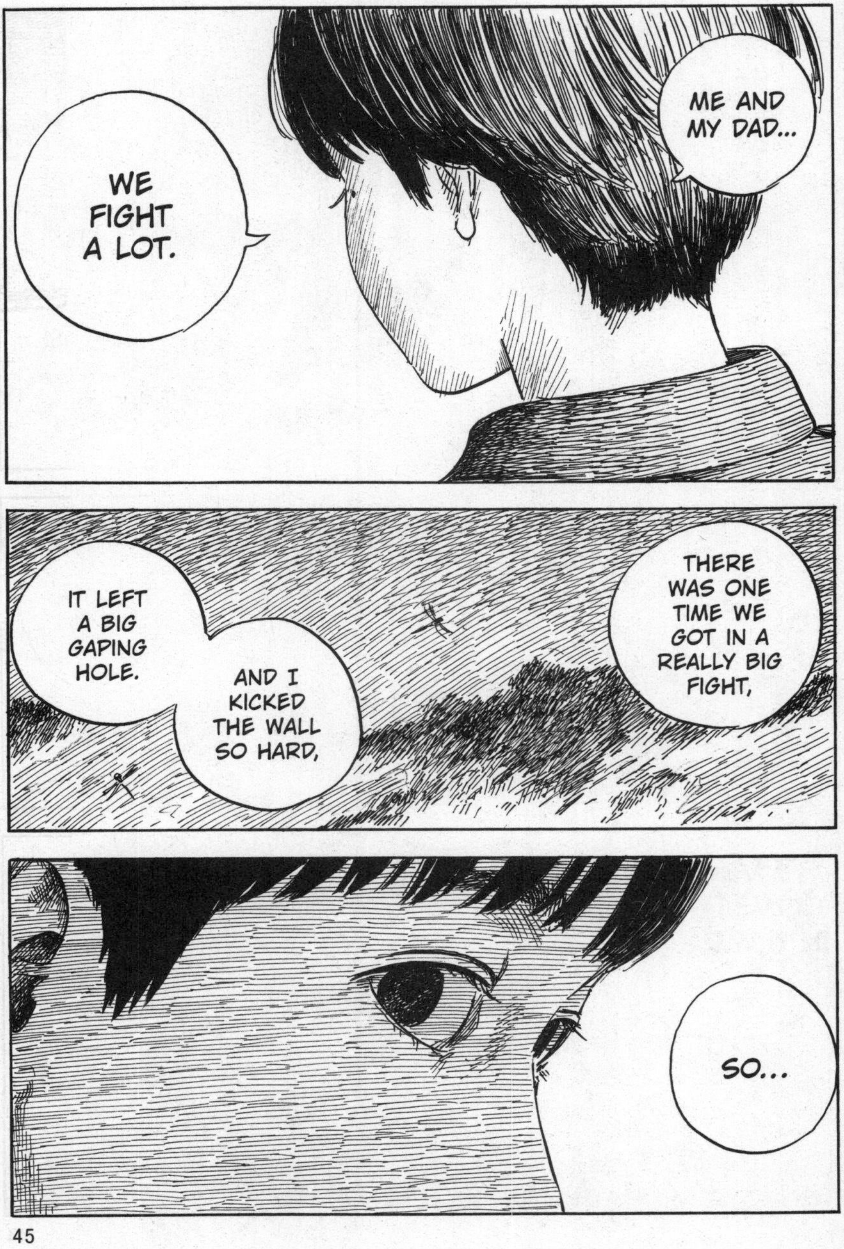

ME AND MY DAD...
WE FIGHT A LOT.
THERE WAS ONE TIME WE GOT IN A REALLY BIG FIGHT,
AND I KICKED THE WALL SO HARD,
IT LEFT A BIG GAPING HOLE.
SO...

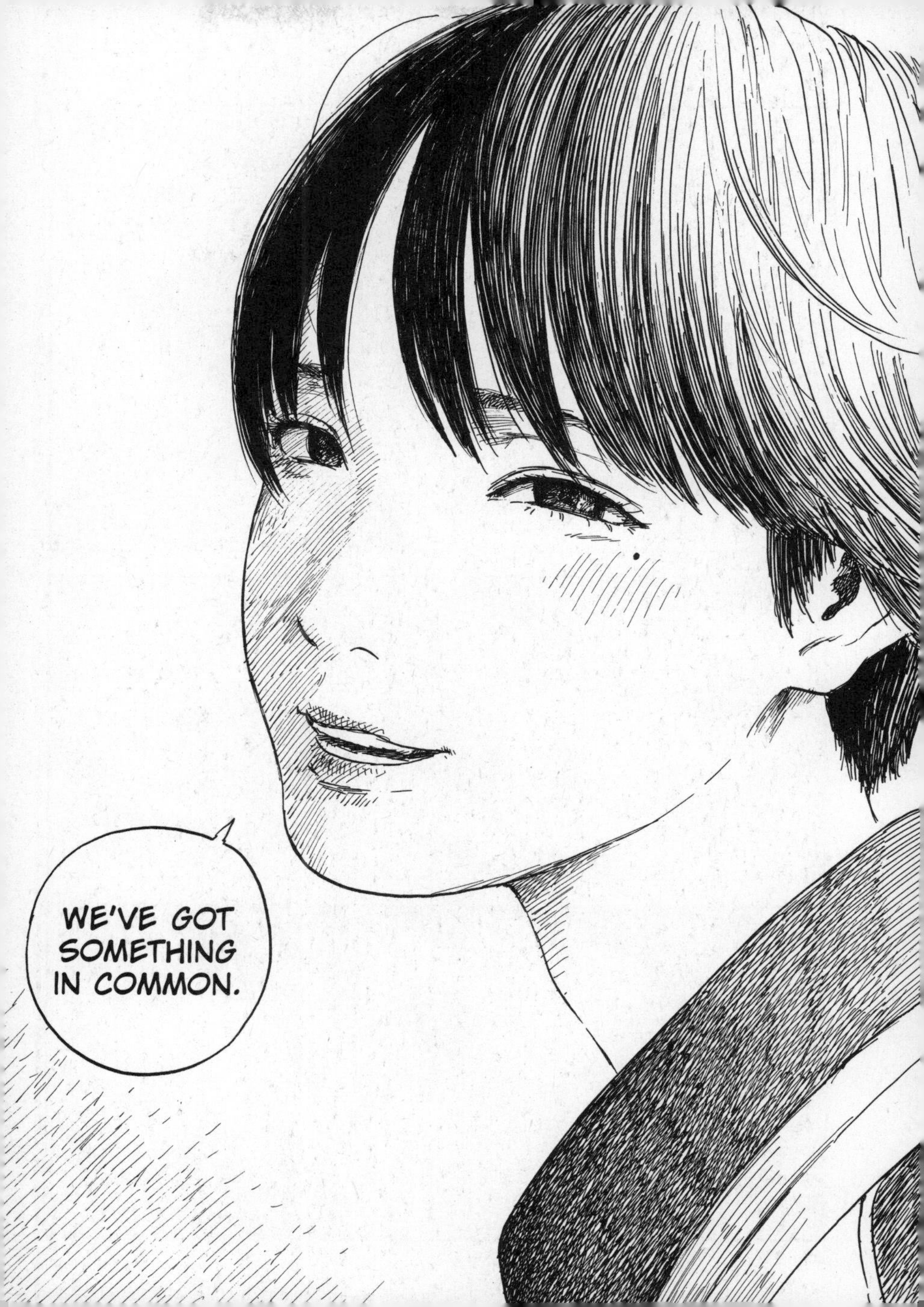
WE'VE GOT SOMETHING IN COMMON.

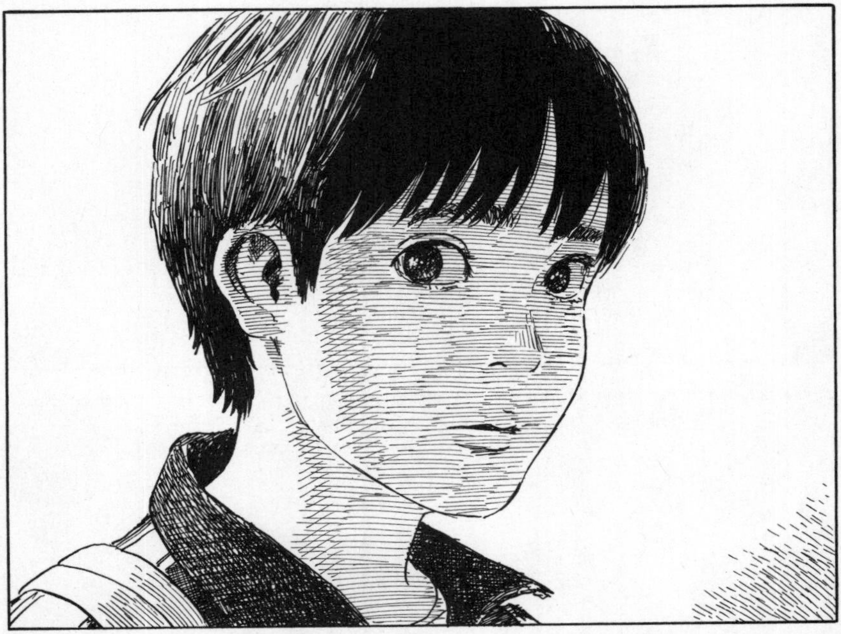
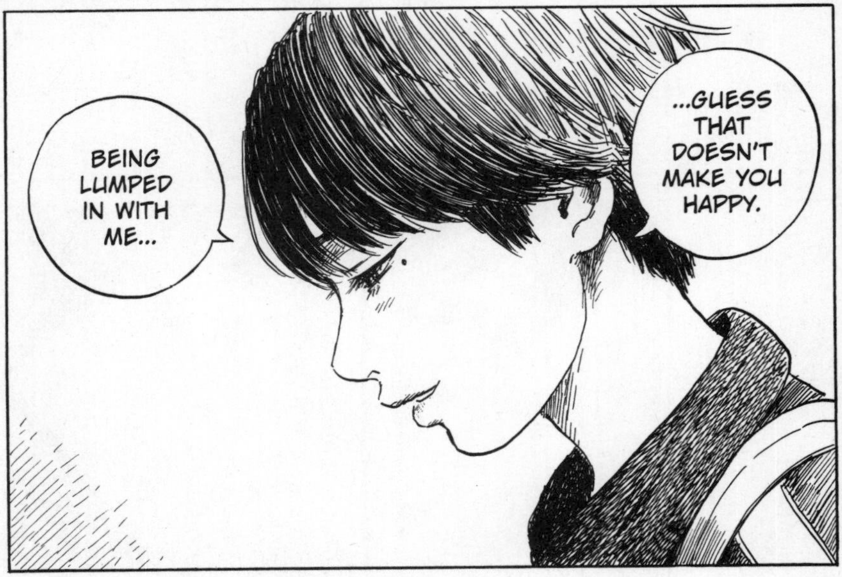
...GUESS THAT DOESN'T MAKE YOU HAPPY.
BEING LUMPED IN WITH ME...

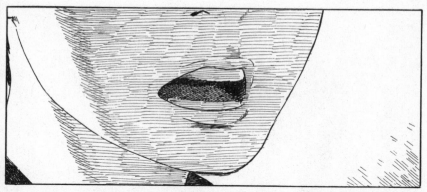

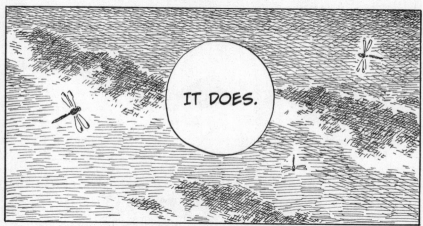

IT DOES.

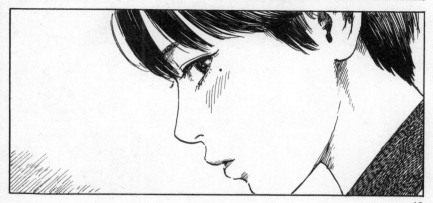

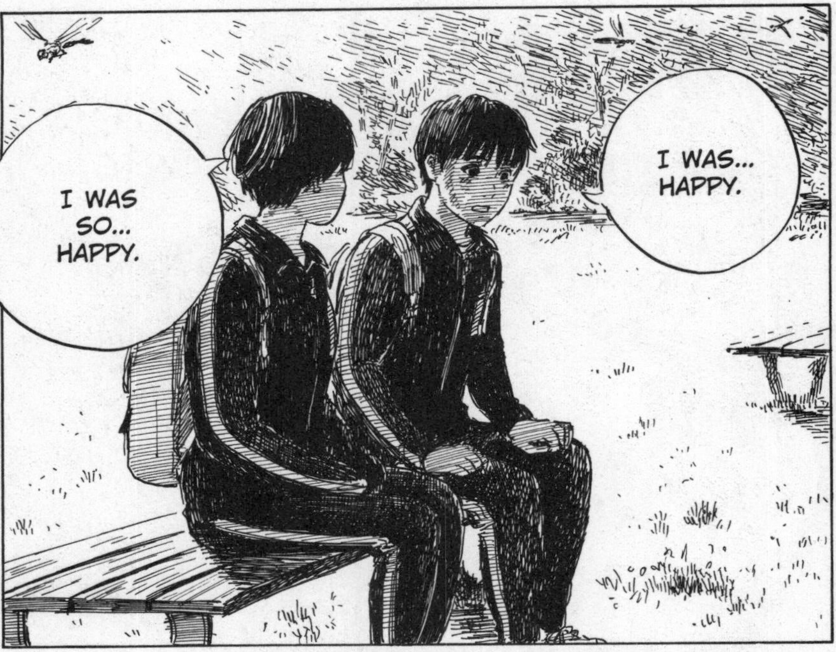
I WAS... HAPPY.
I WAS SO... HAPPY.

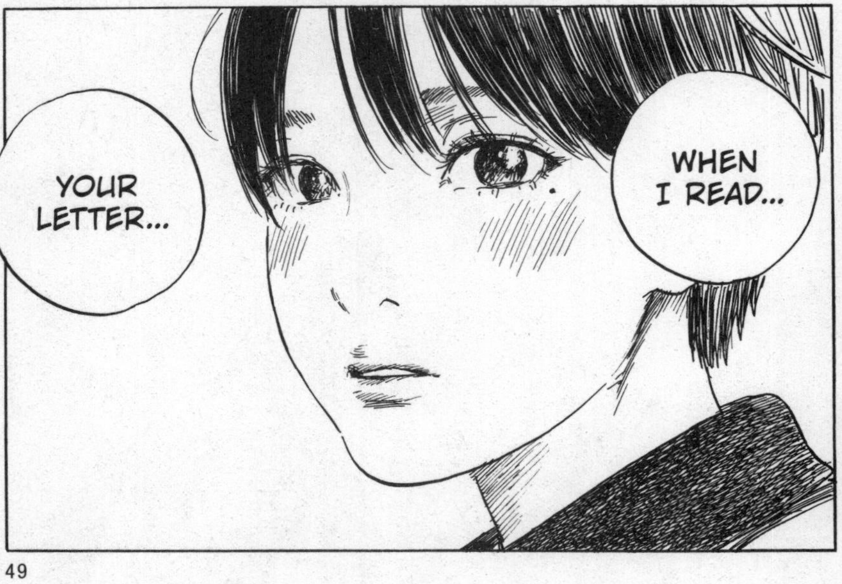
WHEN I READ...
YOUR LETTER...

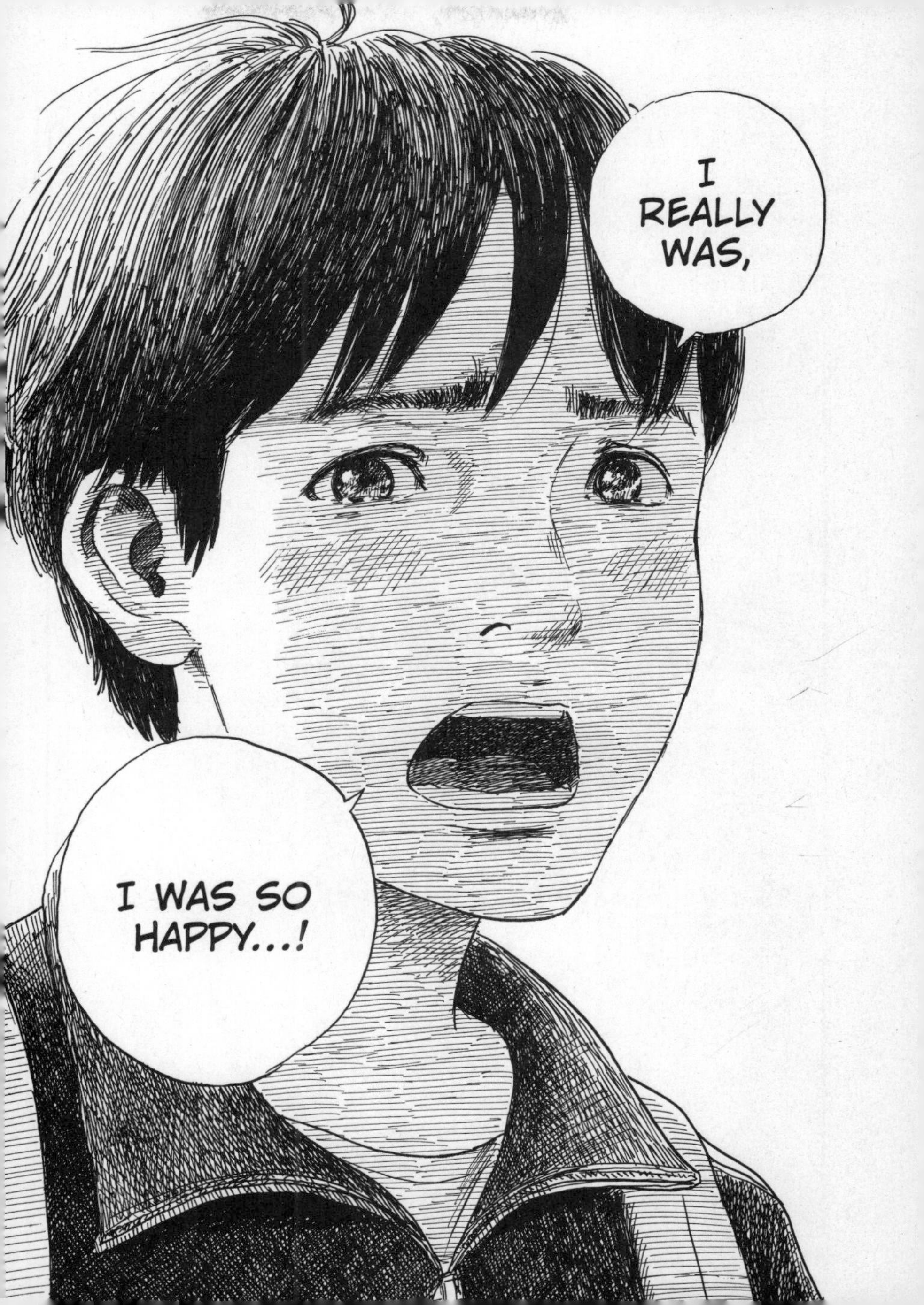
I REALLY WAS,
I WAS SO HAPPY...!

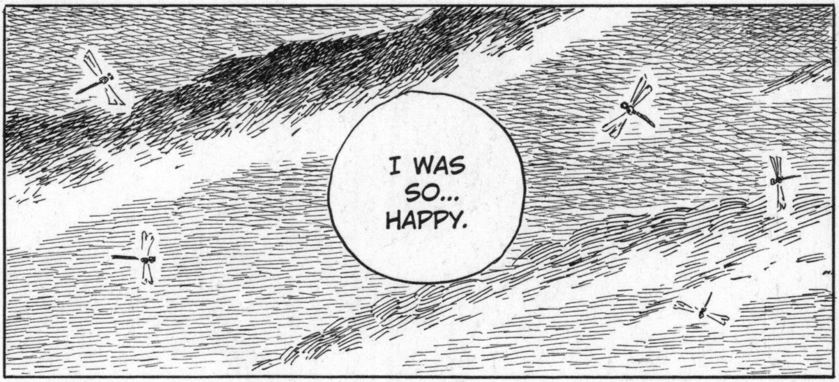
I WAS SO... HAPPY.

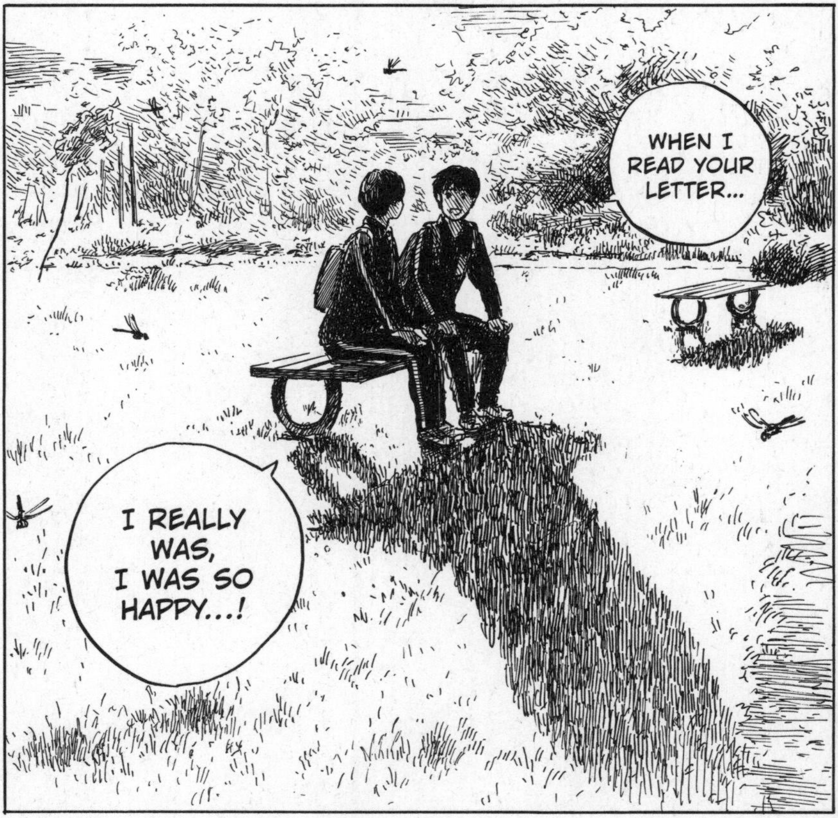
WHEN I READ YOUR LETTER...
I REALLY WAS, I WAS SO HAPPY...!

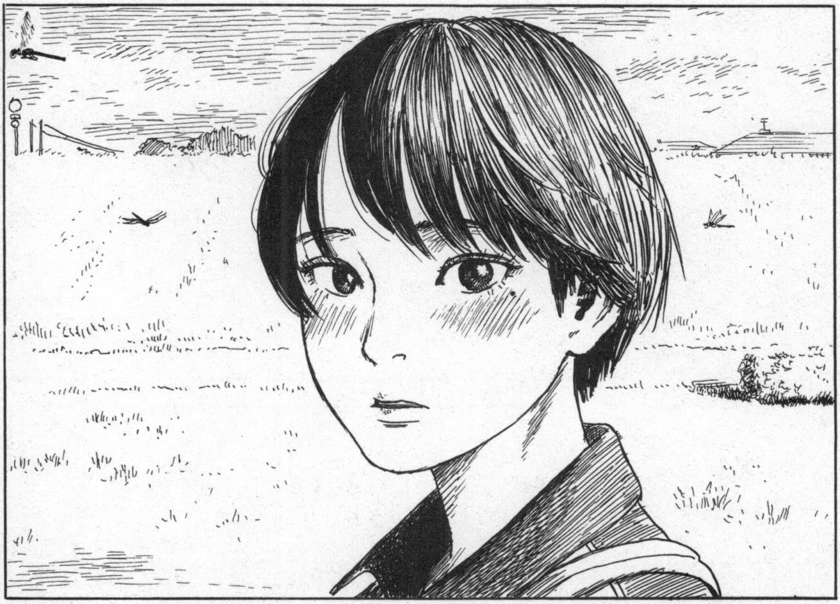

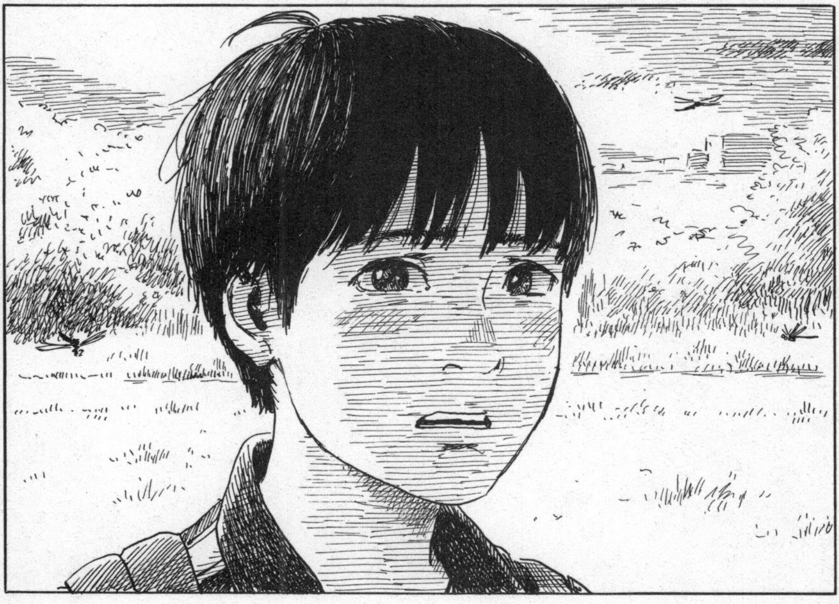

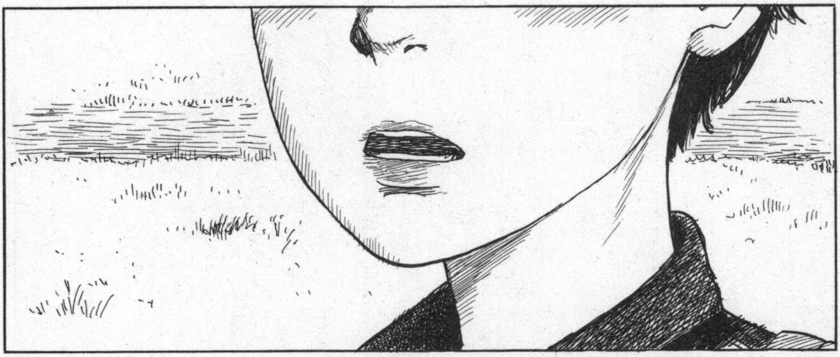
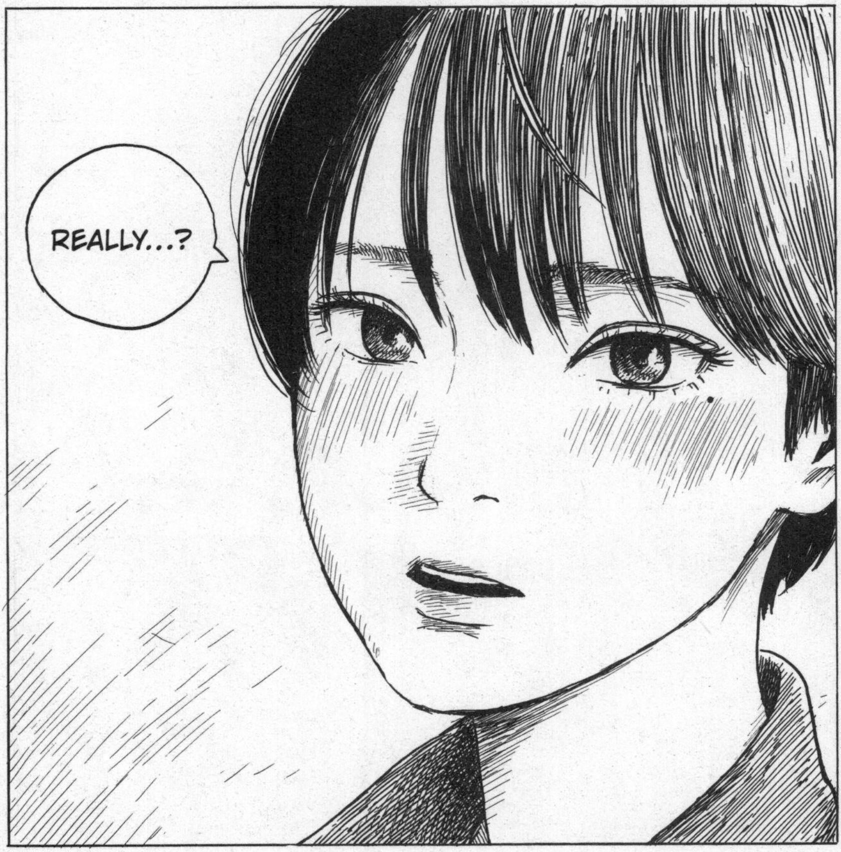
REALLY...?

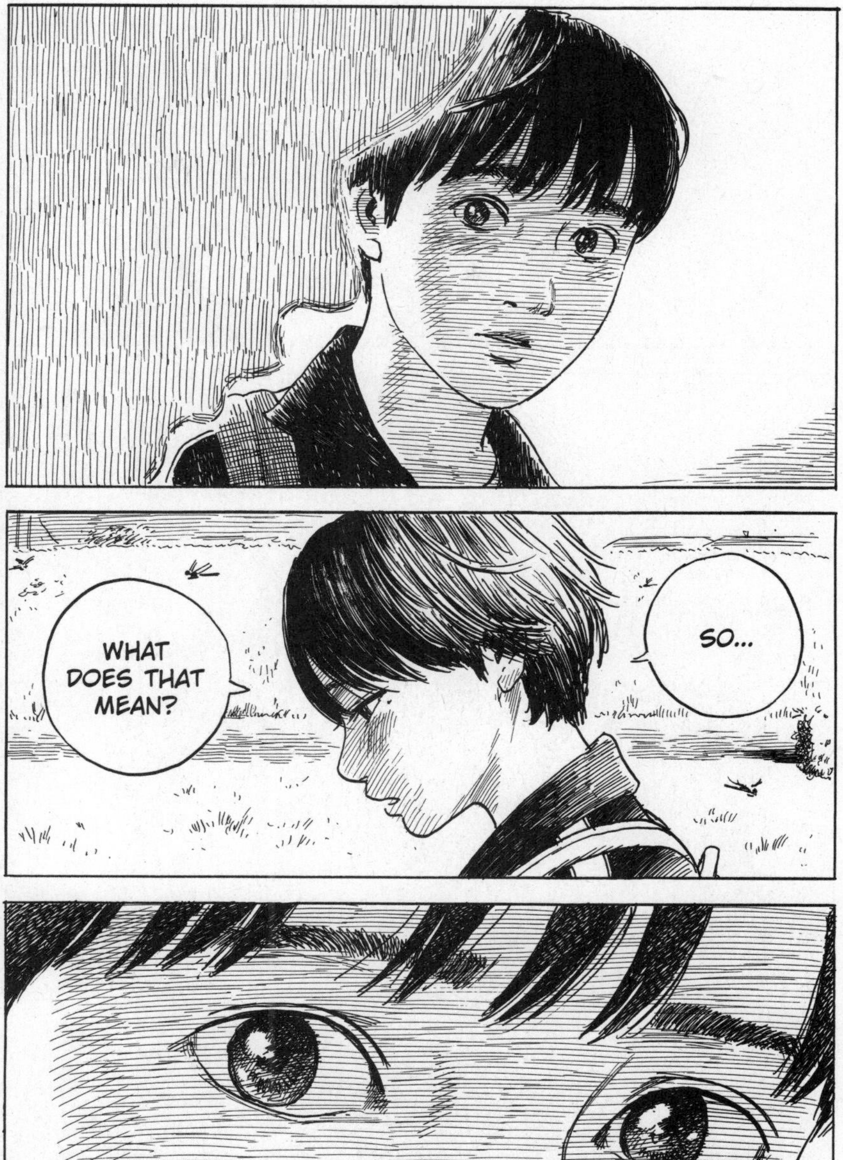
SO...
WHAT DOES THAT MEAN?

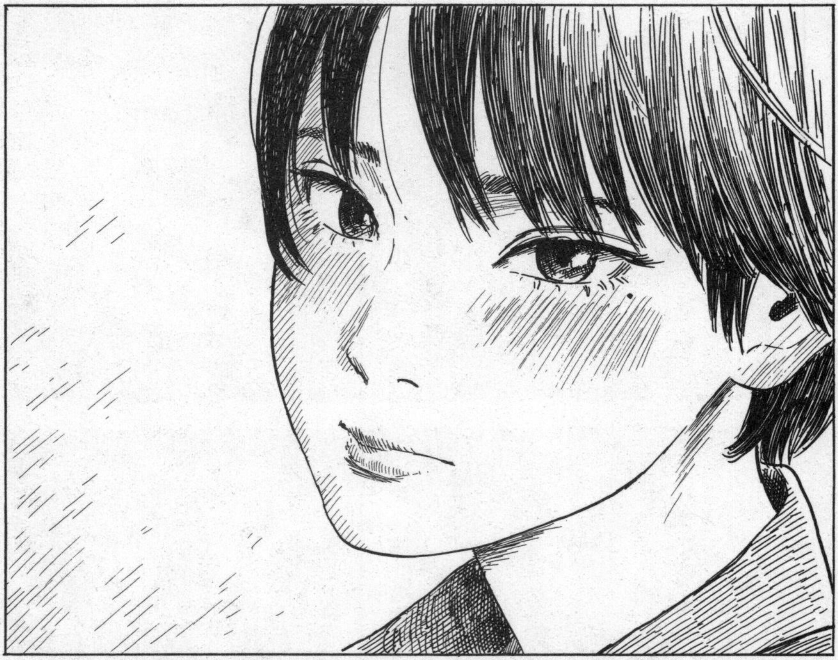
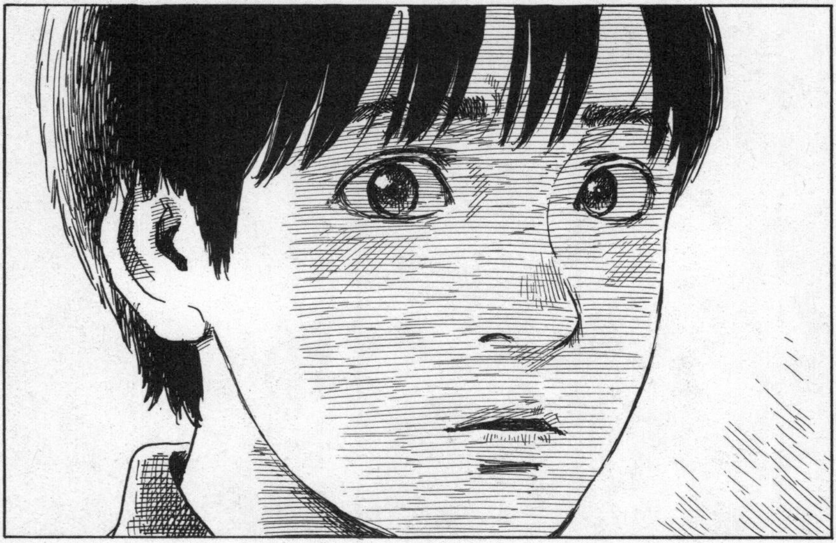

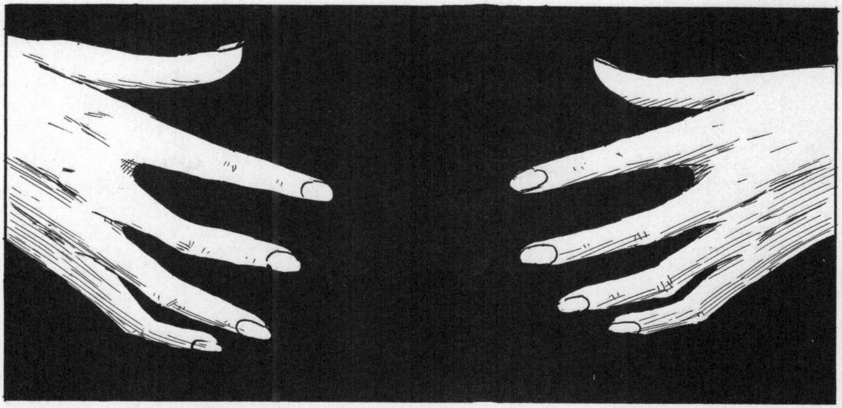

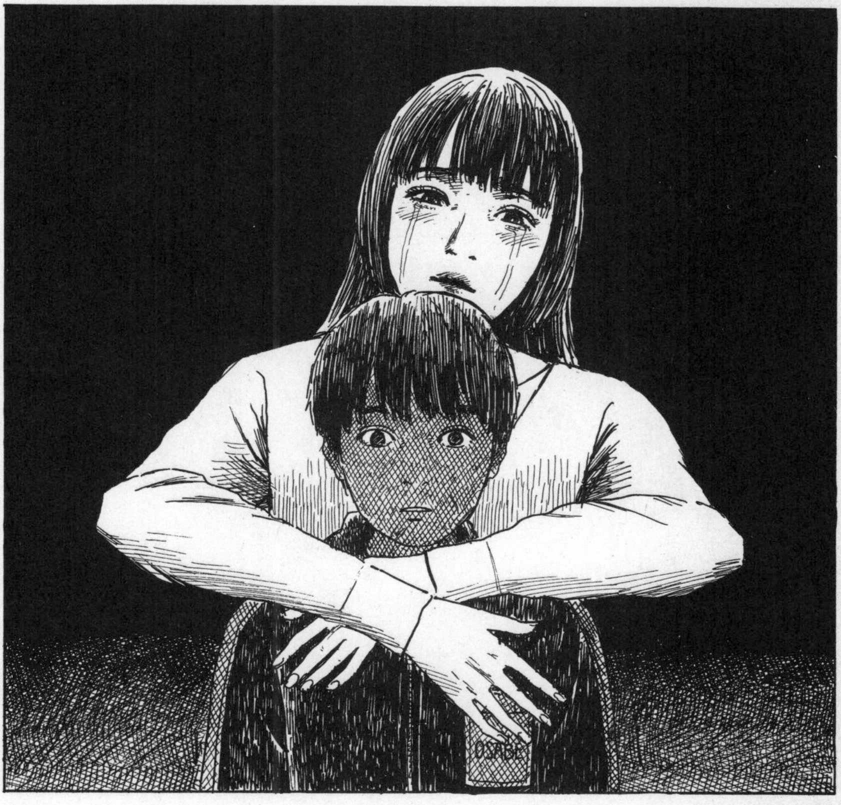

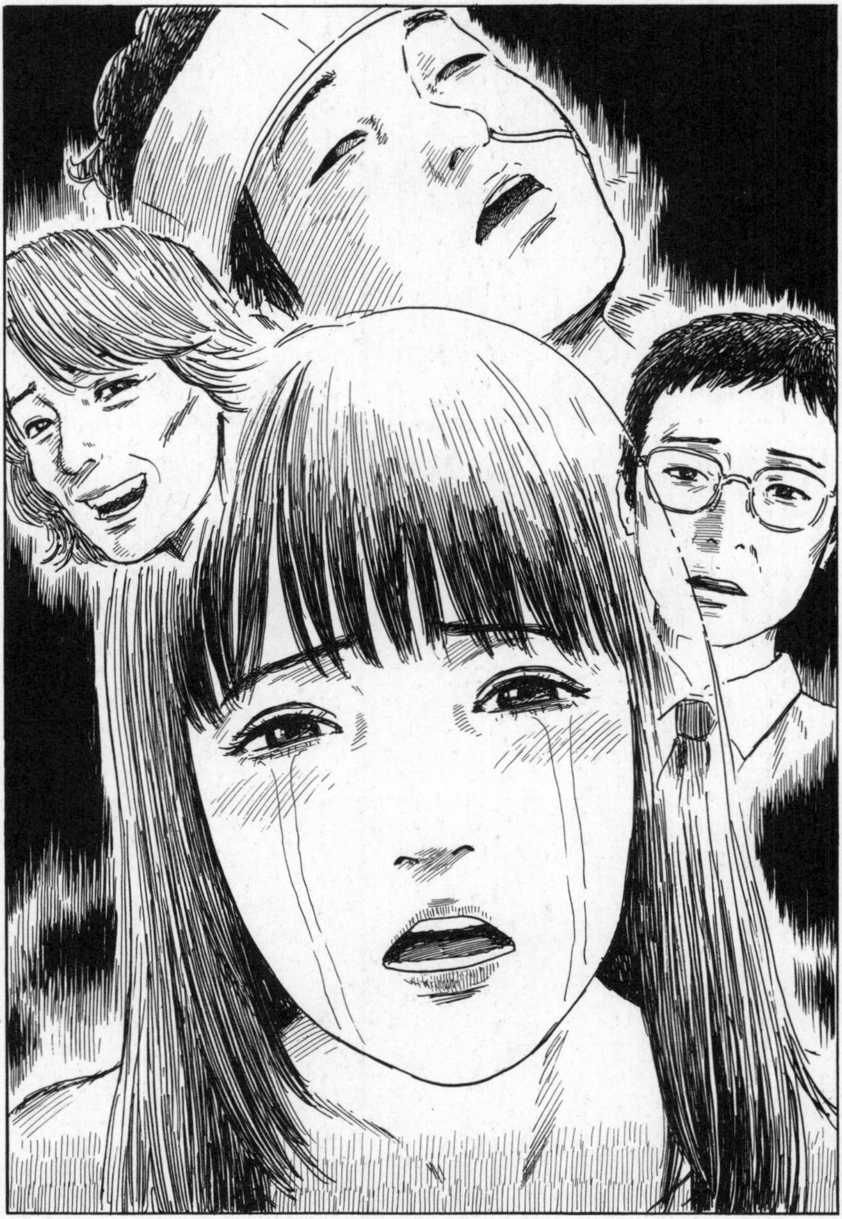

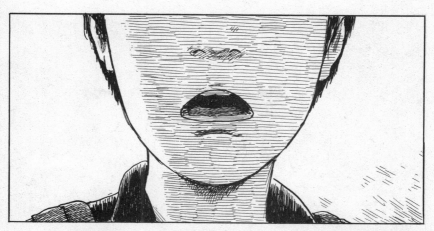

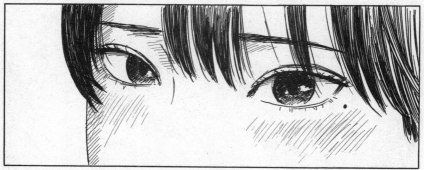

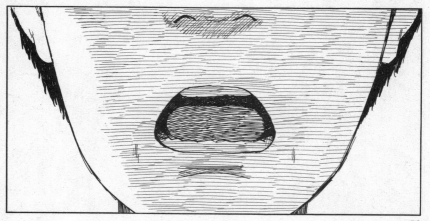

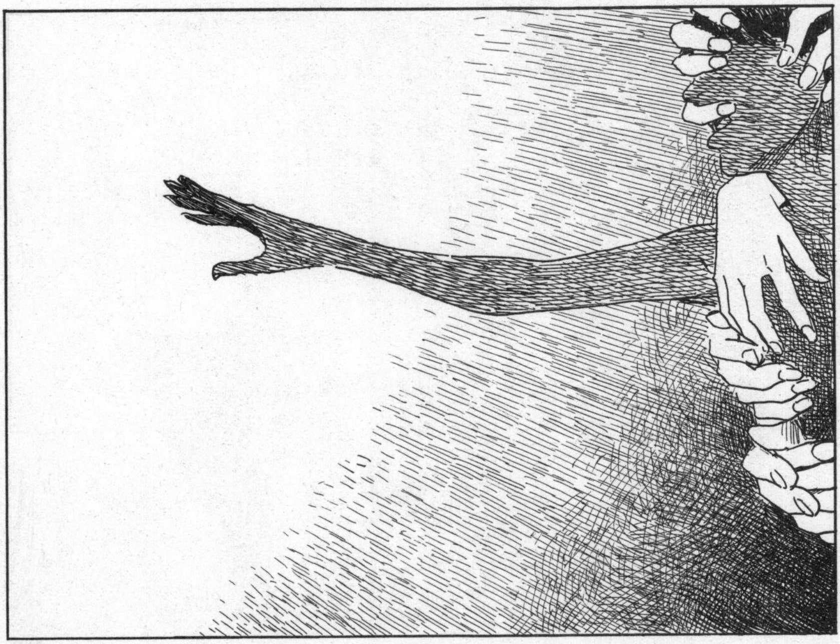

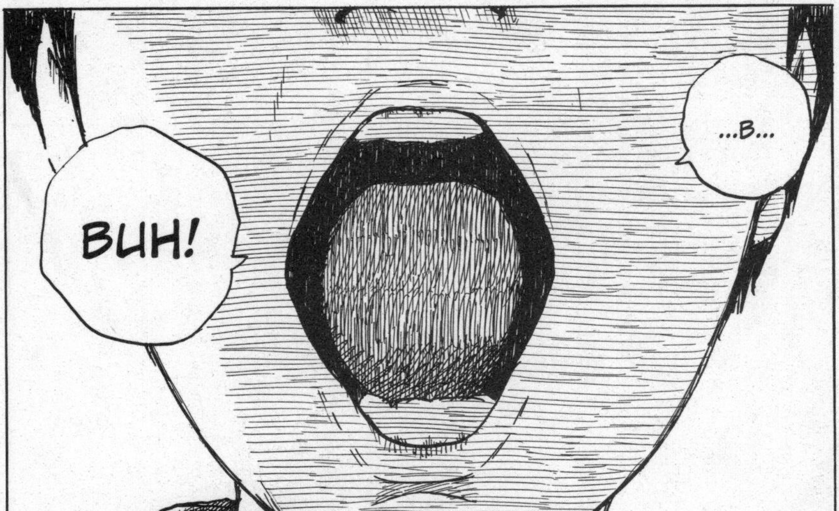
...B...
BUH!

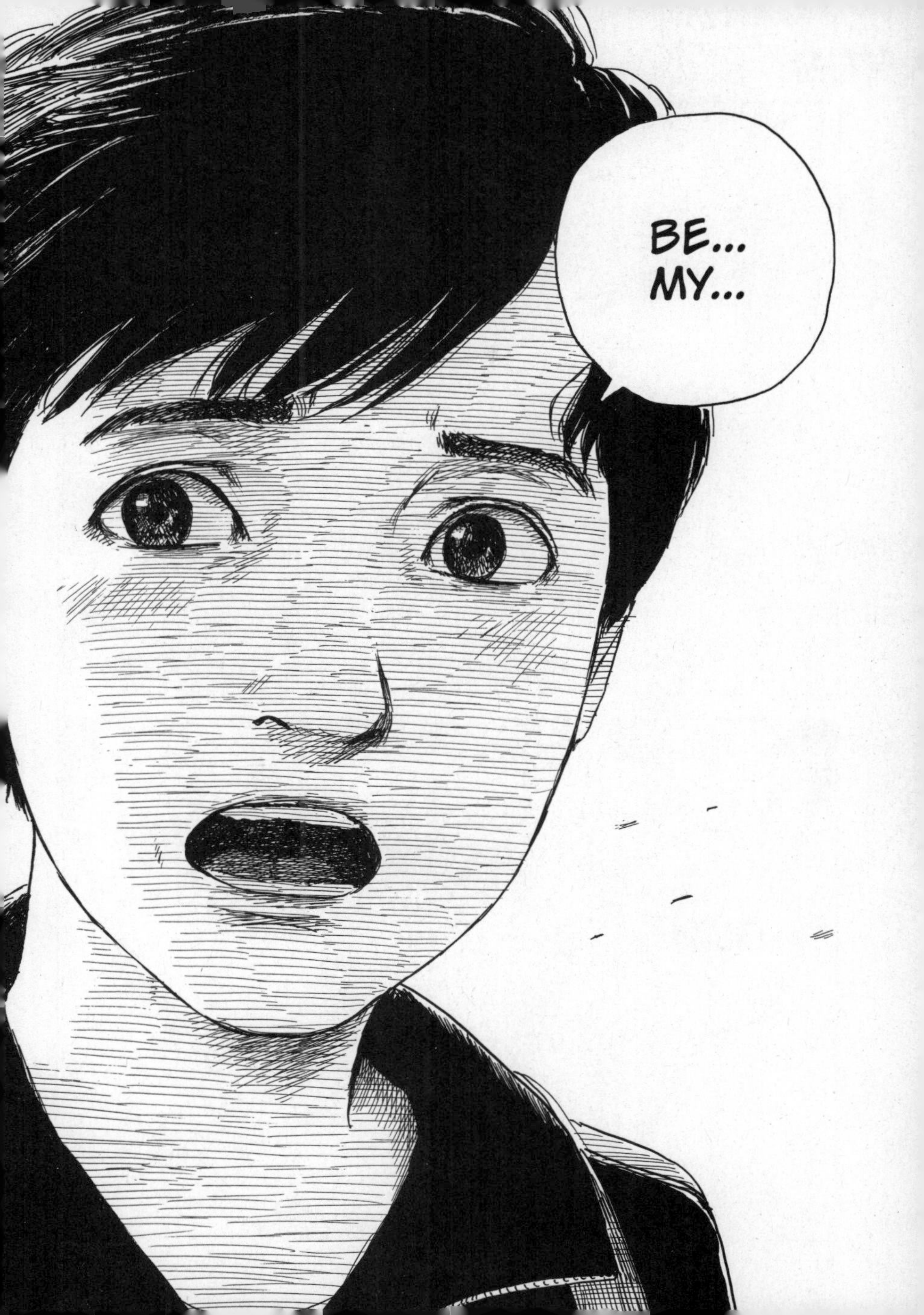
BE...
MY...

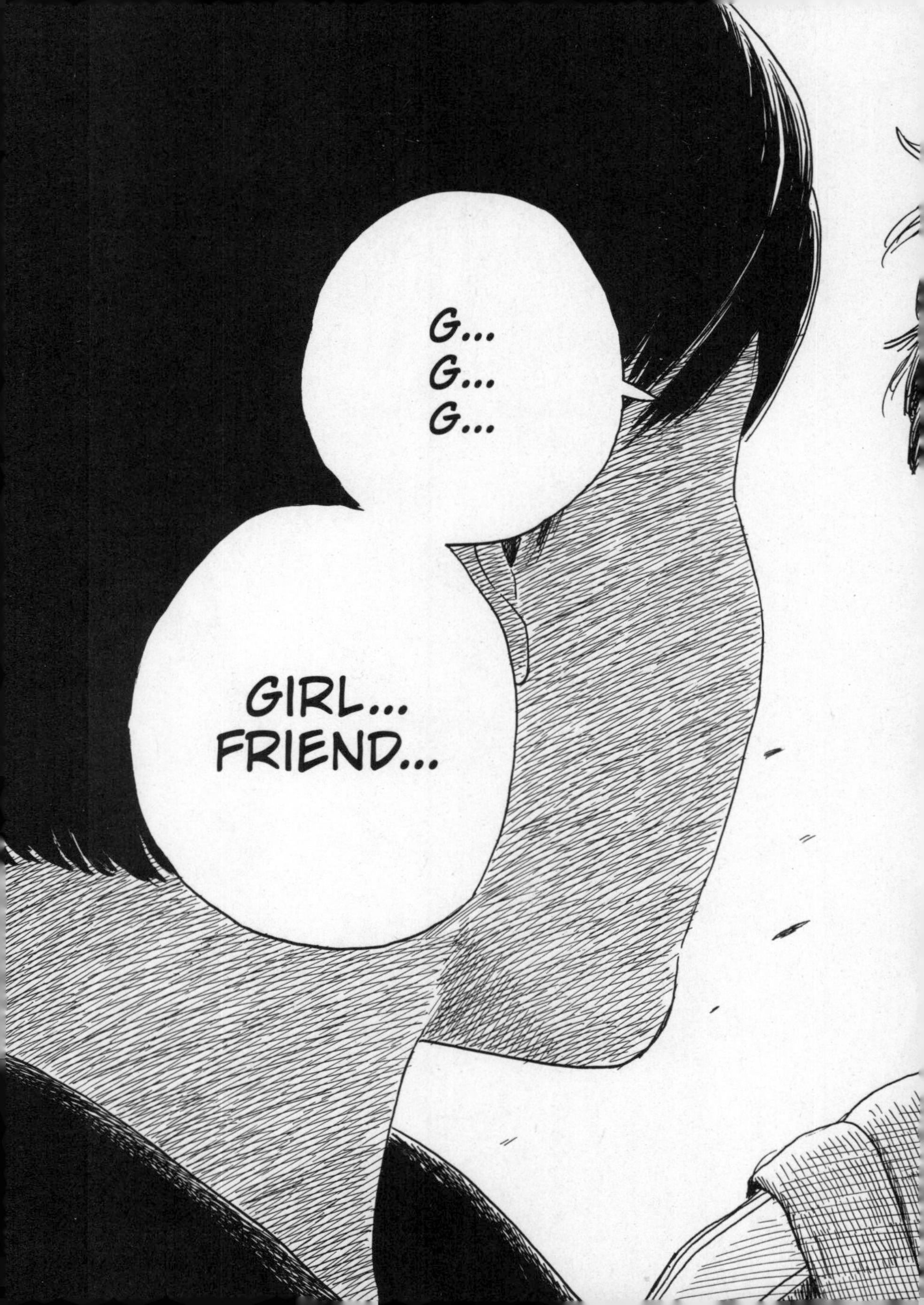
G... G... G...
GIRL... FRIEND...

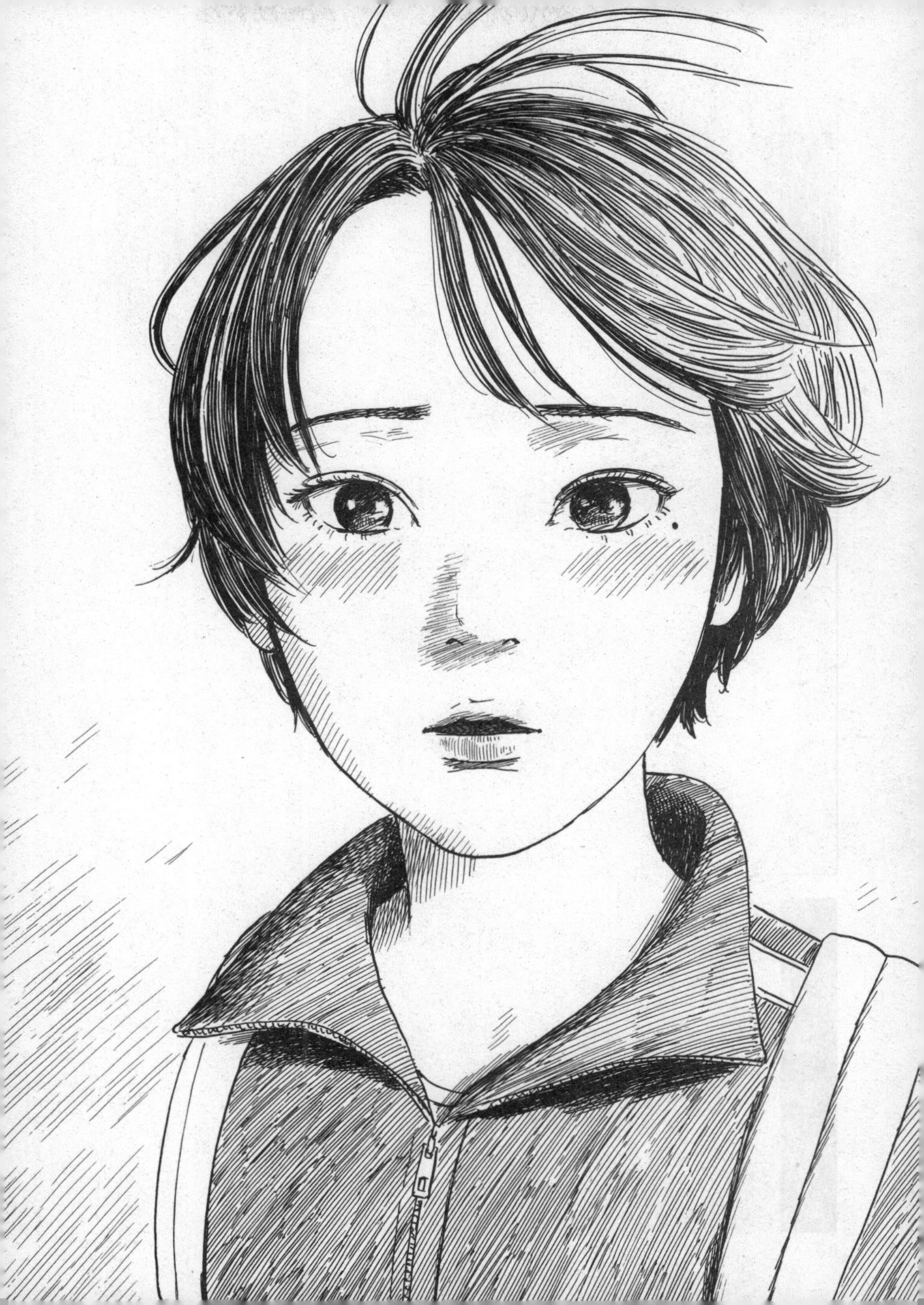

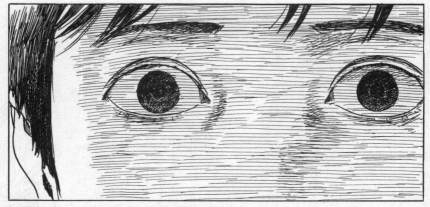

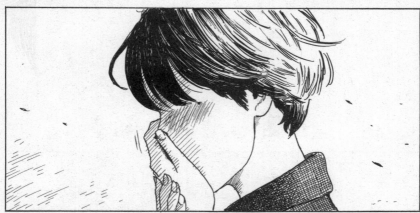

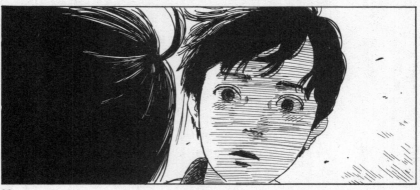

63

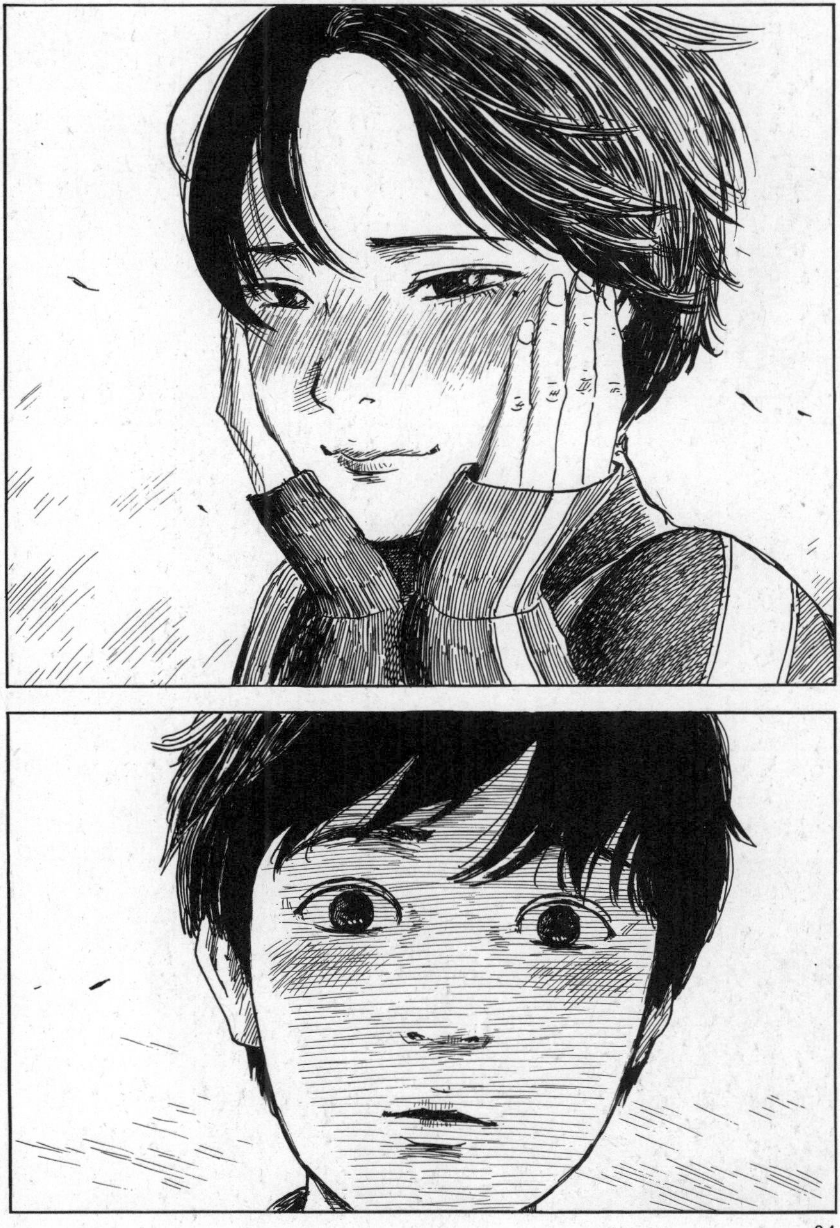

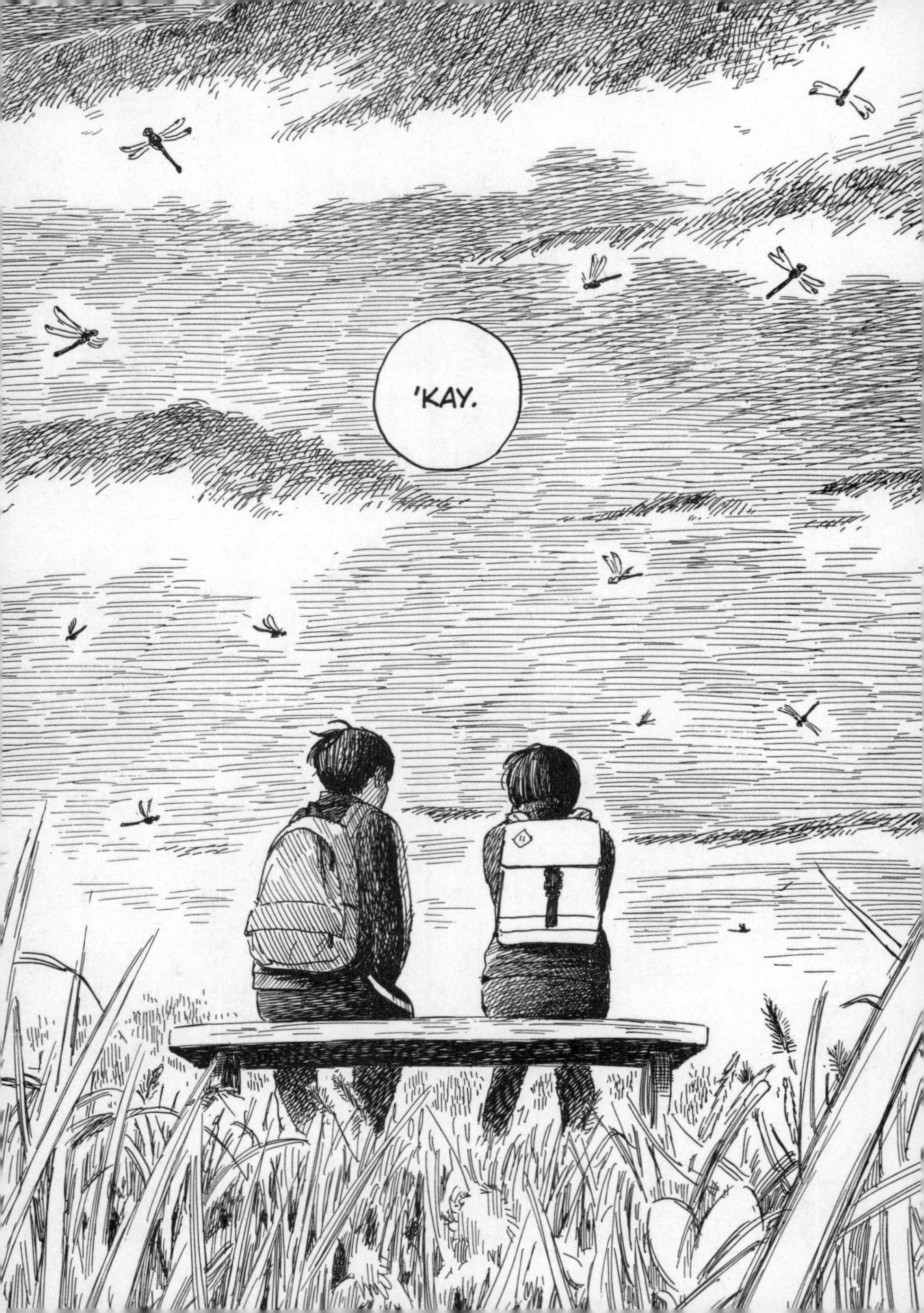
'KAY.

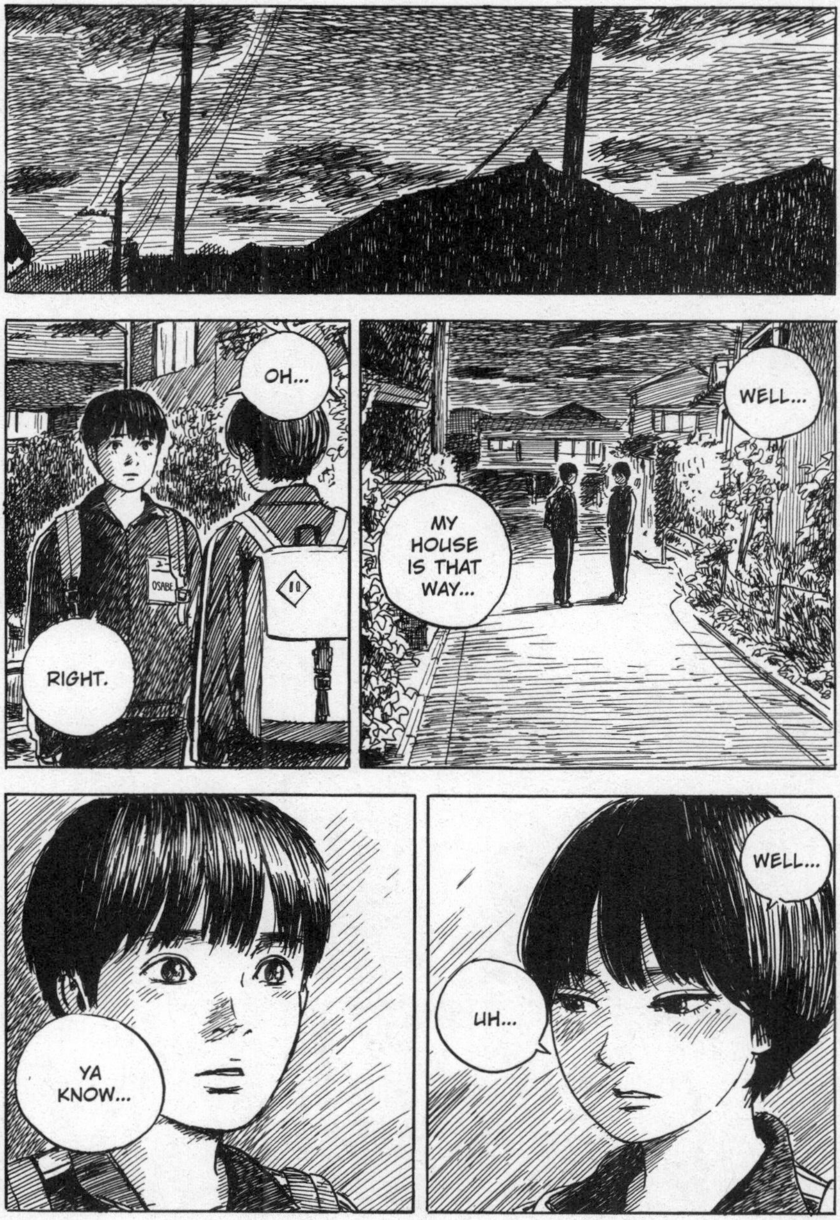
WELL...
MY HOUSE IS THAT WAY...
OH...
RIGHT.
WELL...
UH...
YA KNOW...

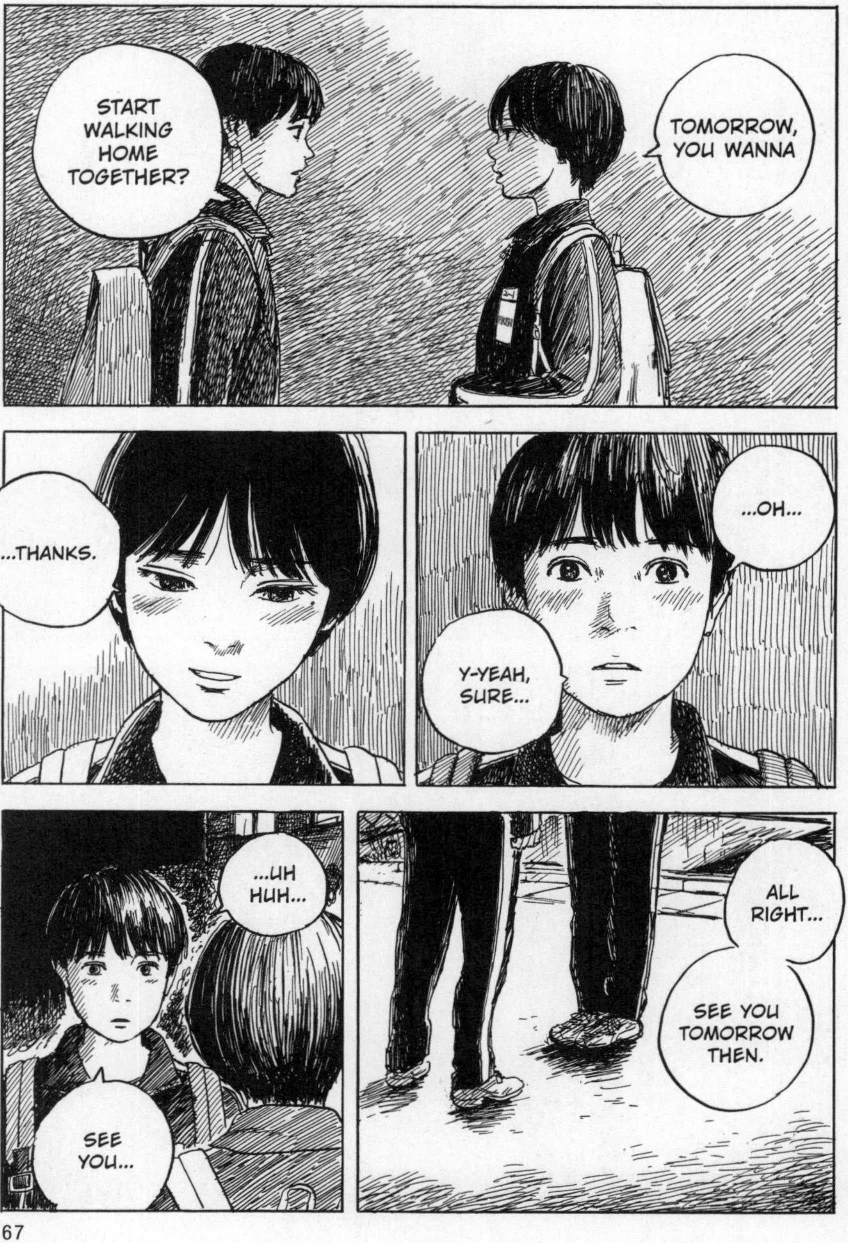
TOMORROW, YOU WANNA
START WALKING HOME TOGETHER?
...OH...
Y-YEAH, SURE...
...THANKS.
ALL RIGHT...
SEE YOU TOMORROW THEN.
...UH HUH...
SEE YOU...

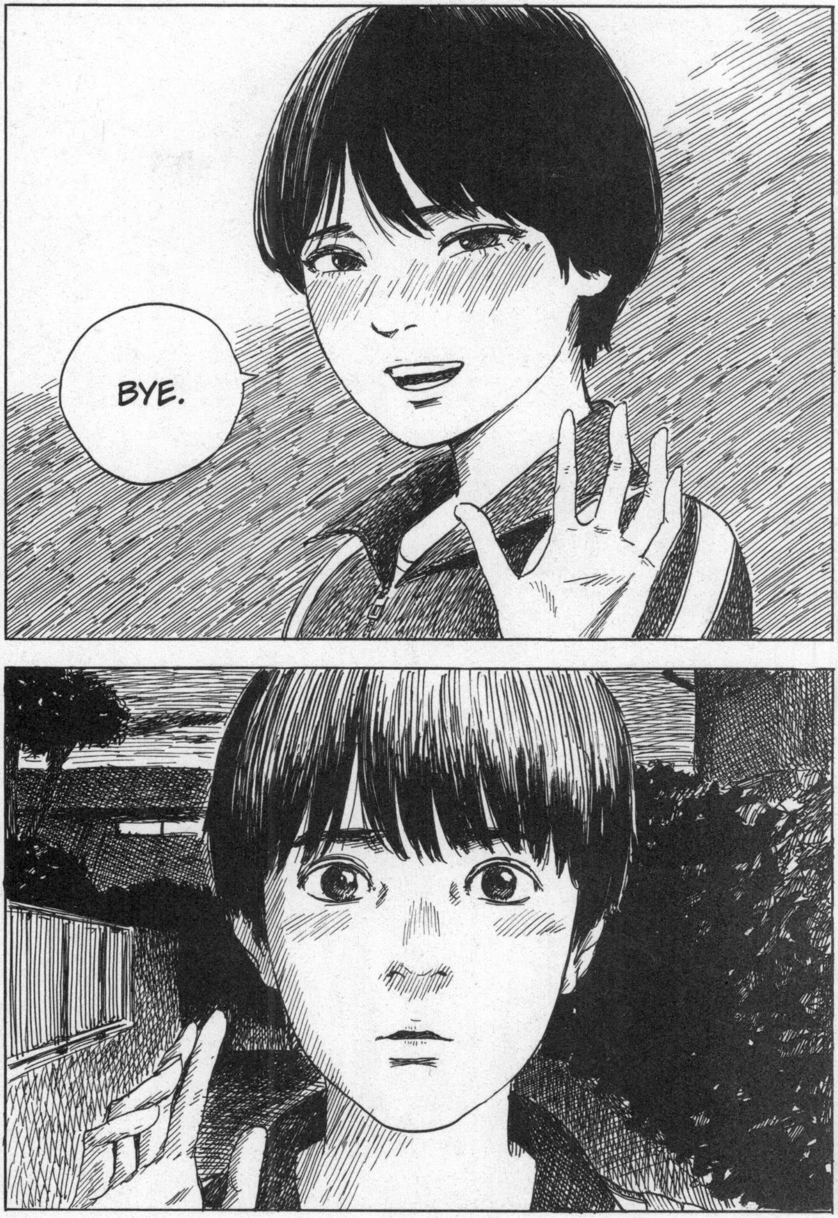
BYE.

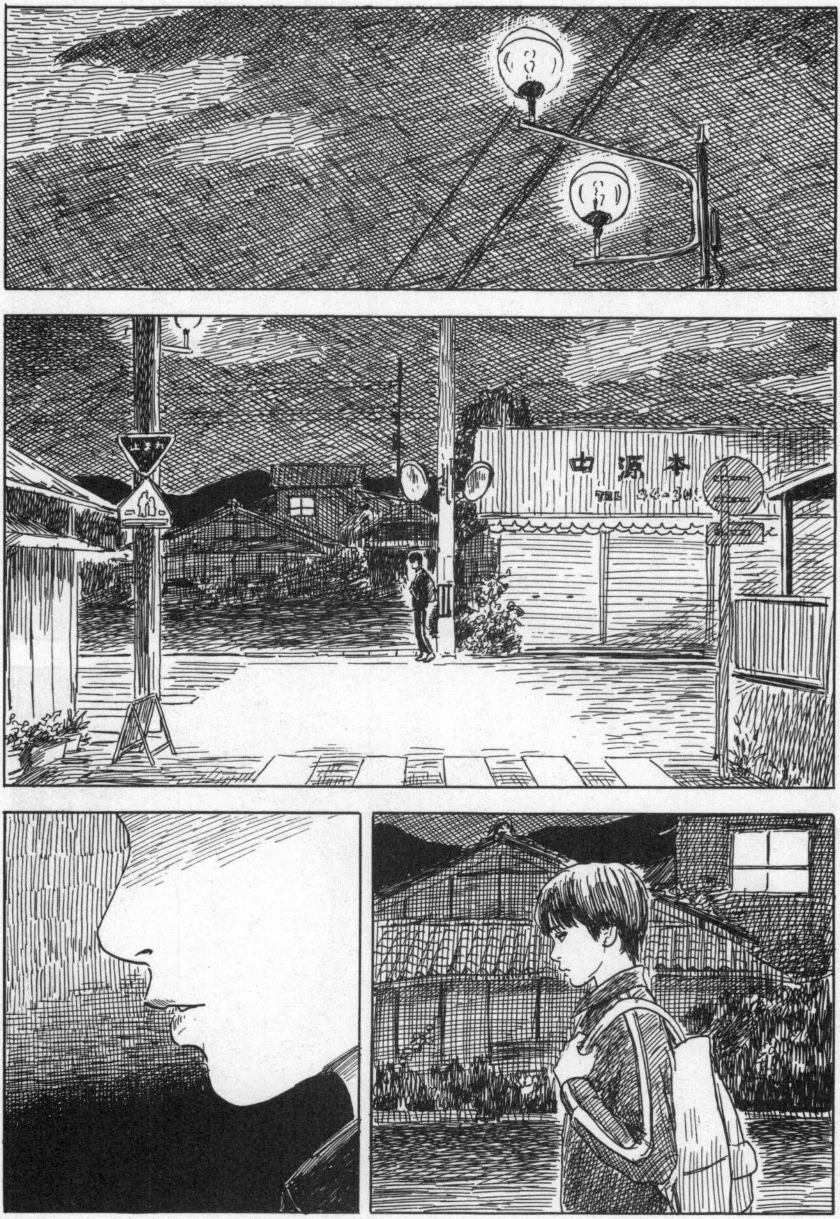

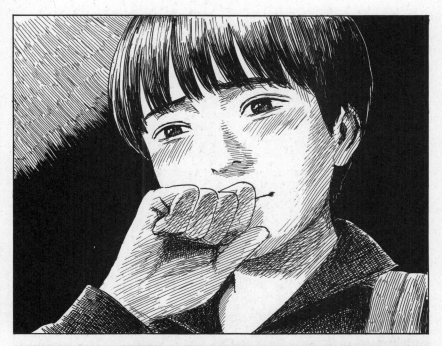

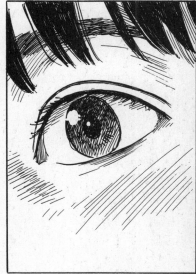

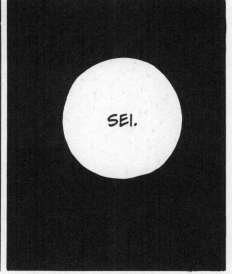

SEI.

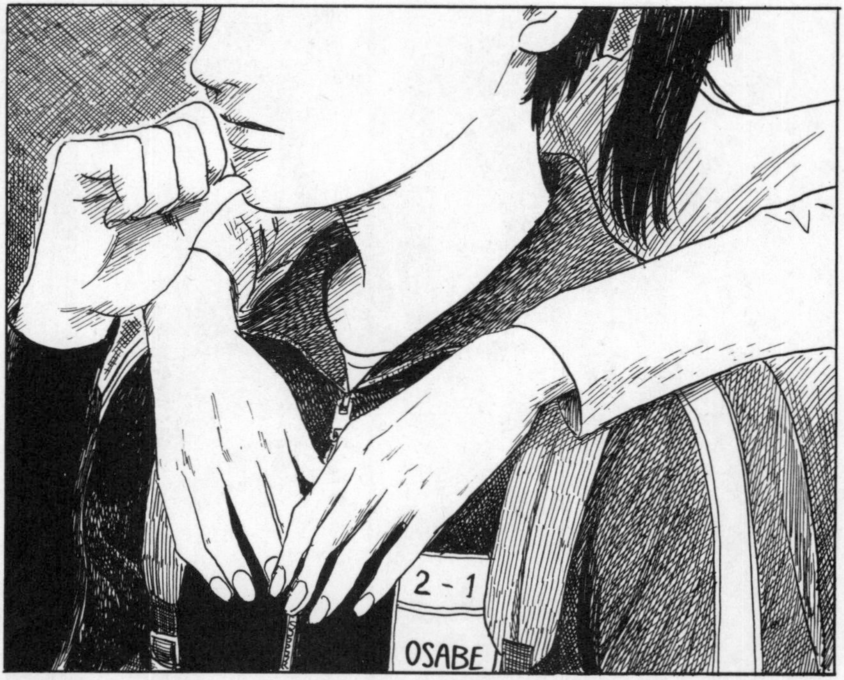
2 - 1
OSABE
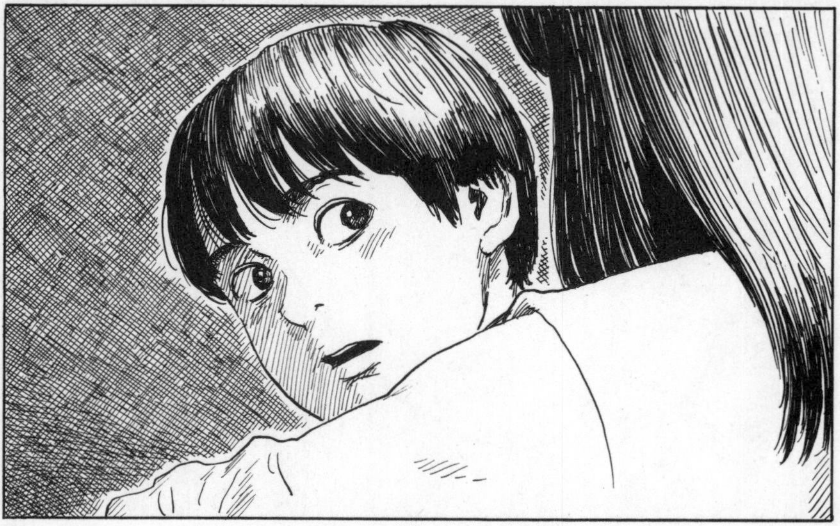

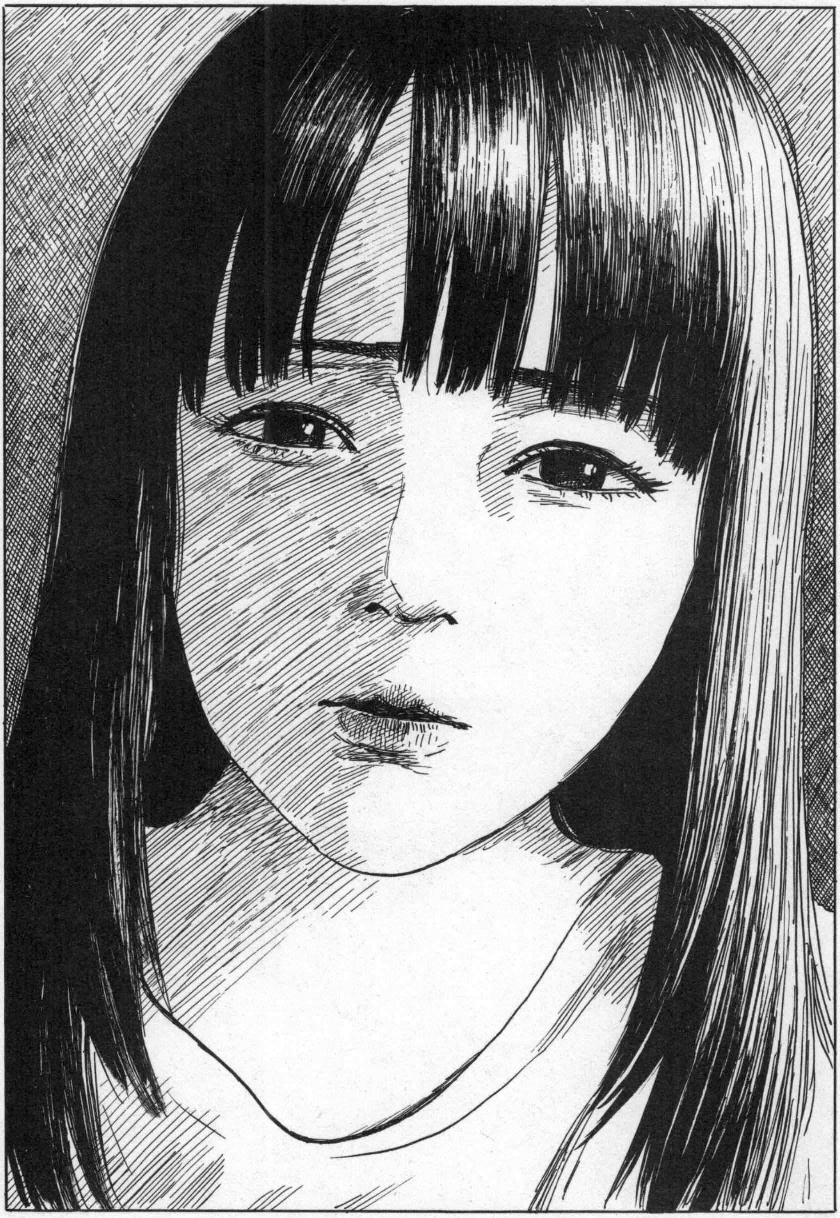

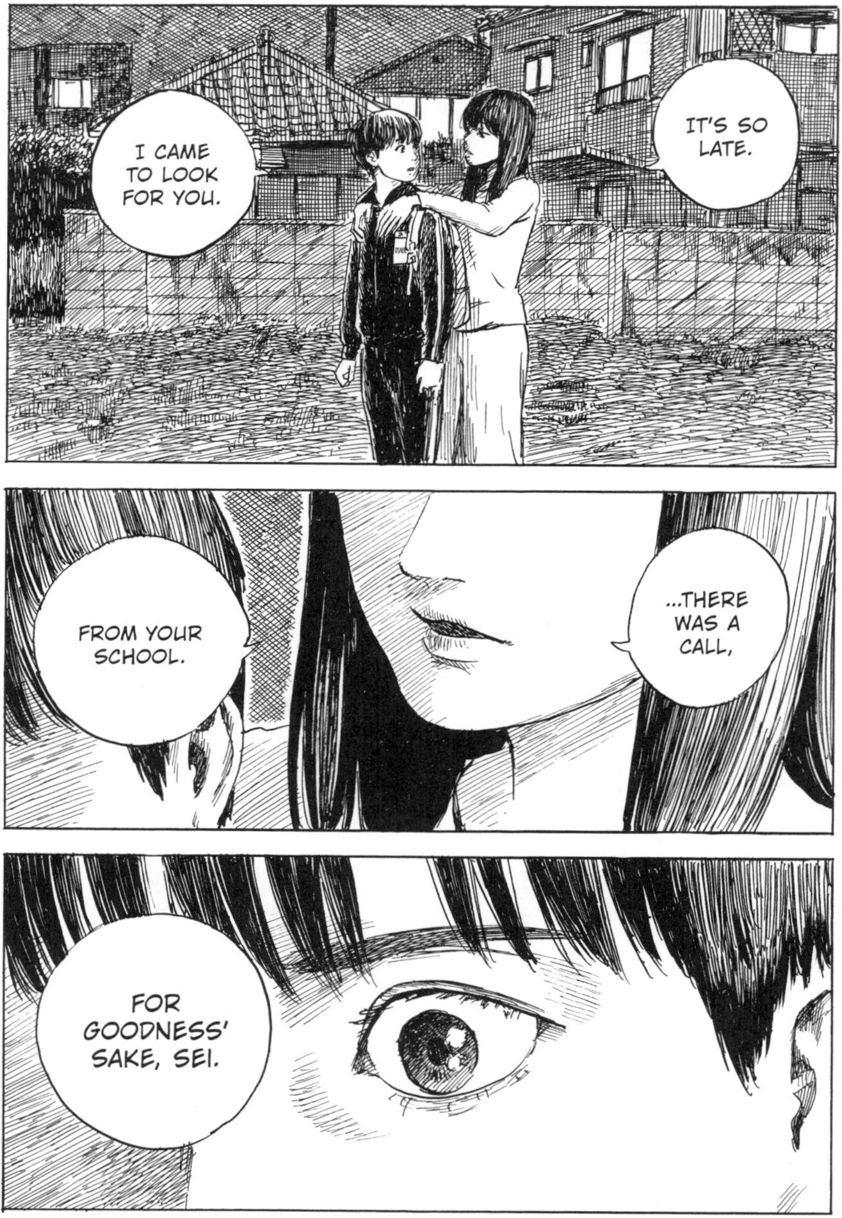
IT'S SO LATE.
I CAME TO LOOK FOR YOU.
...THERE WAS A CALL,
FROM YOUR SCHOOL.
FOR GOODNESS' SAKE, SEI.

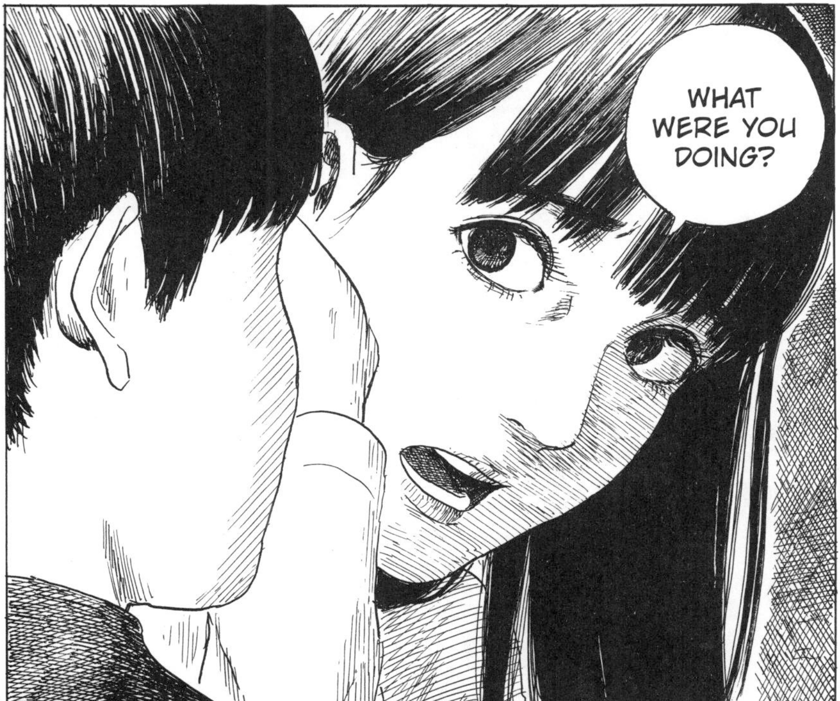
WHAT WERE YOU DOING?

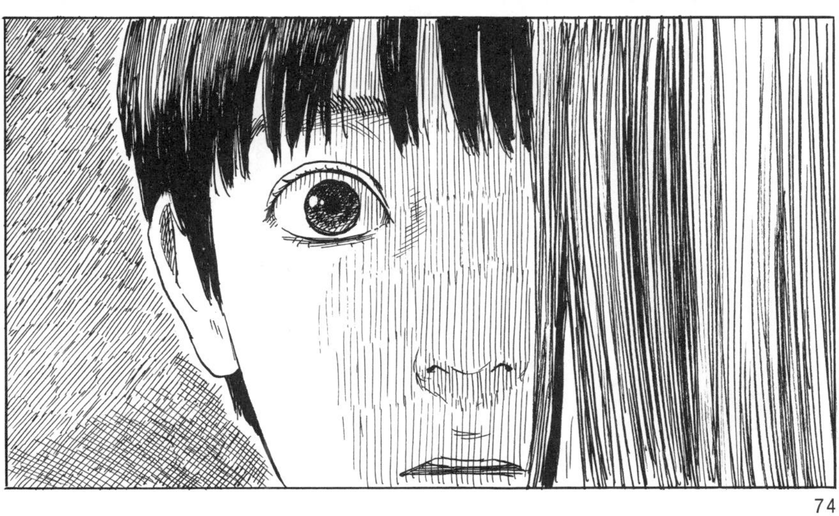

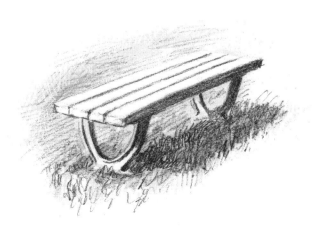

CHAPTER 28 Step

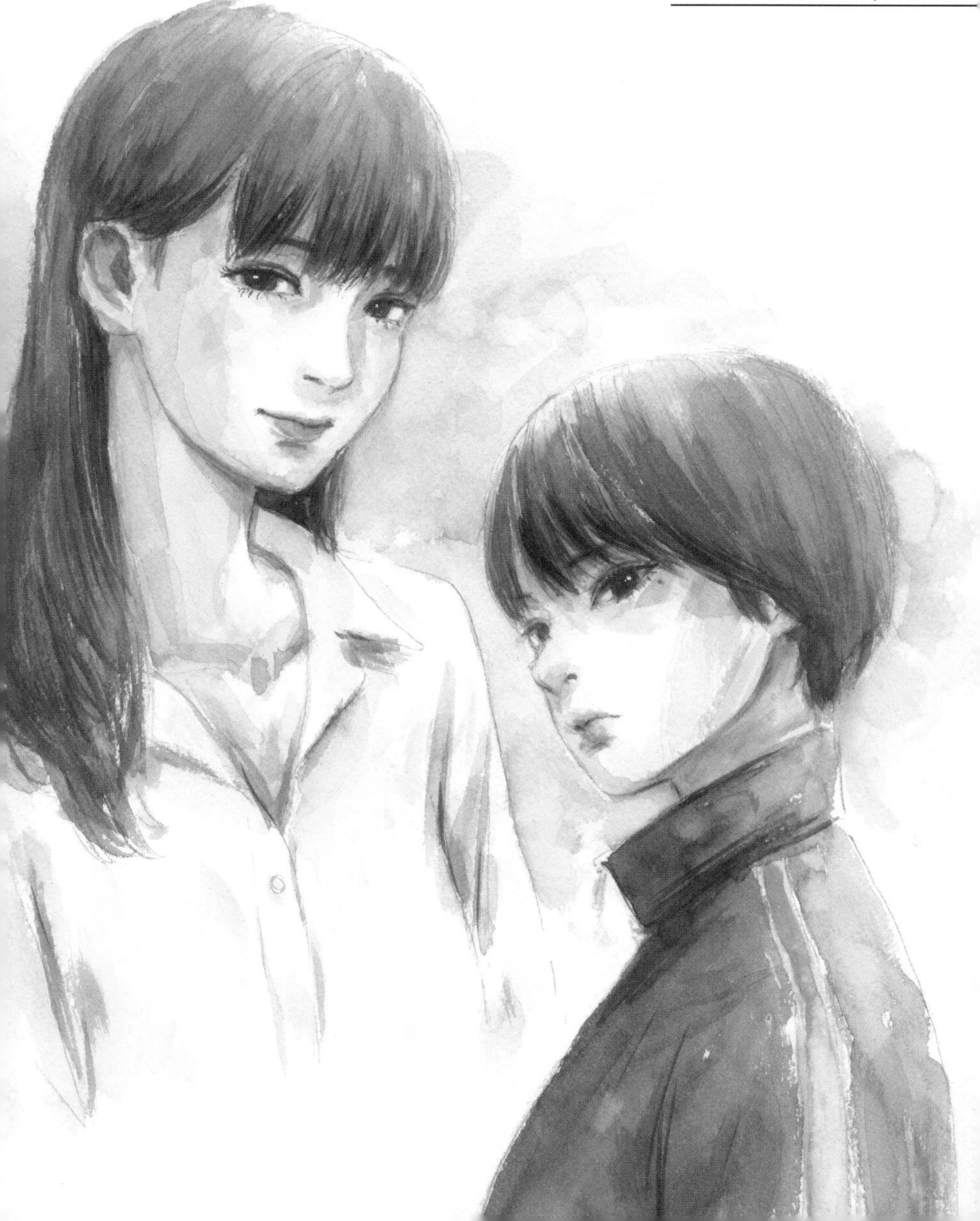

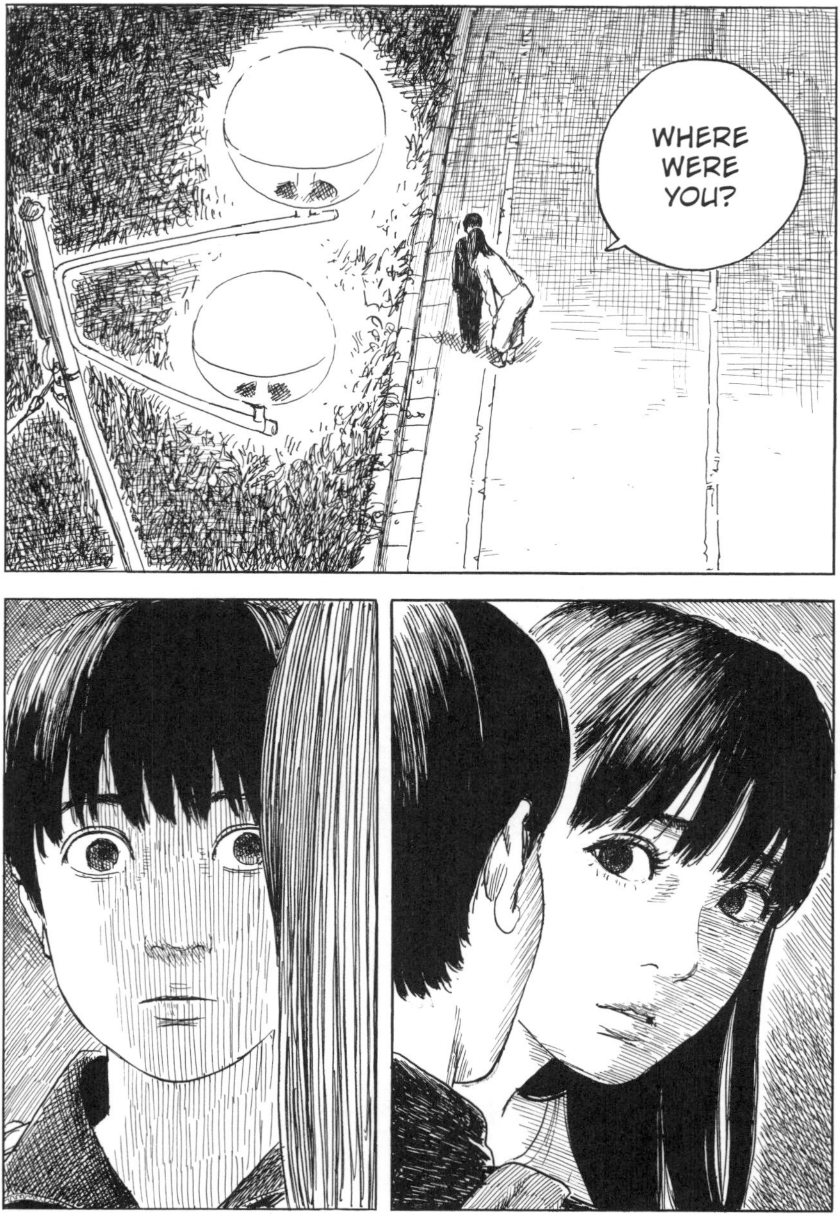
WHERE WERE YOU?

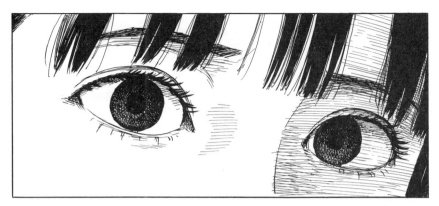

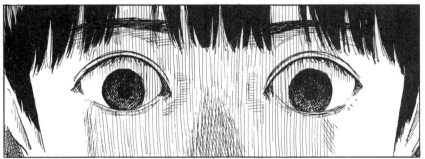

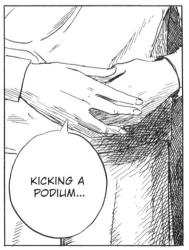

KICKING A
PODIUM...

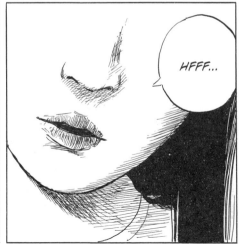

HFFF...

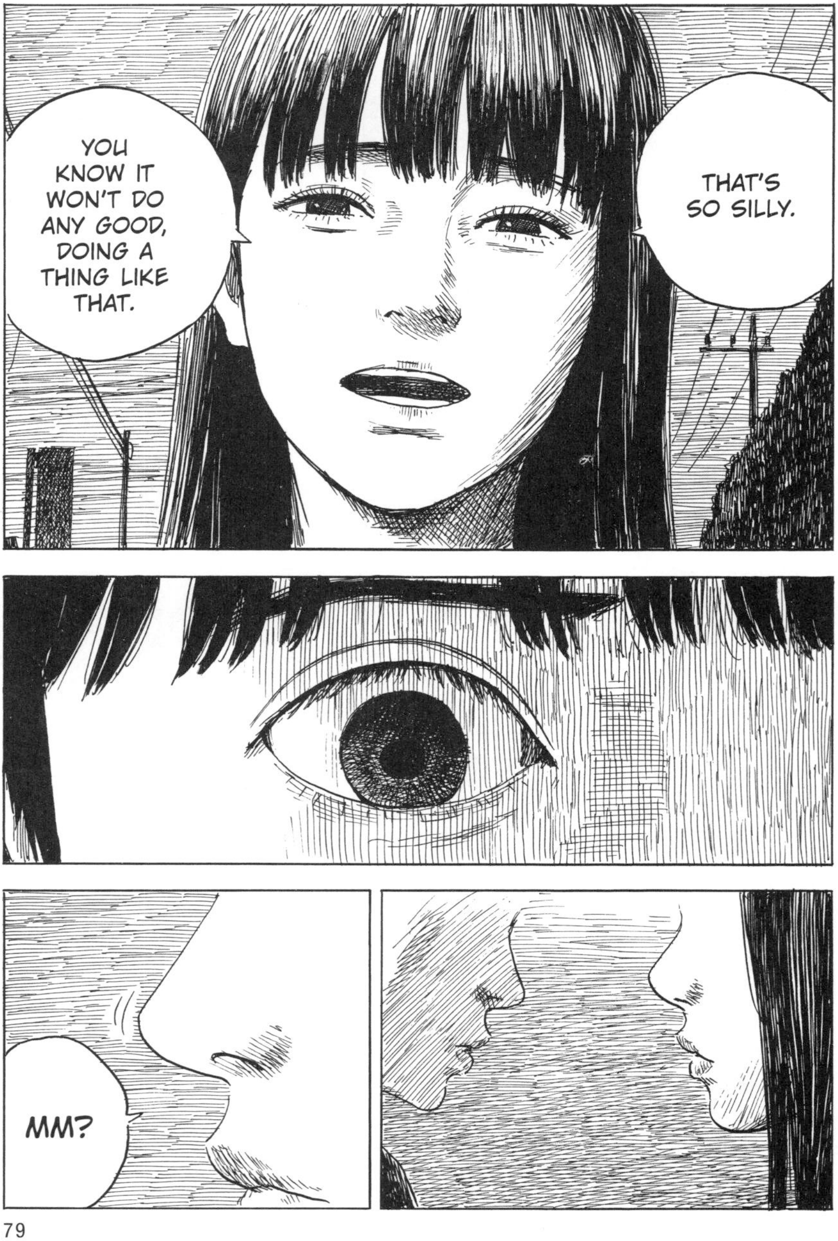
THAT'S SO SILLY.
YOU KNOW IT WON'T DO ANY GOOD, DOING A THING LIKE THAT.
MM?

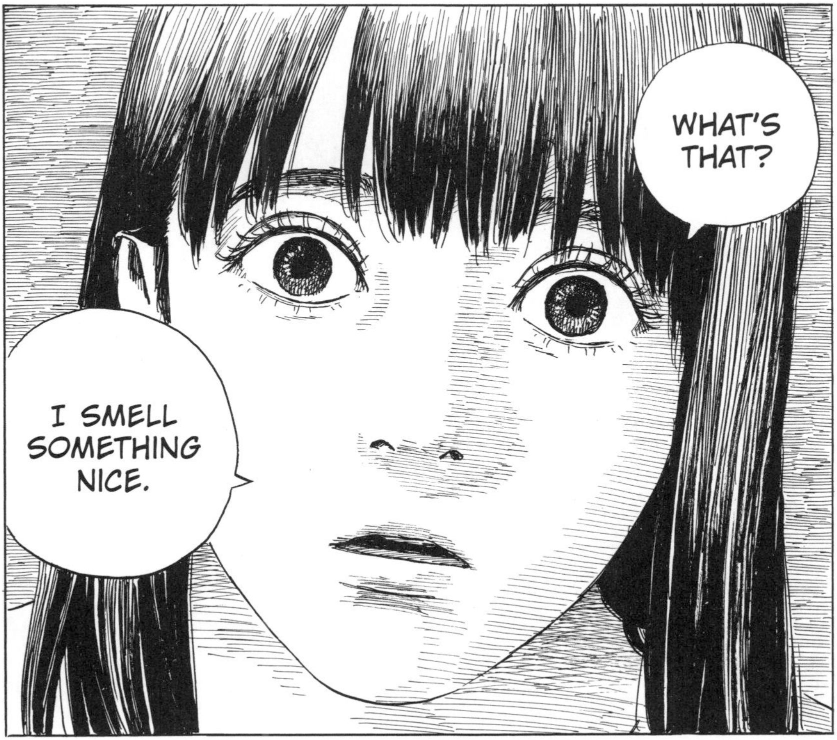
WHAT'S THAT?
I SMELL SOMETHING NICE.

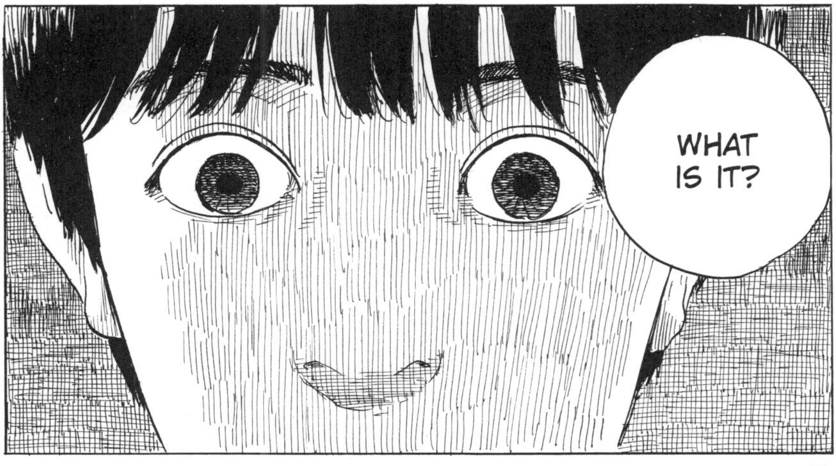
WHAT IS IT?

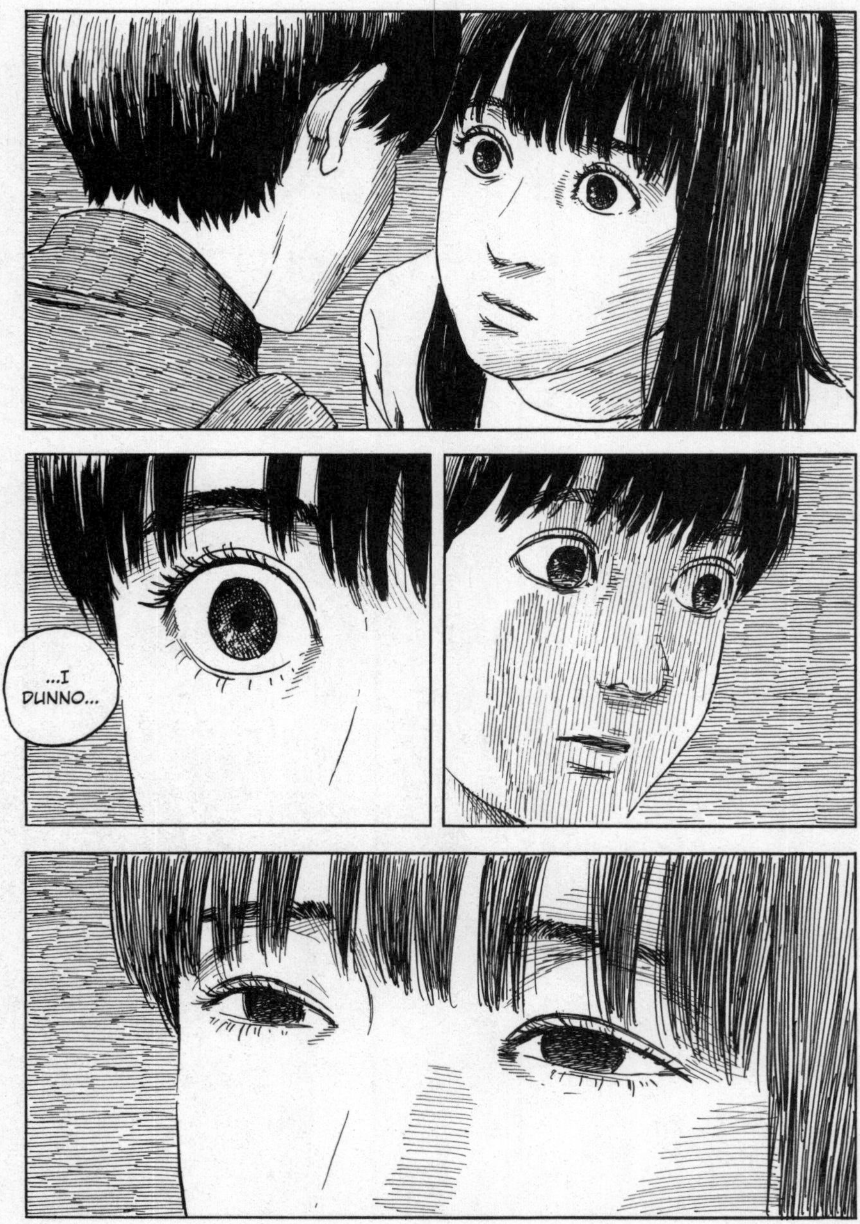
...I DUNNO...

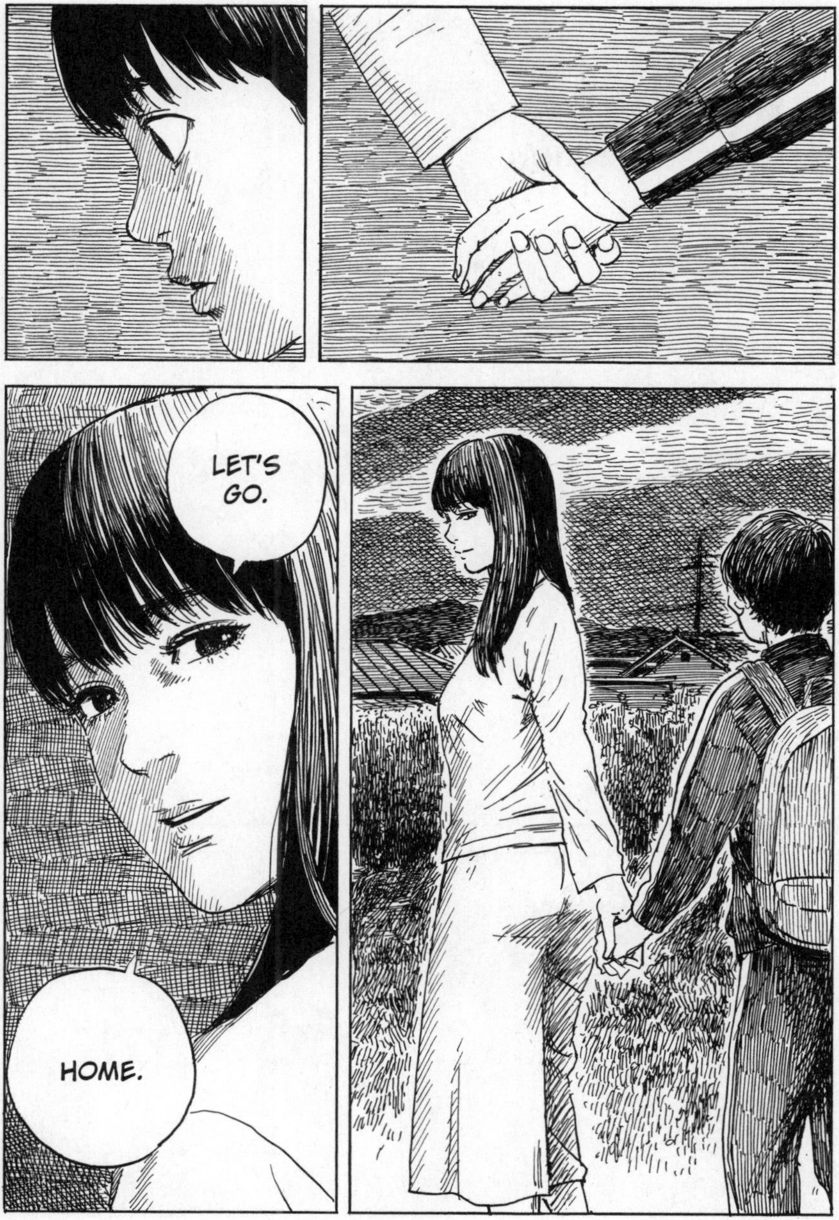
LET'S GO.
HOME.

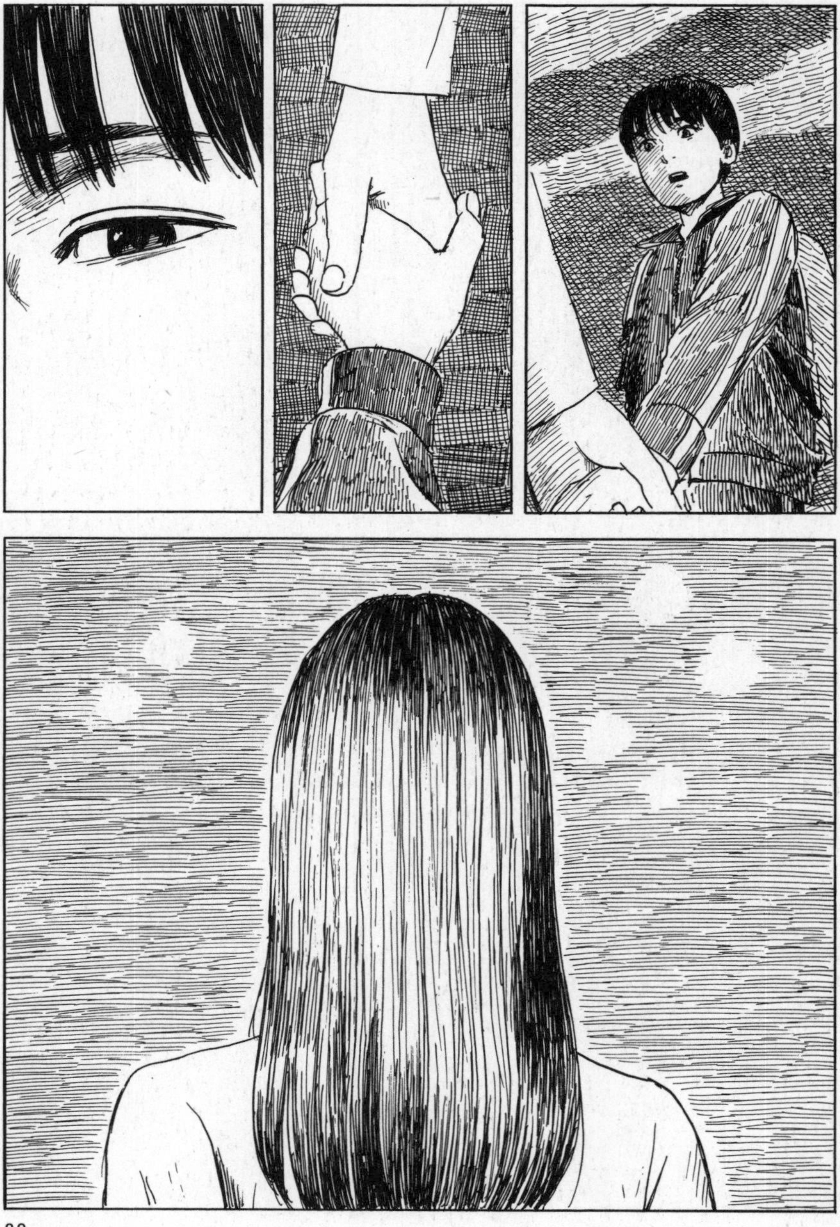

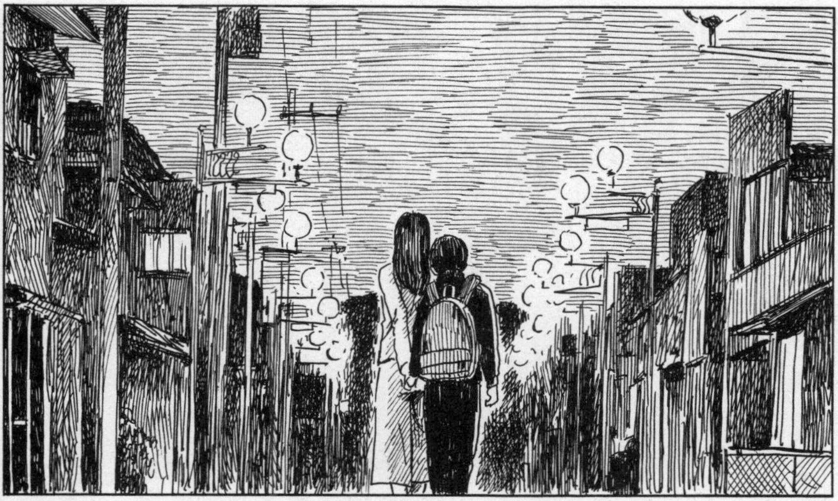

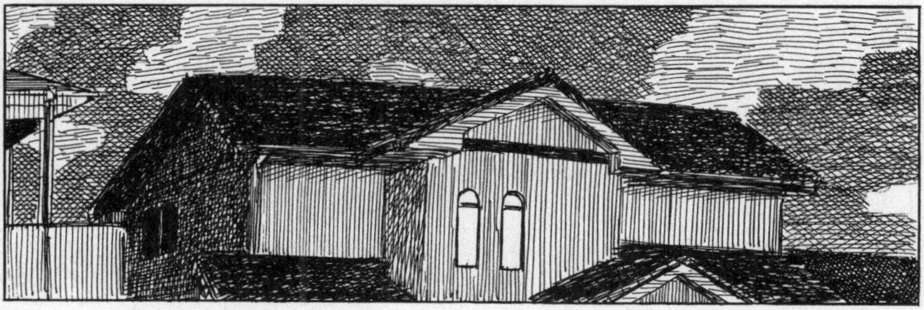

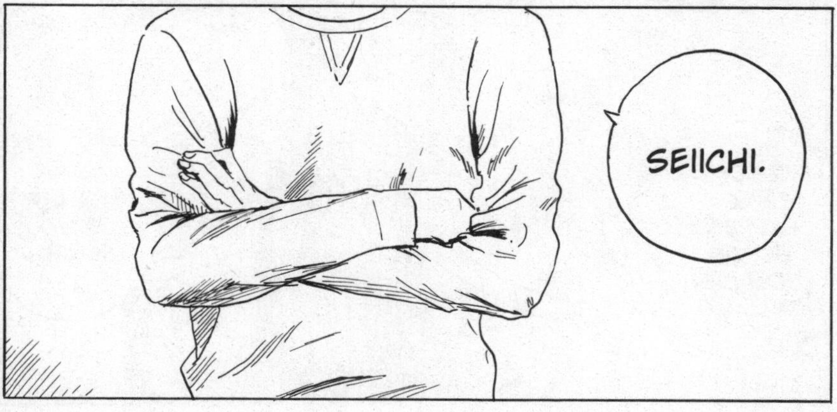
SEIICHI.

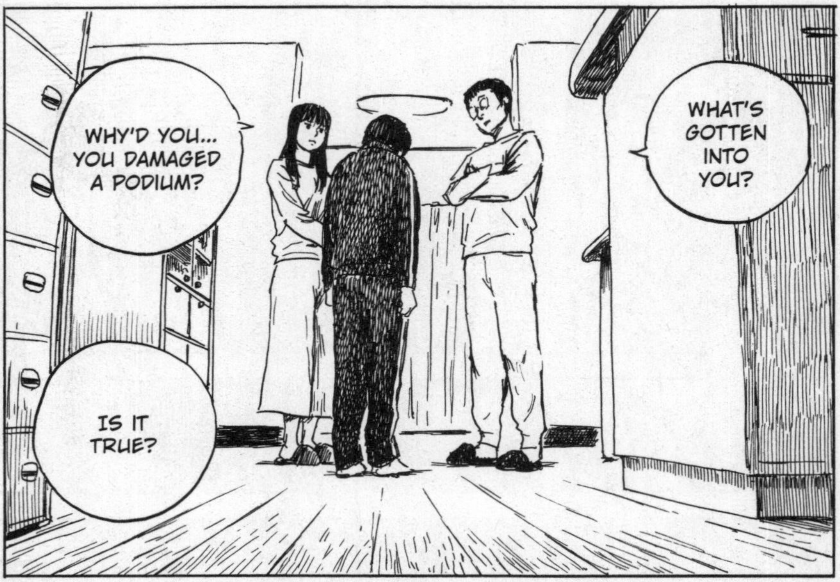
WHAT'S GOTTEN INTO YOU?
WHY'D YOU... YOU DAMAGED A PODIUM?
IS IT TRUE?

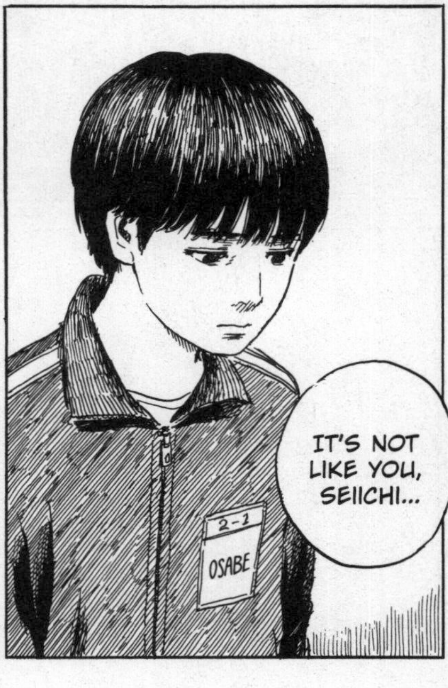
IT'S NOT LIKE YOU, SEIICHI...
2-1
OSABE

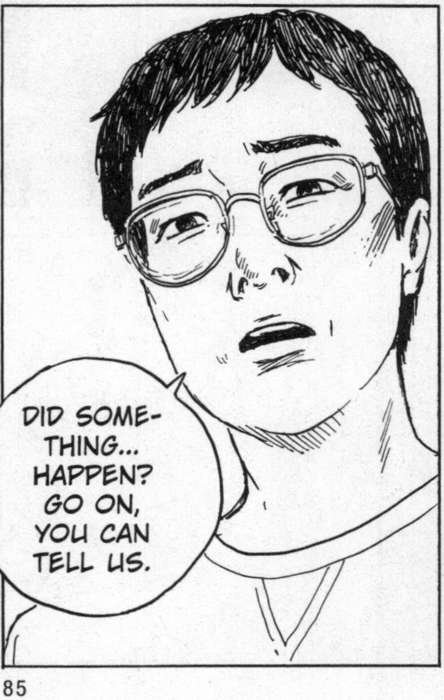
DID SOME-THING... HAPPEN? GO ON, YOU CAN TELL US.

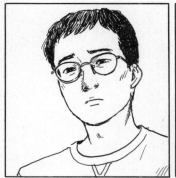

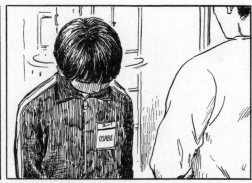

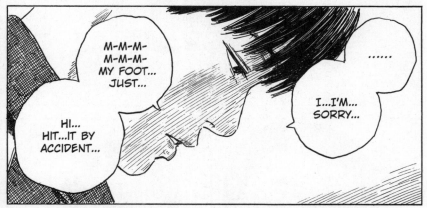

M-M-M-
M-M-M-
MY FOOT...
JUST...

HI...
HIT...IT BY
ACCIDENT...

......

I...I'M...
SORRY...

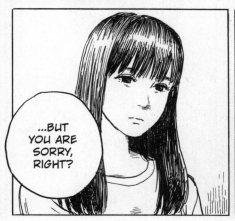

...BUT
YOU ARE
SORRY,
RIGHT?

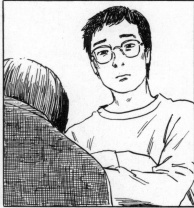

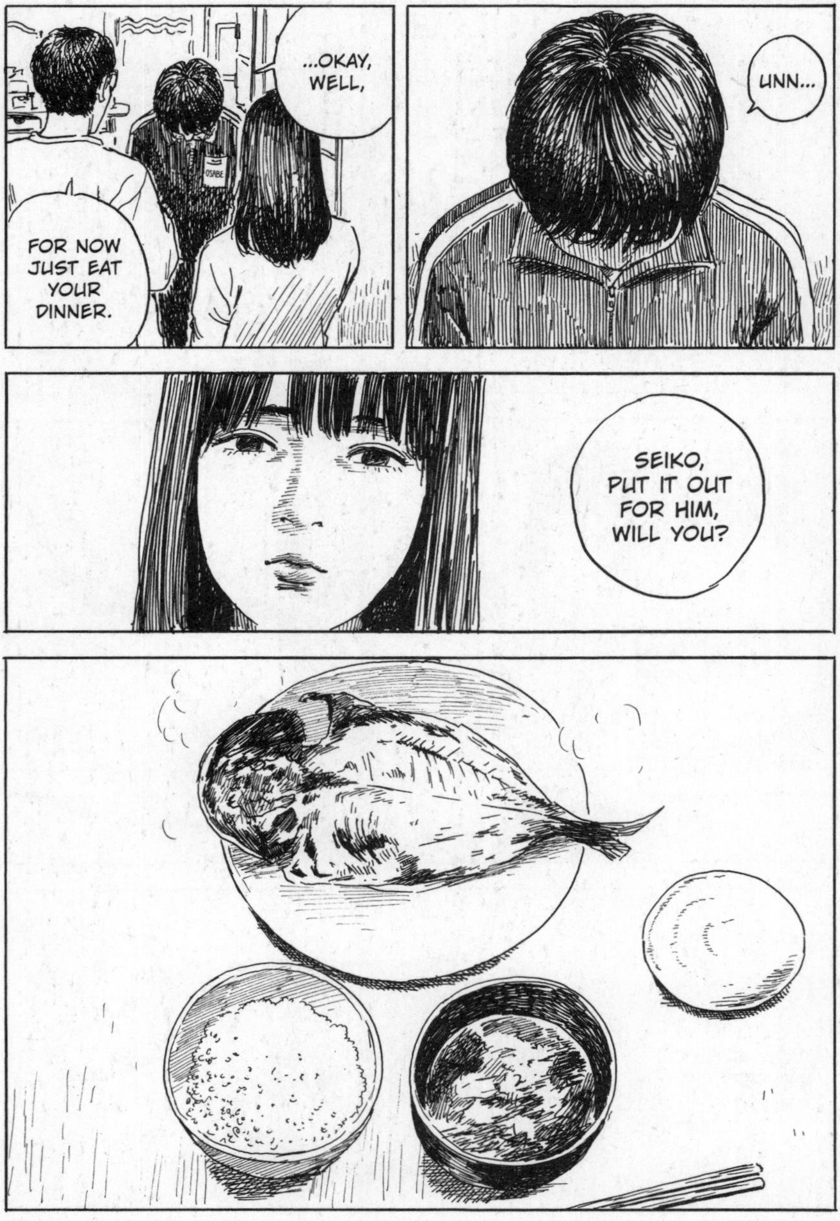
UNN...
...OKAY, WELL,
OSABE
FOR NOW JUST EAT YOUR DINNER.
SEIKO, PUT IT OUT FOR HIM, WILL YOU?

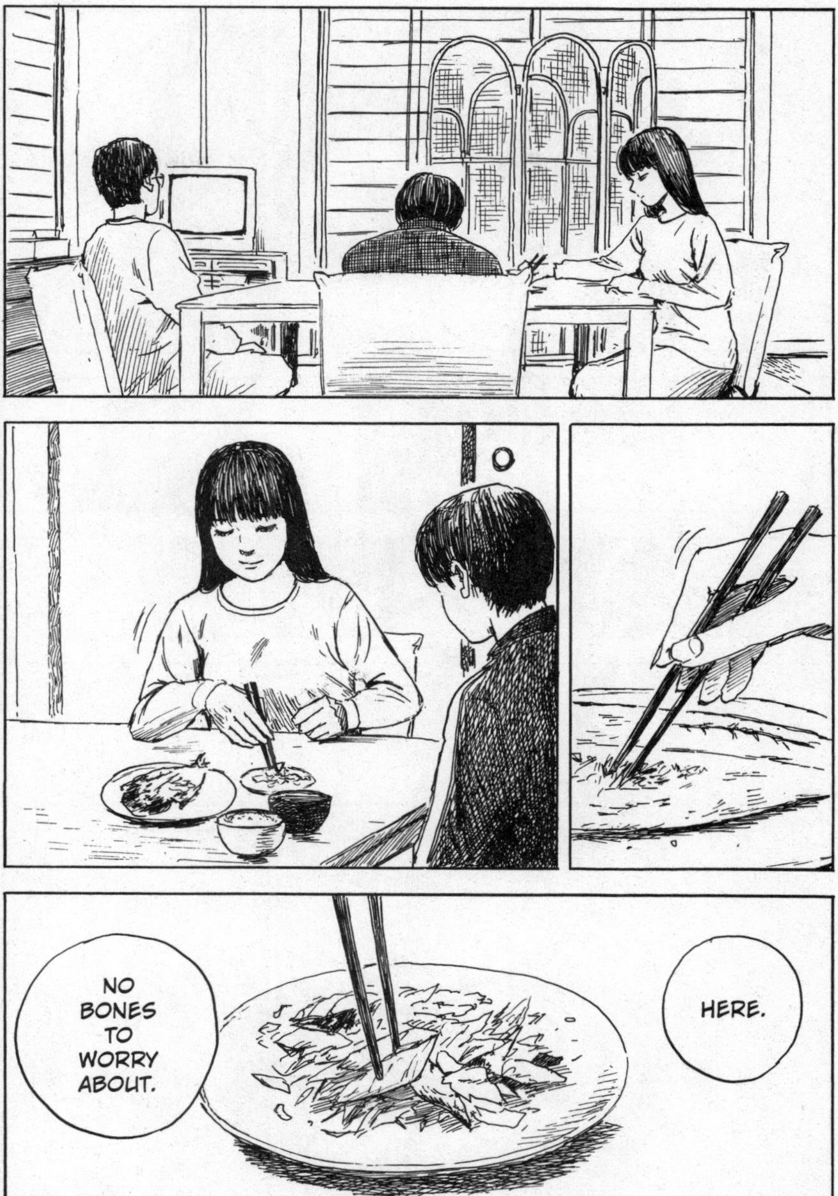
HERE.
NO BONES TO WORRY ABOUT.

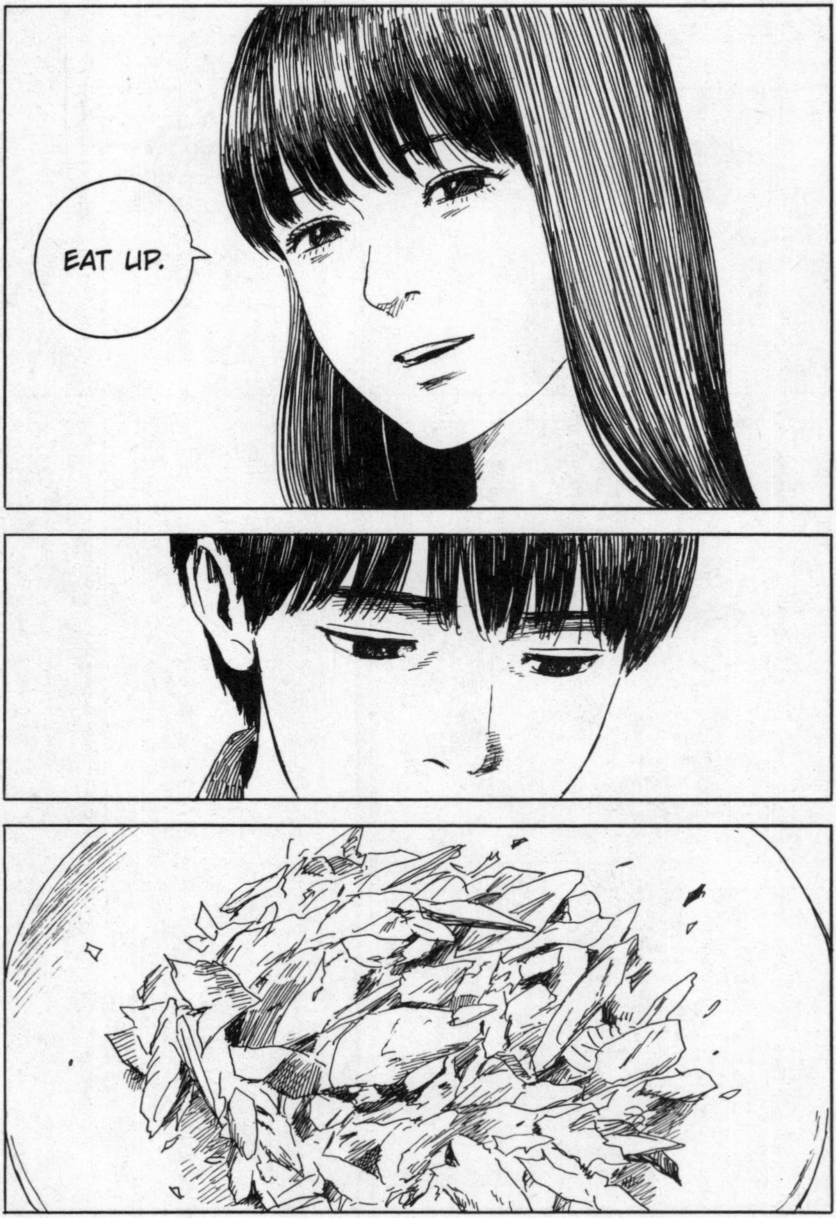
EAT UP.

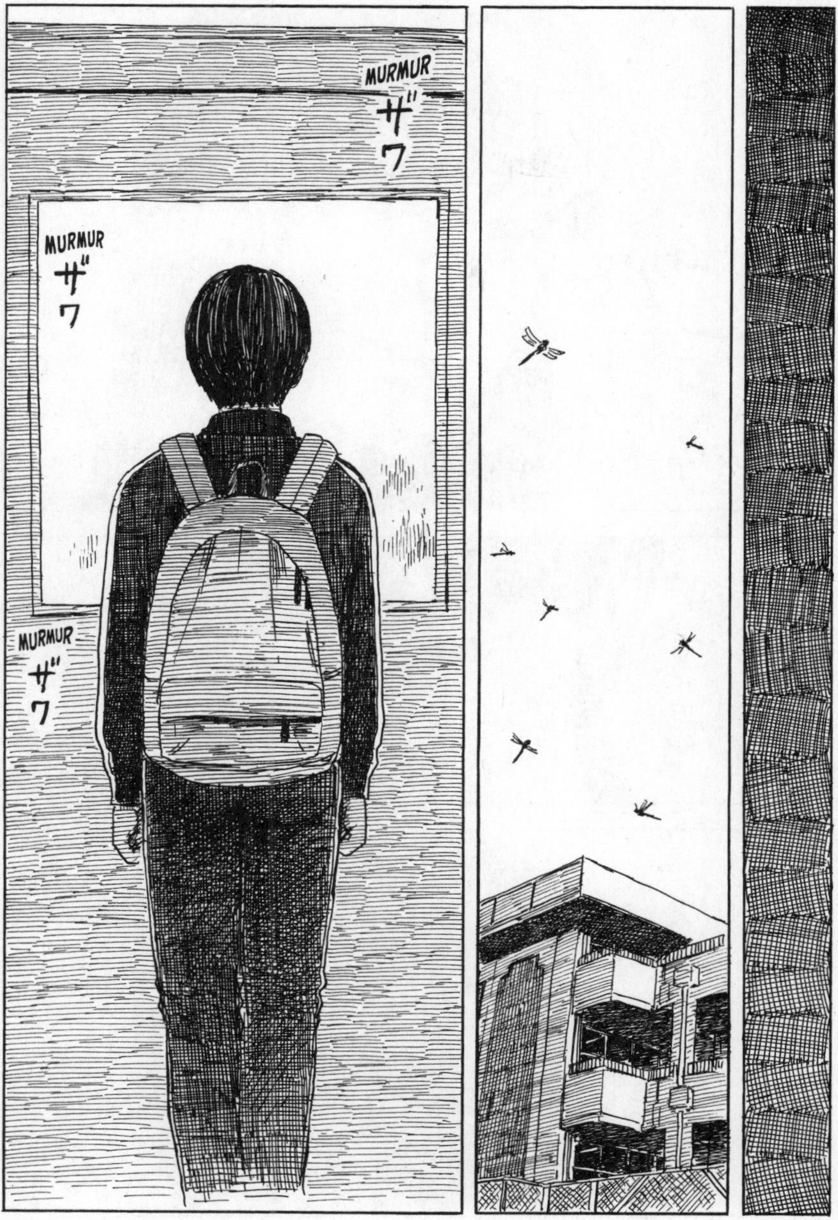
MURMUR
ザワ
MURMUR
ザワ
MURMUR
ザワ

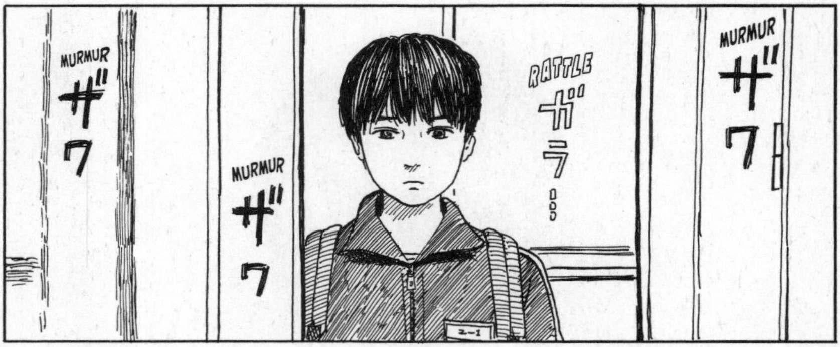
MURMUR
ザワ
RATTLE
ガラ…
MURMUR
ザワ
MURMUR
ザワ

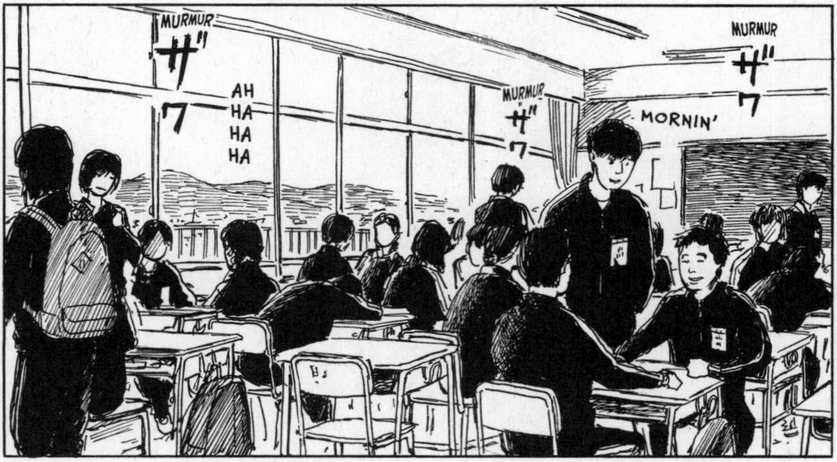
MURMUR
ザワ
MORNIN'
MURMUR
ザワ
AH HA HA HA
MURMUR
ザワ

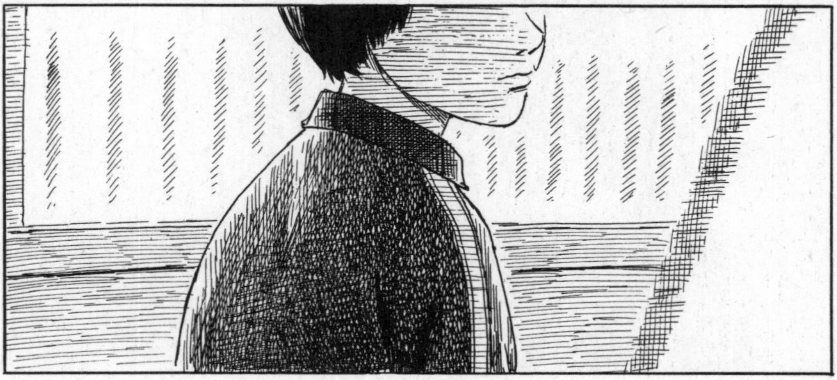

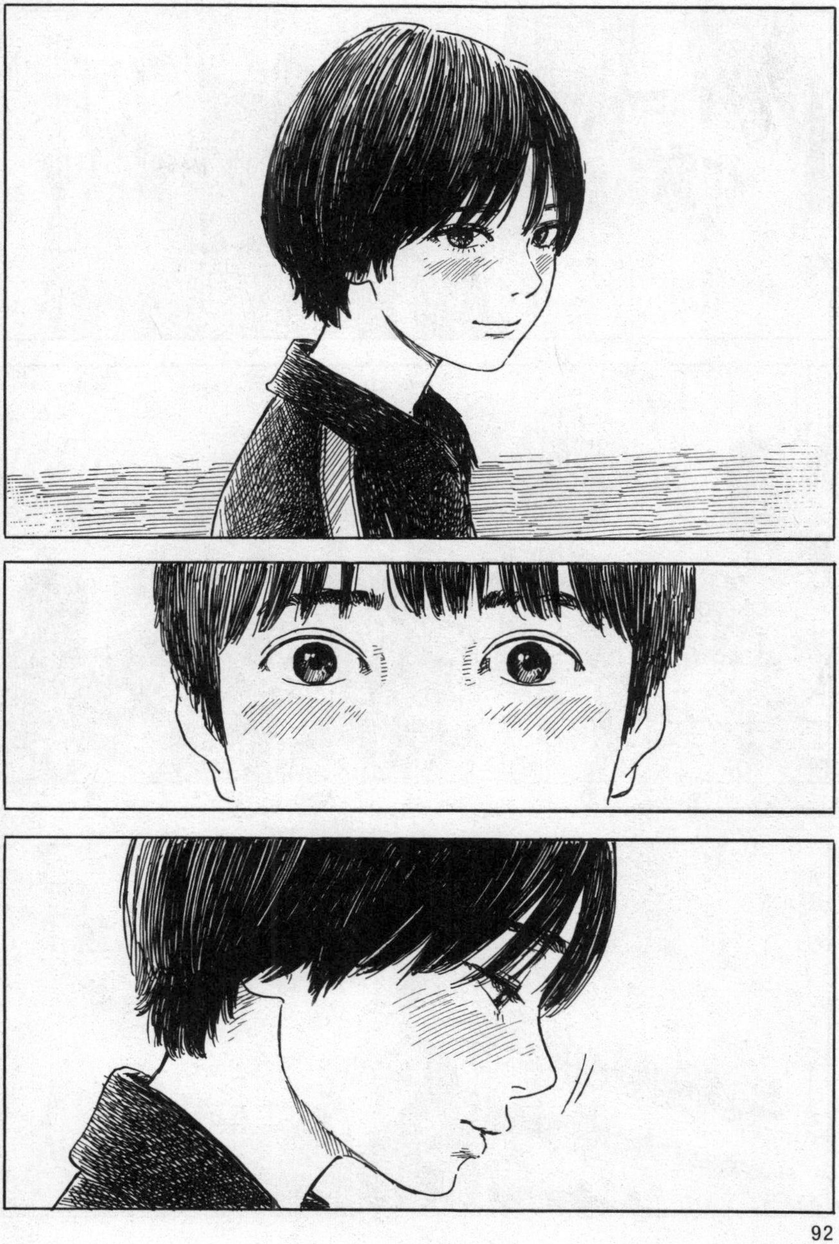

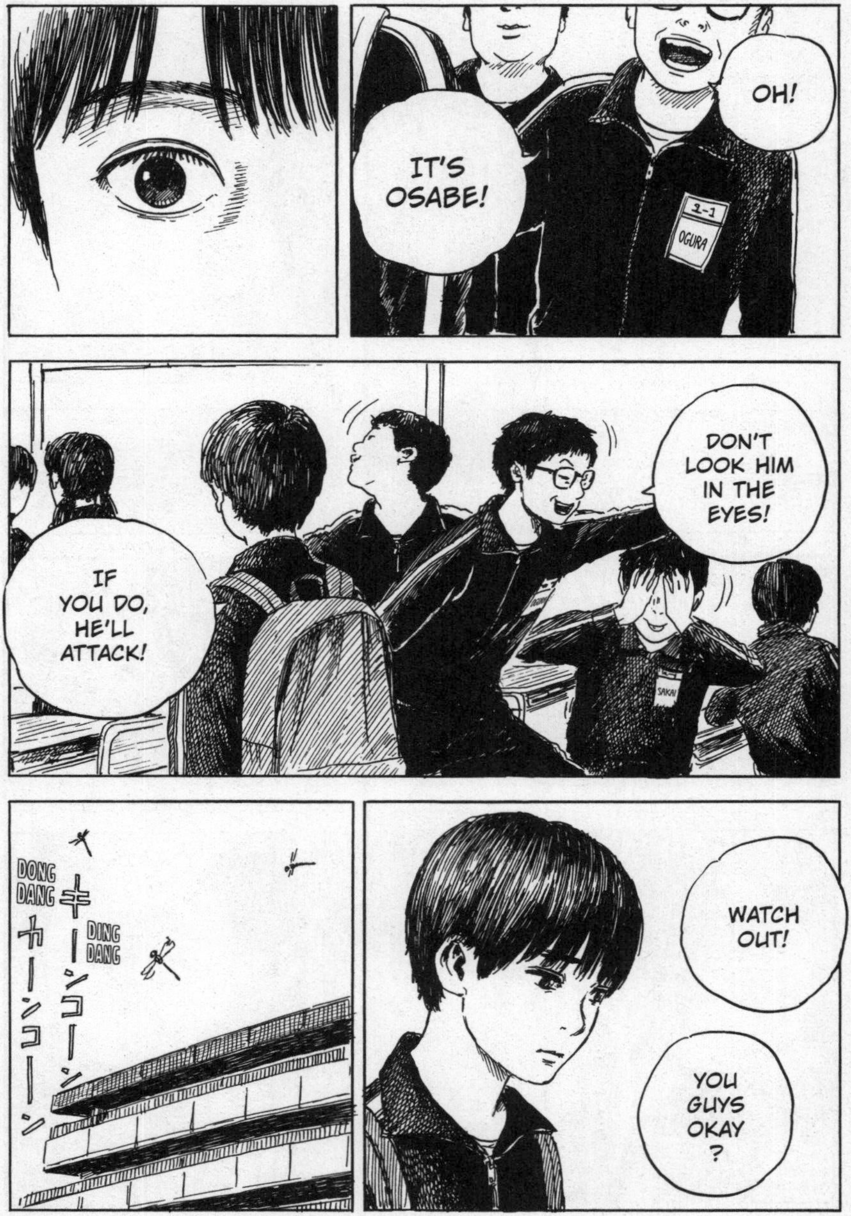
OH!
IT'S OSABE!
1-1 OGURA
DON'T LOOK HIM IN THE EYES!
IF YOU DO, HE'LL ATTACK!
SAKAI
WATCH OUT!
YOU GUYS OKAY?
キーンコーン
DING DANG
カーンコーン
DONG DANG

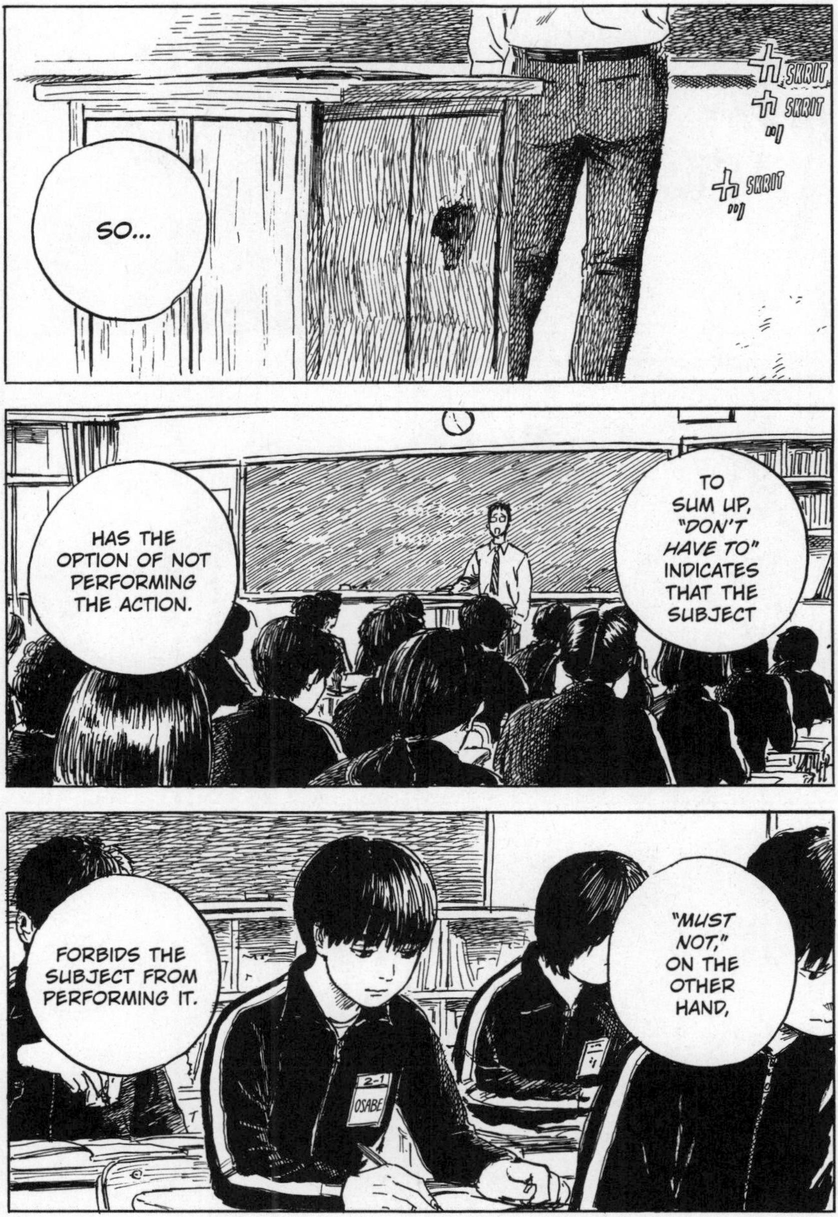
SKRIT
SKRIT
SKRIT
SO...
TO SUM UP, "DON'T HAVE TO" INDICATES THAT THE SUBJECT
HAS THE OPTION OF NOT PERFORMING THE ACTION.
"MUST NOT," ON THE OTHER HAND,
FORBIDS THE SUBJECT FROM PERFORMING IT.
2-1
OSABE

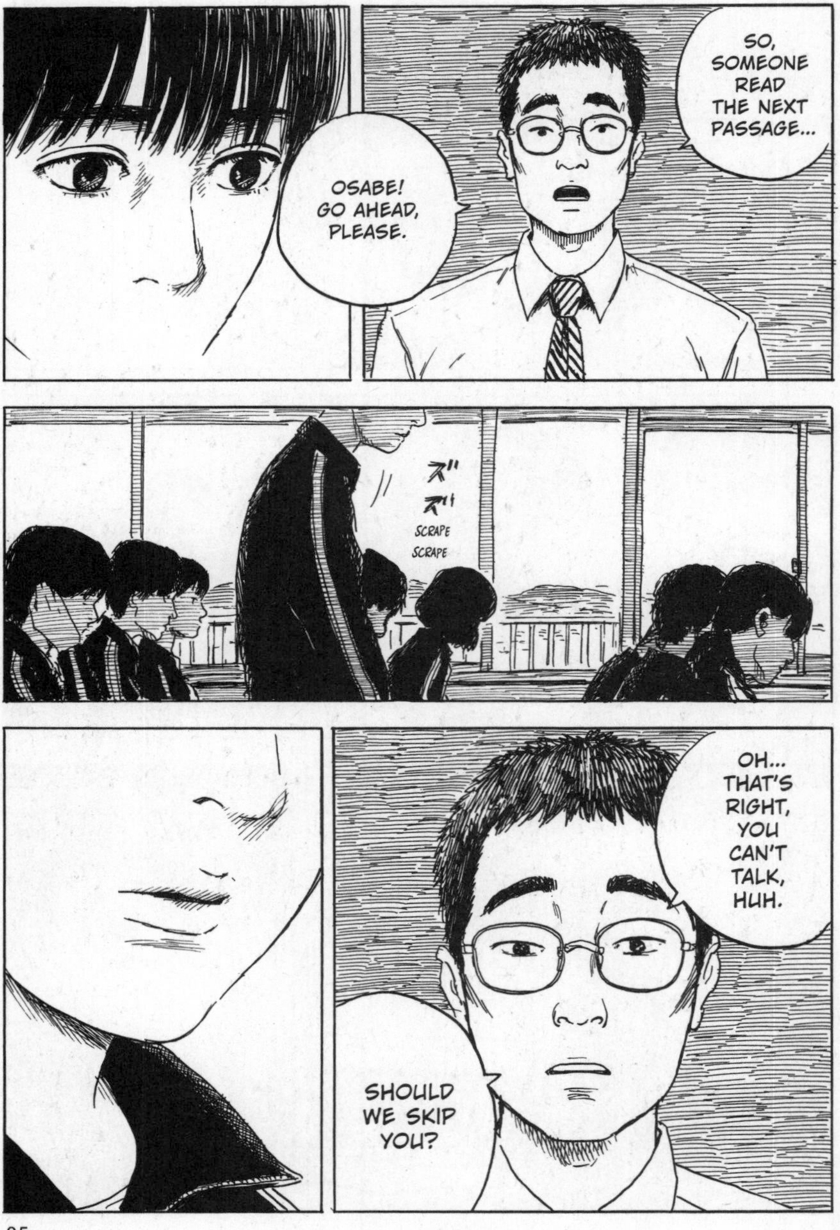
SO, SOMEONE READ THE NEXT PASSAGE...
OSABE! GO AHEAD, PLEASE.
ズズ
SCRAPE SCRAPE
OH... THAT'S RIGHT, YOU CAN'T TALK, HUH.
SHOULD WE SKIP YOU?

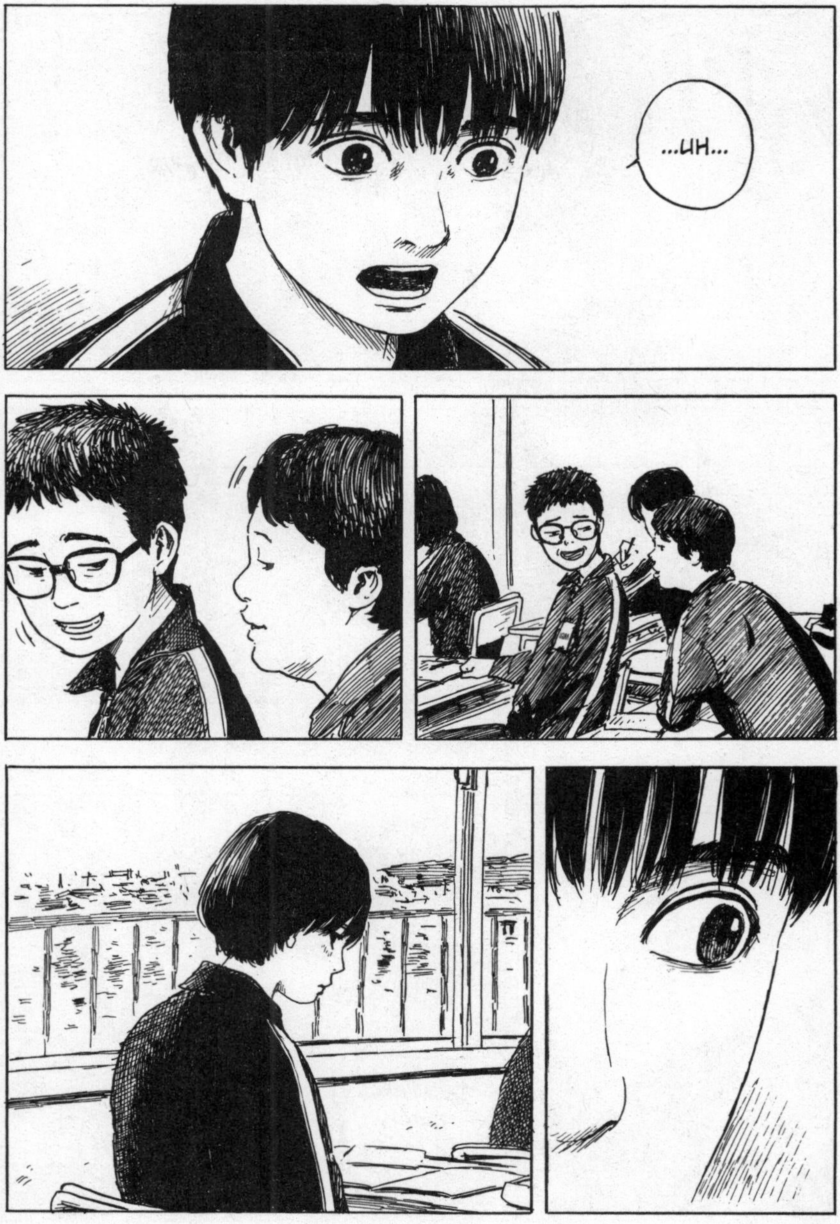
...UH...

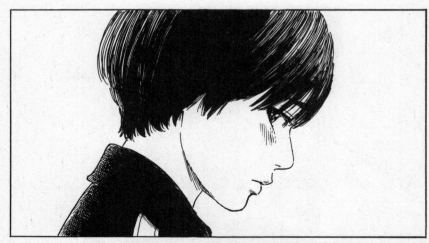

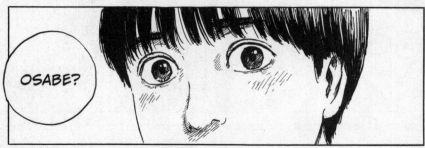

OSABE?

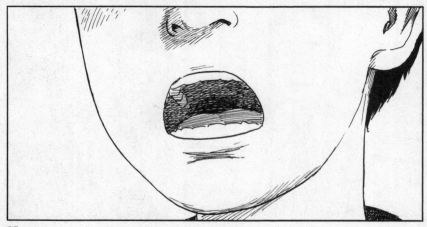

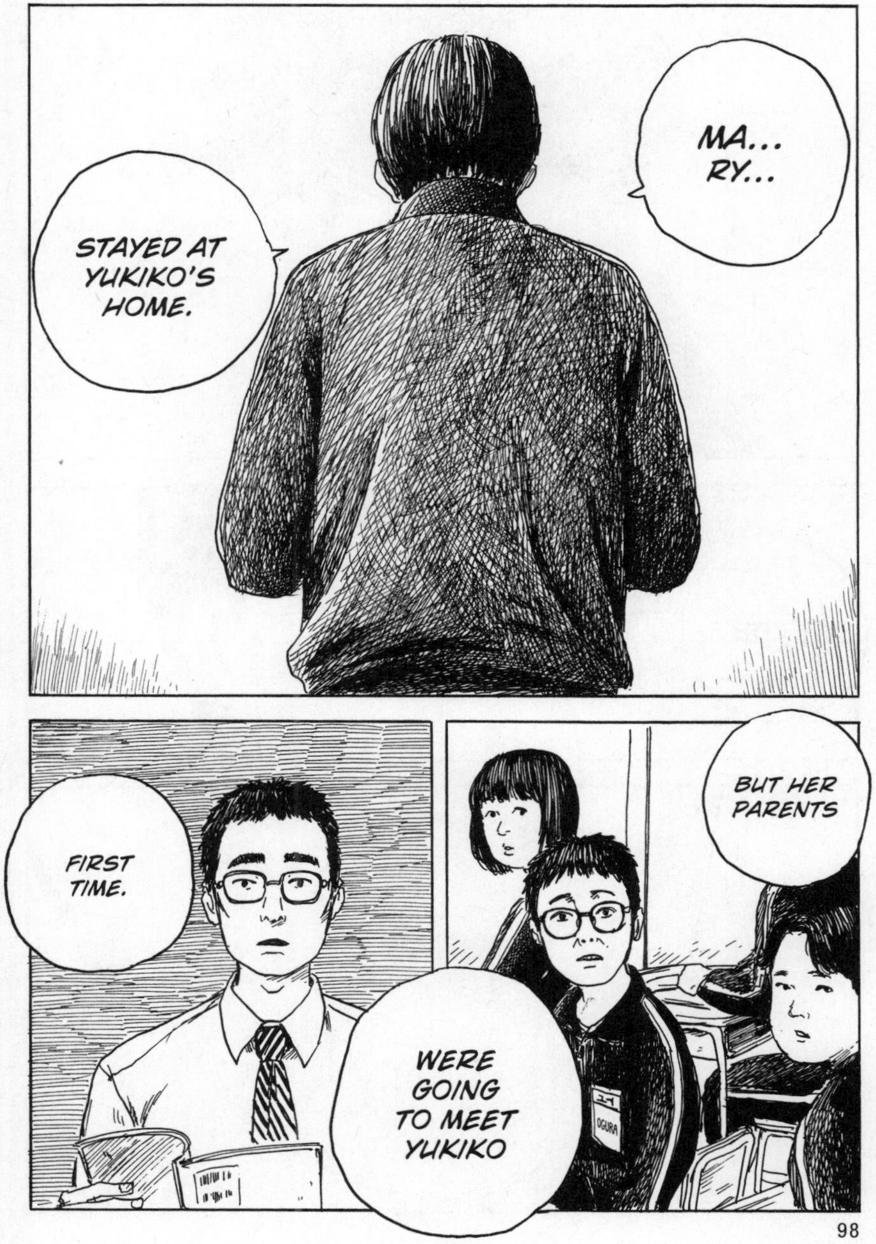
MA... RY...
STAYED AT YUKIKO'S HOME.
BUT HER PARENTS
WERE GOING TO MEET YUKIKO
FIRST TIME.

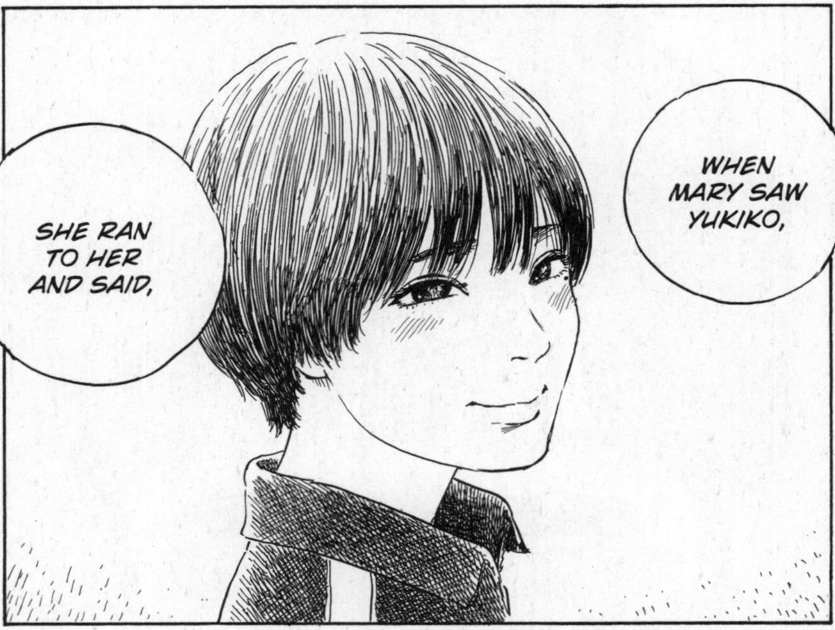
WHEN MARY SAW YUKIKO,
SHE RAN TO HER AND SAID,

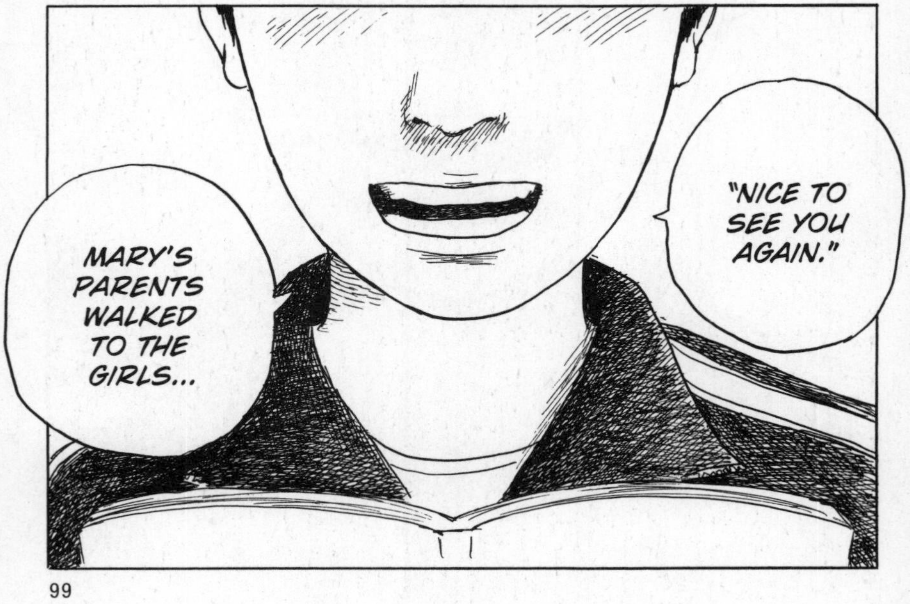
"NICE TO SEE YOU AGAIN."
MARY'S PARENTS WALKED TO THE GIRLS...

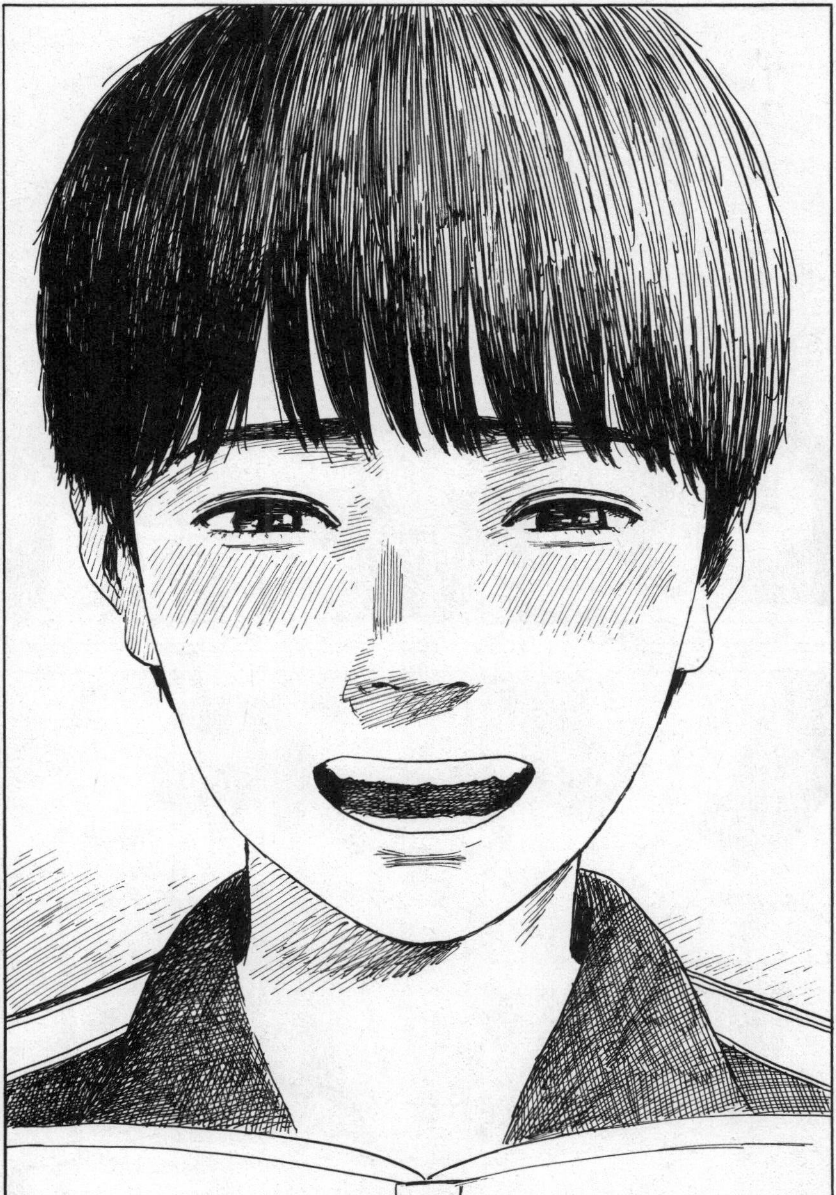

CHAPTER 29 Springtime of the Afternoon

ザワ
MURMUR
ザワ
MURMUR
ザワ
MURMUR
ザワ
MURMUR
ザワ
MURMUR
NEXT PERIOD'S IN THE HOME EC ROOM.
LET'S MOVE IT.
2-1
OSABE
TMP
トン

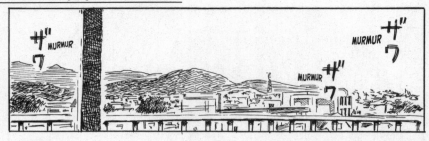

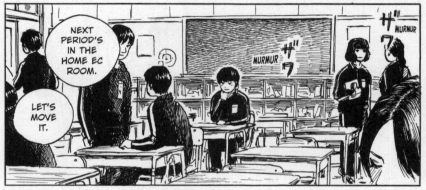

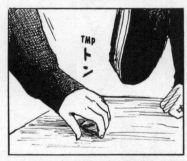

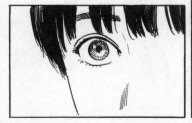

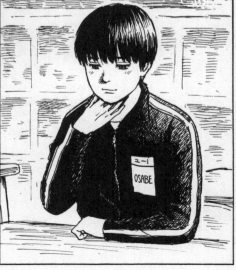

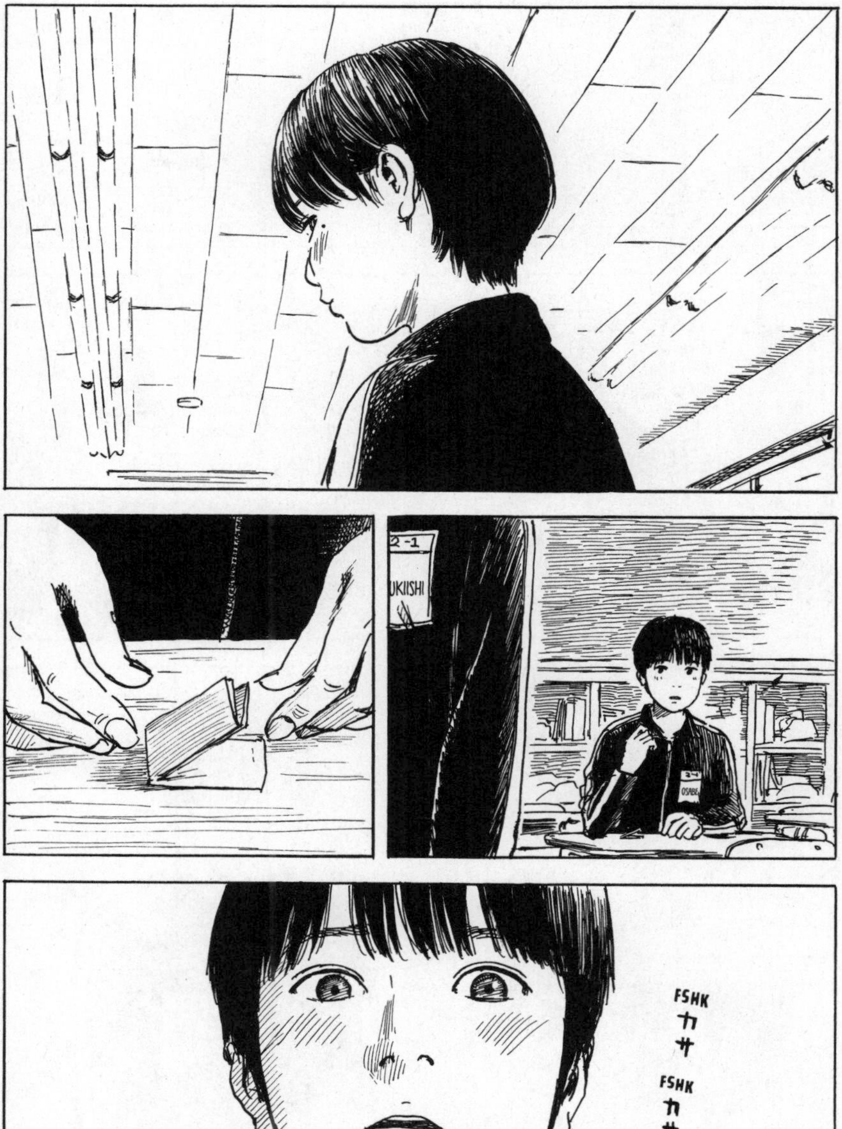
2-1
UKIISHI
FSHK
カサ
FSHK
カサ

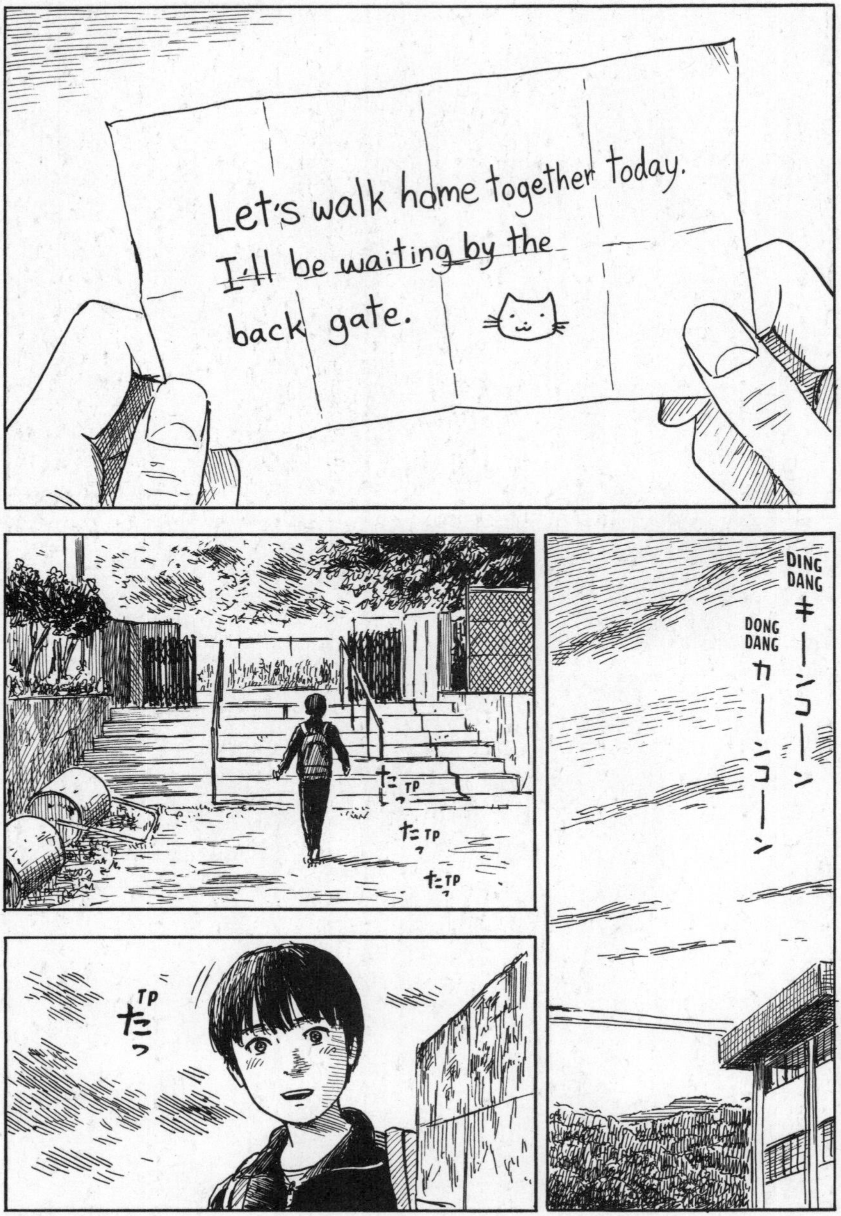
Let's walk home together today. I'll be waiting by the back gate.
DING DANG キーンコーン
DONG DANG カーンコーン
TP たっ
TP たっ
TP たっ
TP たっ

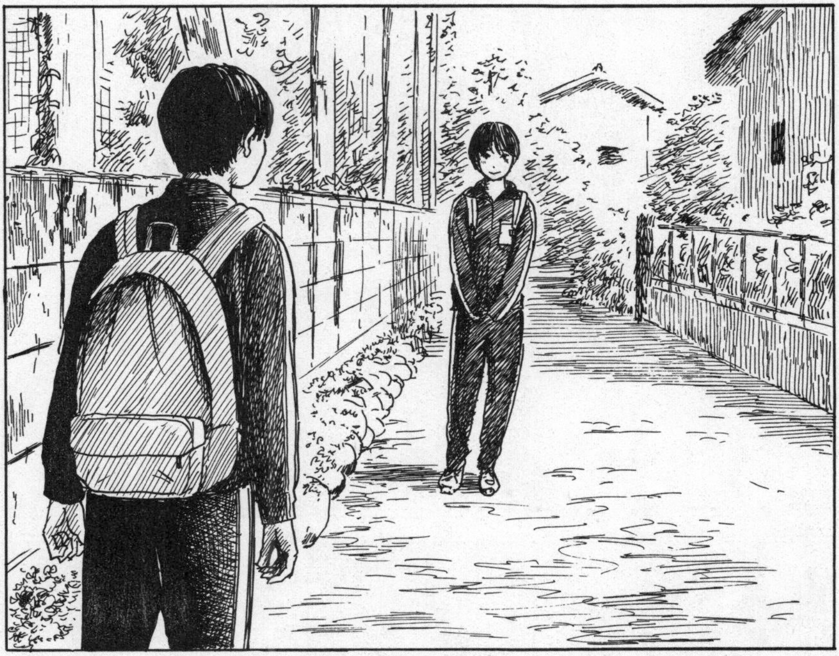
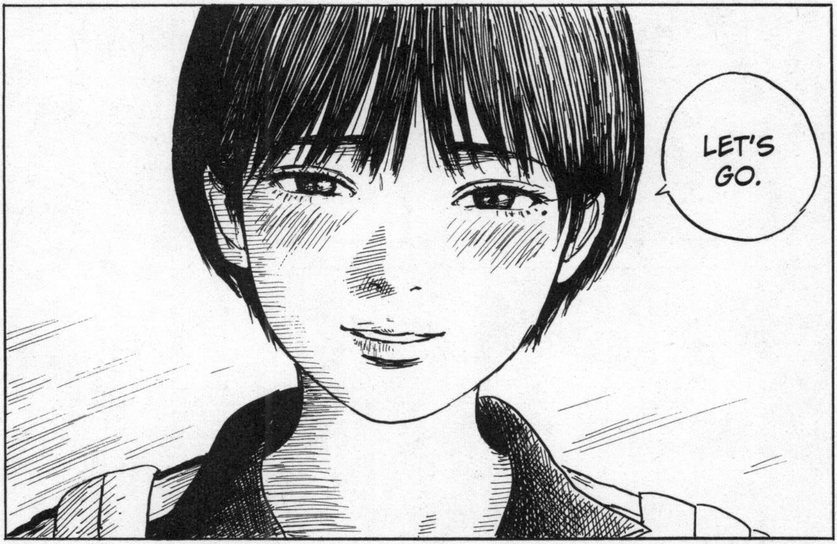
LET'S GO.

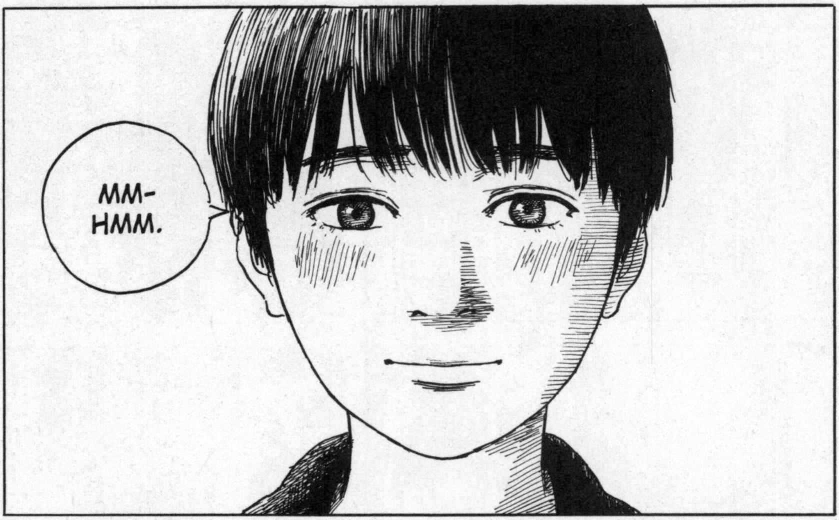
MM-
HMM.
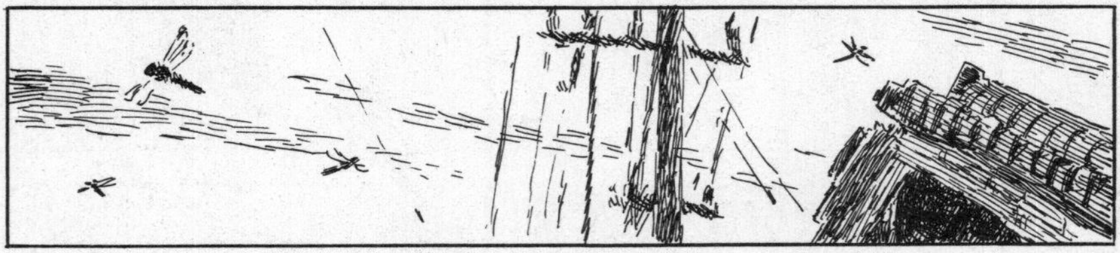
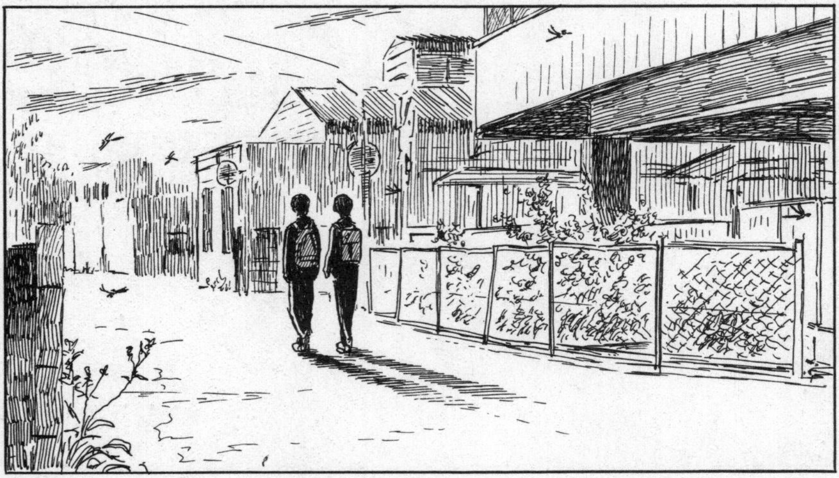

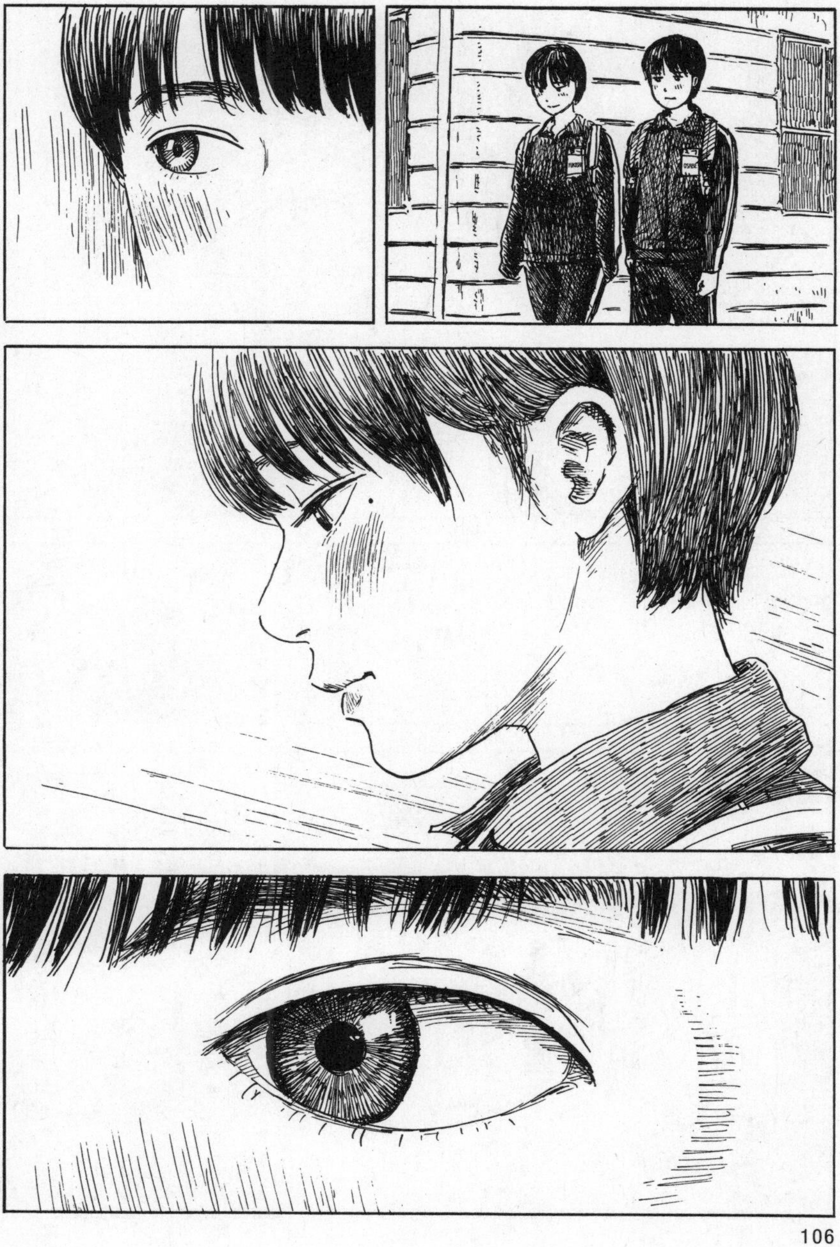
OSABE

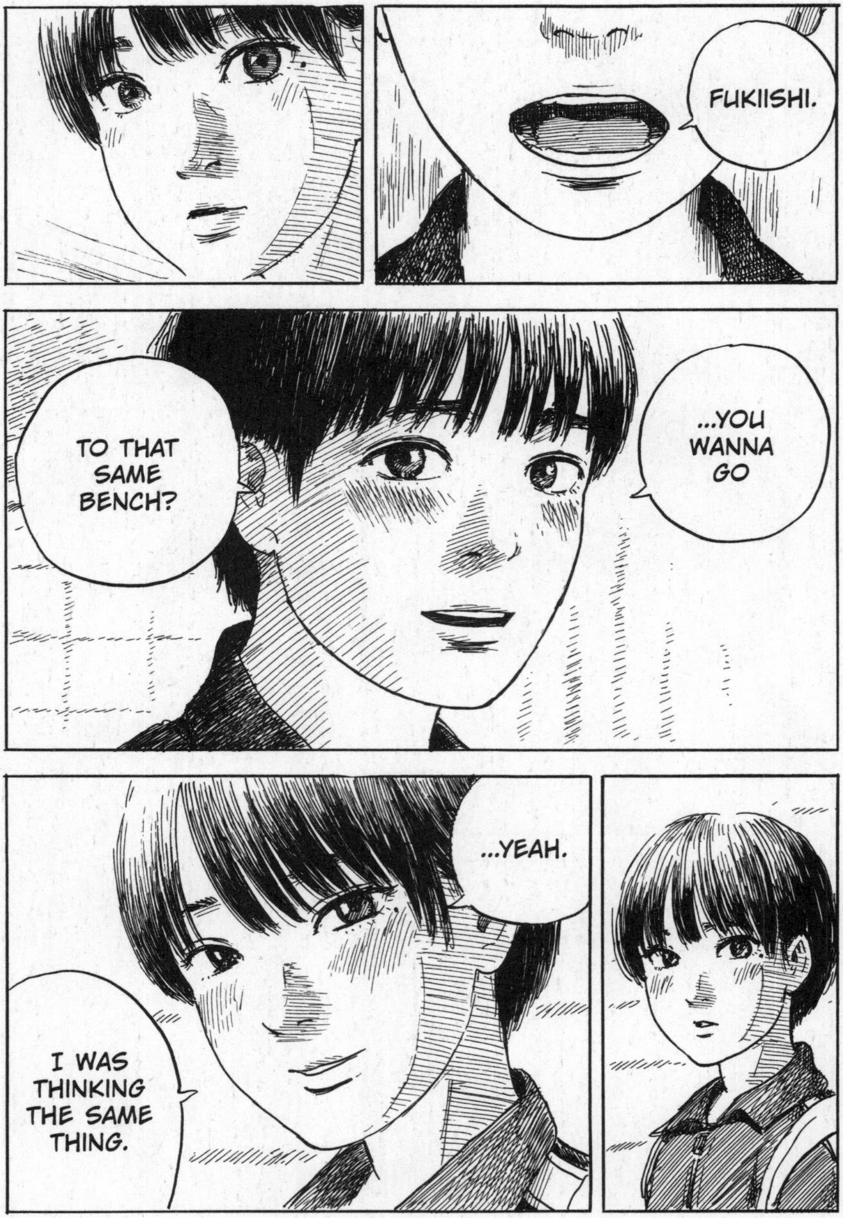
FUKIISHI.
...YOU WANNA GO
TO THAT SAME BENCH?
...YEAH.
I WAS THINKING THE SAME THING.

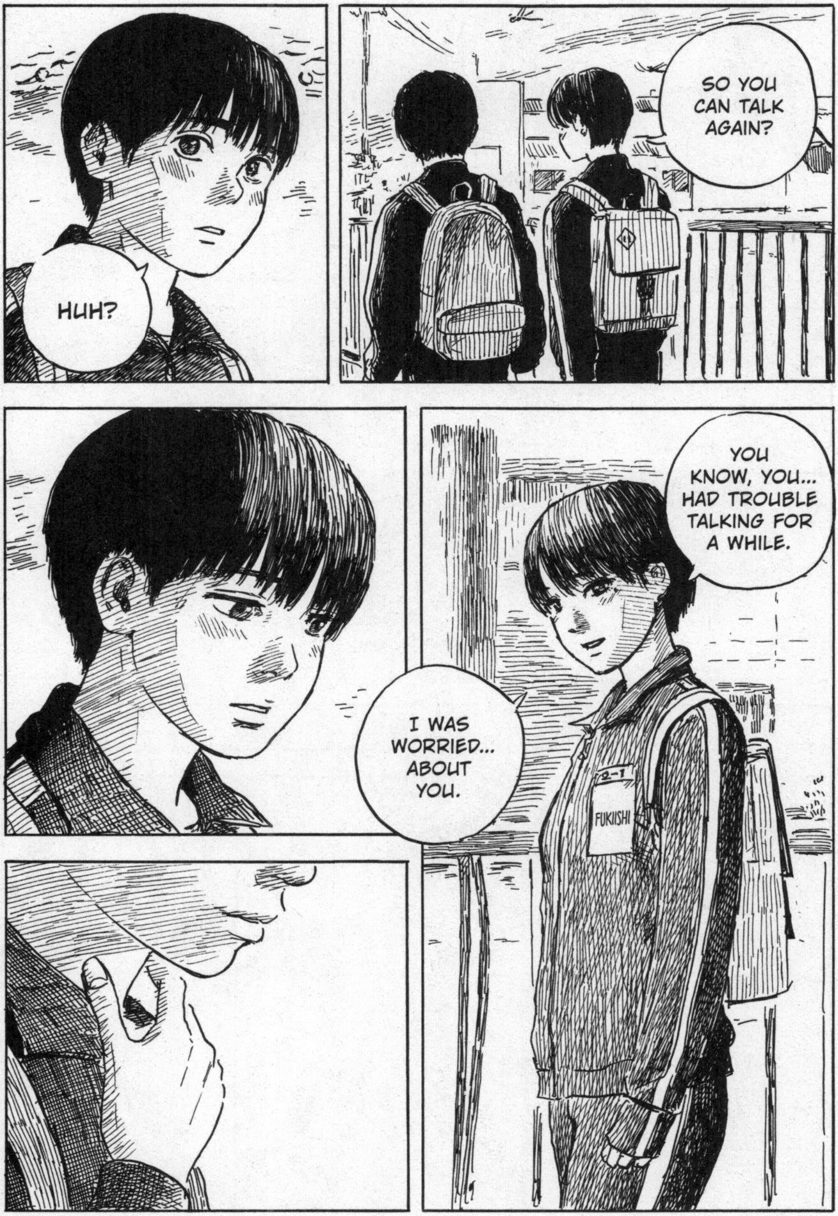
SO YOU CAN TALK AGAIN?
HUH?
YOU KNOW, YOU... HAD TROUBLE TALKING FOR A WHILE.
I WAS WORRIED... ABOUT YOU.
2-1
FUKIISHI

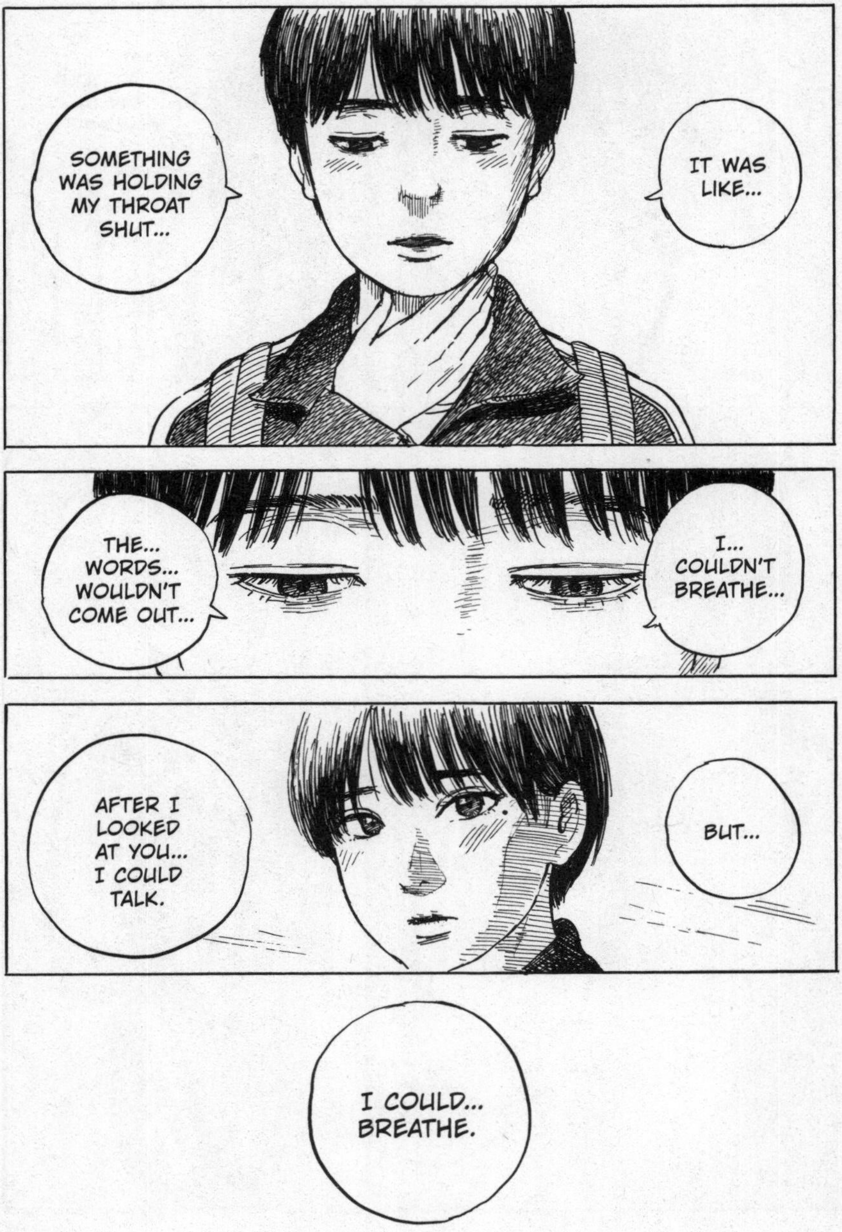
IT WAS LIKE...
SOMETHING WAS HOLDING MY THROAT SHUT...
I... COULDN'T BREATHE...
THE... WORDS... WOULDN'T COME OUT...
BUT...
AFTER I LOOKED AT YOU... I COULD TALK.
I COULD... BREATHE.

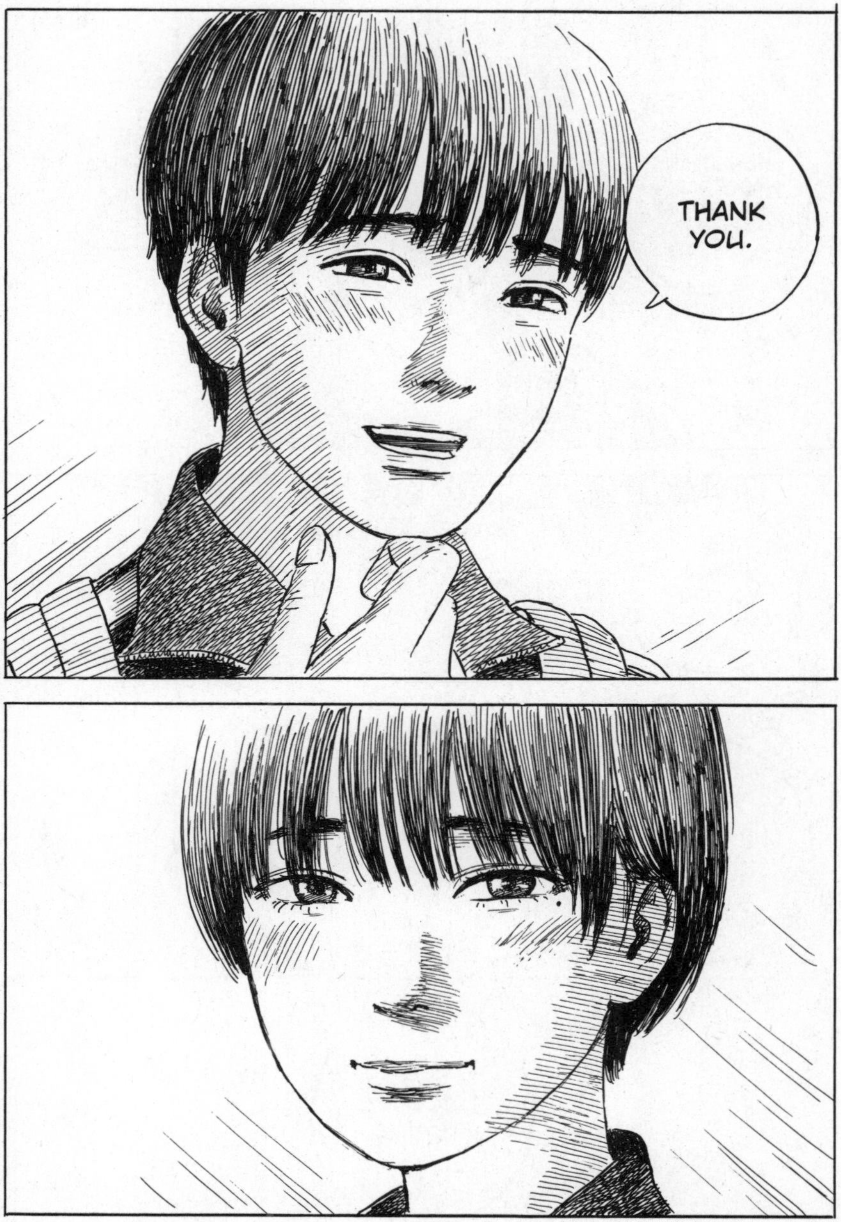
THANK YOU.

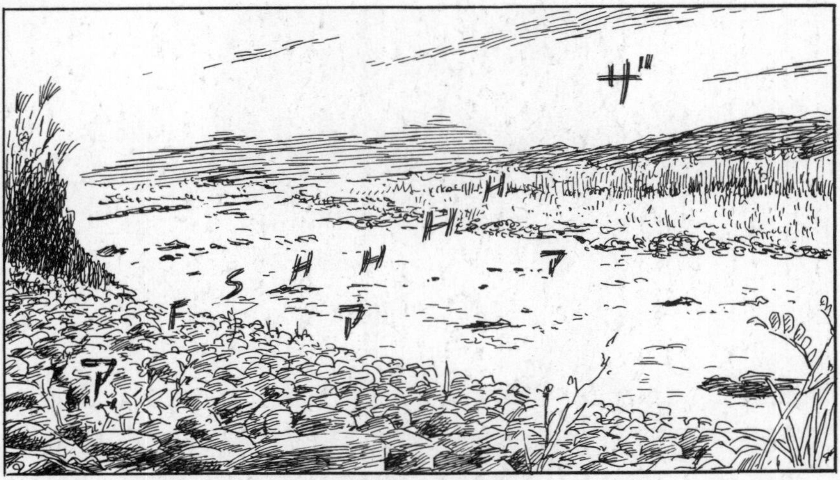
FSHHHH

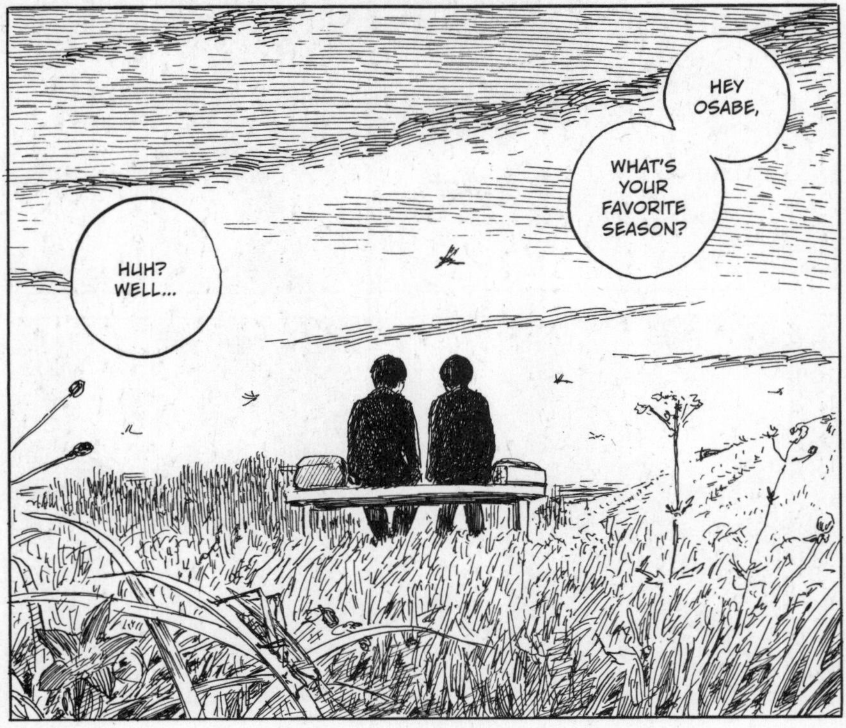
HEY OSABE,
WHAT'S YOUR FAVORITE SEASON?
HUH? WELL...

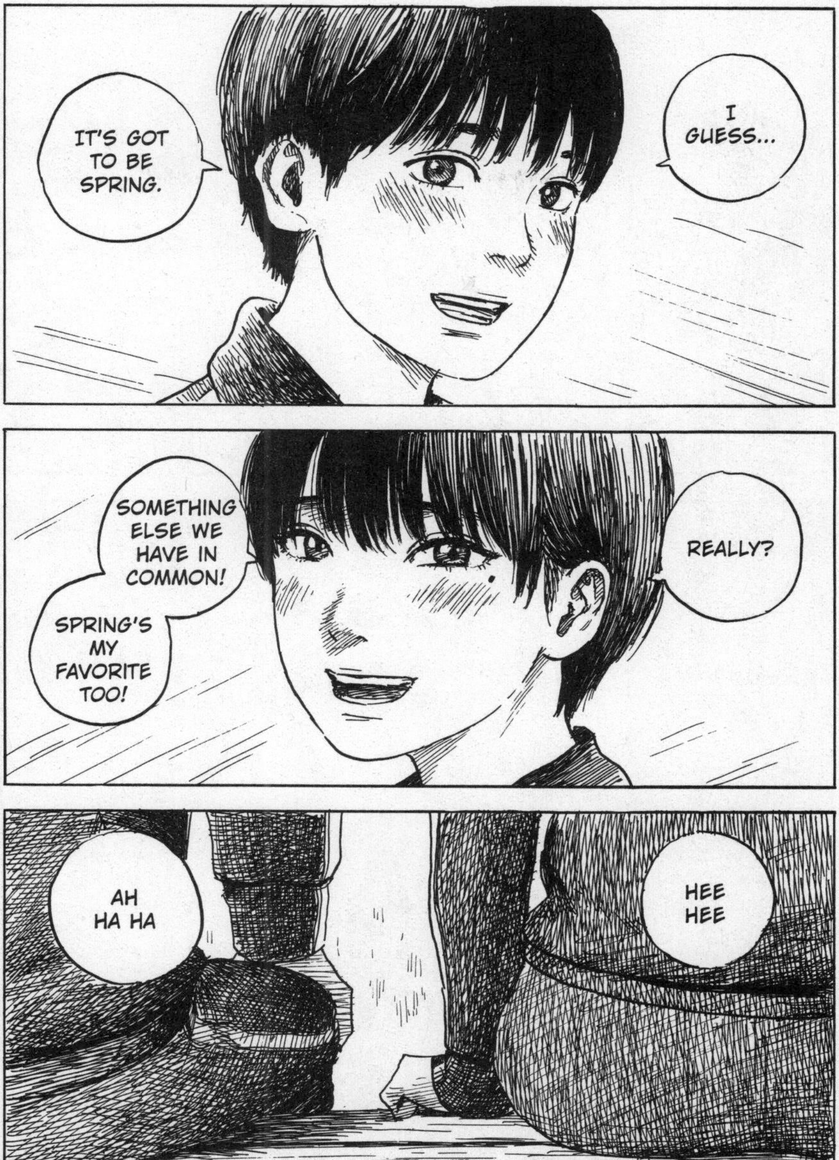

I GUESS...
IT'S GOT TO BE SPRING.
REALLY?
SOMETHING ELSE WE HAVE IN COMMON!
SPRING'S MY FAVORITE TOO!
HEE HEE
AH HA HA

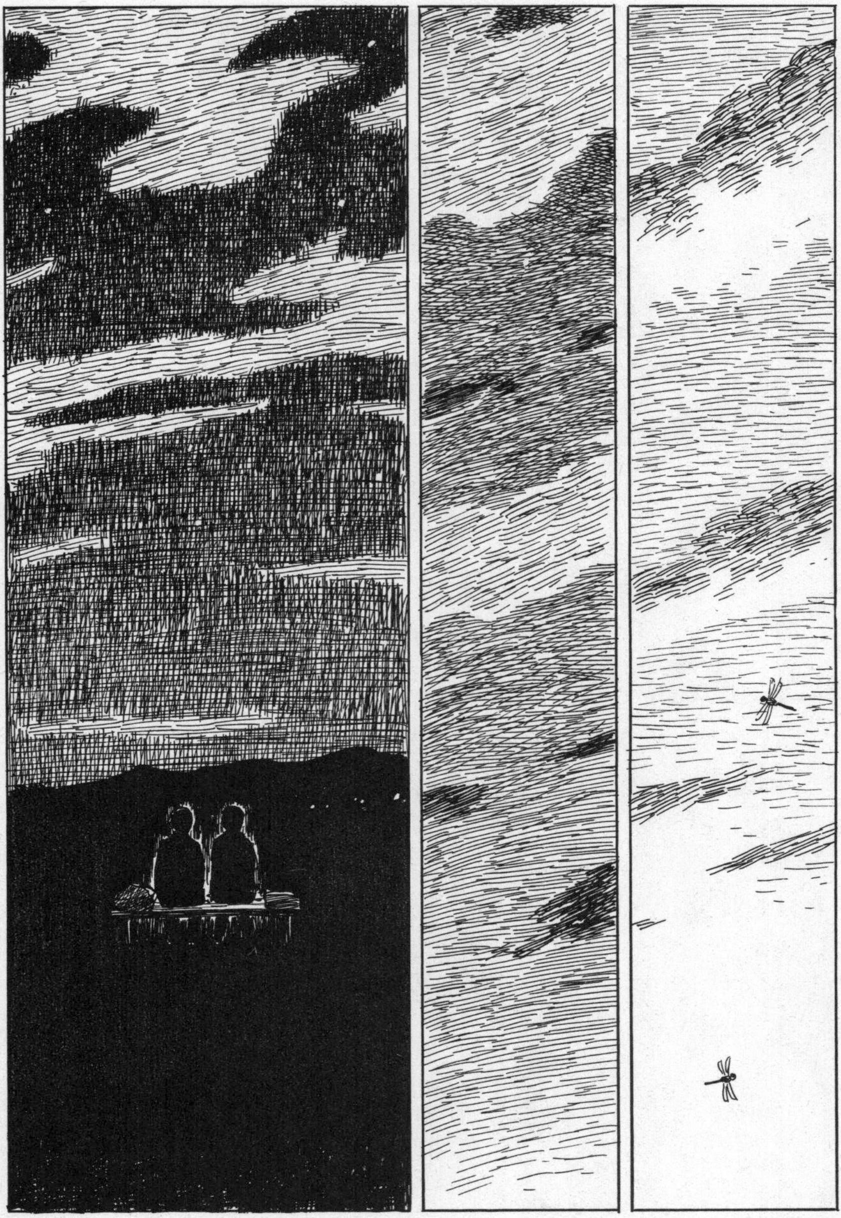

...GUESS IT'S TIME TO GO?
IT GOT DARK, HUH.
OUR PARENTS MIGHT GET MAD.
YOUR DAD...
...OH...
YEAH... GUESS SO...
WHAT ABOUT YOU?
DON'T WORRY ABOUT ME.
I DON'T CARE IF HE'S MAD.

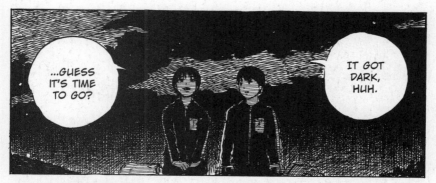

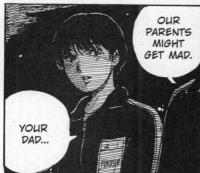

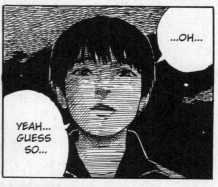

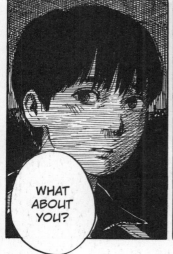

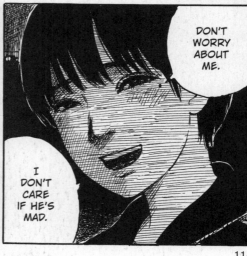

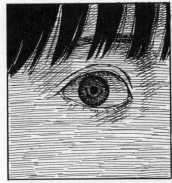

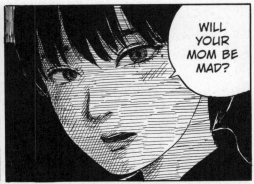

WILL YOUR MOM BE MAD?

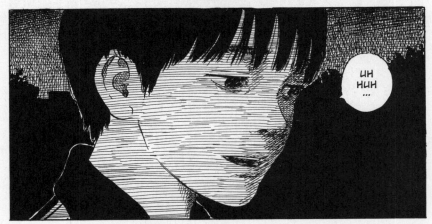

UH HUH ...

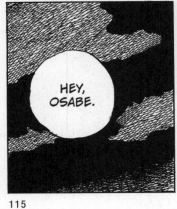

HEY, OSABE.

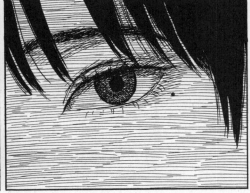

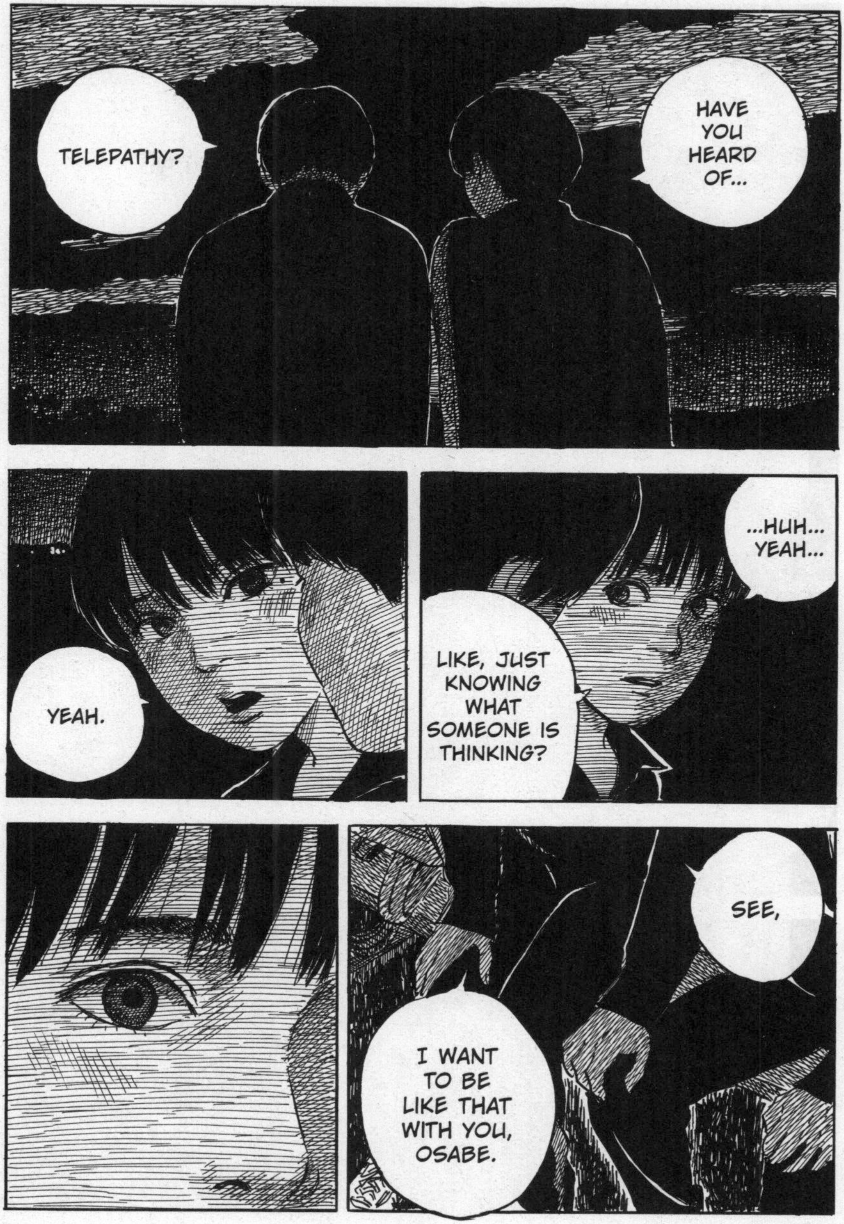
HAVE YOU HEARD OF...
TELEPATHY?
...HUH... YEAH...
LIKE, JUST KNOWING WHAT SOMEONE IS THINKING?
YEAH.
SEE,
I WANT TO BE LIKE THAT WITH YOU, OSABE.

I WANT TO KNOW...
EVERYTHING ABOUT YOU.
AND I HOPE
2-1
FUKIISHI
YOU'LL KNOW ME THE SAME WAY.
KNOW IT ALL...
NO MATTER HOW PAINFUL.

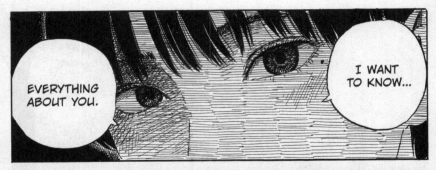

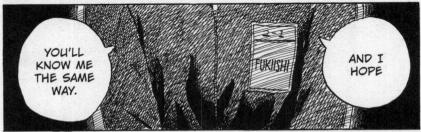

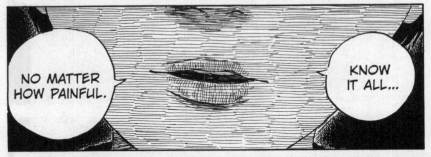

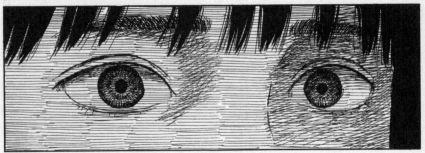

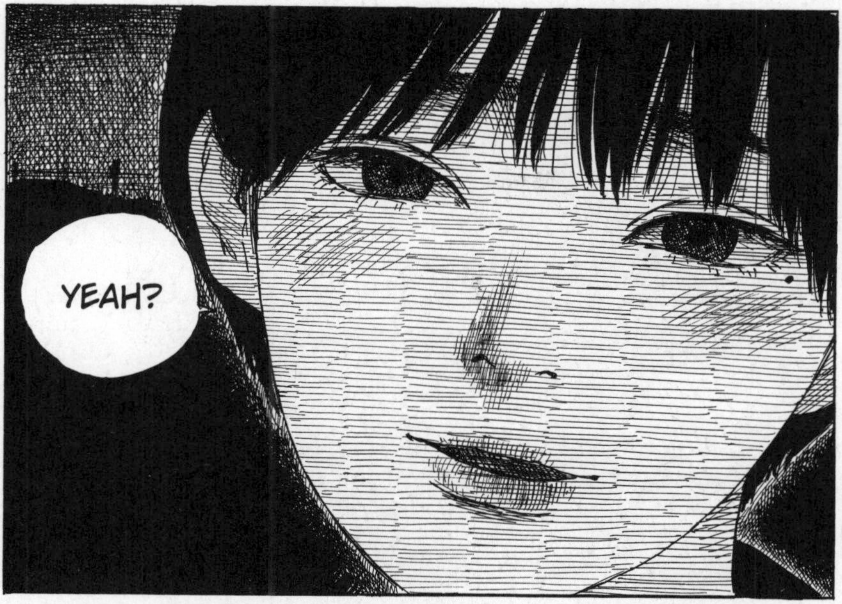
YEAH?
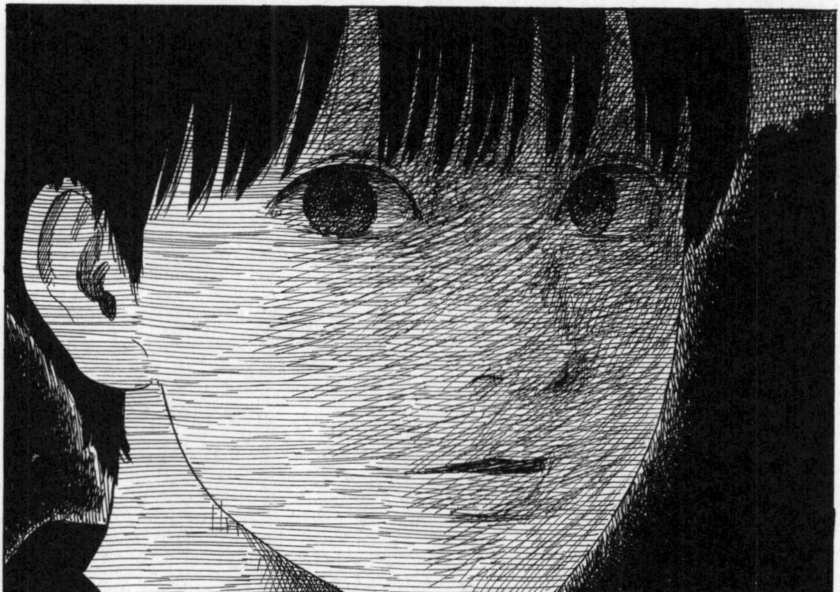

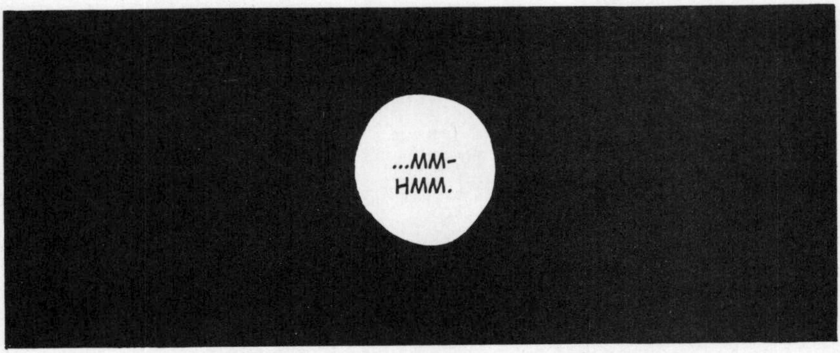
...MM-
HMM.

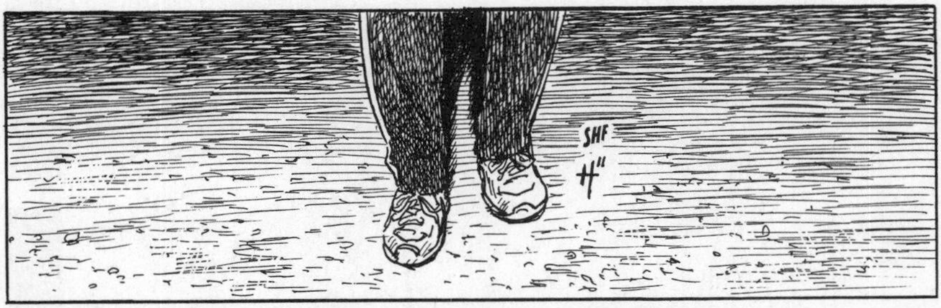
SHF

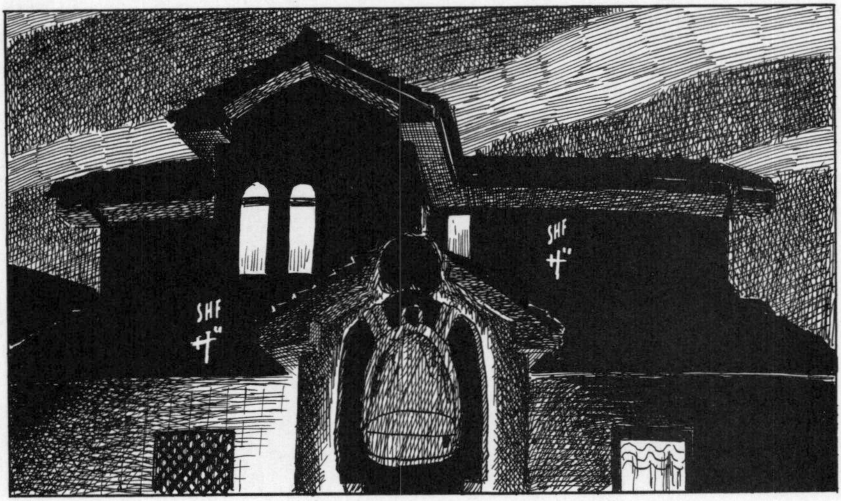
SHF
SHF

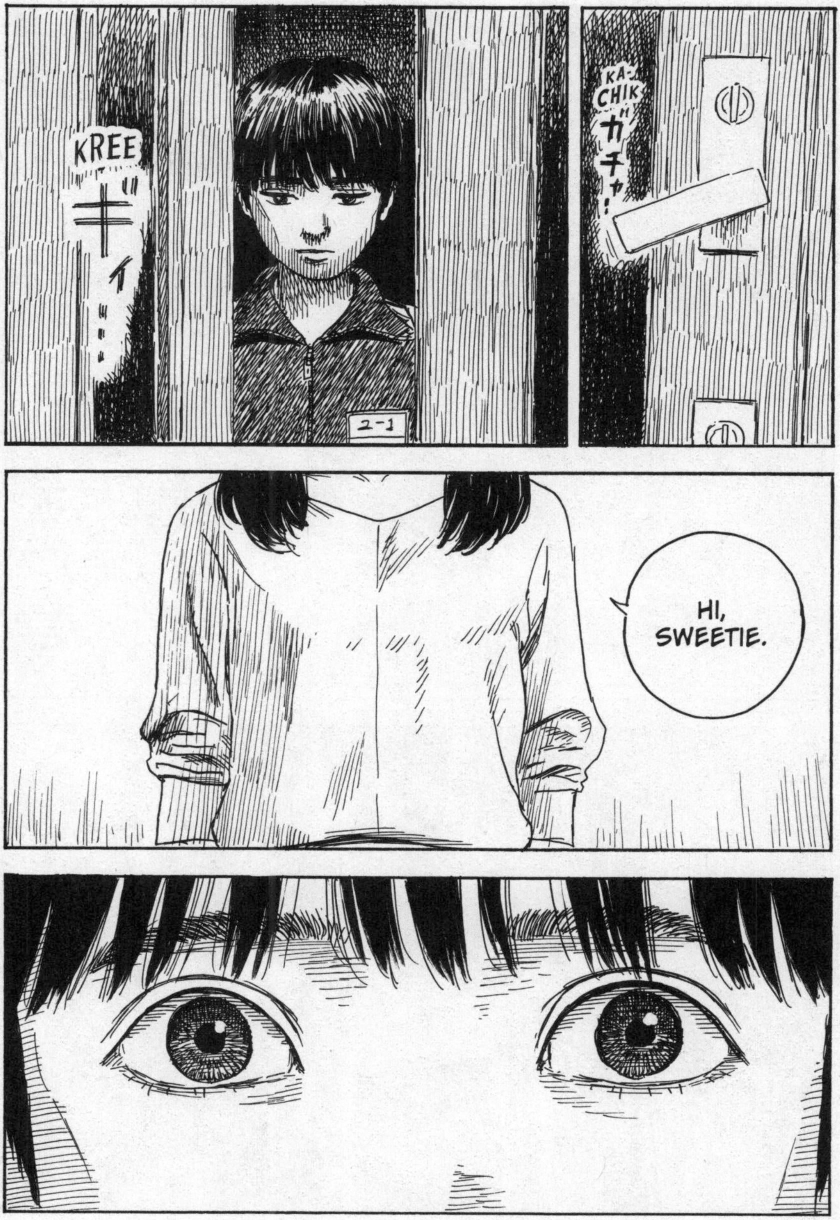
KA-CHIK
ガチャ!
KREE
ギィ……
HI, SWEETIE.

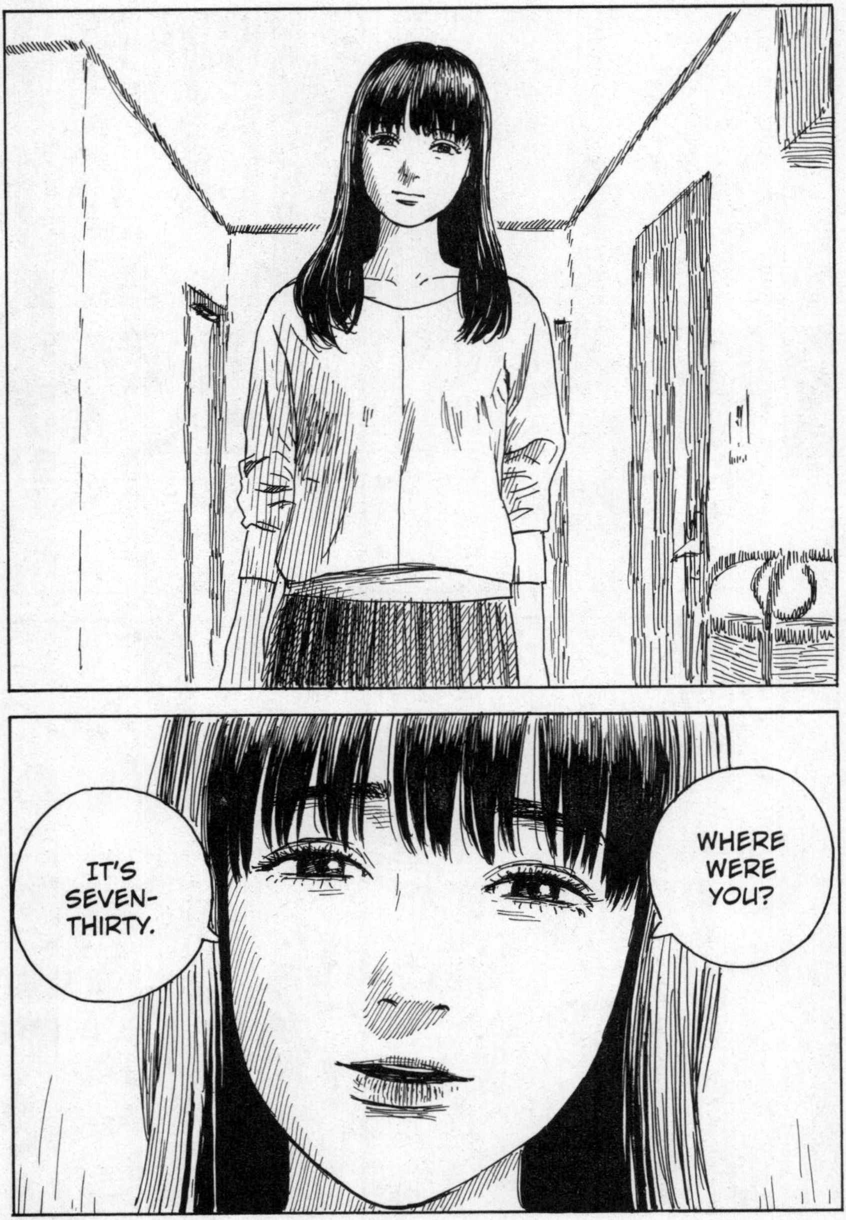
WHERE WERE YOU?
IT'S SEVEN-THIRTY.

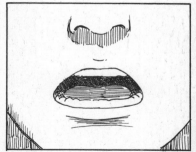

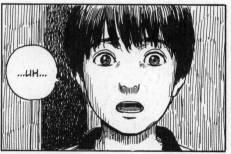

...ин...

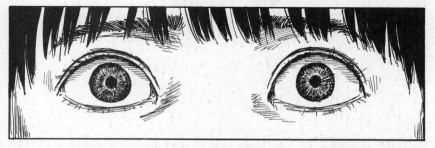

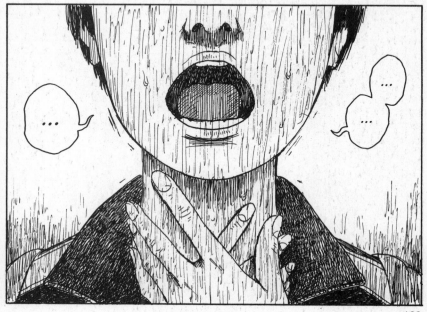

...

...

...

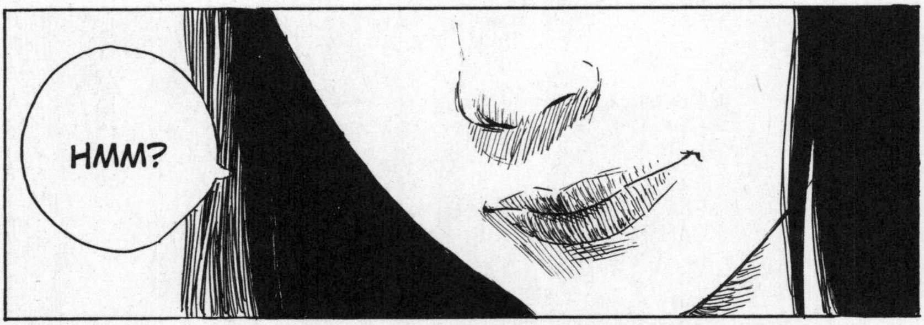
HMM?
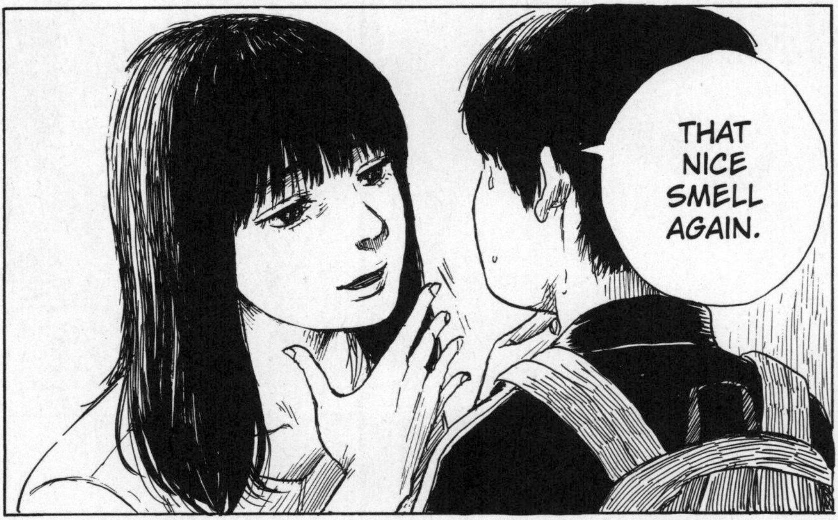
THAT NICE SMELL AGAIN.
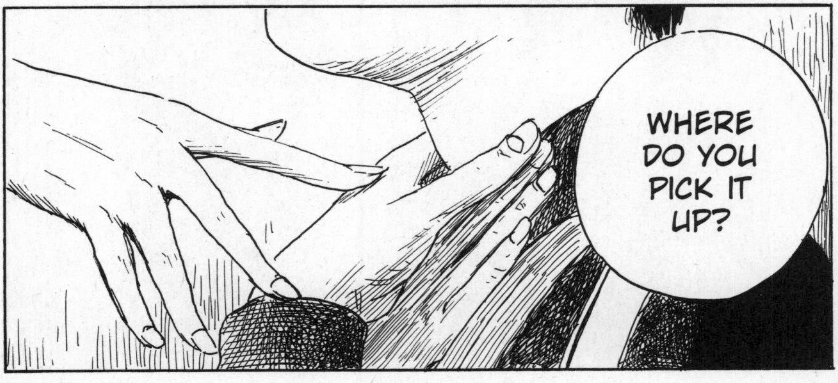
WHERE DO YOU PICK IT UP?

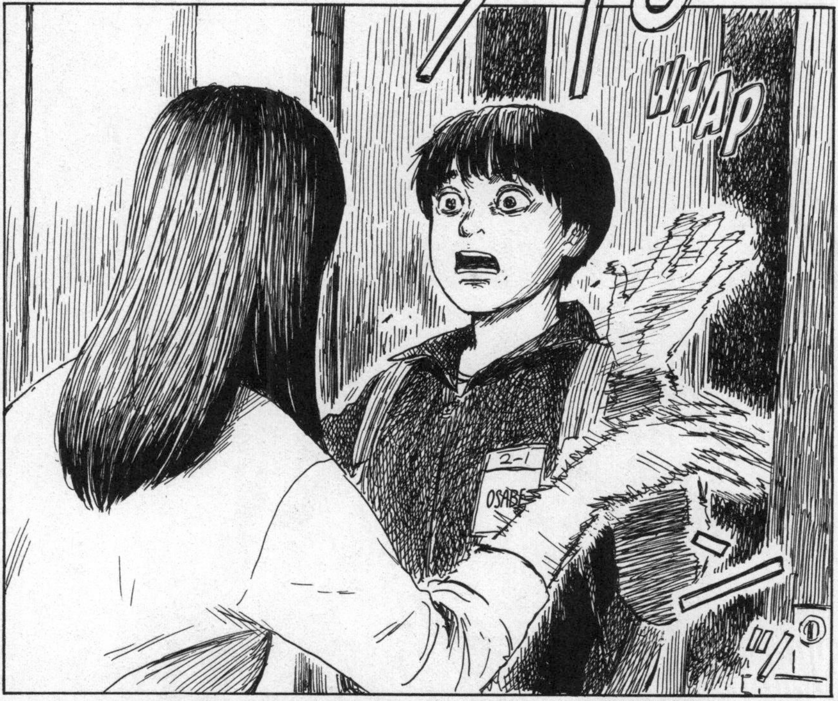
WHAP
2-1
OSABE

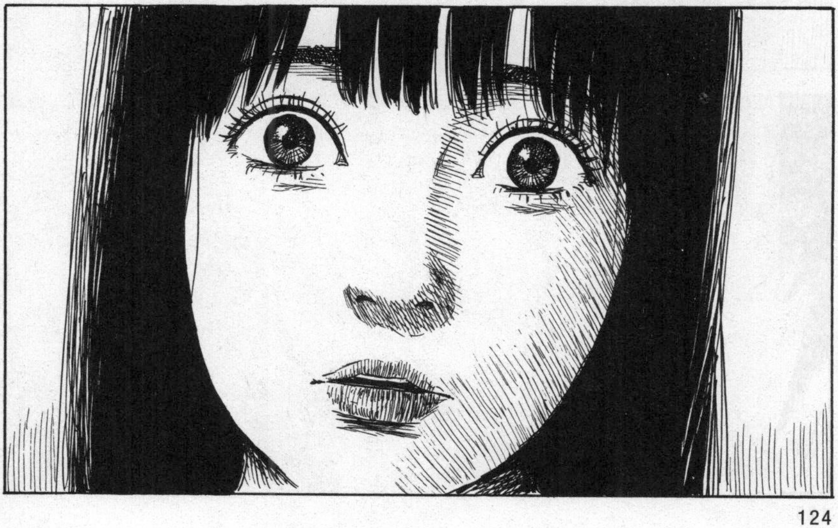

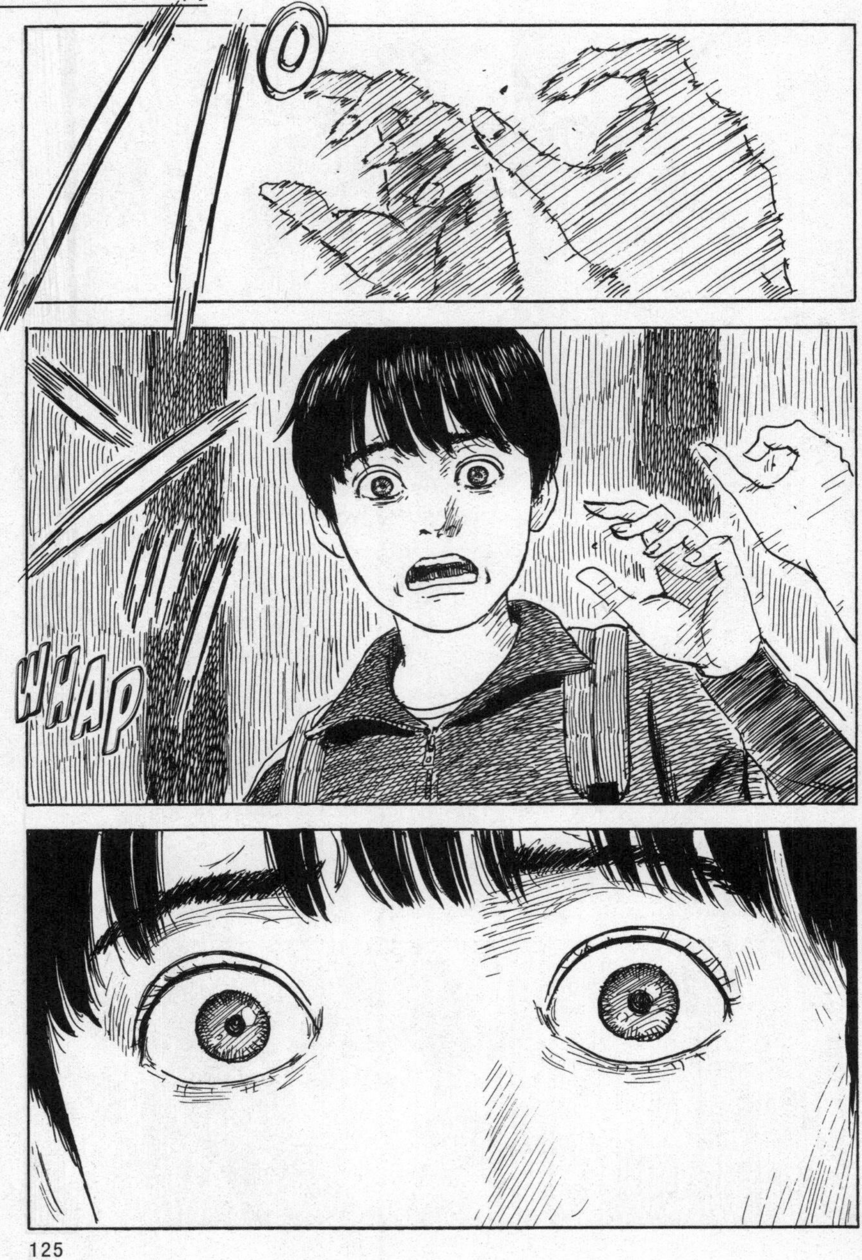
WHAP

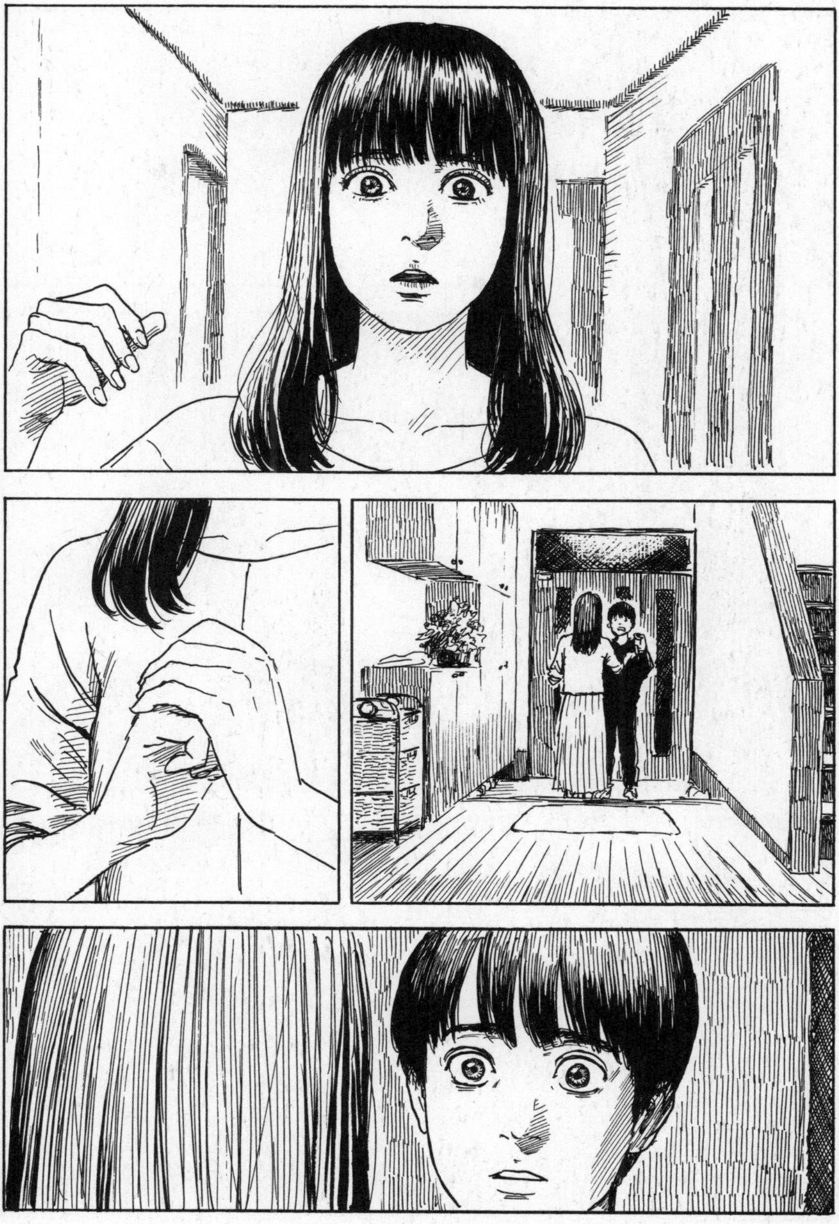

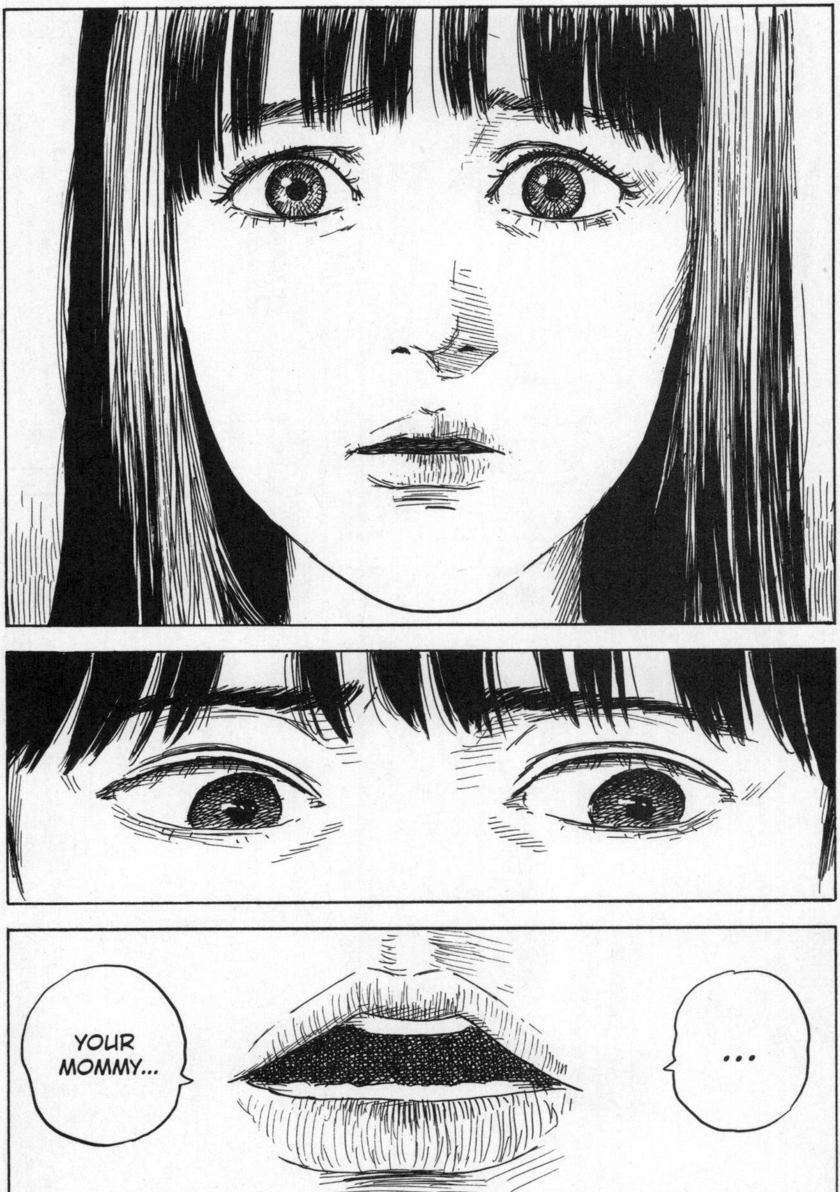
...
YOUR MOMMY...

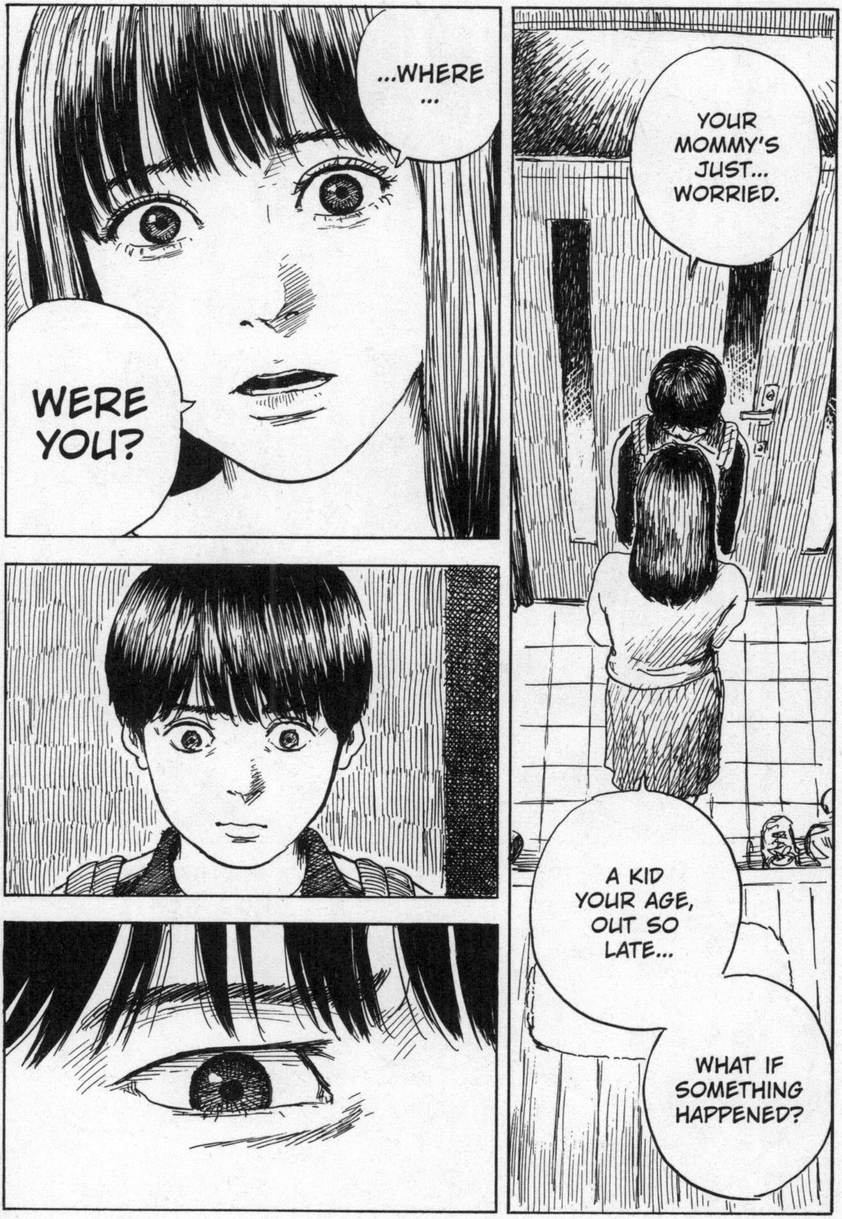
YOUR MOMMY'S JUST... WORRIED.
A KID YOUR AGE, OUT SO LATE...
WHAT IF SOMETHING HAPPENED?
...WHERE ...
WERE YOU?

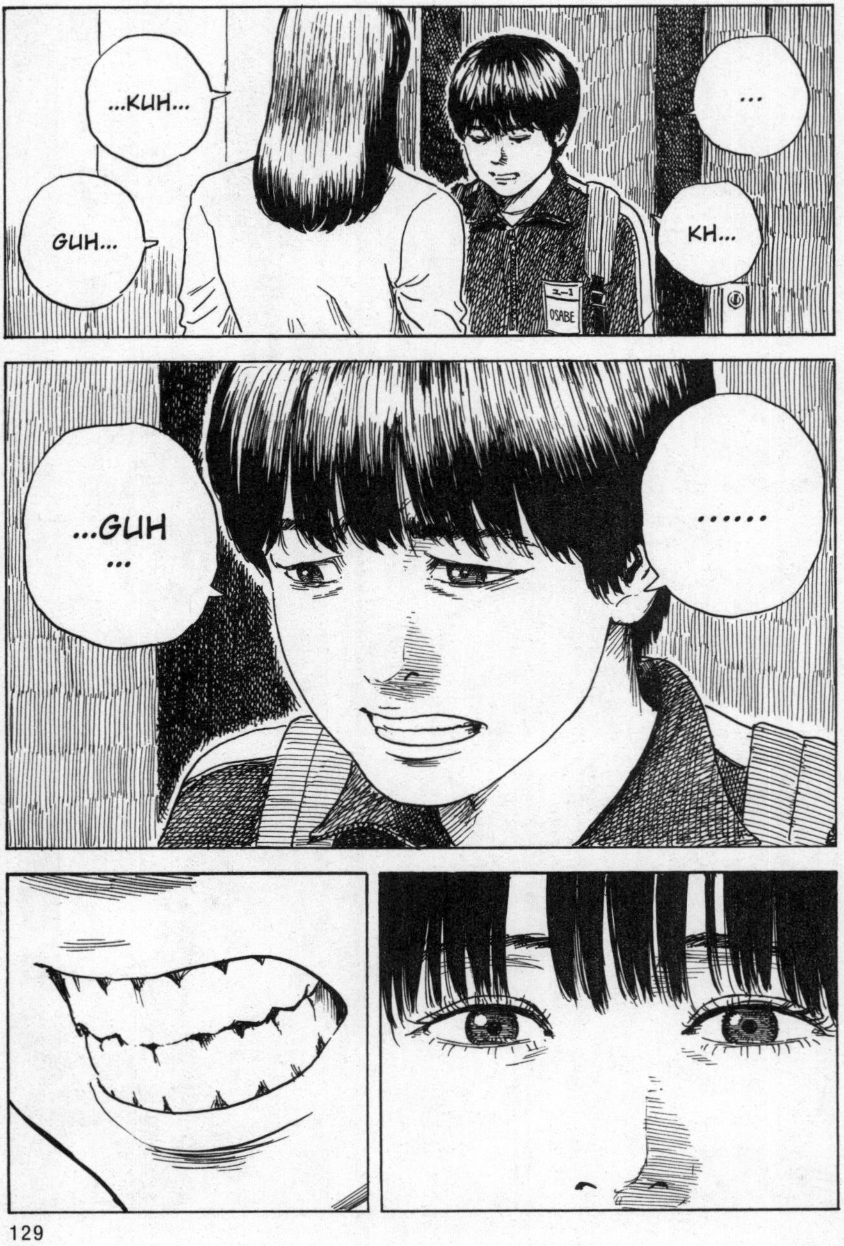
...
...KUH...
KH...
GUH...
OSABE
......
...GUH ...

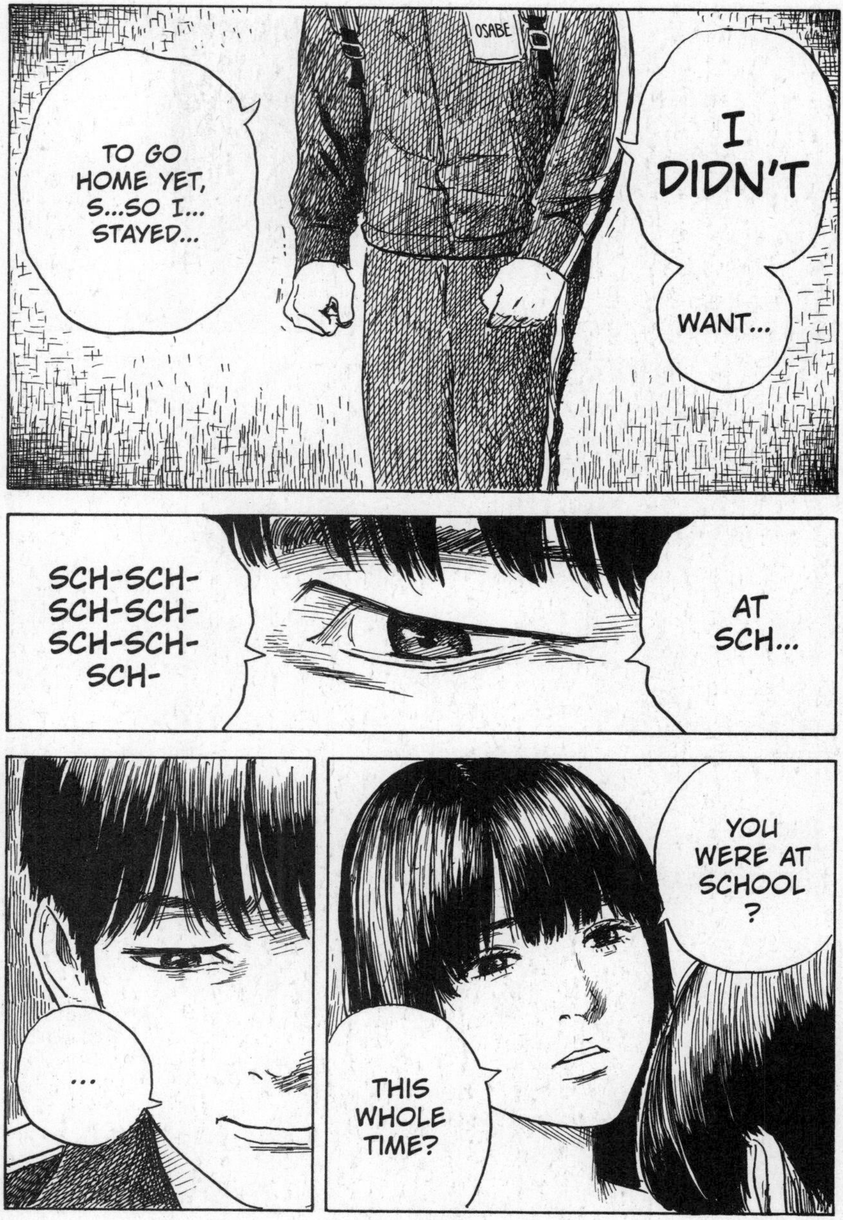
OSABE
I DIDN'T WANT...
TO GO HOME YET, S...SO I... STAYED...
AT SCH...
SCH-SCH-SCH-SCH-SCH-SCH-SCH-
YOU WERE AT SCHOOL ?
THIS WHOLE TIME?
...

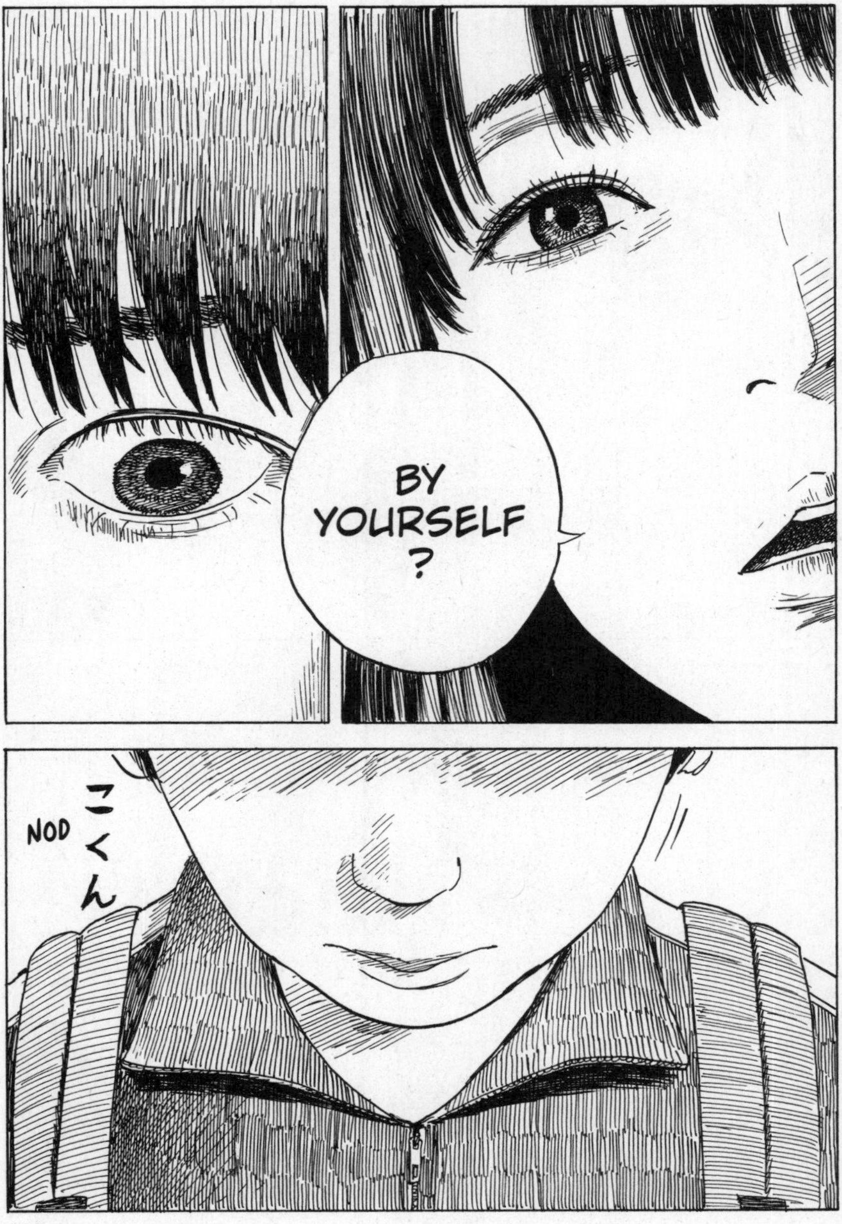
BY YOURSELF ?
こくん
NOD

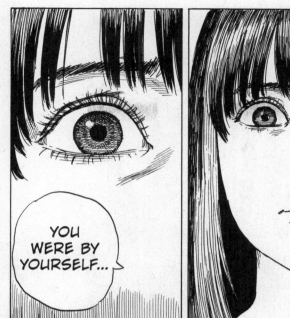

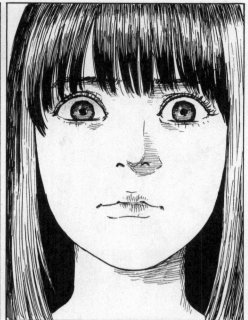

YOU
WERE BY
YOURSELF...

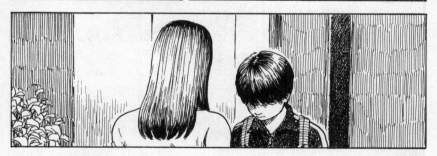

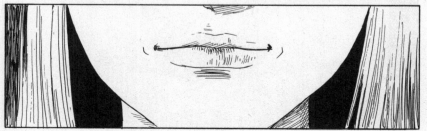

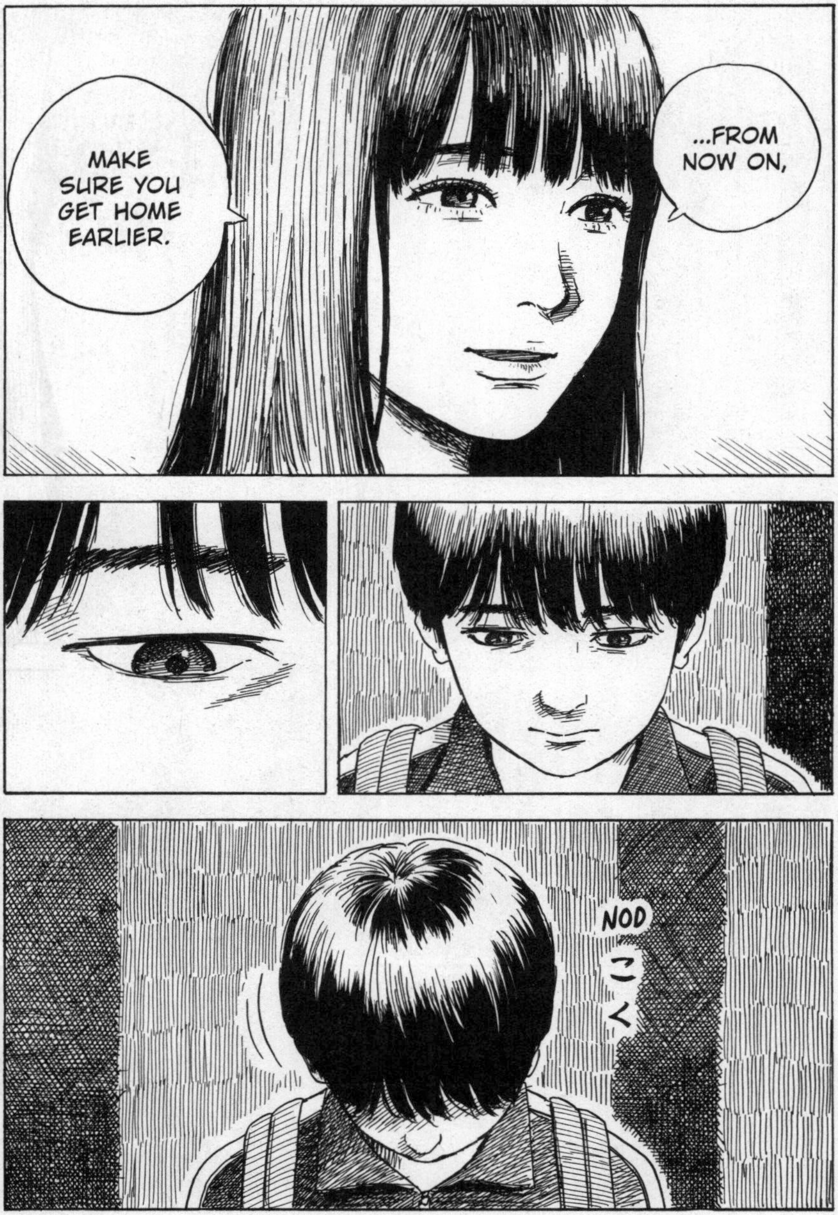
...FROM NOW ON,
MAKE SURE YOU GET HOME EARLIER.
NOD
こく

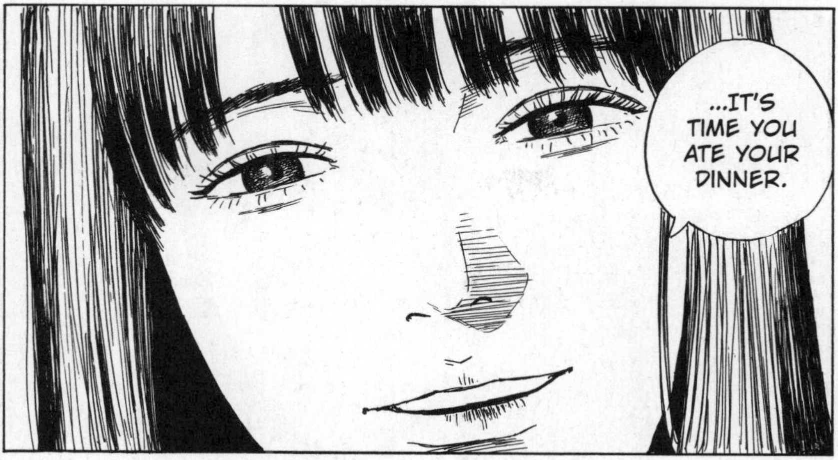
...IT'S TIME YOU ATE YOUR DINNER.

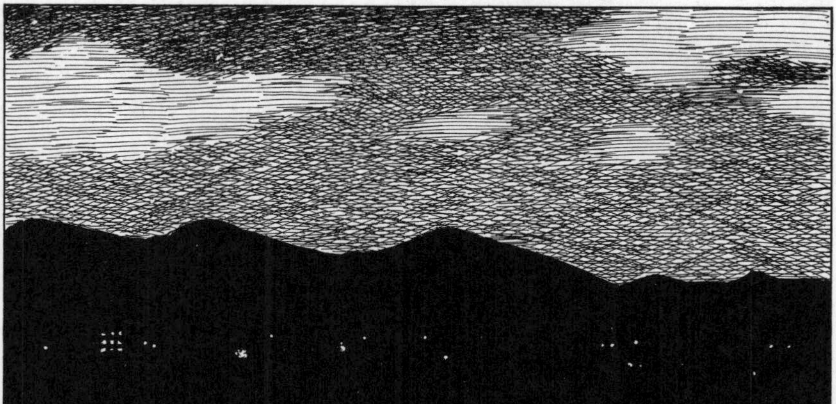

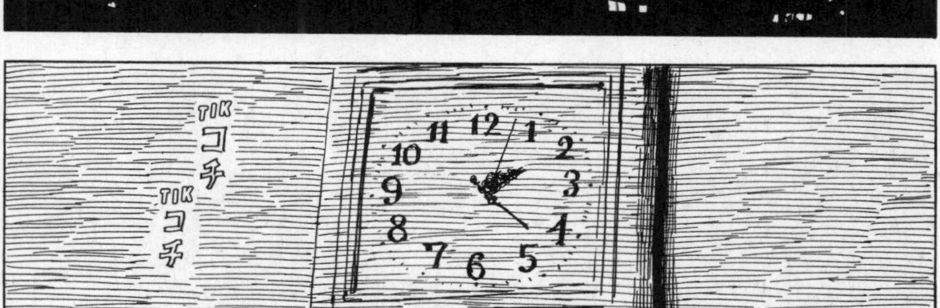
TIK
コチ
TIK
コチ

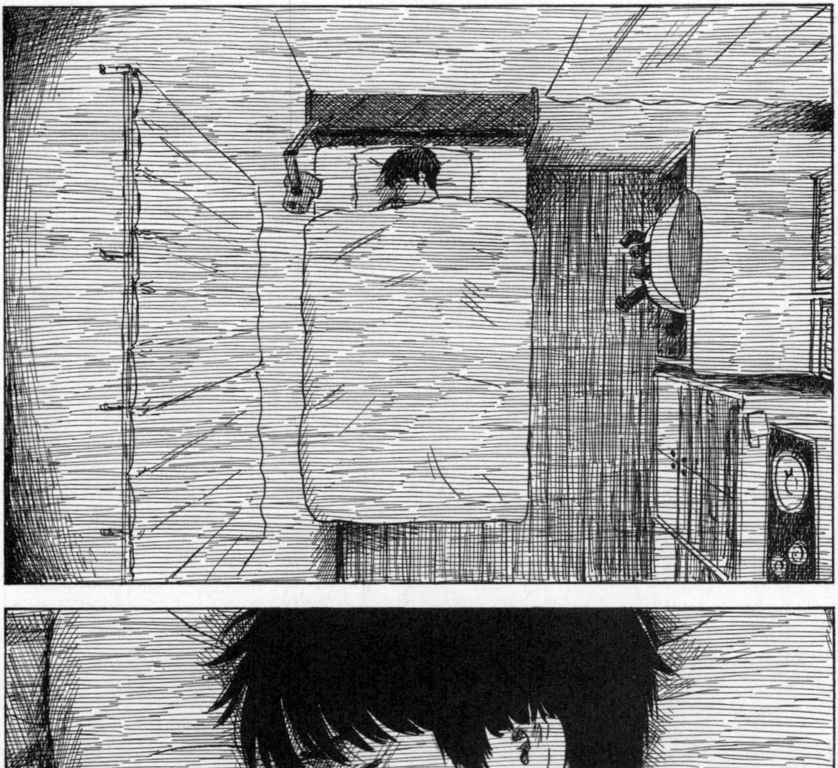
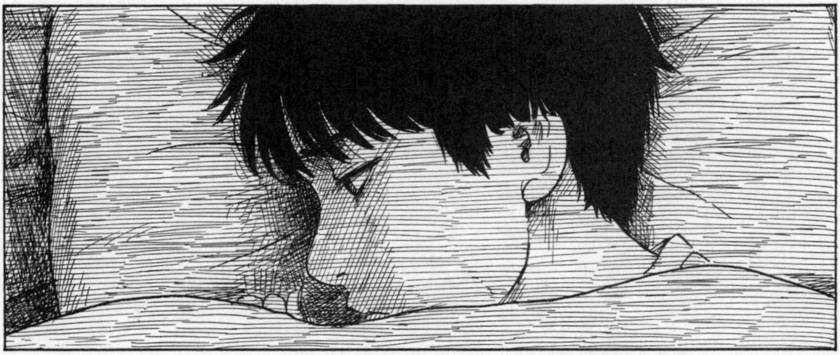
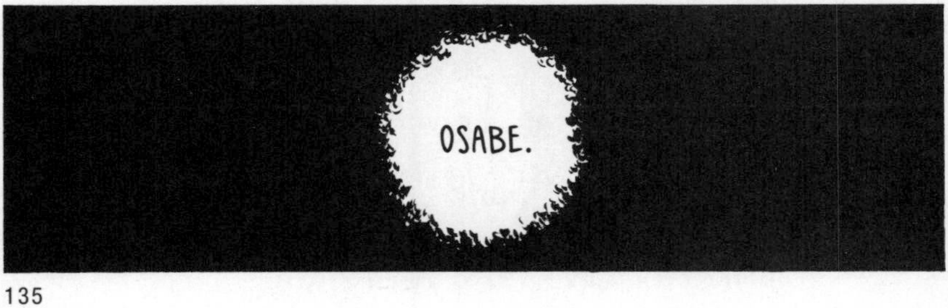
OSABE.

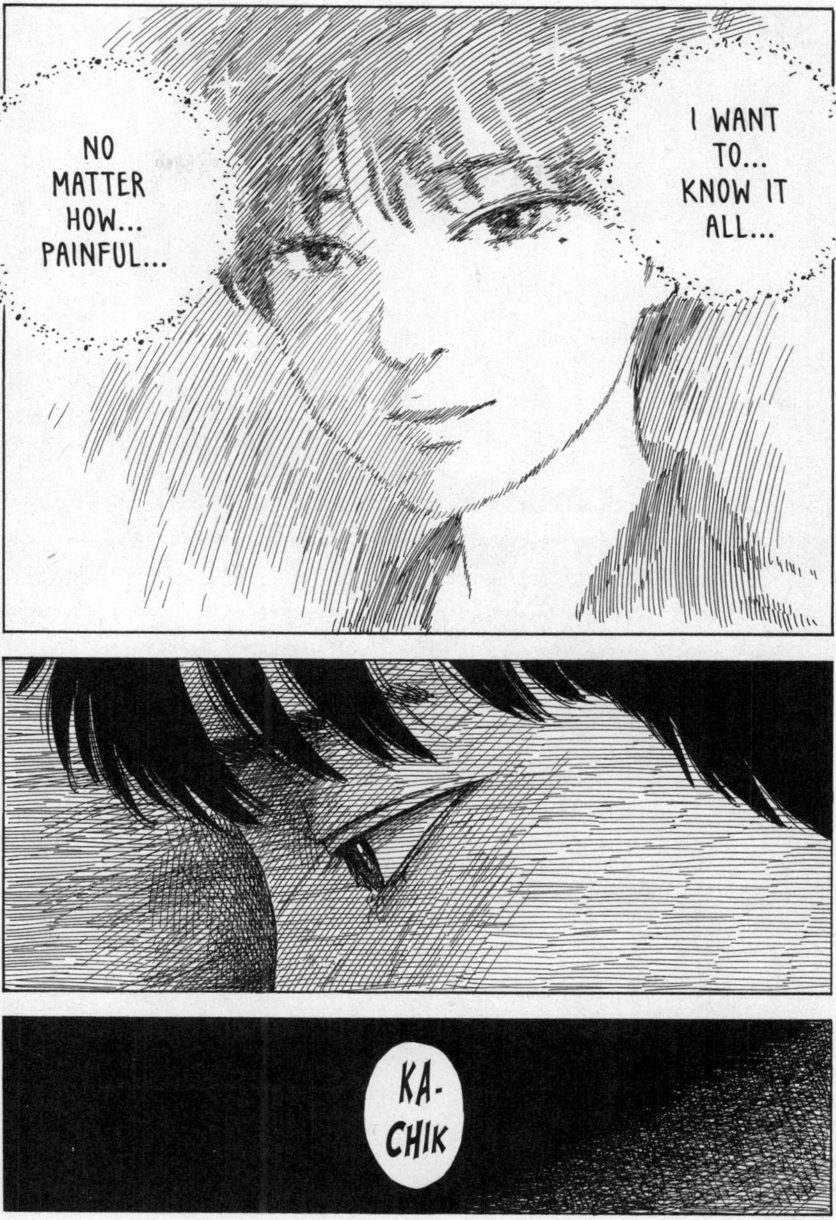
I WANT TO... KNOW IT ALL...
NO MATTER HOW... PAINFUL...
KA-CHIK

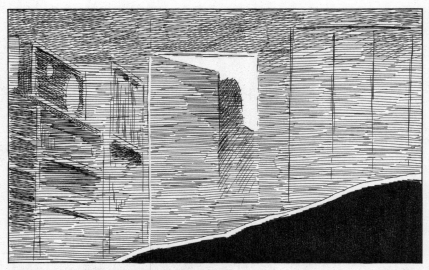

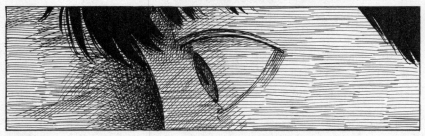

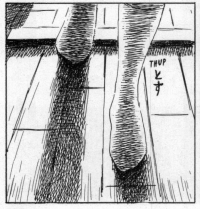

THUP
とす

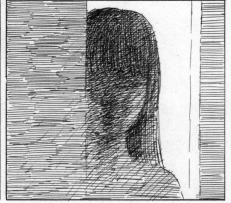

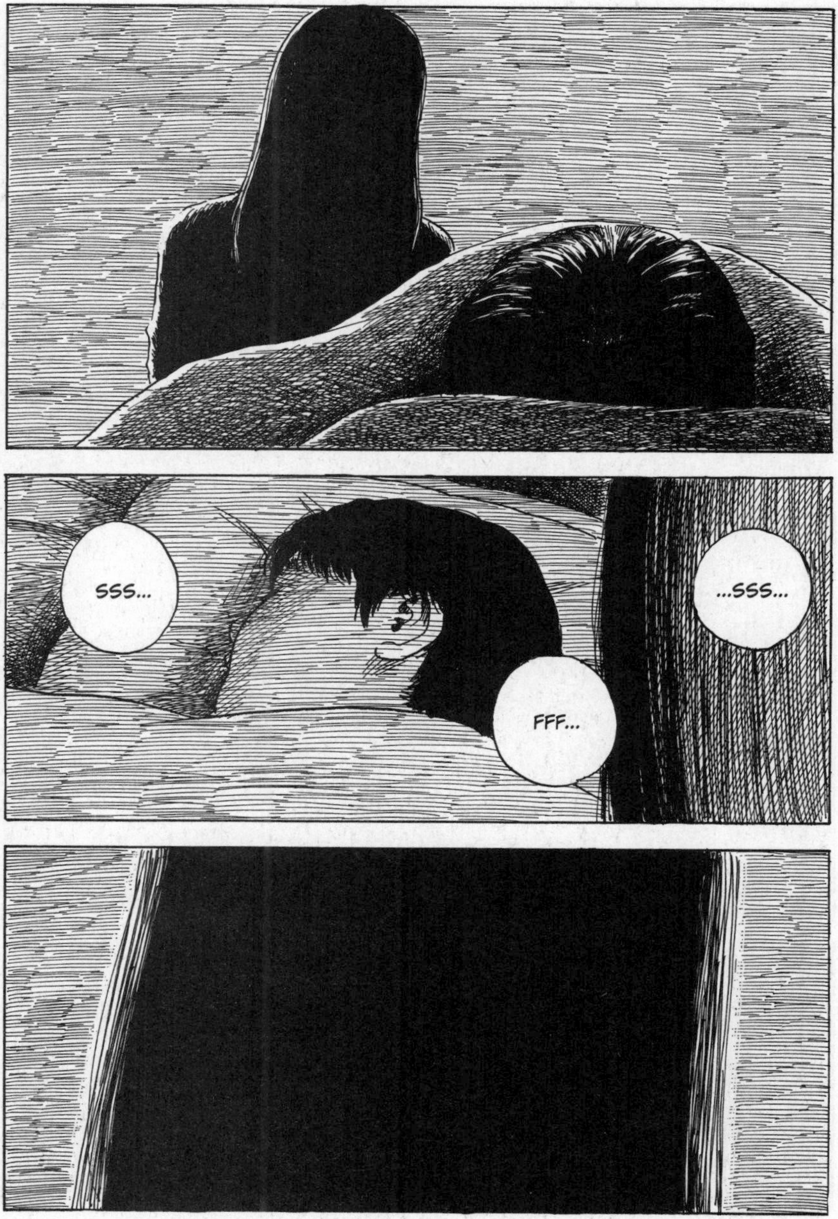
...SSS...
FFF...
SSS...

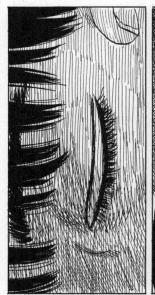
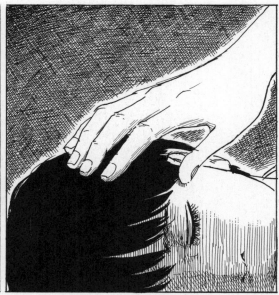
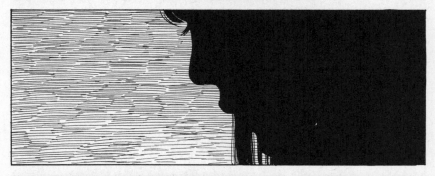
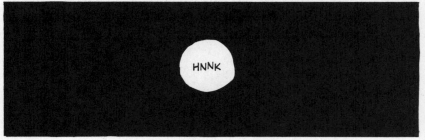

HNNK

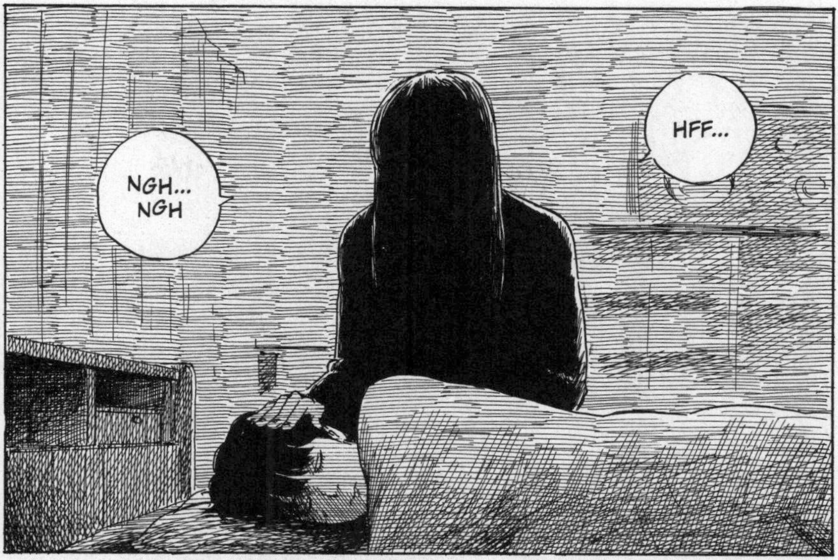
HFF...
NGH... NGH

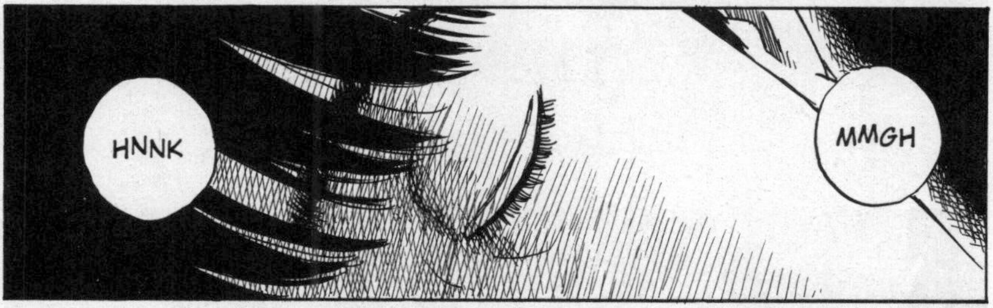
MMGH
HNNK

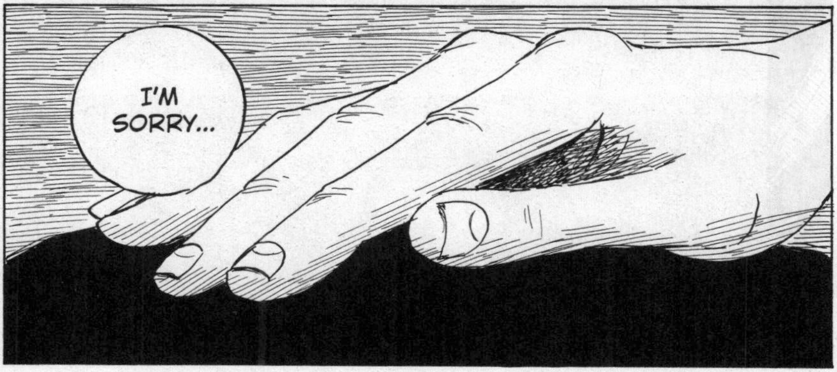
I'M SORRY...

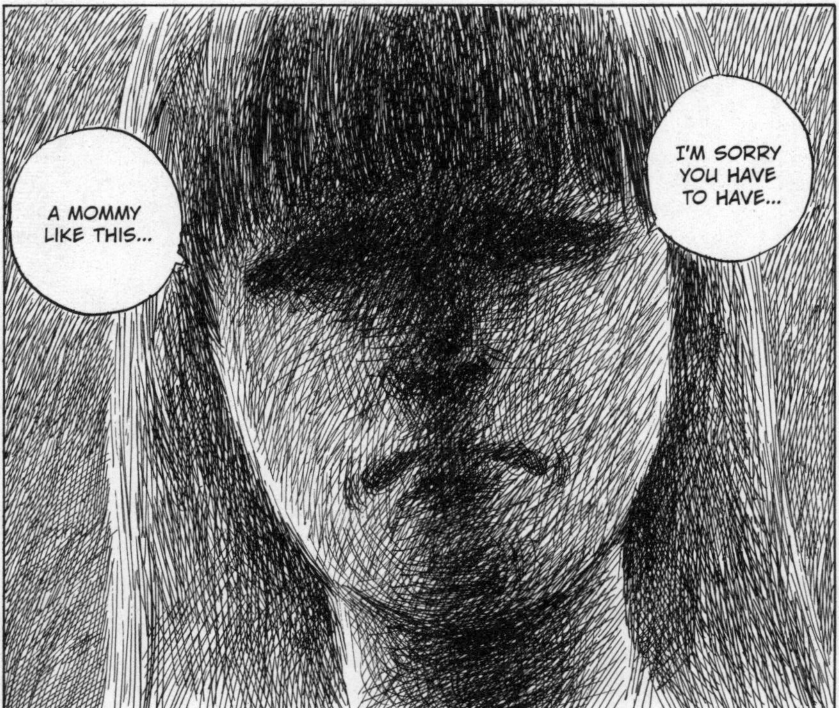
I'M SORRY YOU HAVE TO HAVE...
A MOMMY LIKE THIS...

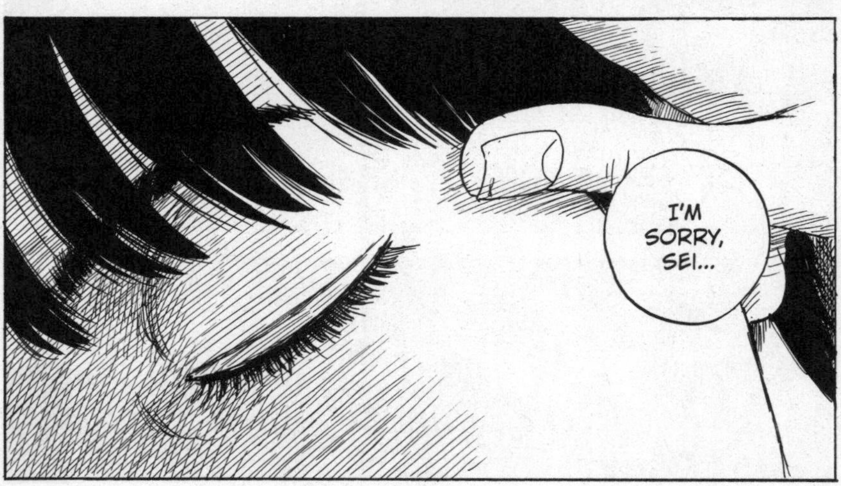
I'M SORRY, SEI...

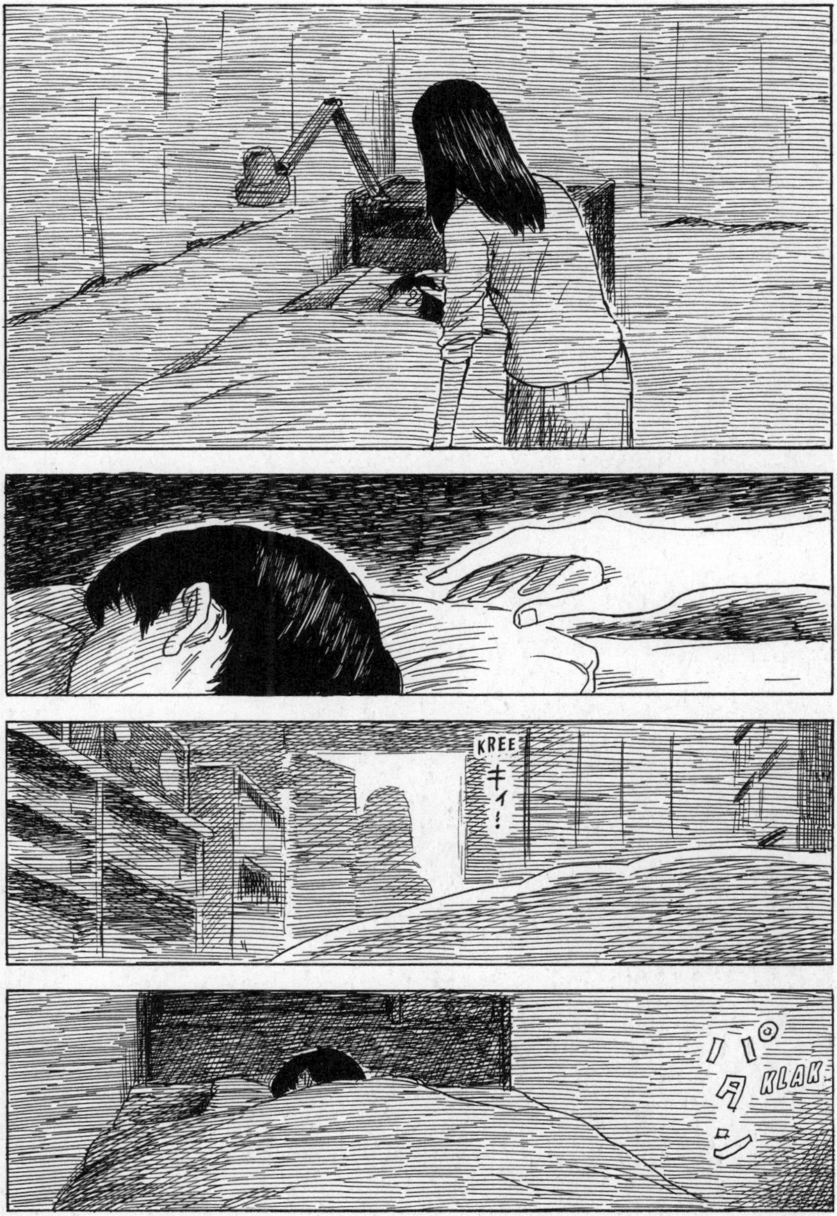
KREE
キィ!!
パタン
KLAK

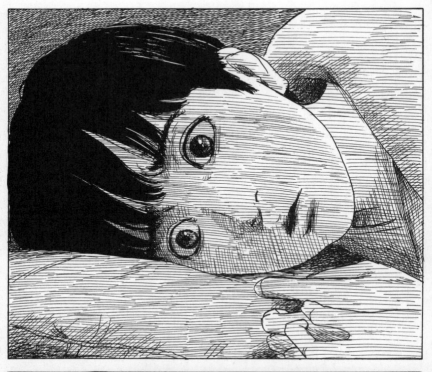

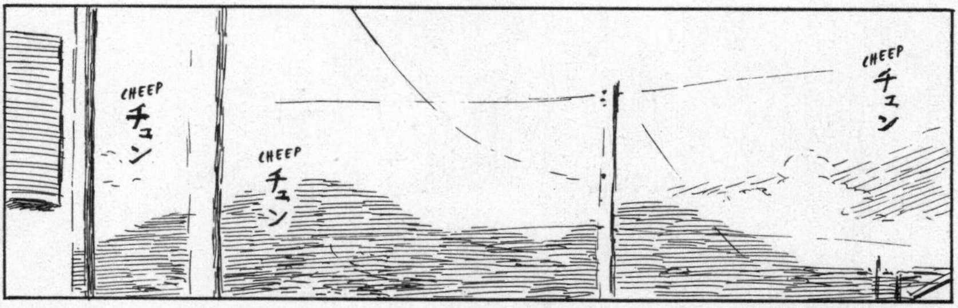
CHEEP
チュン
CHEEP
チュン
CHEEP
チュン

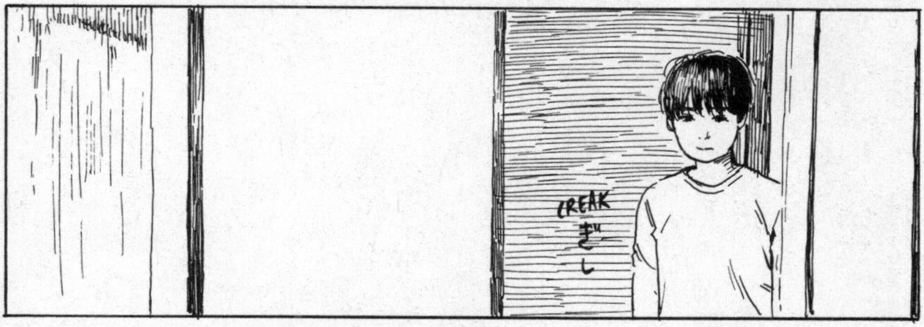
CREAK
ぎし

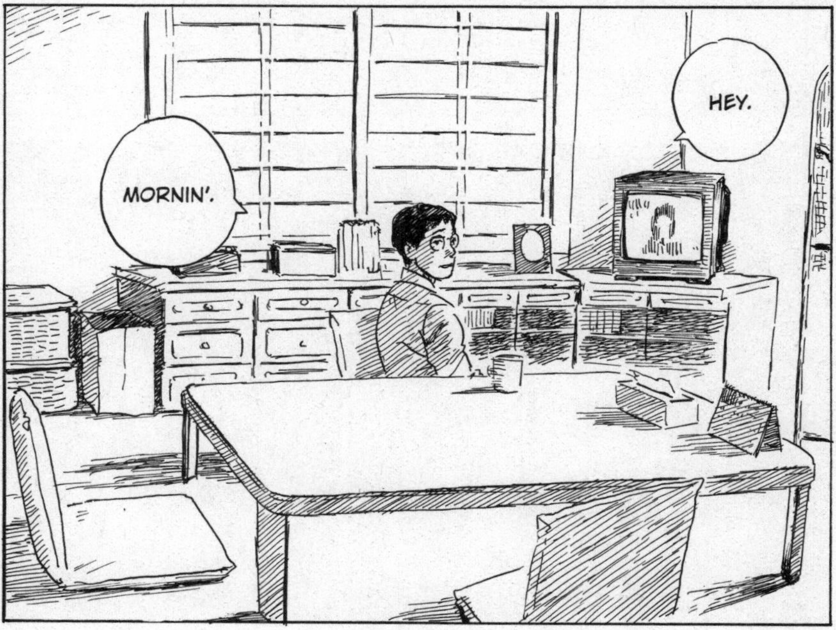
HEY.
MORNIN'.

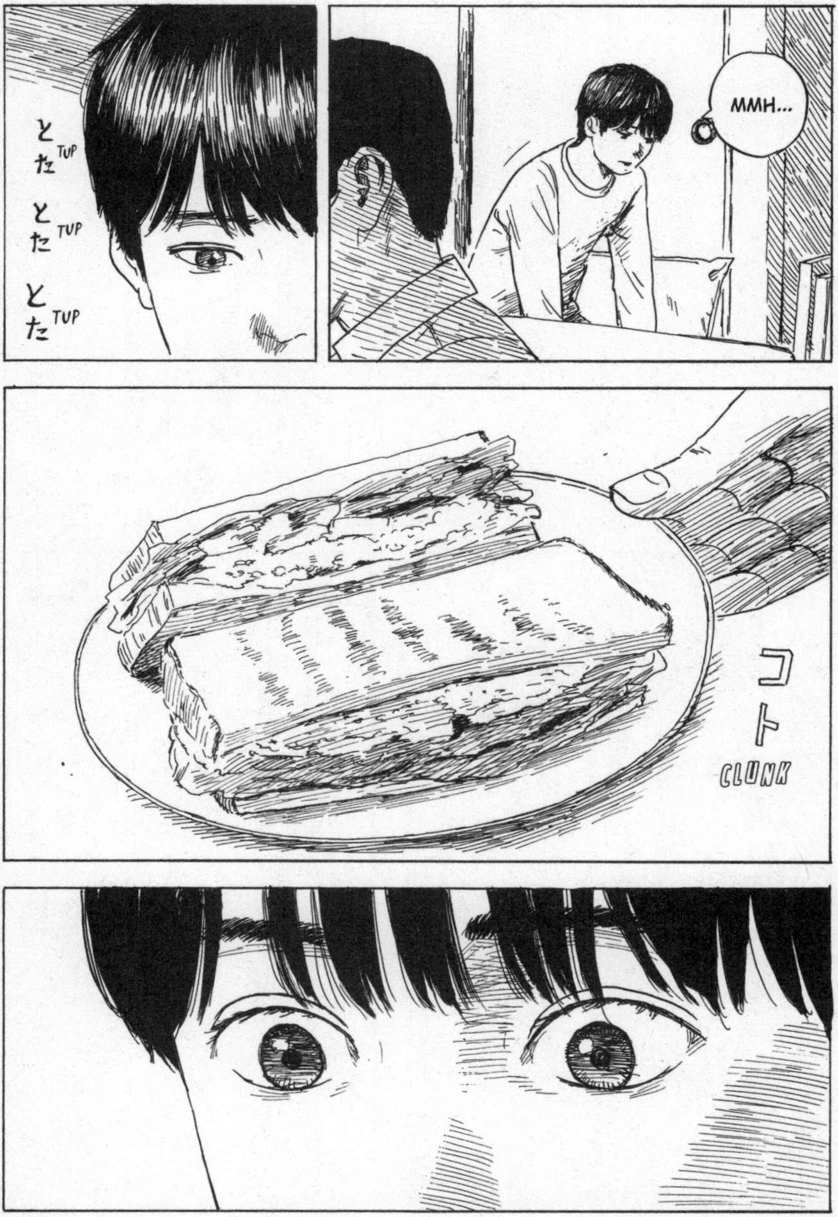
MMH...
とた TUP
とた TUP
とた TUP
コト
CLUNK

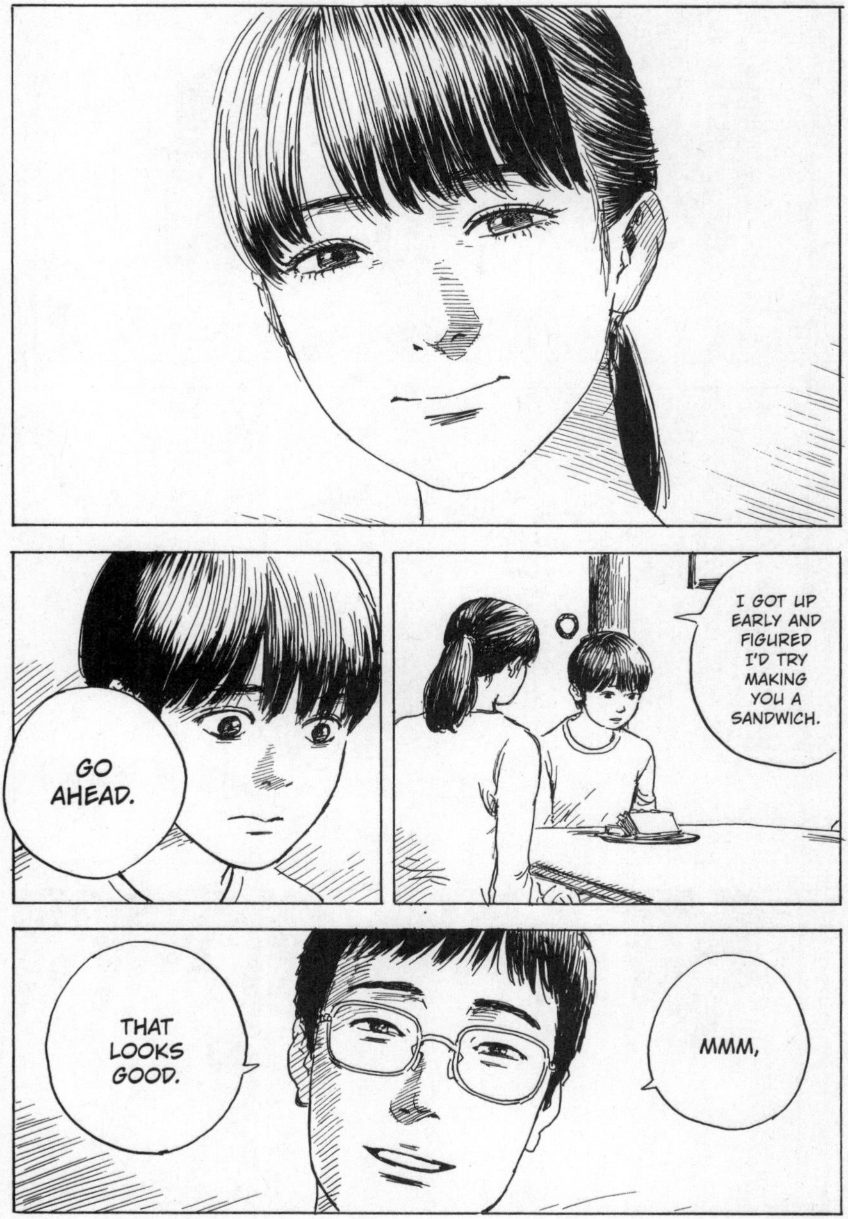
I GOT UP EARLY AND FIGURED I'D TRY MAKING YOU A SANDWICH.
GO AHEAD.
MMM,
THAT LOOKS GOOD.

WOULD YOU LIKE ONE TOO?
YOU DON'T MIND?
THEN YES, PLEASE.
GO AHEAD, SEI.
TRY IT.

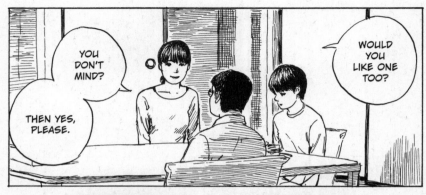

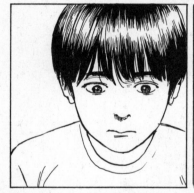

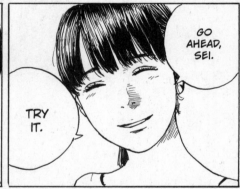

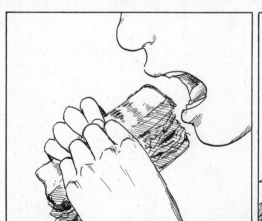

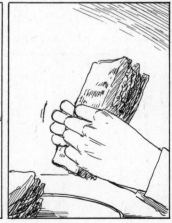

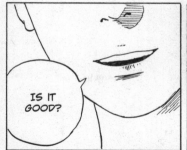

IS IT GOOD?

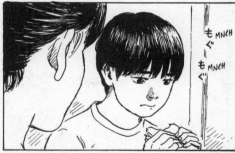

もぐ MNCH
もぐ MNCH

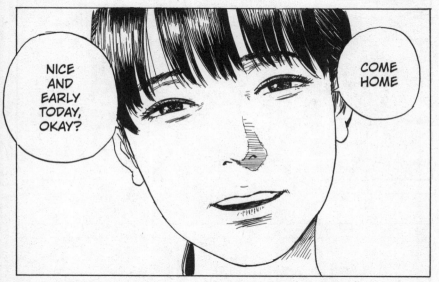

NICE AND EARLY TODAY, OKAY?

COME HOME

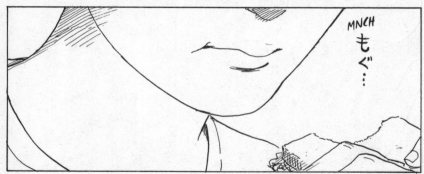

MNCH
もぐ…

CHAPTER 31 Aroma

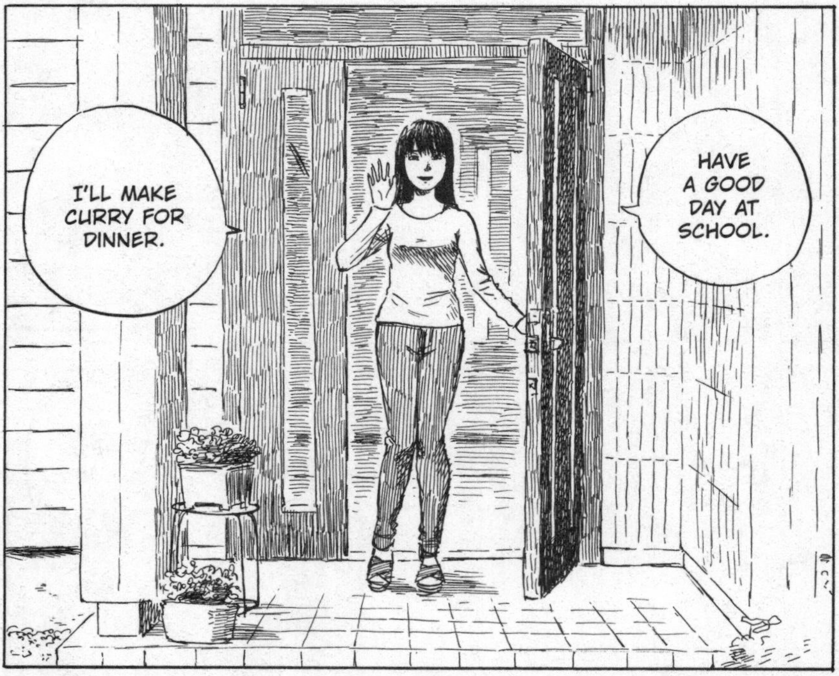
HAVE A GOOD DAY AT SCHOOL.
I'LL MAKE CURRY FOR DINNER.

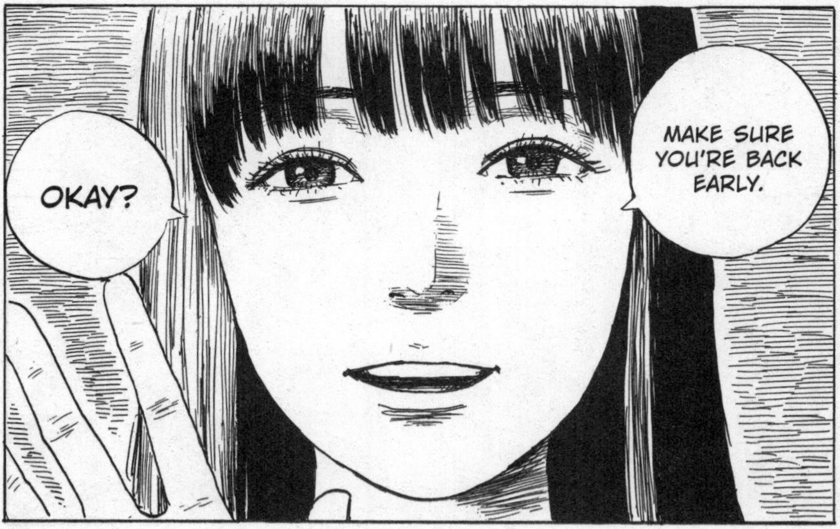
MAKE SURE YOU'RE BACK EARLY.
OKAY?

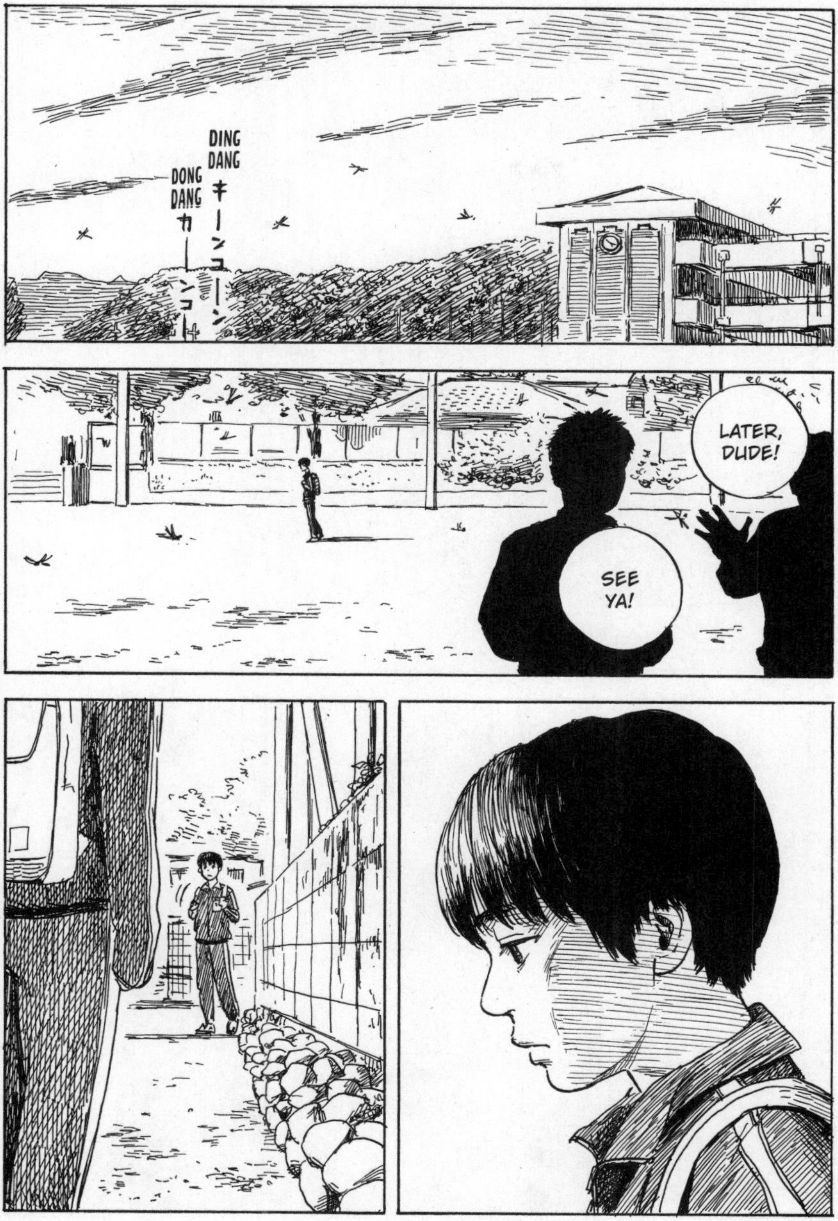
DING DANG
キーンコーン
DONG DANG
カーンコン
LATER, DUDE!
SEE YA!

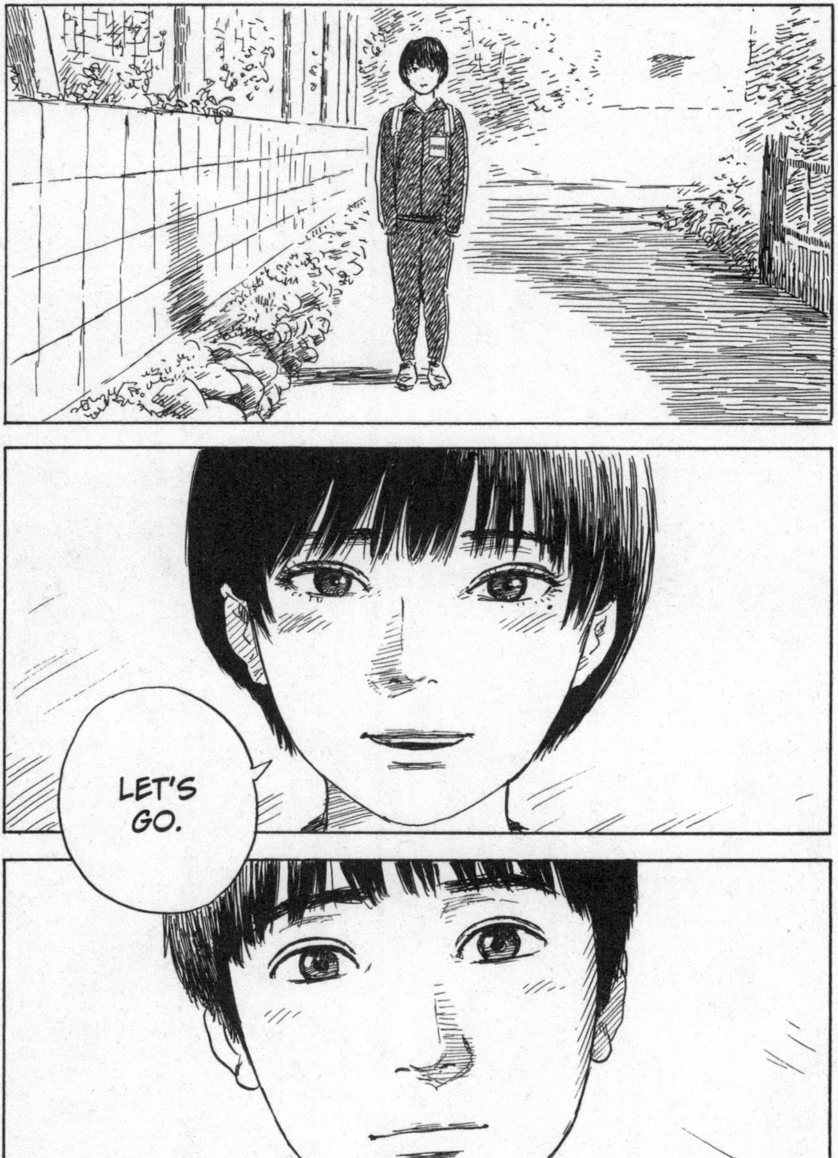
LET'S GO.

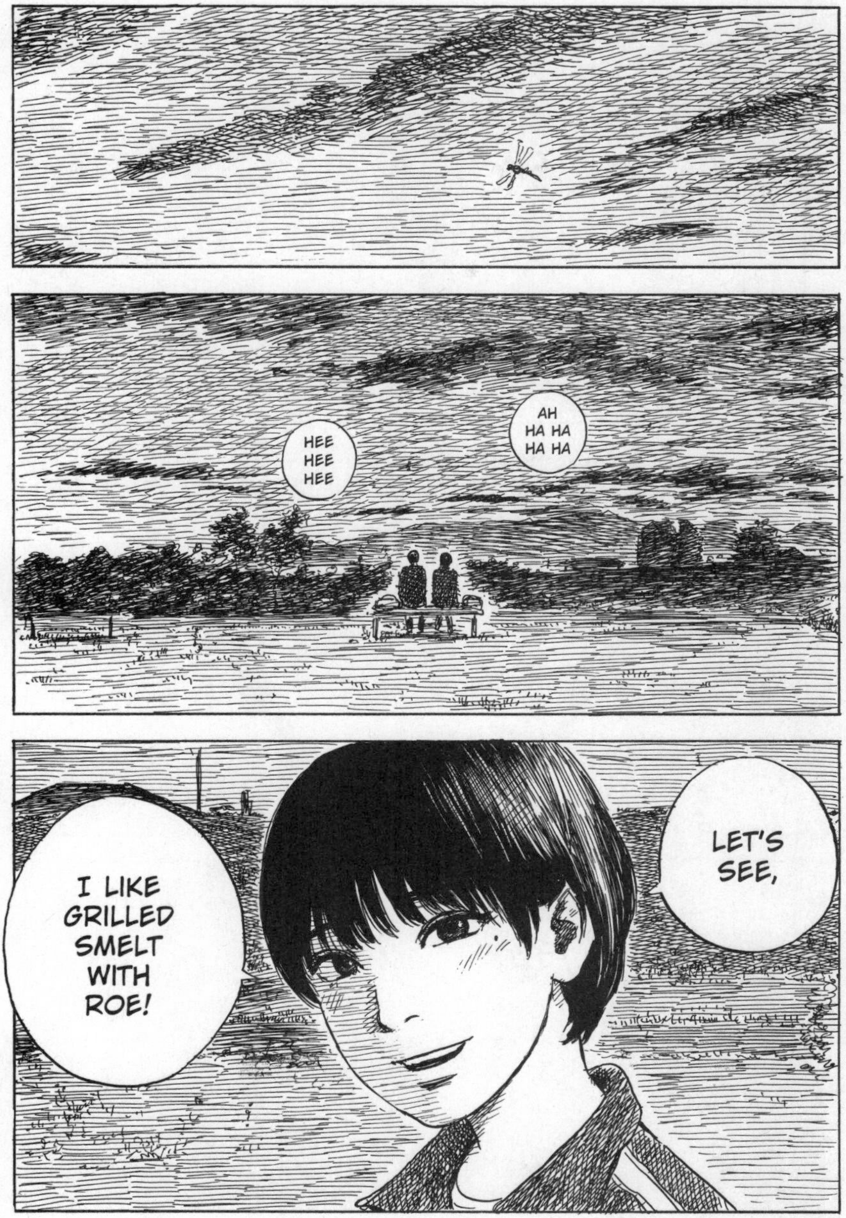
AH HA HA HA HA
HEE HEE HEE
LET'S SEE,
I LIKE GRILLED SMELT WITH ROE!

IT'S SO GOOD!
NICE, I LIKE SMELT TOO.
OH, AND YOU KNOW WHAT ELSE, KIMCHI NATTO!
I HAD IT AT A RESTAURANT THIS ONE TIME, AND IT WAS DELICIOUS!
I'VE NEVER HAD THAT.
WHOA.
I'M SORRY.

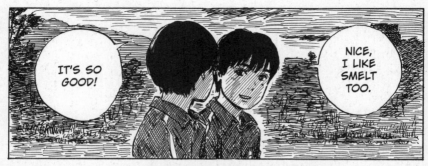

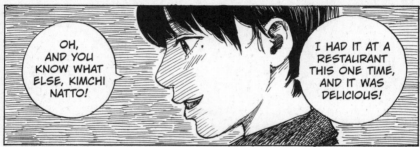

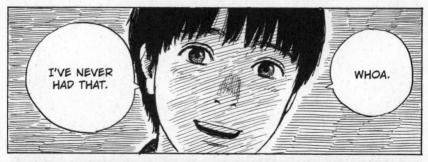

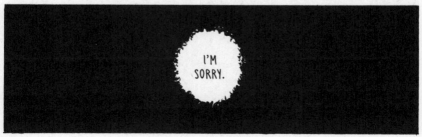

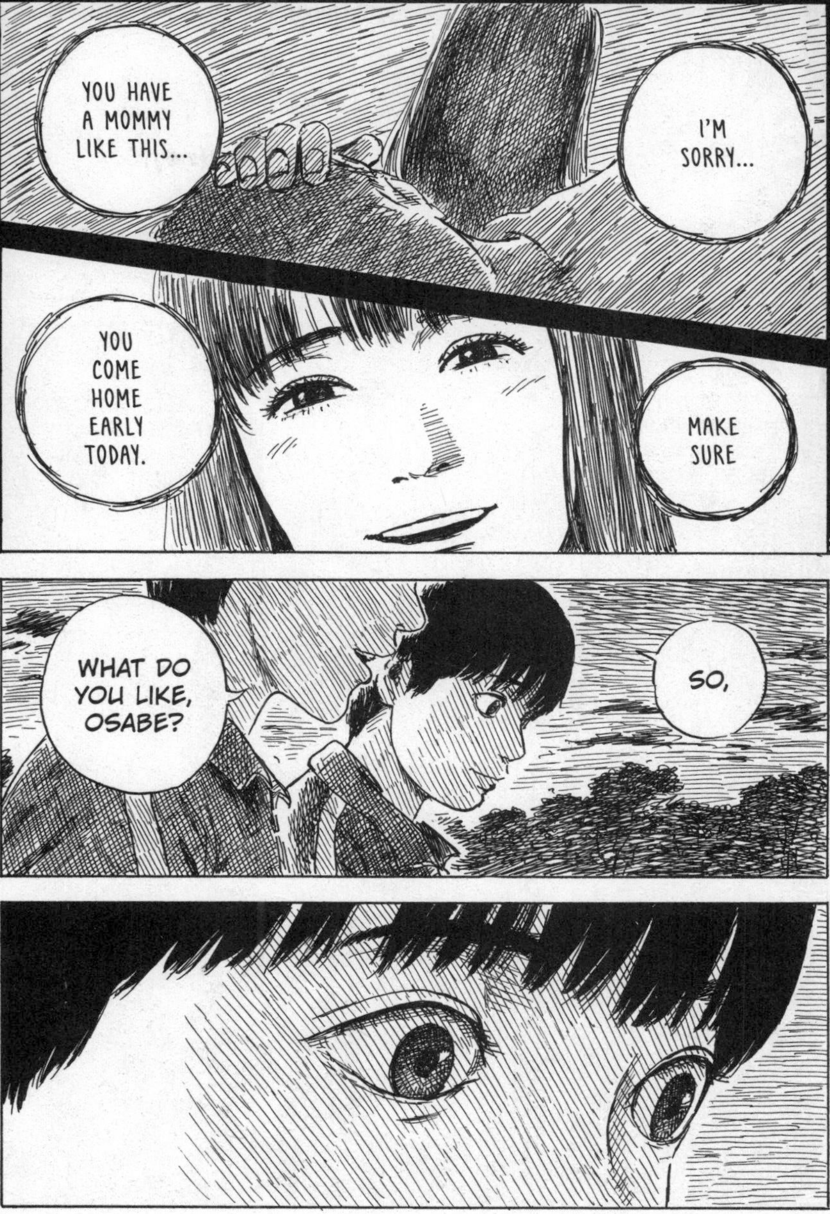
I'M SORRY...
YOU HAVE A MOMMY LIKE THIS...
MAKE SURE
YOU COME HOME EARLY TODAY.
SO,
WHAT DO YOU LIKE, OSABE?

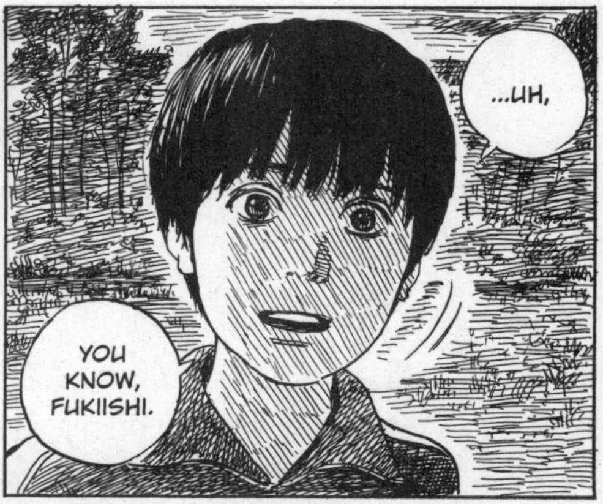
...UH,
YOU KNOW, FUKIISHI.
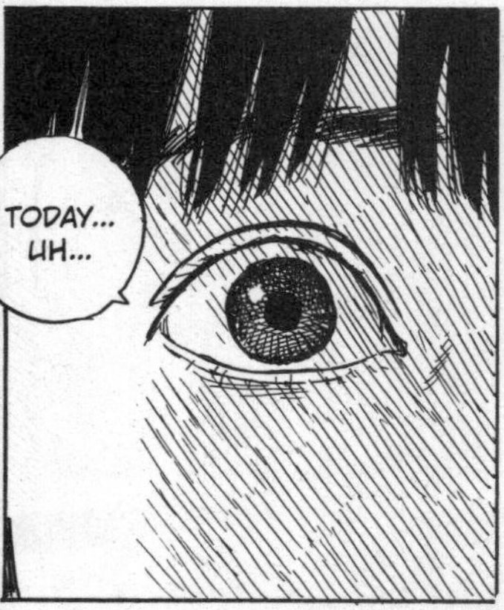
TODAY... UH...
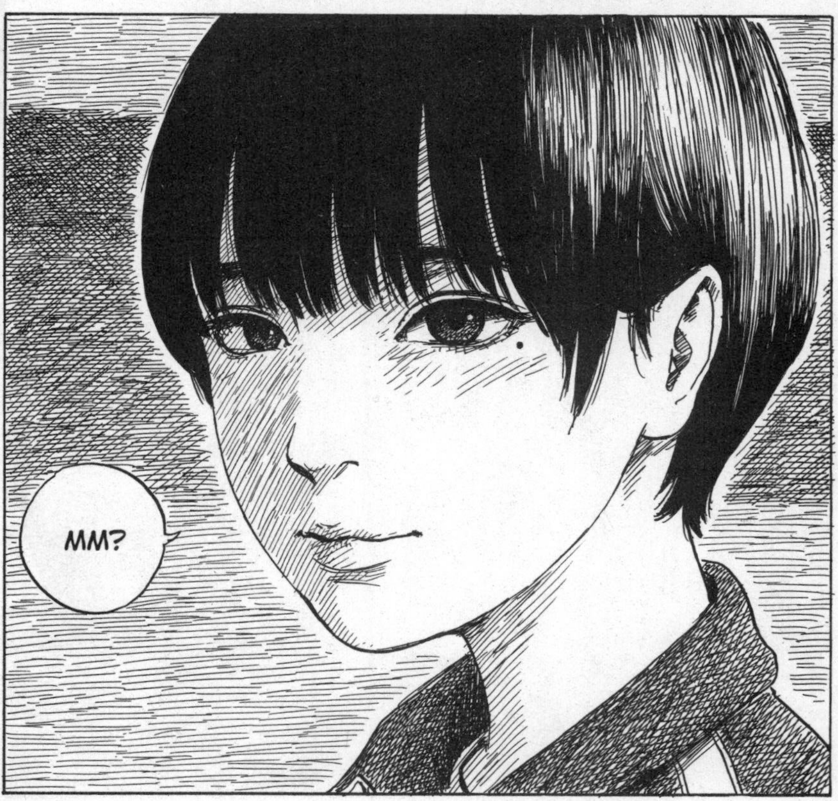
MM?

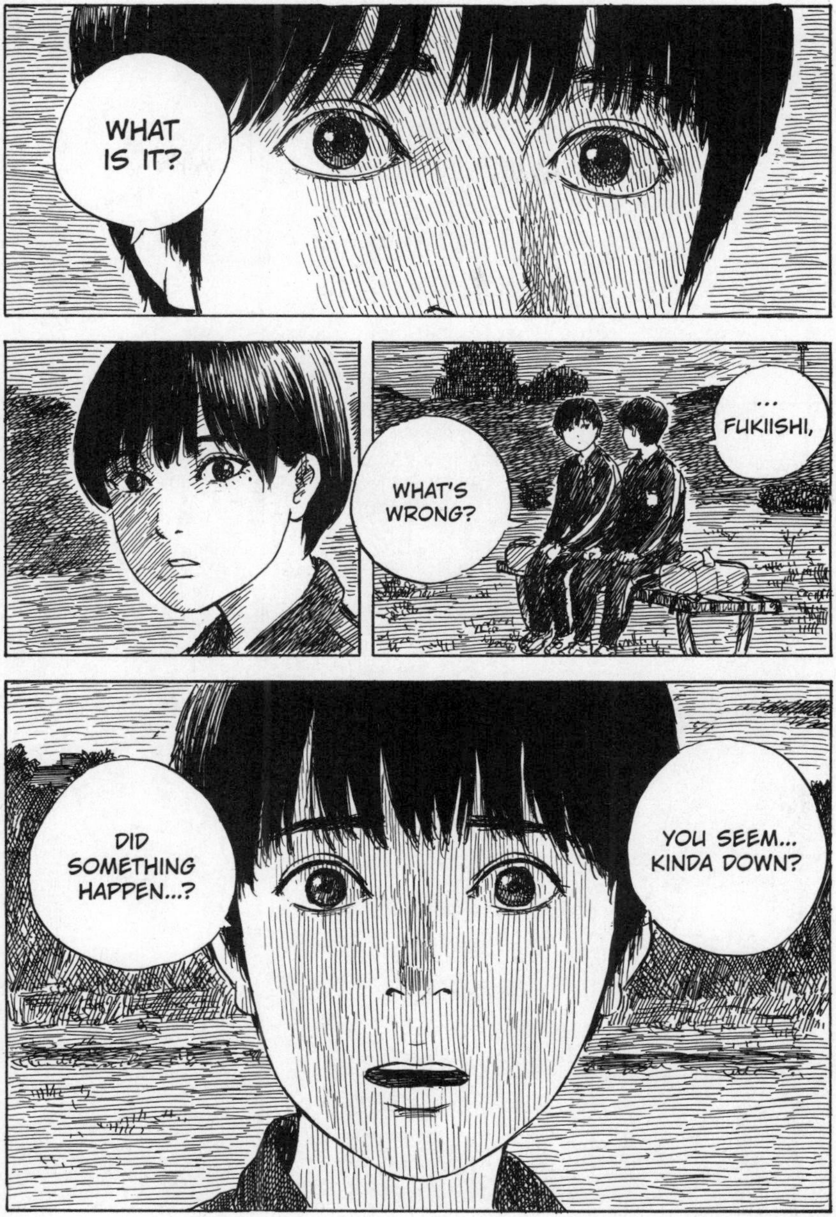
WHAT IS IT?
... FUKIISHI,
WHAT'S WRONG?
YOU SEEM... KINDA DOWN?
DID SOMETHING HAPPEN...?

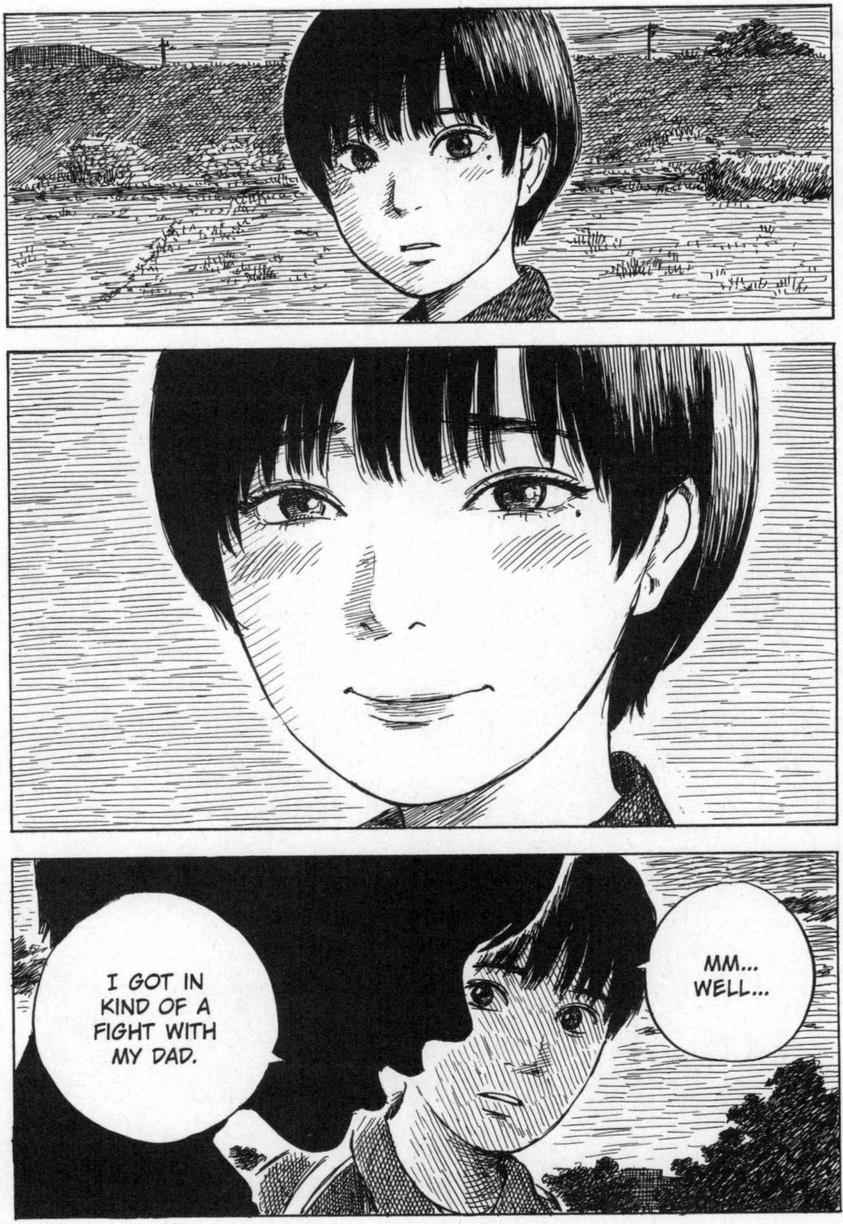
MM... WELL...
I GOT IN KIND OF A FIGHT WITH MY DAD.

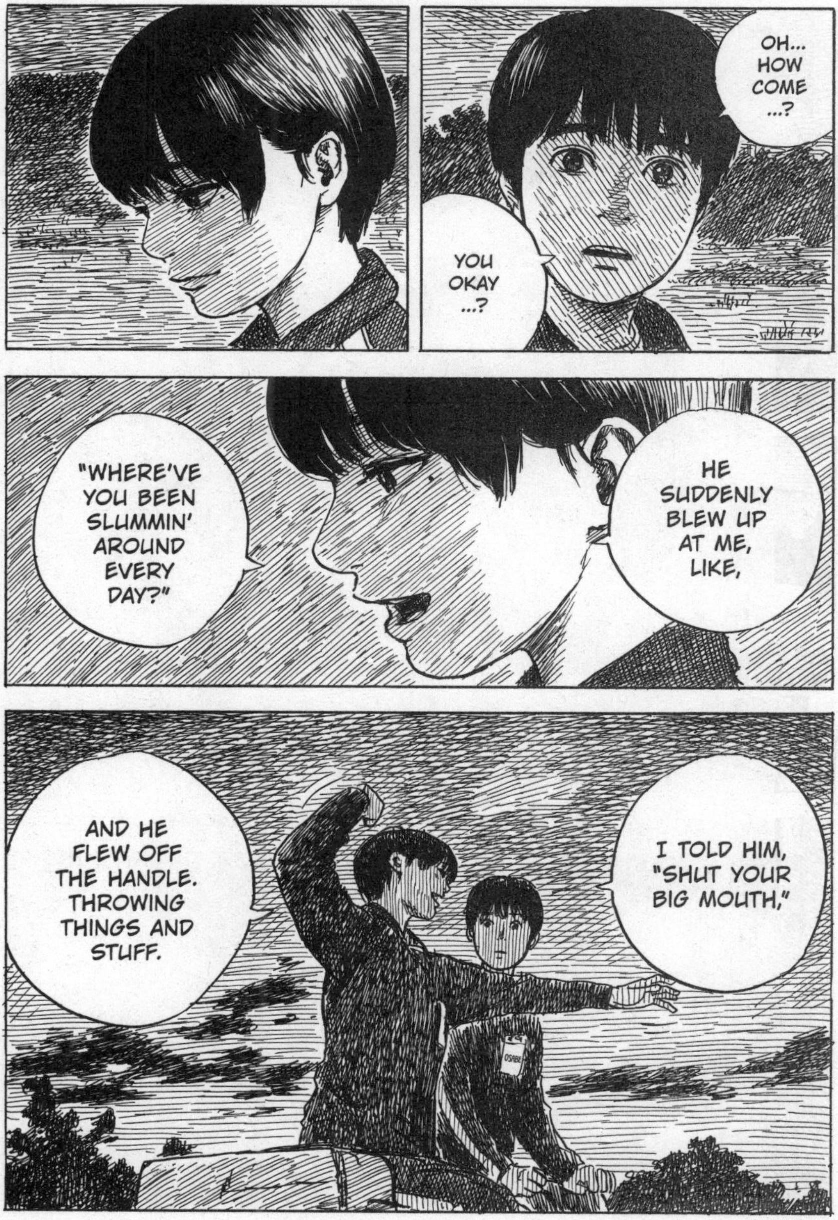
OH... HOW COME ...?
YOU OKAY ...?
HE SUDDENLY BLEW UP AT ME, LIKE,
"WHERE'VE YOU BEEN SLUMMIN' AROUND EVERY DAY?"
I TOLD HIM, "SHUT YOUR BIG MOUTH,"
AND HE FLEW OFF THE HANDLE. THROWING THINGS AND STUFF.

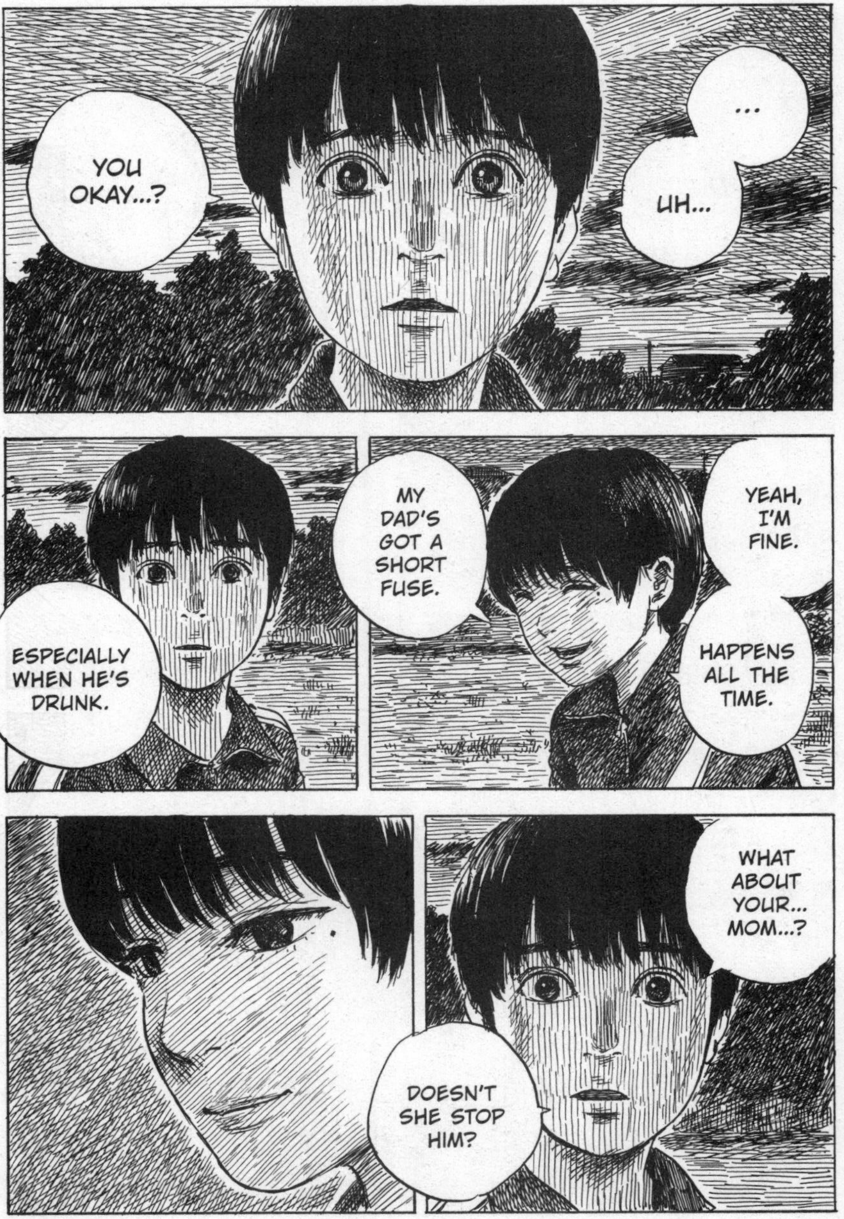
...
UH...
YOU OKAY...?
YEAH, I'M FINE.
HAPPENS ALL THE TIME.
MY DAD'S GOT A SHORT FUSE.
ESPECIALLY WHEN HE'S DRUNK.
WHAT ABOUT YOUR... MOM...?
DOESN'T SHE STOP HIM?

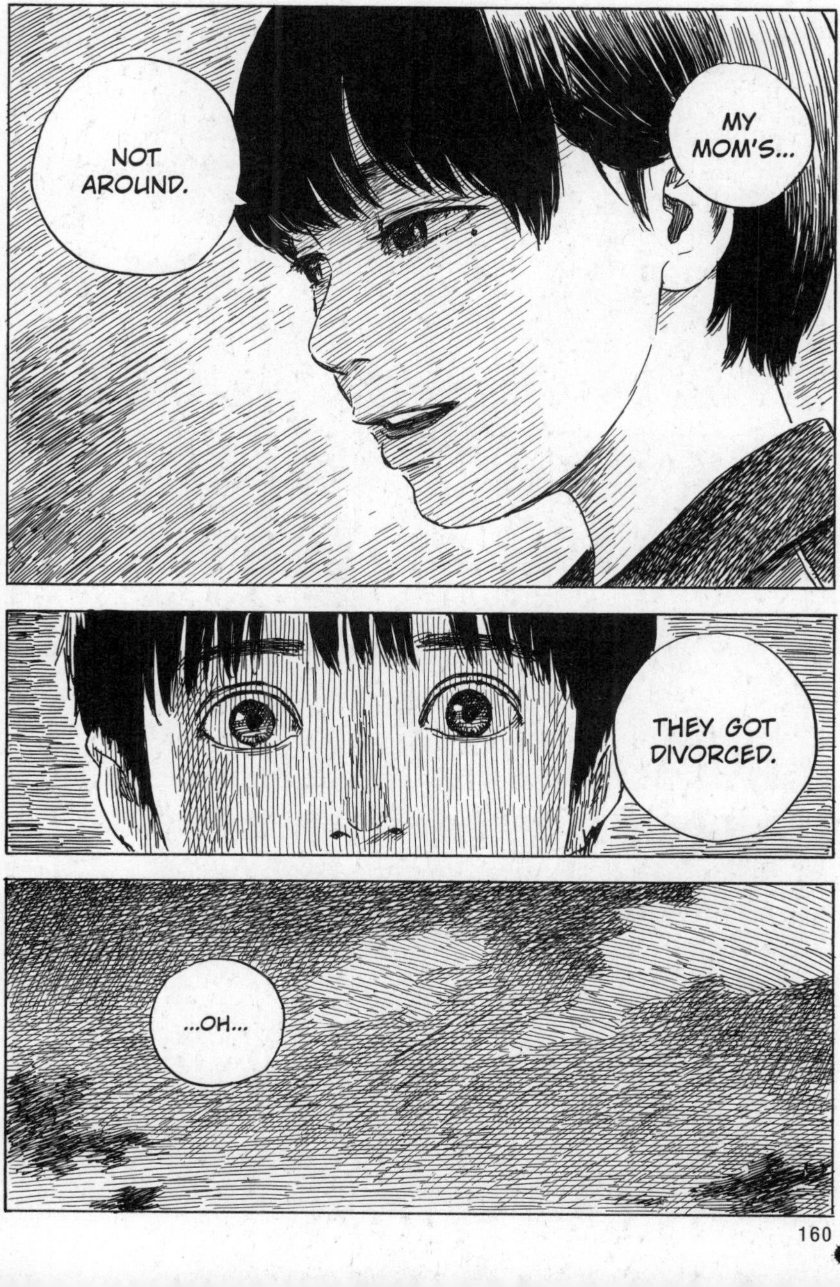
MY MOM'S...
NOT AROUND.
THEY GOT DIVORCED.
...OH...

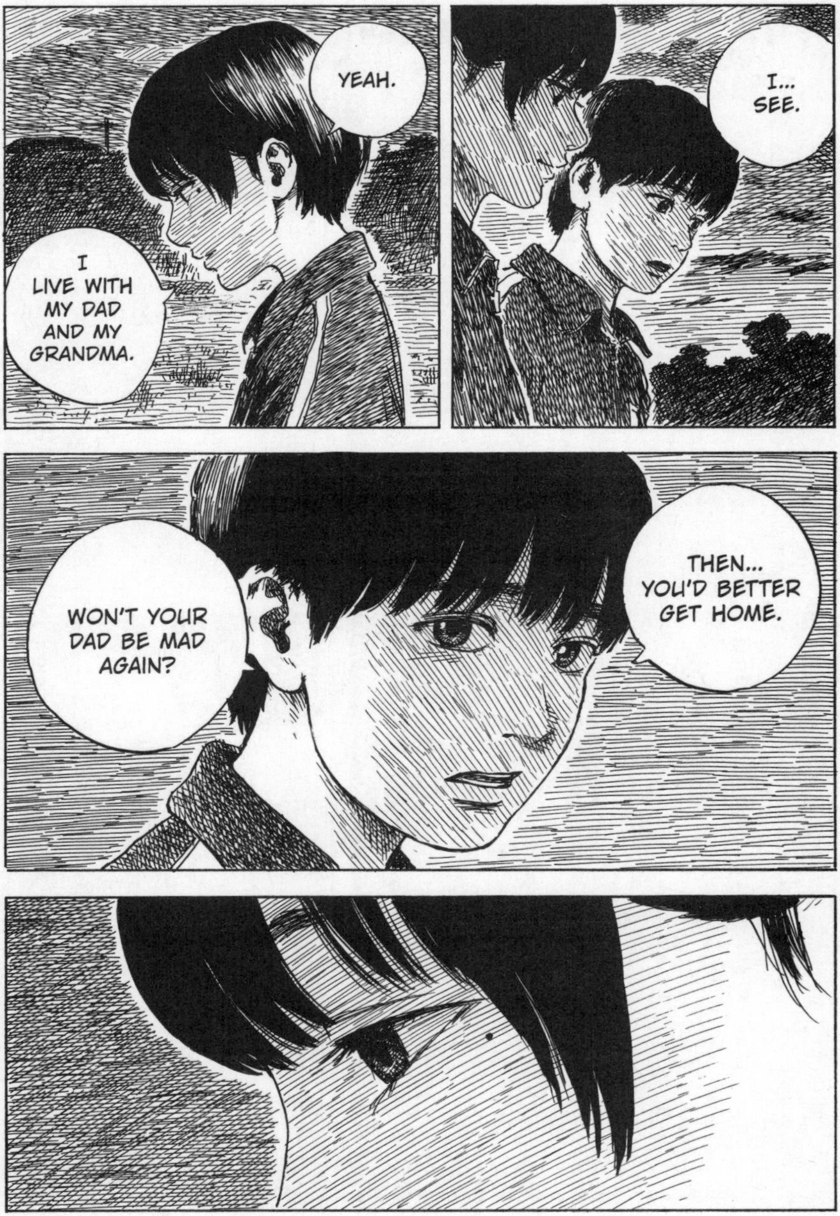
YEAH.
I LIVE WITH MY DAD AND MY GRANDMA.
I... SEE.
WON'T YOUR DAD BE MAD AGAIN?
THEN... YOU'D BETTER GET HOME.

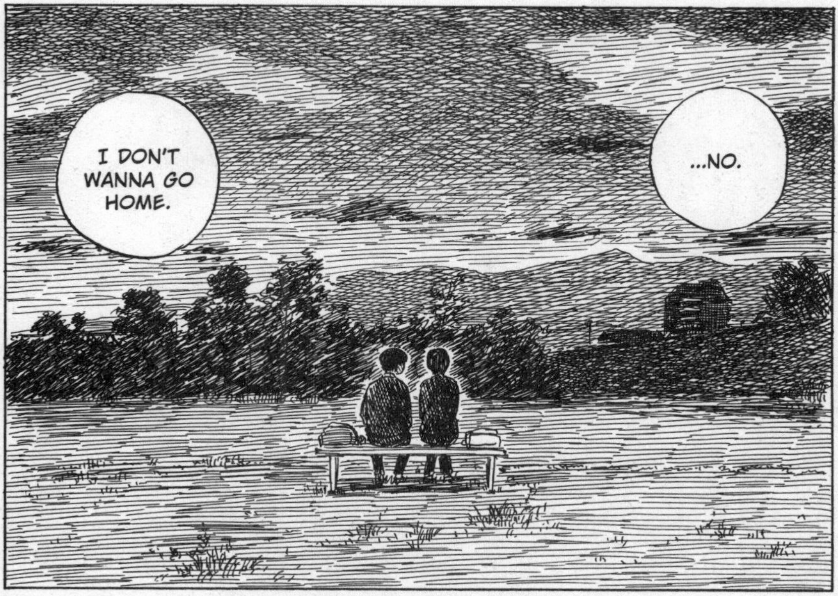
...NO.
I DON'T WANNA GO HOME.
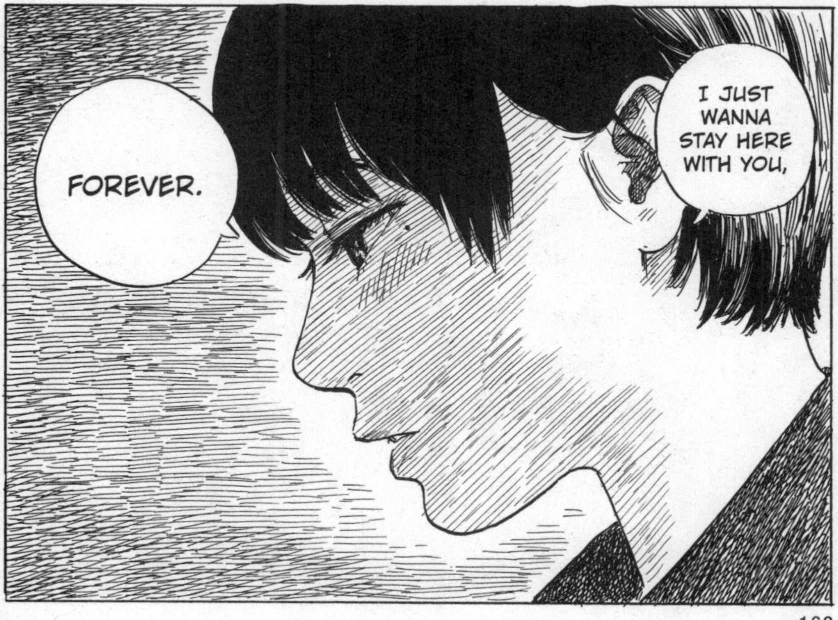
I JUST WANNA STAY HERE WITH YOU,
FOREVER.

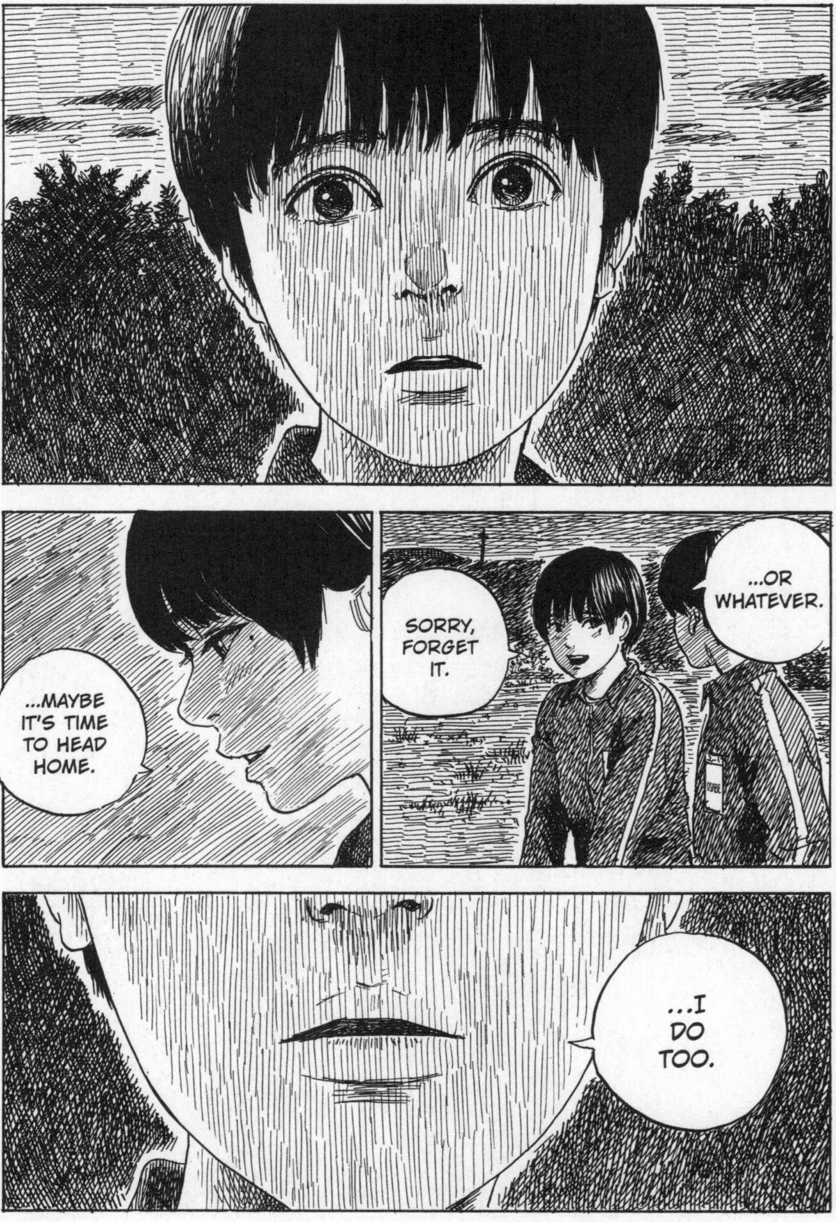
...OR WHATEVER.
SORRY, FORGET IT.
...MAYBE IT'S TIME TO HEAD HOME.
...I DO TOO.

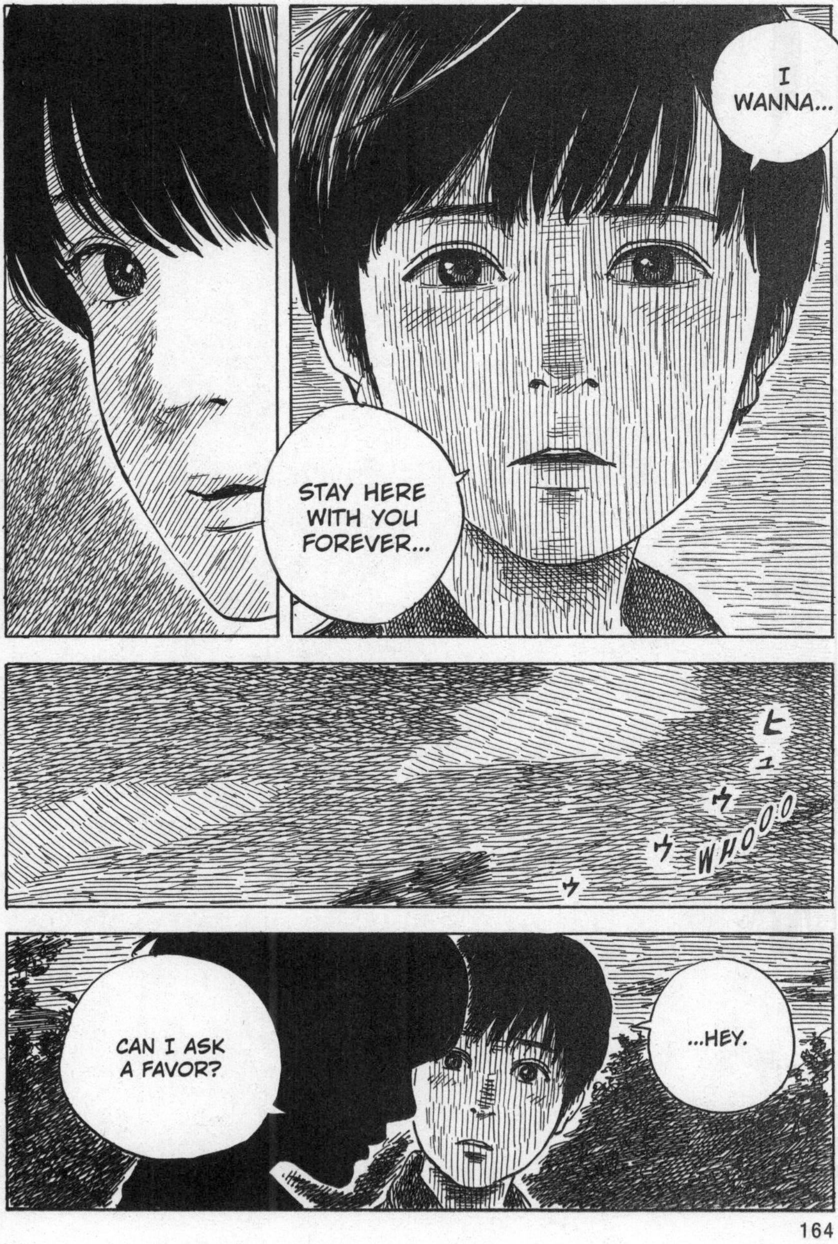

I WANNA...
STAY HERE WITH YOU FOREVER...
ヒュウウウ
WHOOOO
...HEY.
CAN I ASK A FAVOR?

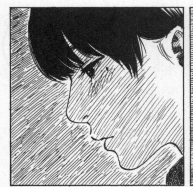

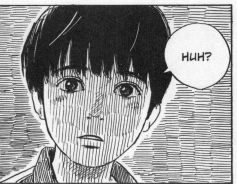

HUH?

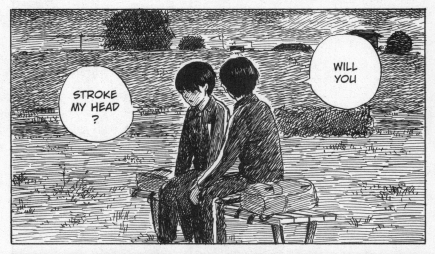

STROKE MY HEAD?

WILL YOU

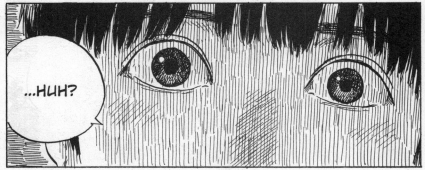

...HUH?

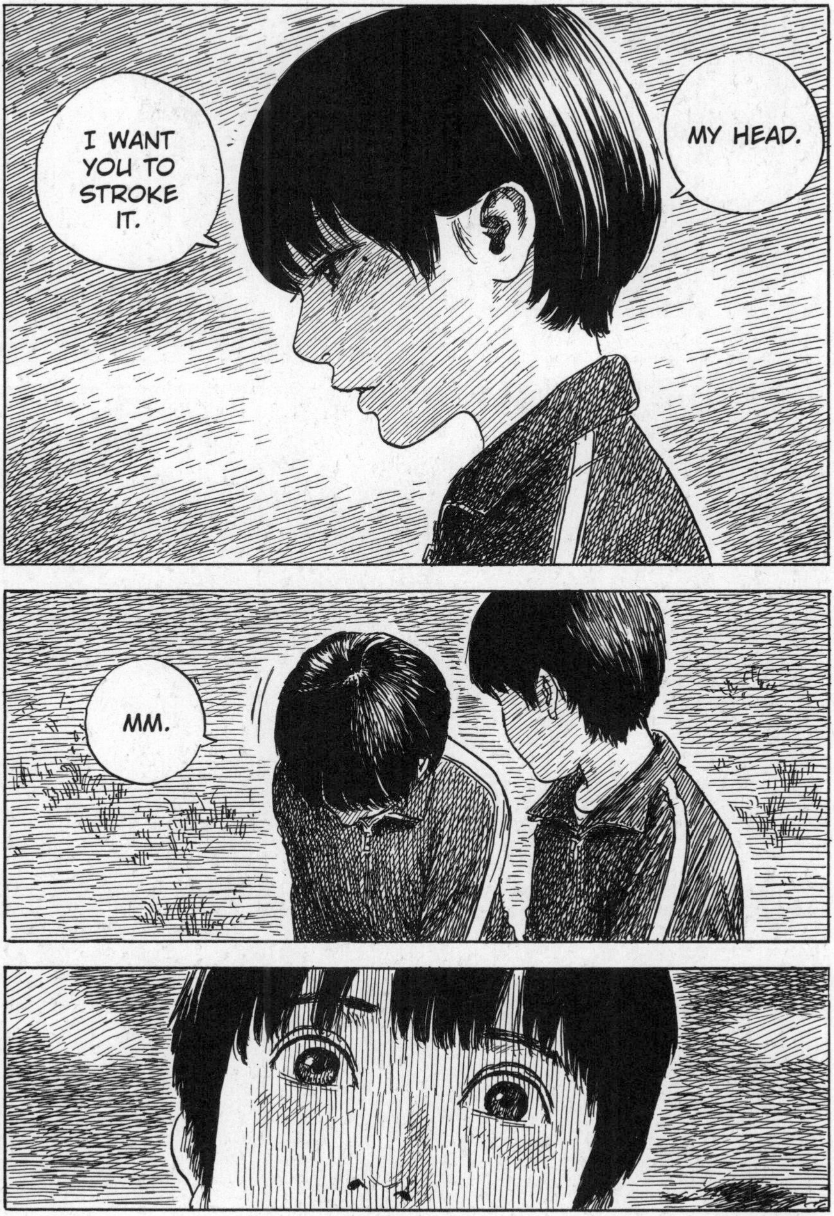
MY HEAD.
I WANT YOU TO STROKE IT.
MM.

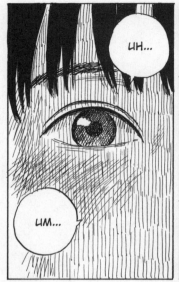

UH...

UM...

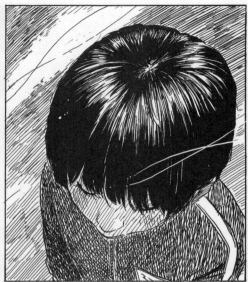

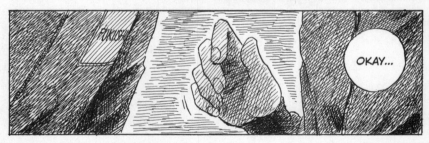

OKAY...

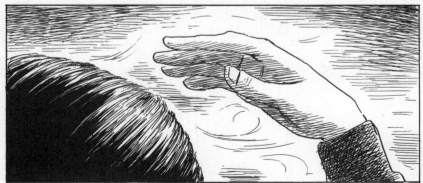

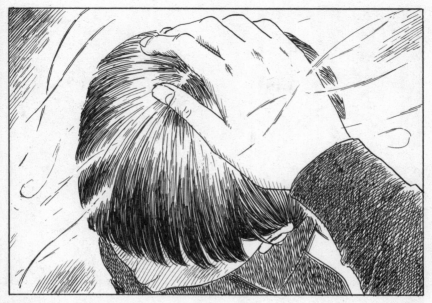

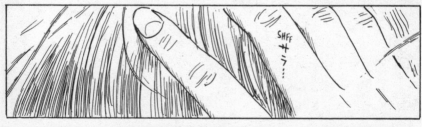

SHFF
サラ…

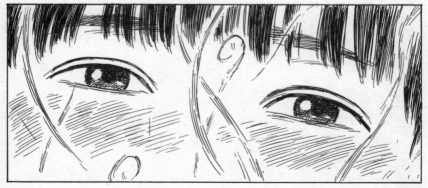

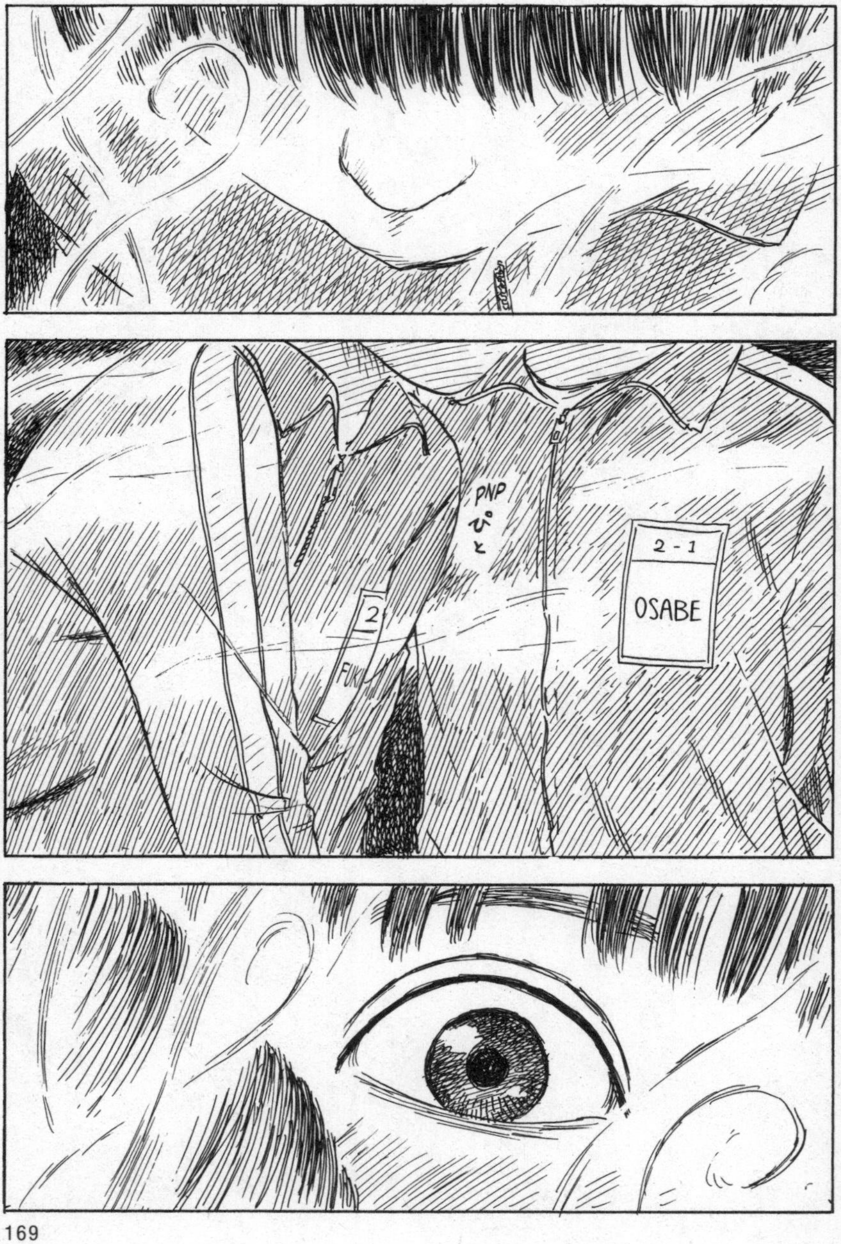
PNP
ぴと
2 - 1
OSABE

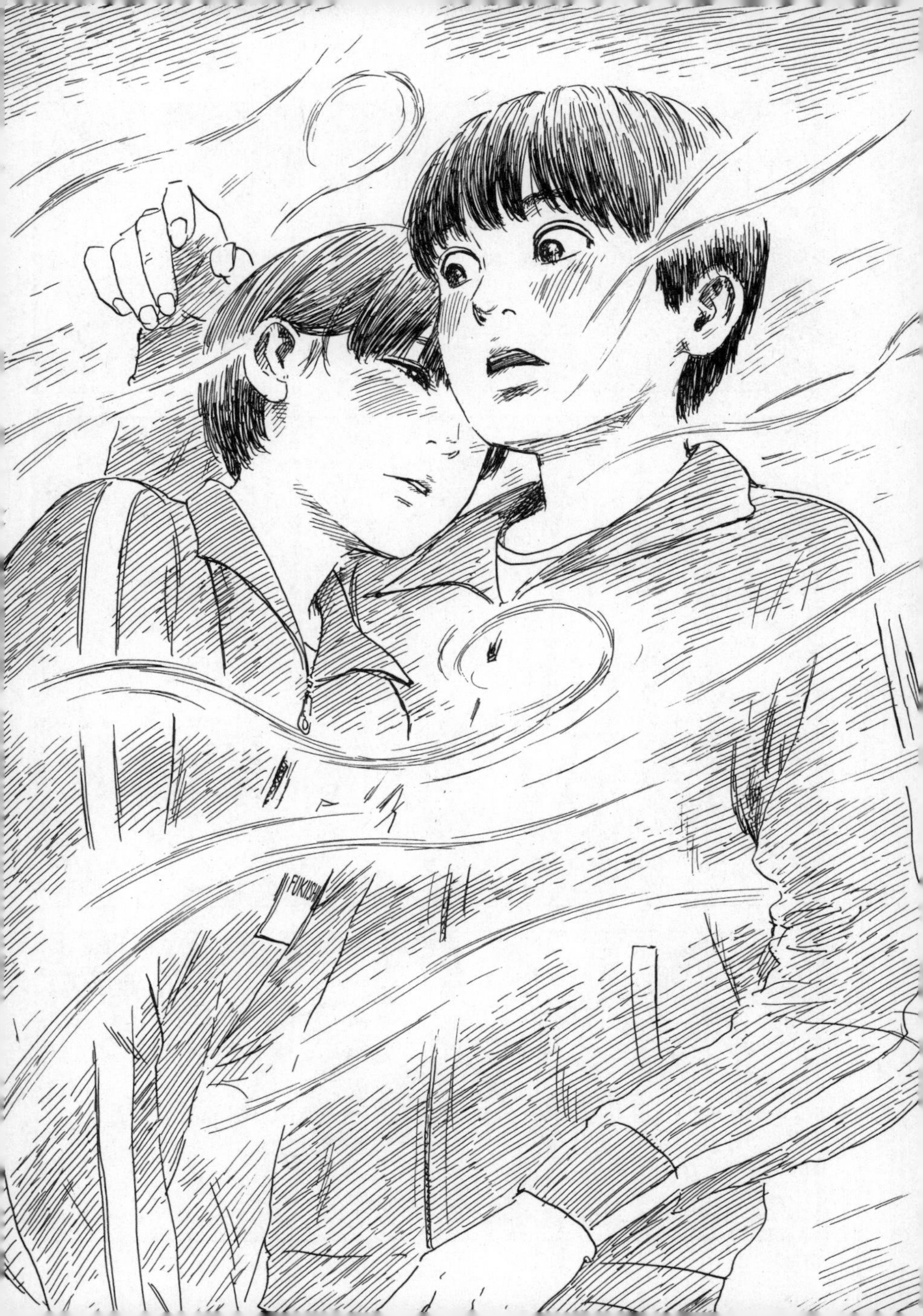

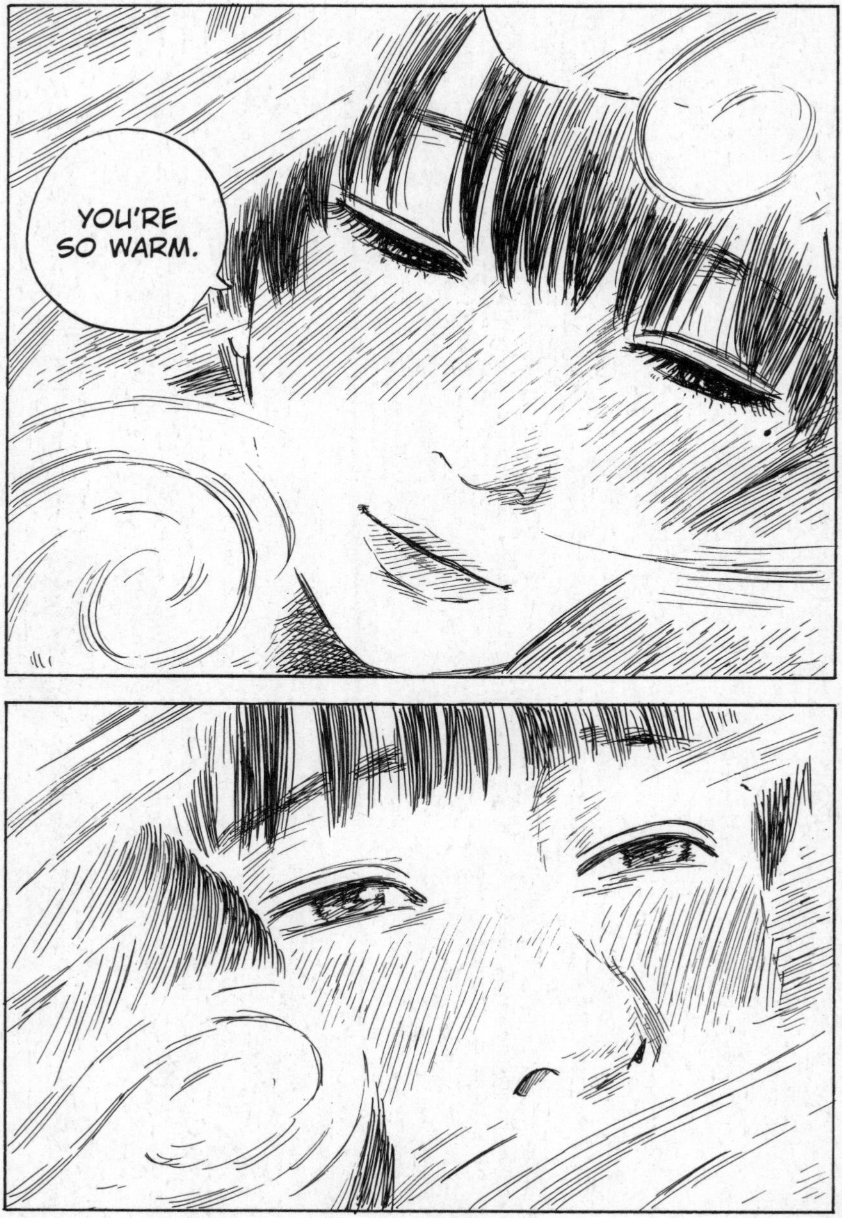
YOU'RE SO WARM.

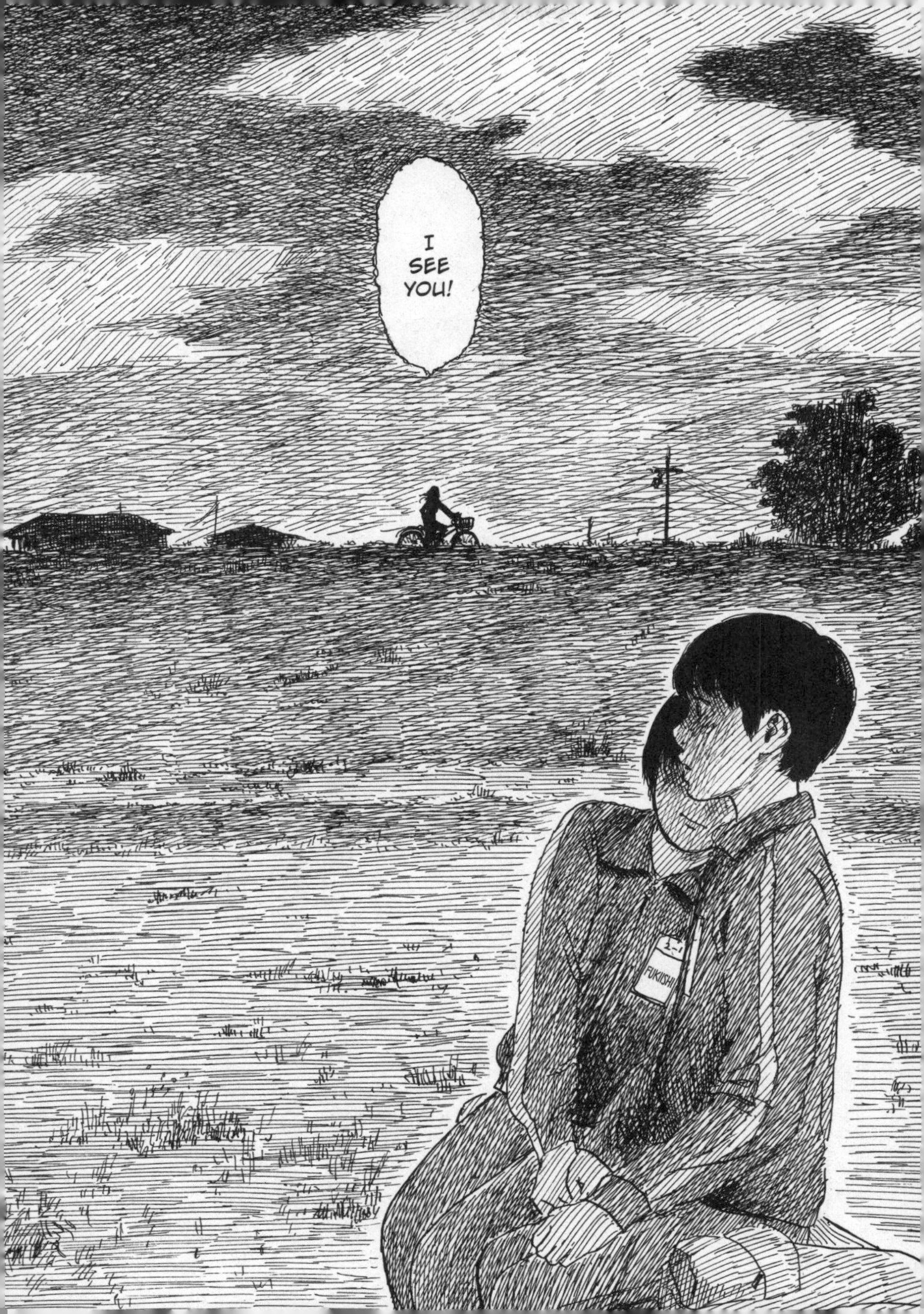
I SEE YOU!
2-1
FUKIISHI

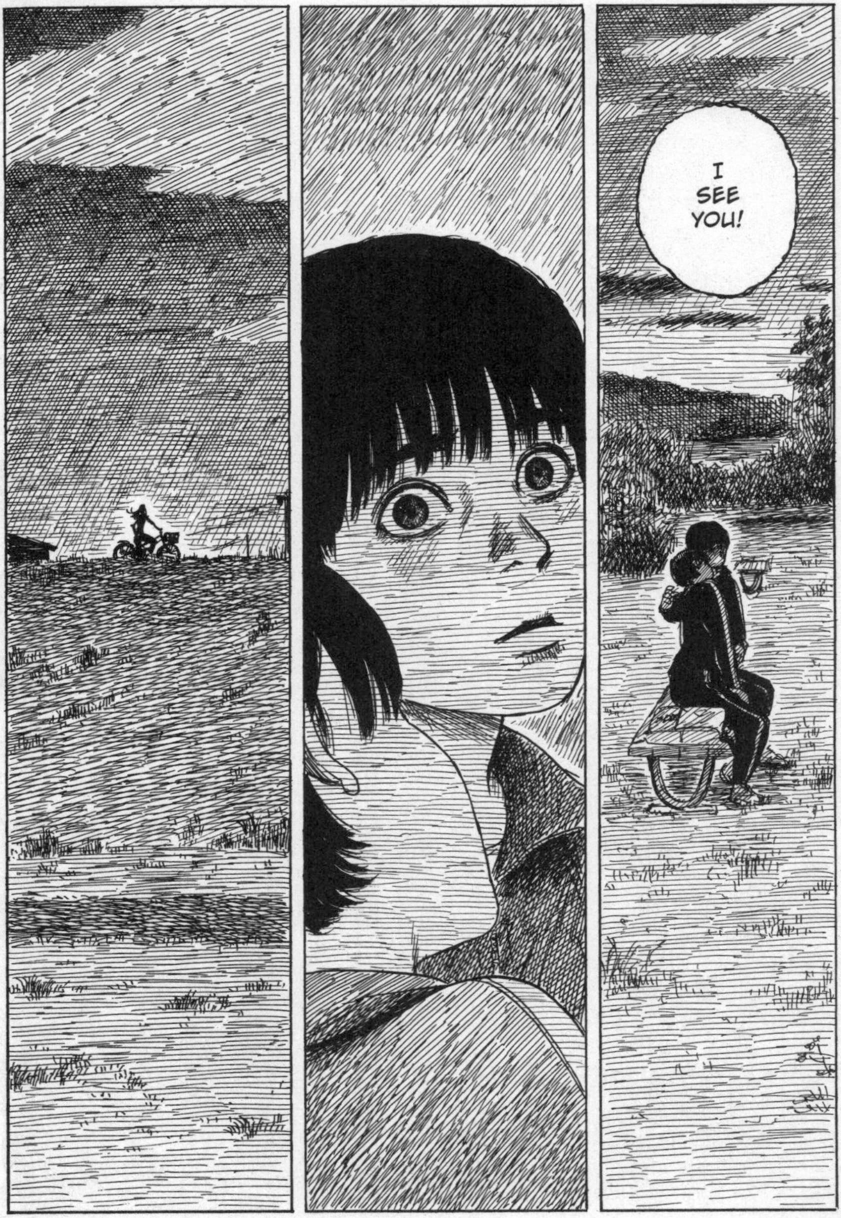
I SEE YOU!

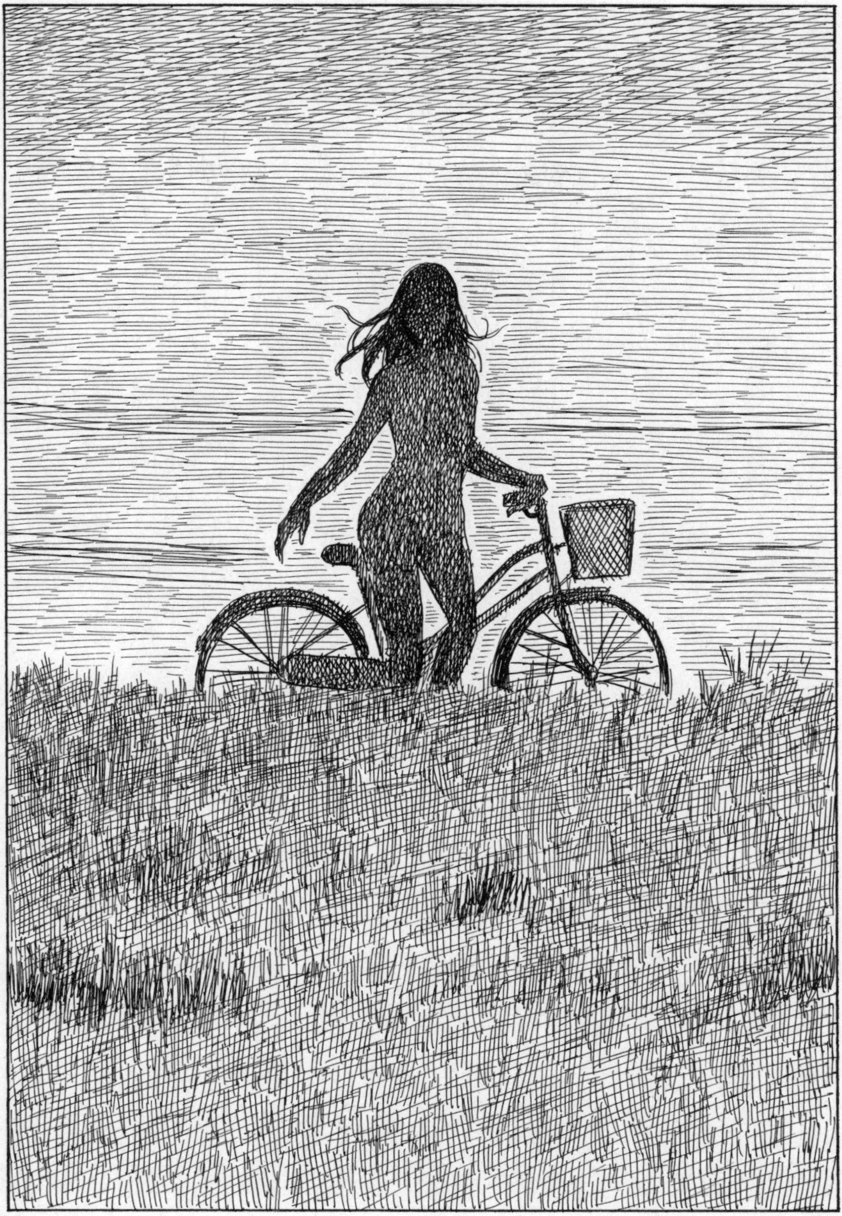

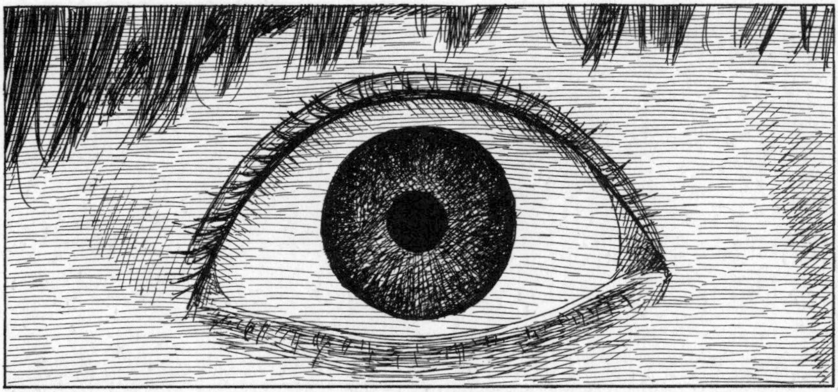

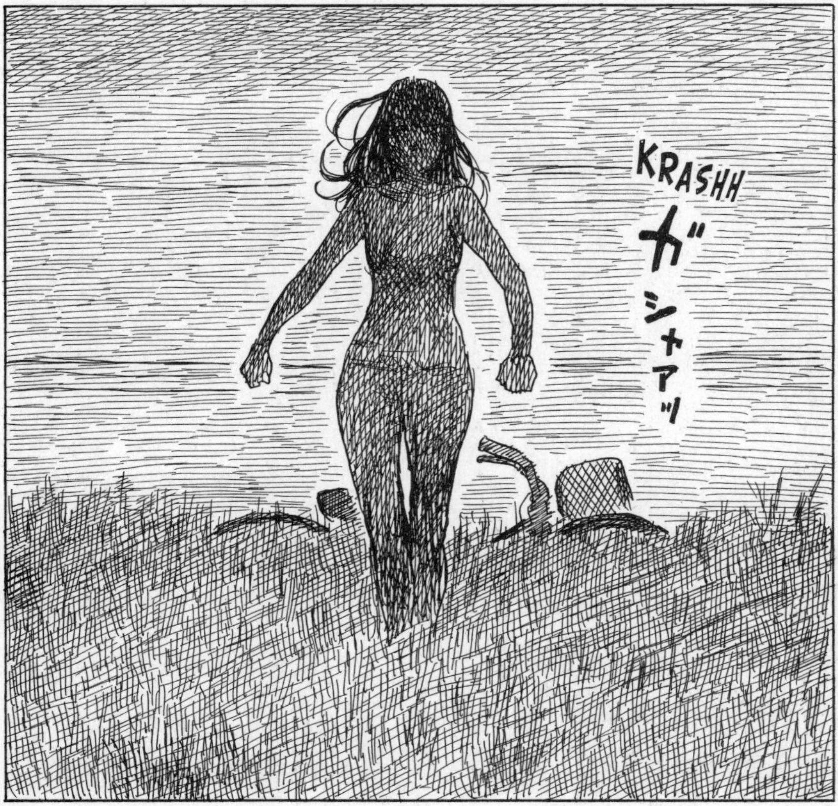
KRASHH
ガシャアッ

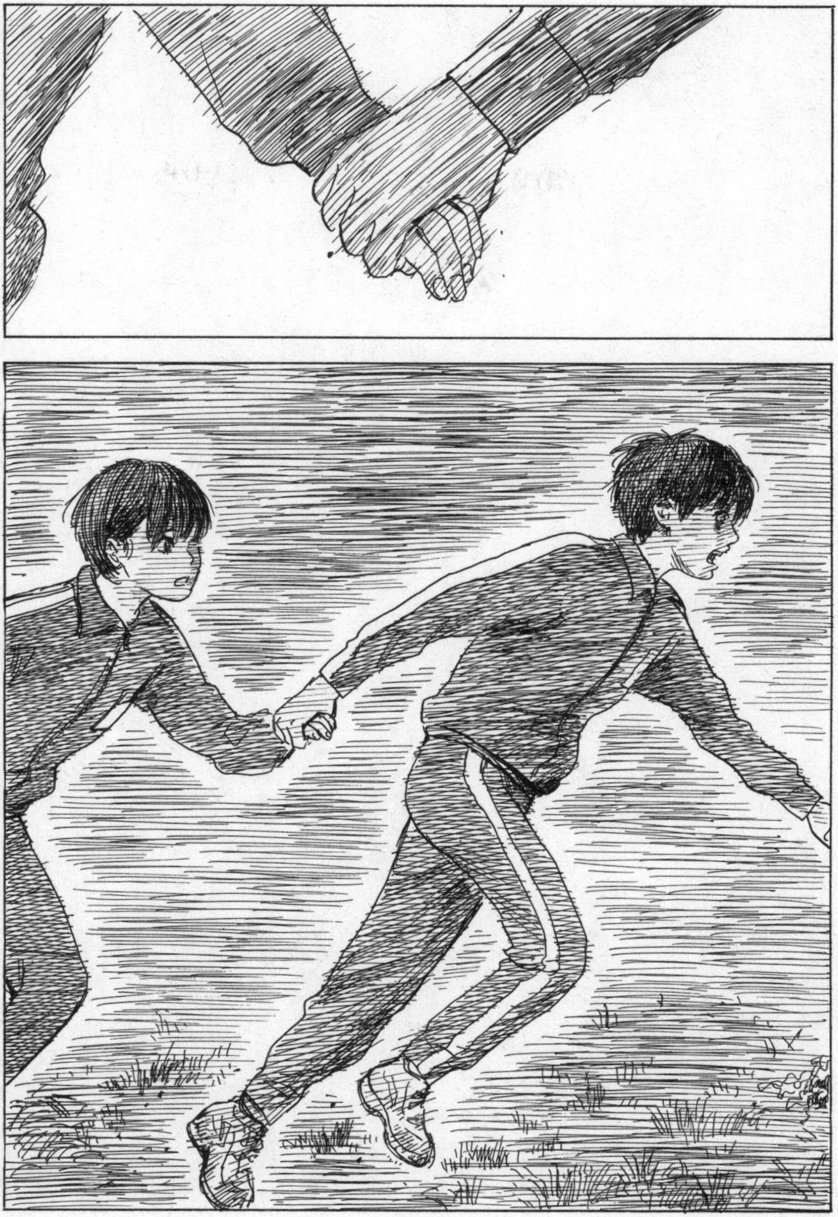

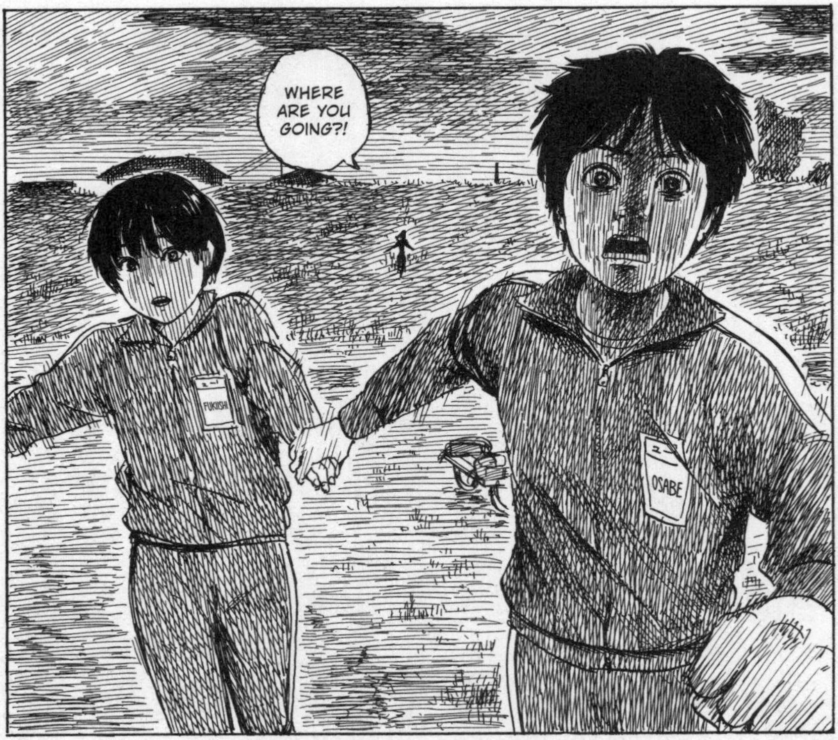
WHERE ARE YOU GOING?!
FUKIISHI
OSABE
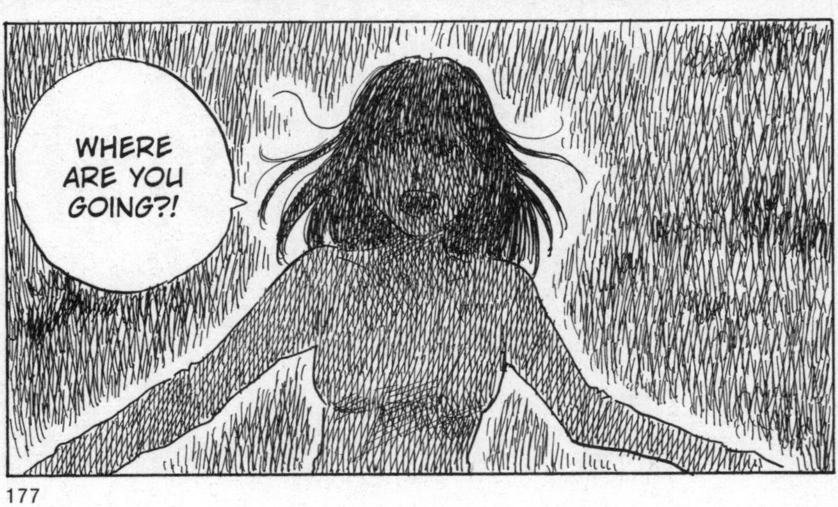
WHERE ARE YOU GOING?!

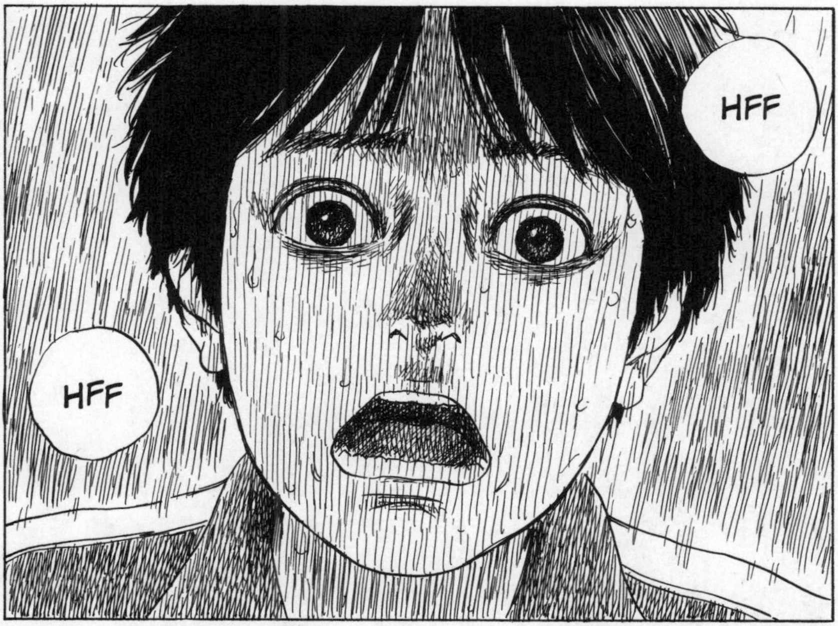
HFF
HFF

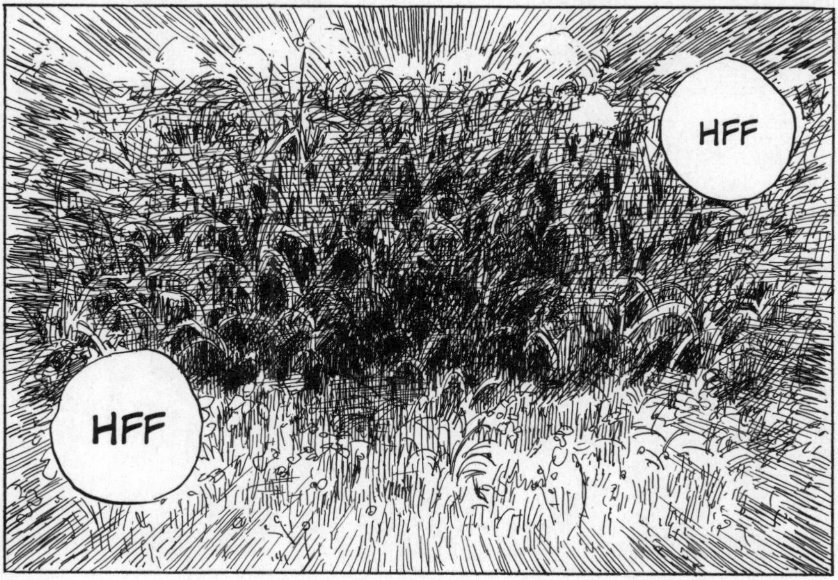
HFF
HFF

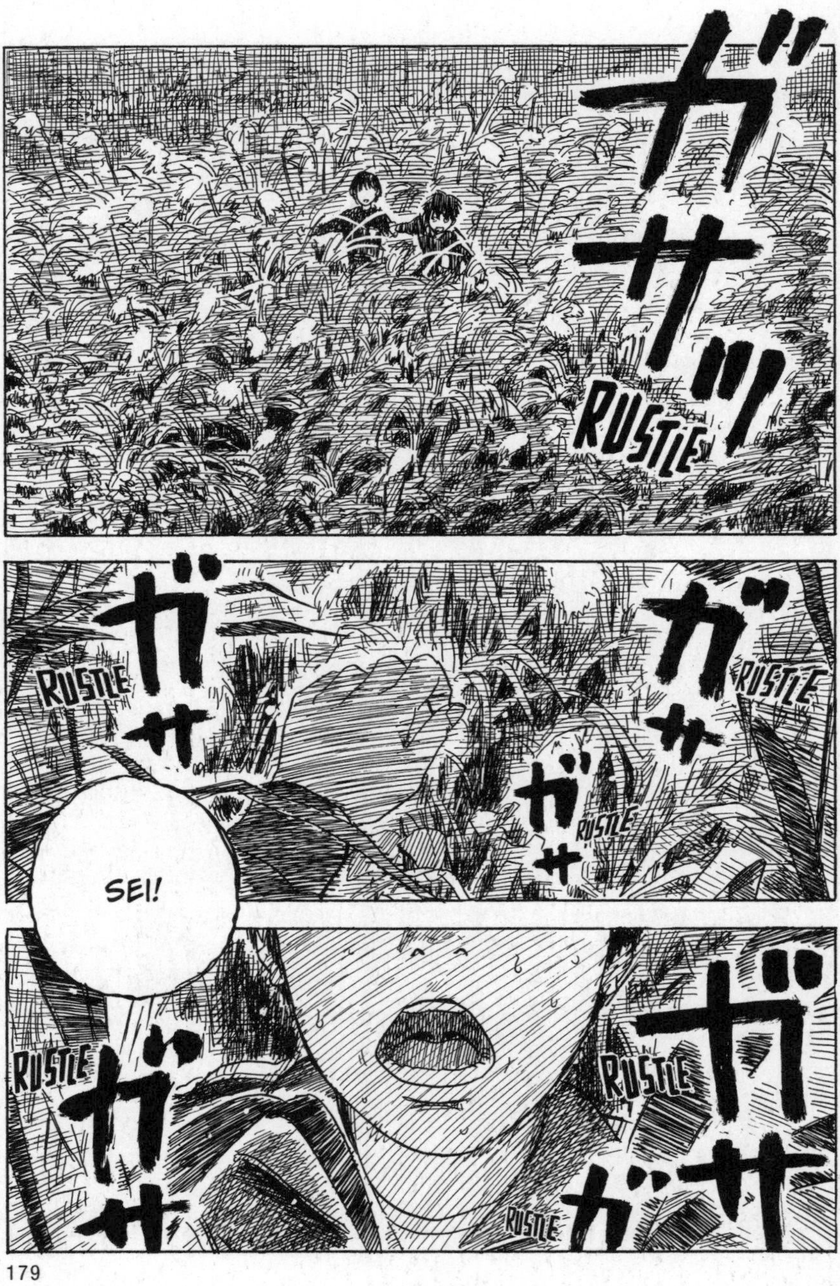
ガサッ
RUSTLE
ガサ
RUSTLE
ガサ
RUSTLE
ガサ
RUSTLE
SEI!
ガザ
RUSTLE
ガ
RUSTLE
ガサ
RUSTLE

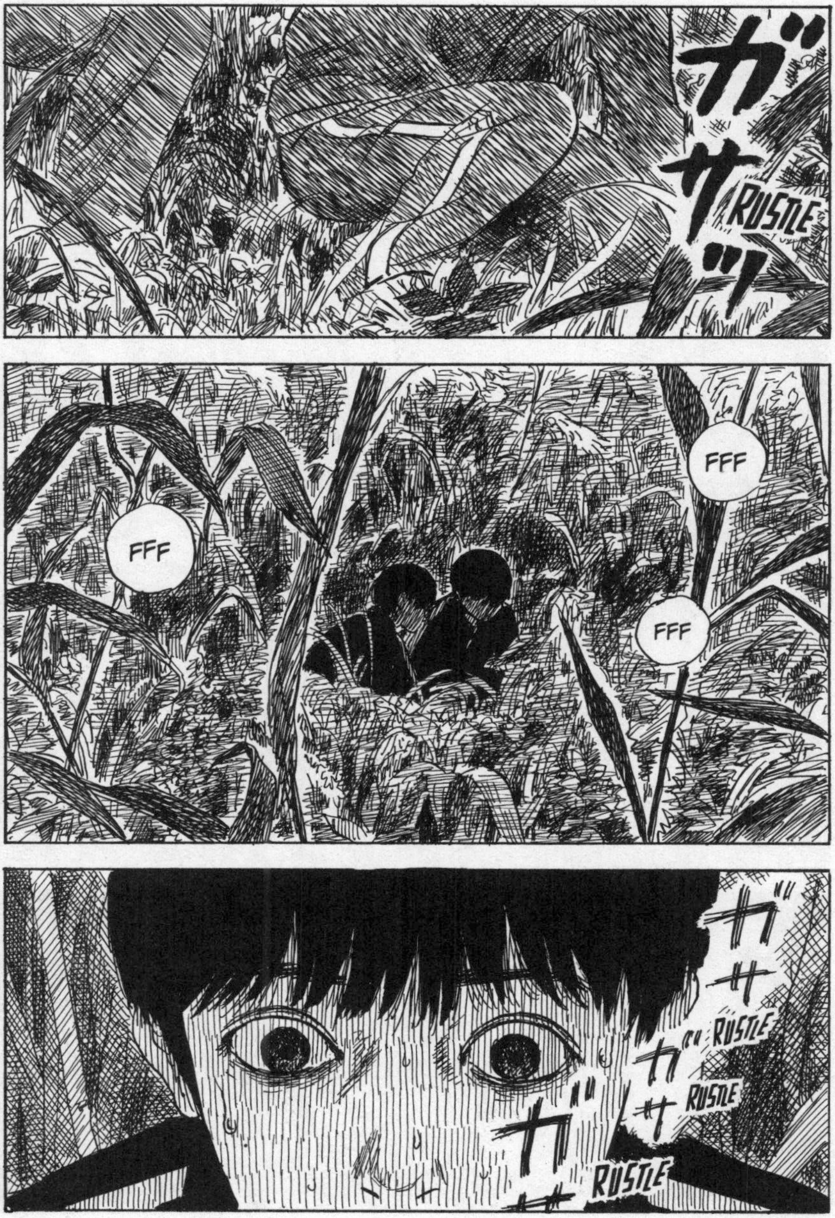
ガサッ
RUSTLE
FFF
FFF
FFF
ガサ
RUSTLE
ガサ
RUSTLE
ガサ
RUSTLE

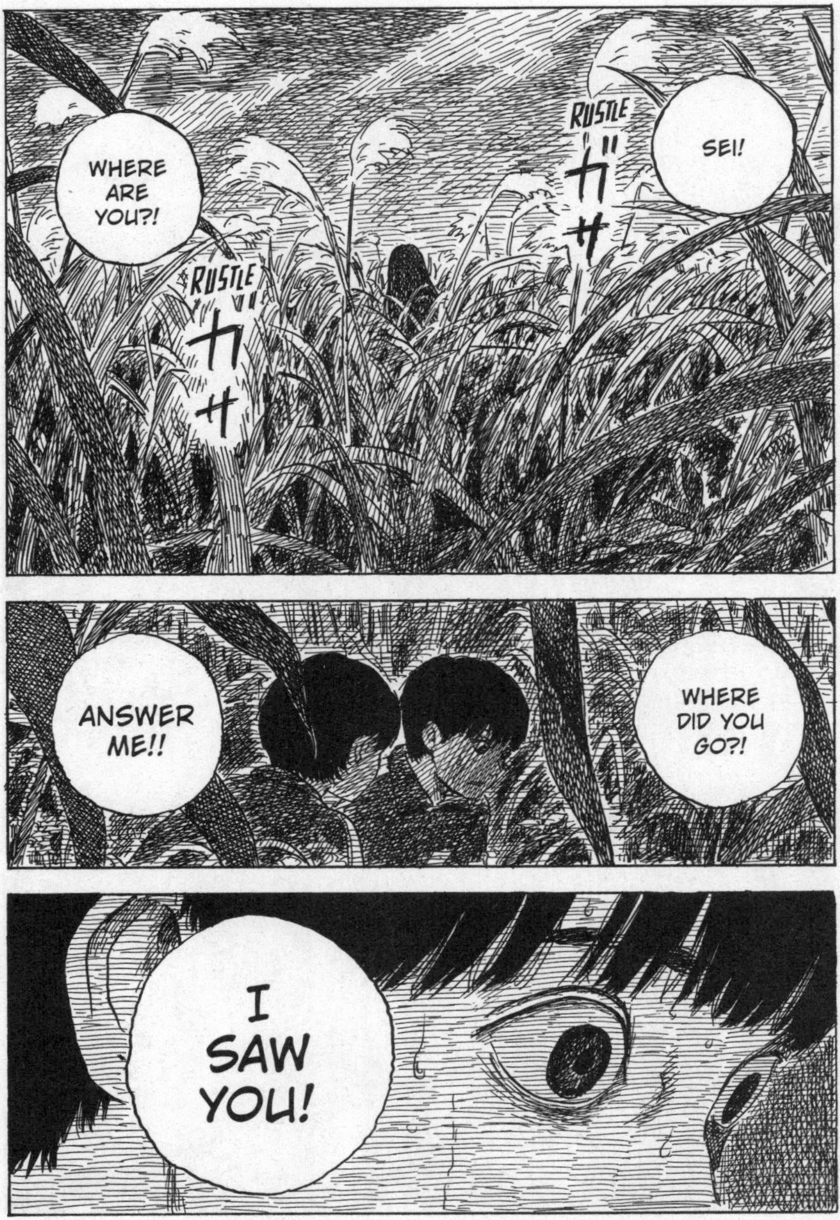
SEI!
RUSTLE
ガサ
WHERE ARE YOU?!
RUSTLE
ガサ
WHERE DID YOU GO?!
ANSWER ME!!
I SAW YOU!

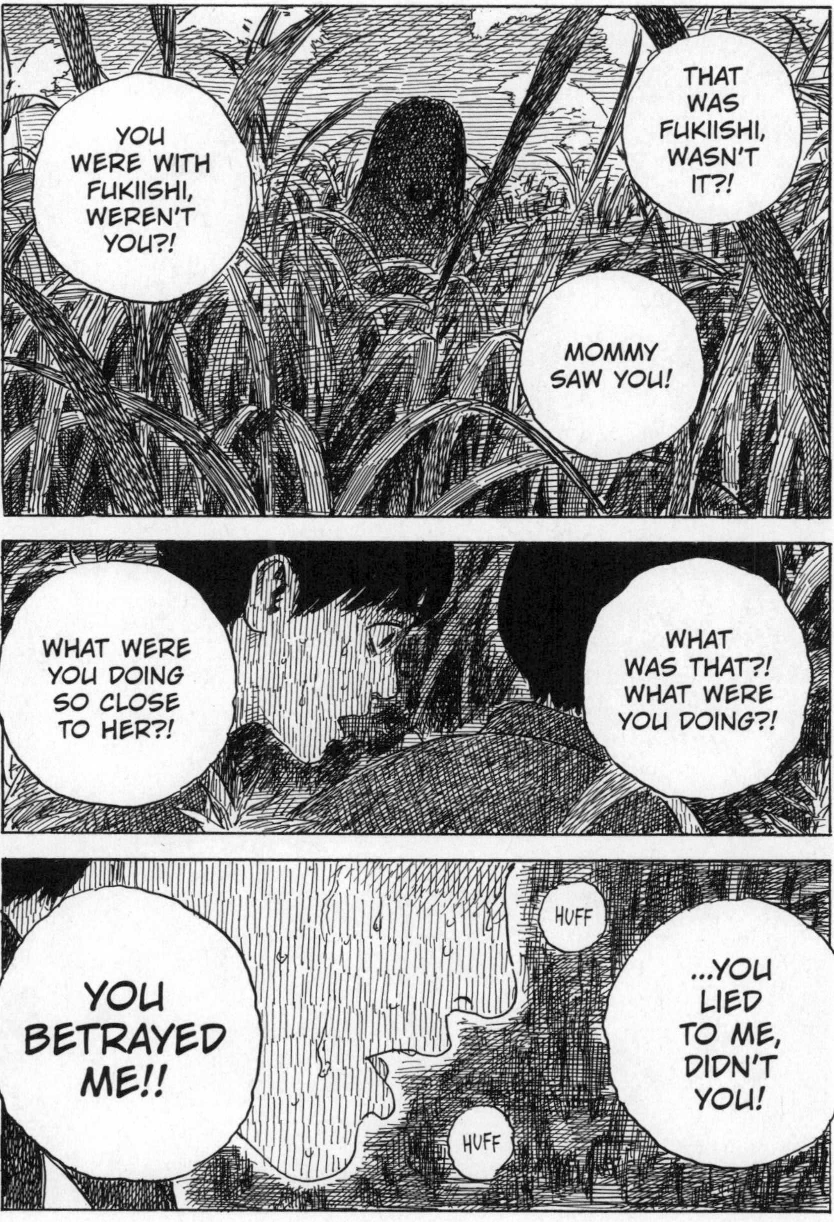
THAT WAS FUKIISHI, WASN'T IT?!
YOU WERE WITH FUKIISHI, WEREN'T YOU?!
MOMMY SAW YOU!
WHAT WAS THAT?! WHAT WERE YOU DOING?!
WHAT WERE YOU DOING SO CLOSE TO HER?!
HUFF
...YOU LIED TO ME, DIDN'T YOU!
YOU BETRAYED ME!!
HUFF

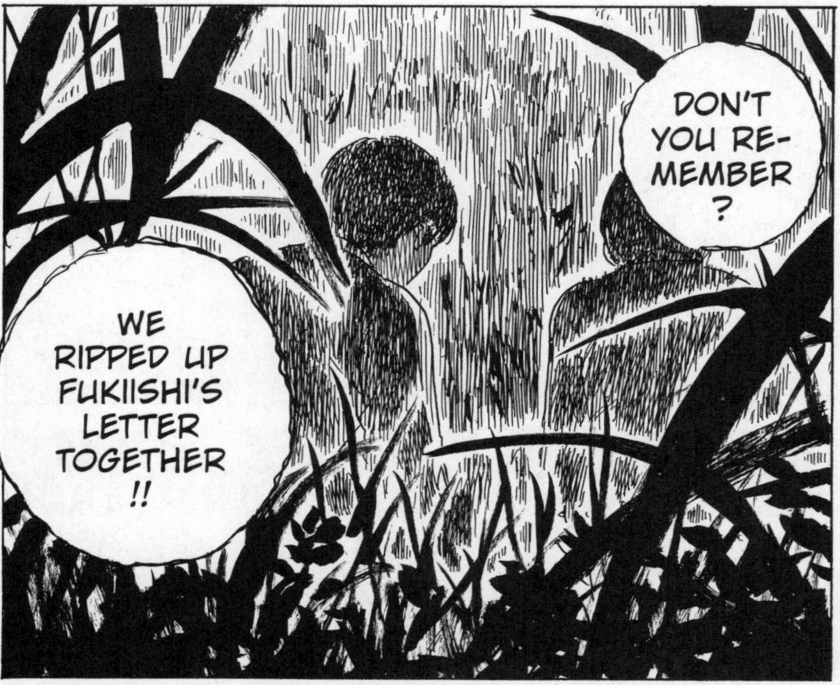
DON'T YOU RE-MEMBER?
WE RIPPED UP FUKIISHI'S LETTER TOGETHER!!
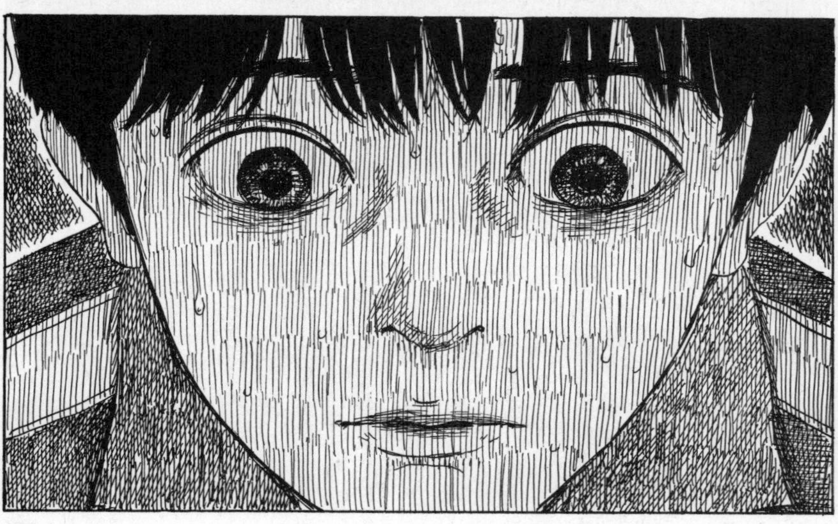

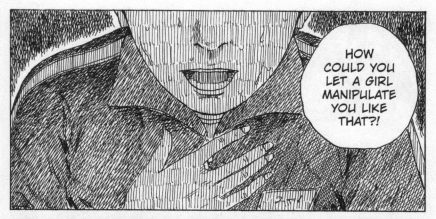

HOW COULD YOU LET A GIRL MANIPULATE YOU LIKE THAT?!

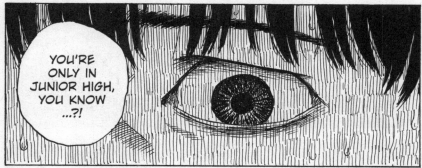

YOU'RE ONLY IN JUNIOR HIGH, YOU KNOW ...?!

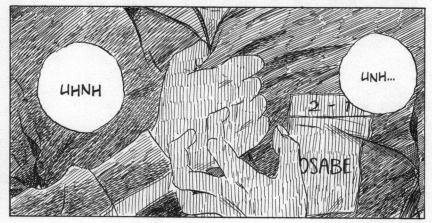

UHNH

UNH...

OSABE

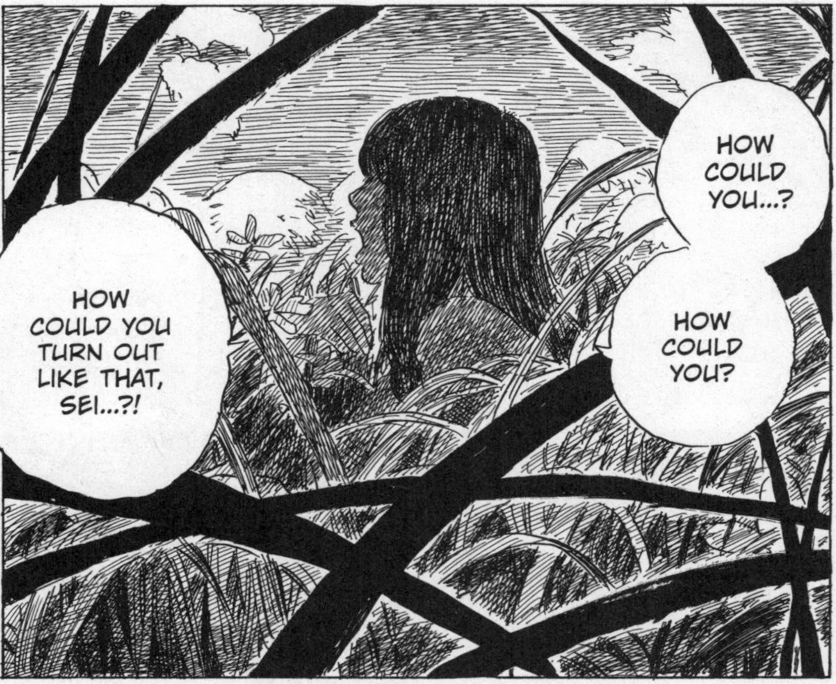
HOW COULD YOU...?
HOW COULD YOU?
HOW COULD YOU TURN OUT LIKE THAT, SEI...?!

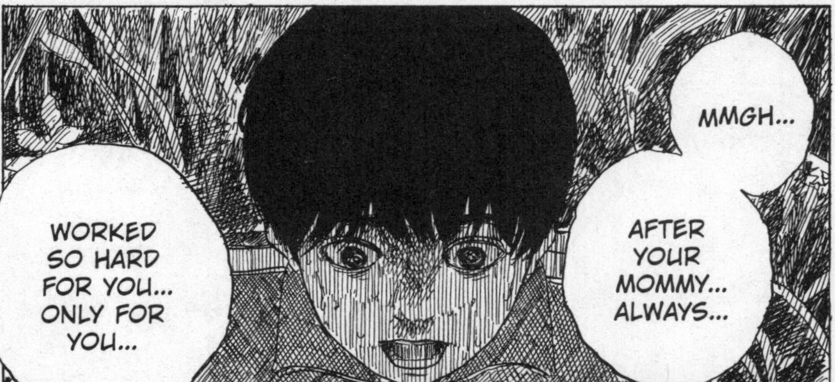
MMGH...
AFTER YOUR MOMMY... ALWAYS...
WORKED SO HARD FOR YOU... ONLY FOR YOU...

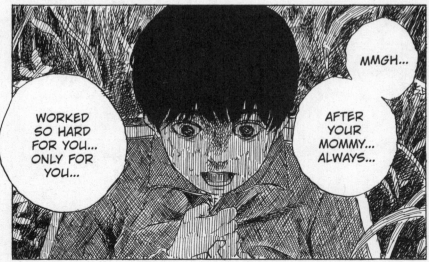

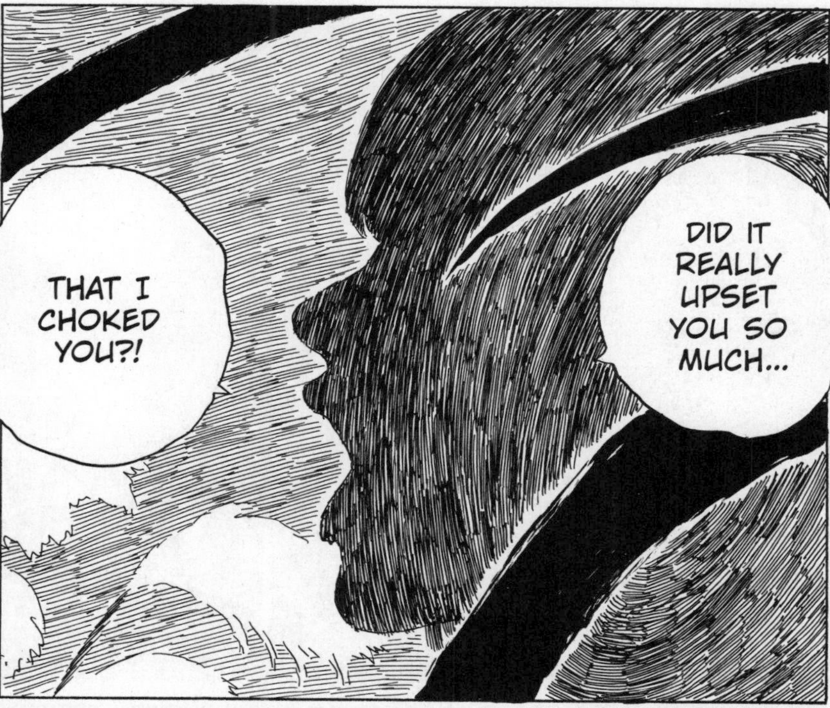
DID IT REALLY UPSET YOU SO MUCH...
THAT I CHOKED YOU?!

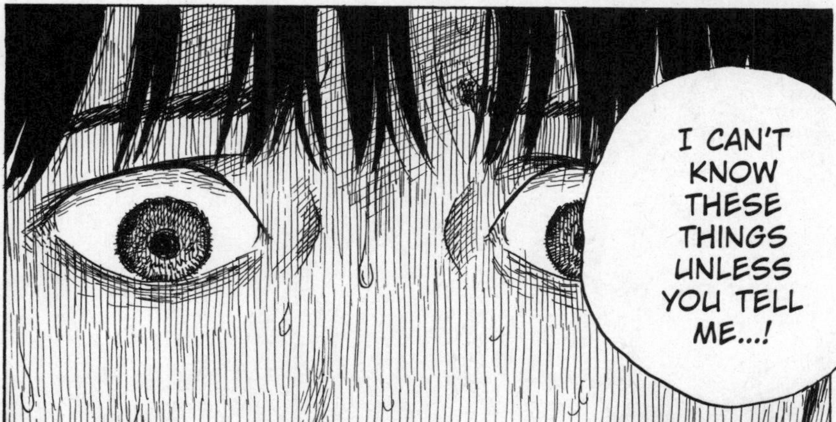
I CAN'T KNOW THESE THINGS UNLESS YOU TELL ME...!

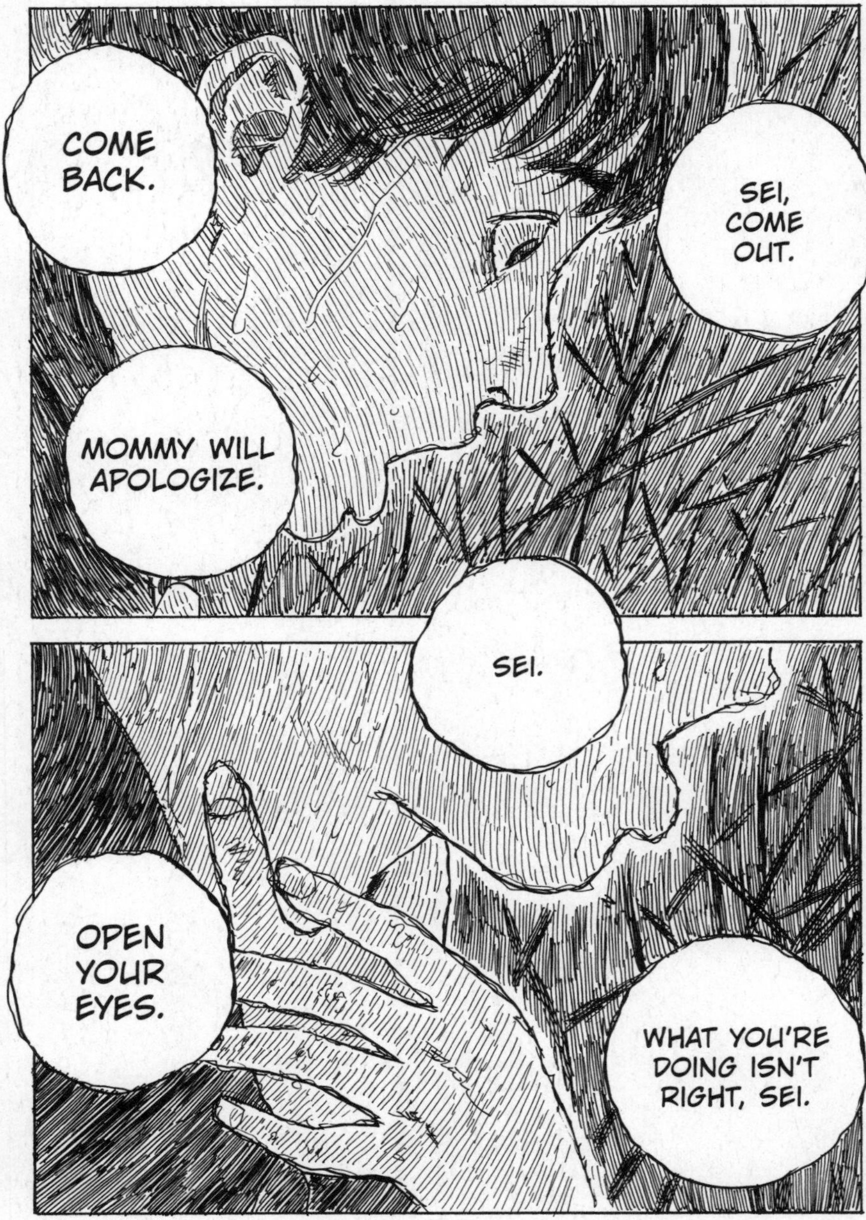
SEI, COME OUT.
COME BACK.
MOMMY WILL APOLOGIZE.
SEI.
OPEN YOUR EYES.
WHAT YOU'RE DOING ISN'T RIGHT, SEI.

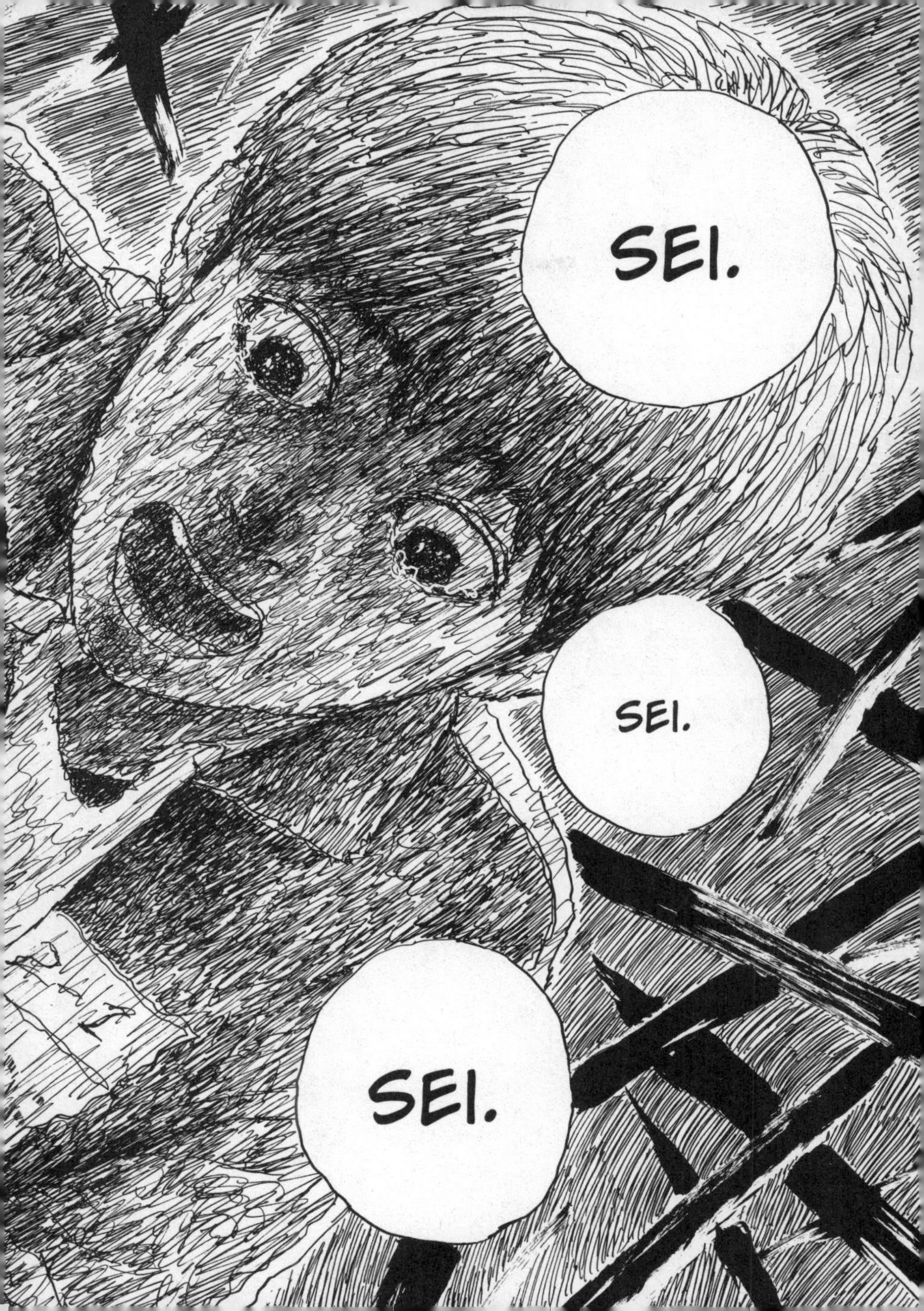
SEI.
SEI.
SEI.

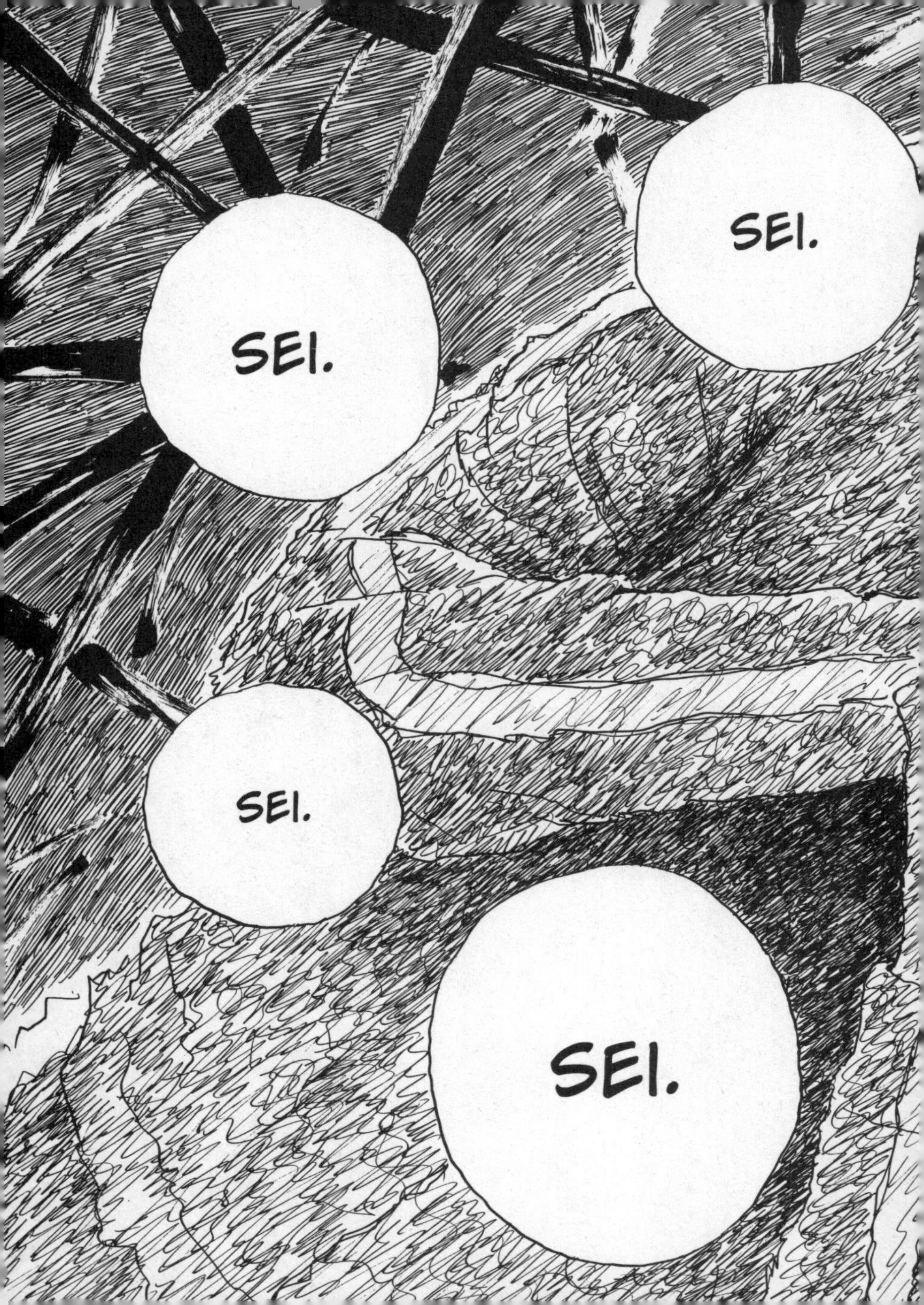
SEI.
SEI.
SEI.
SEI.

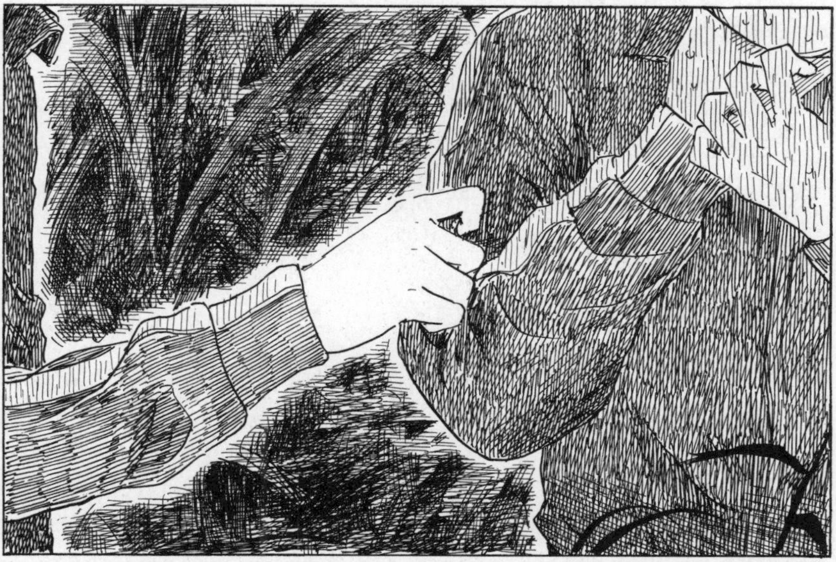
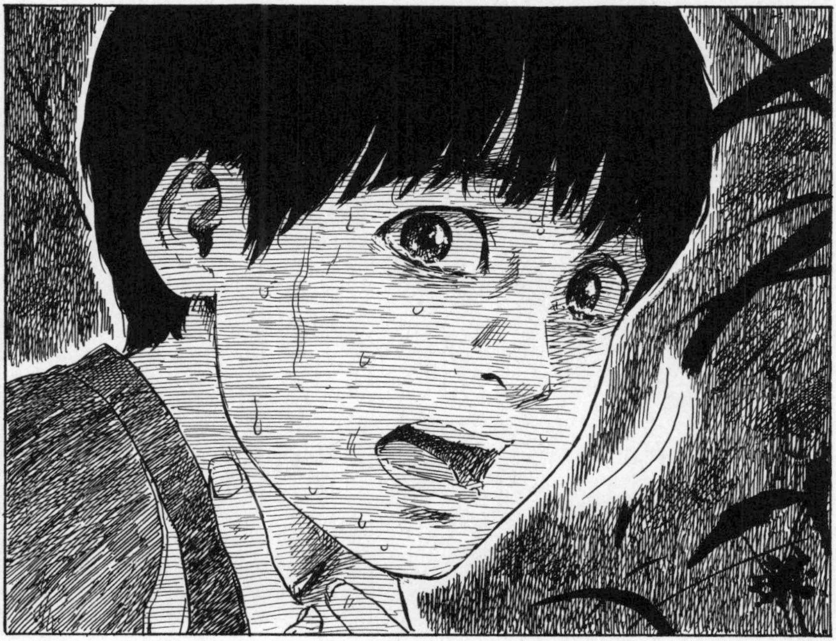

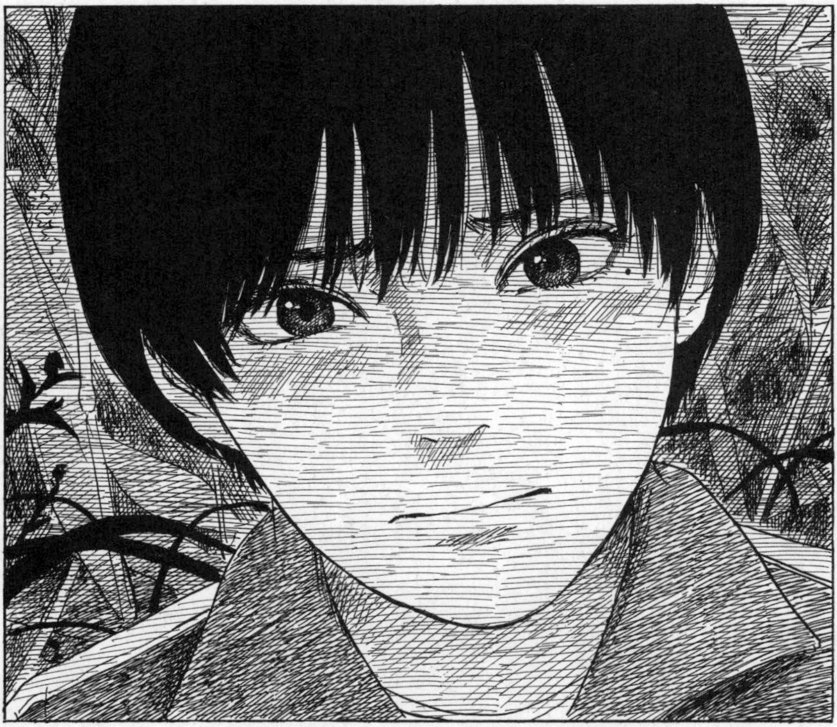

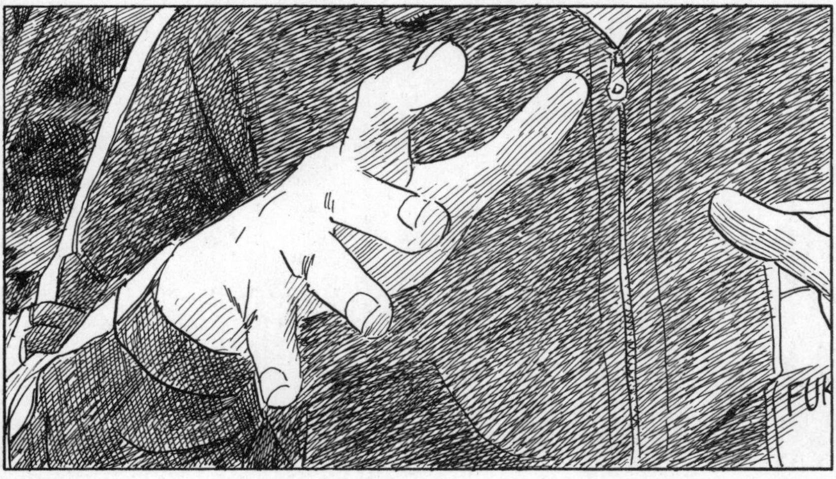
FUK

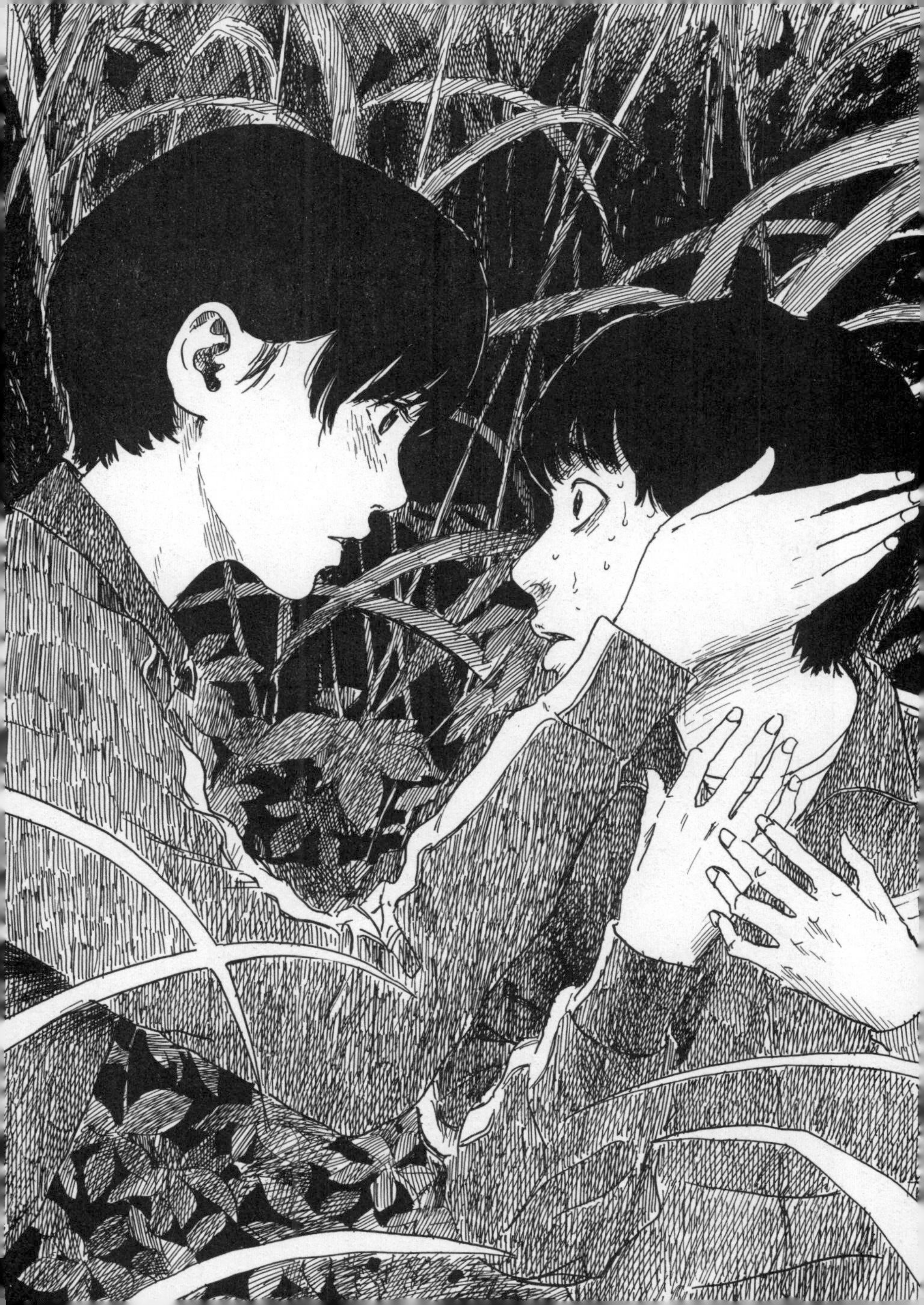

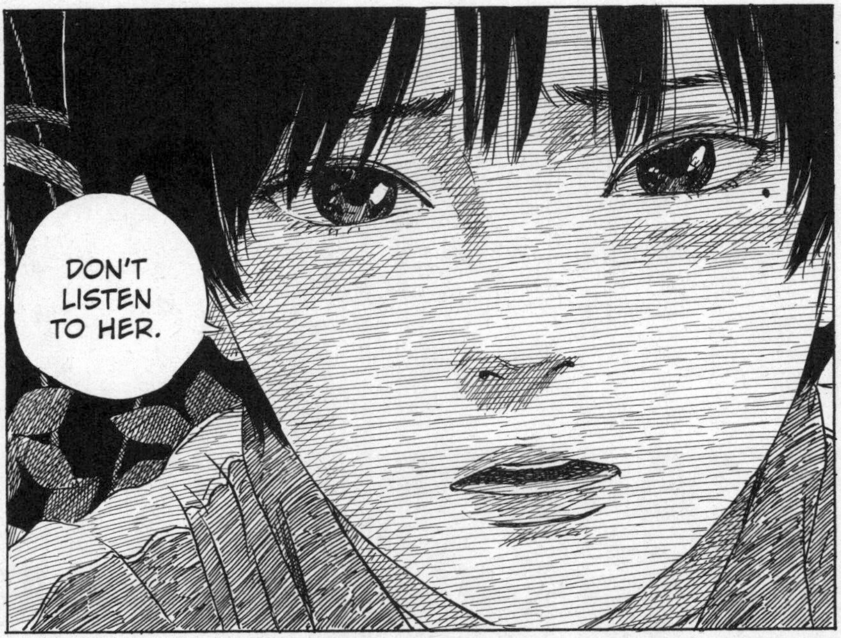
DON'T LISTEN TO HER.

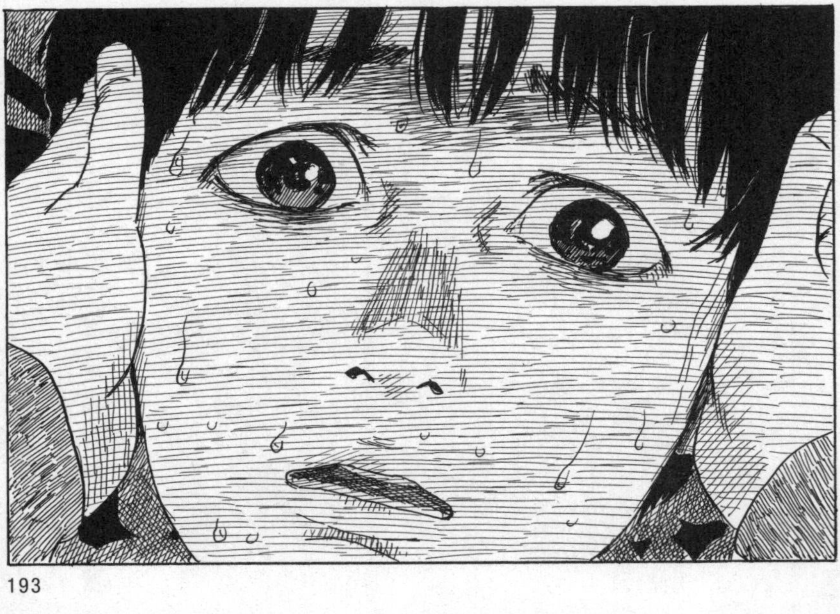

ガサッ
RUSTLE

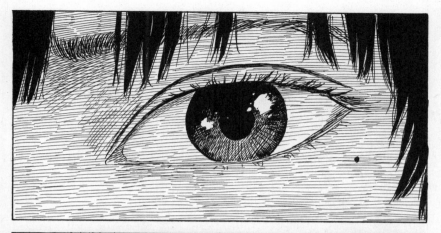

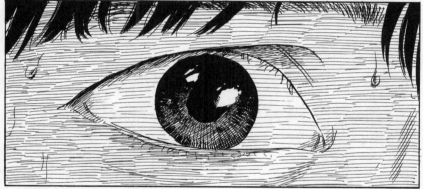

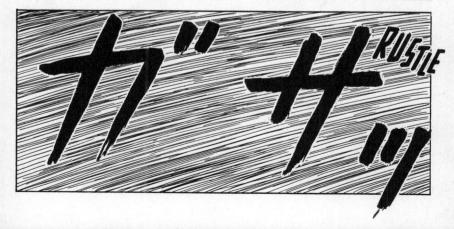

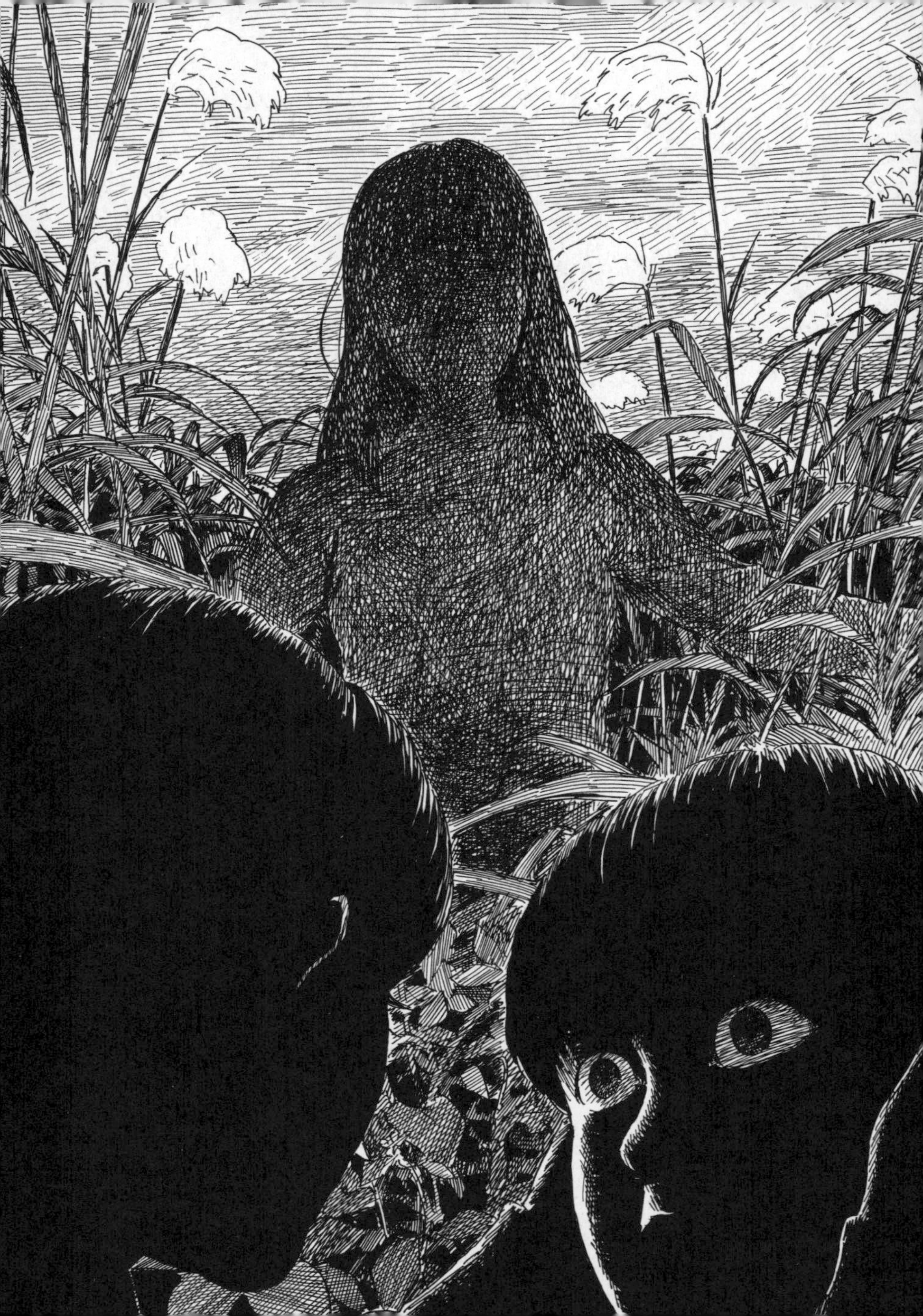

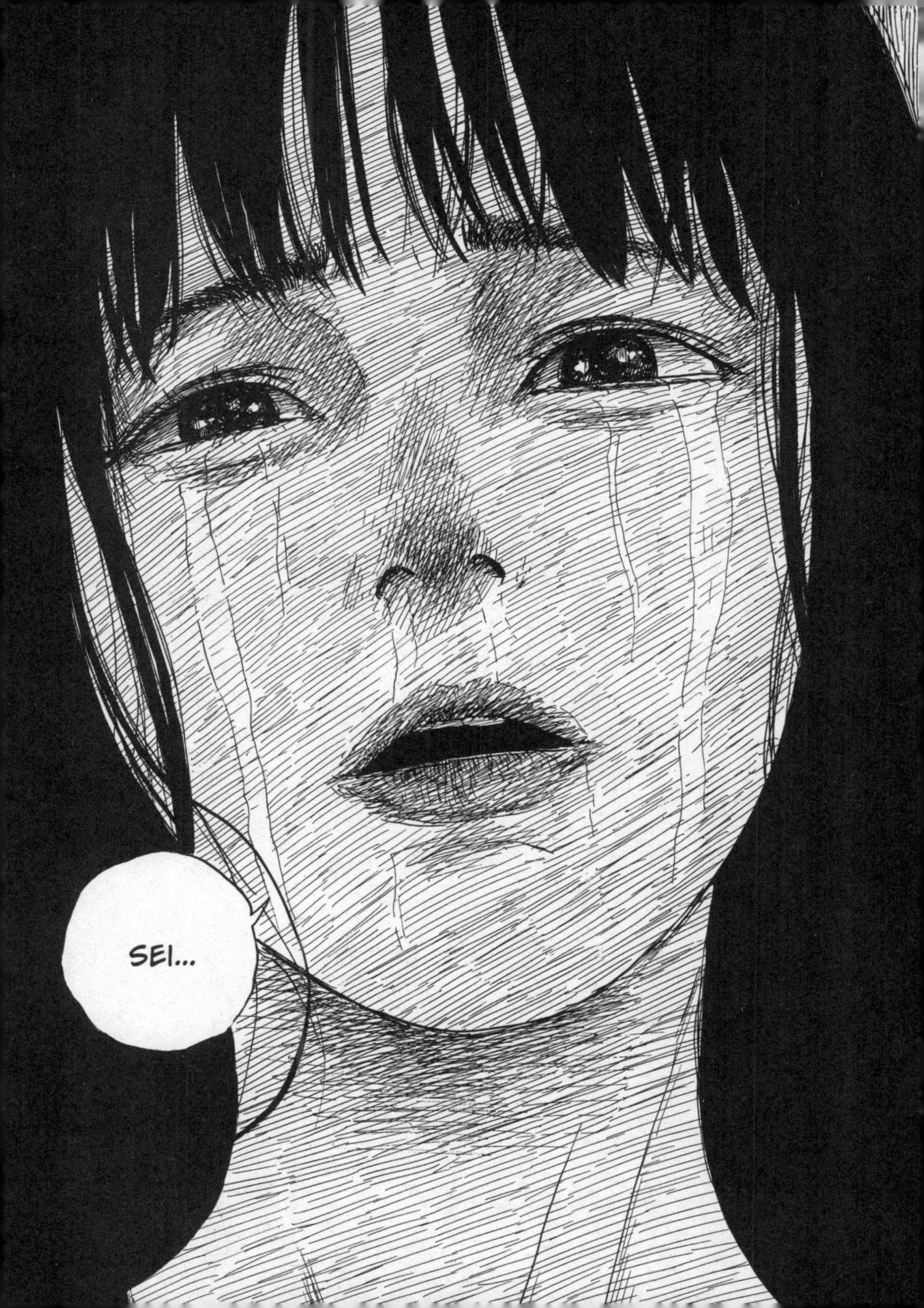
SEI...

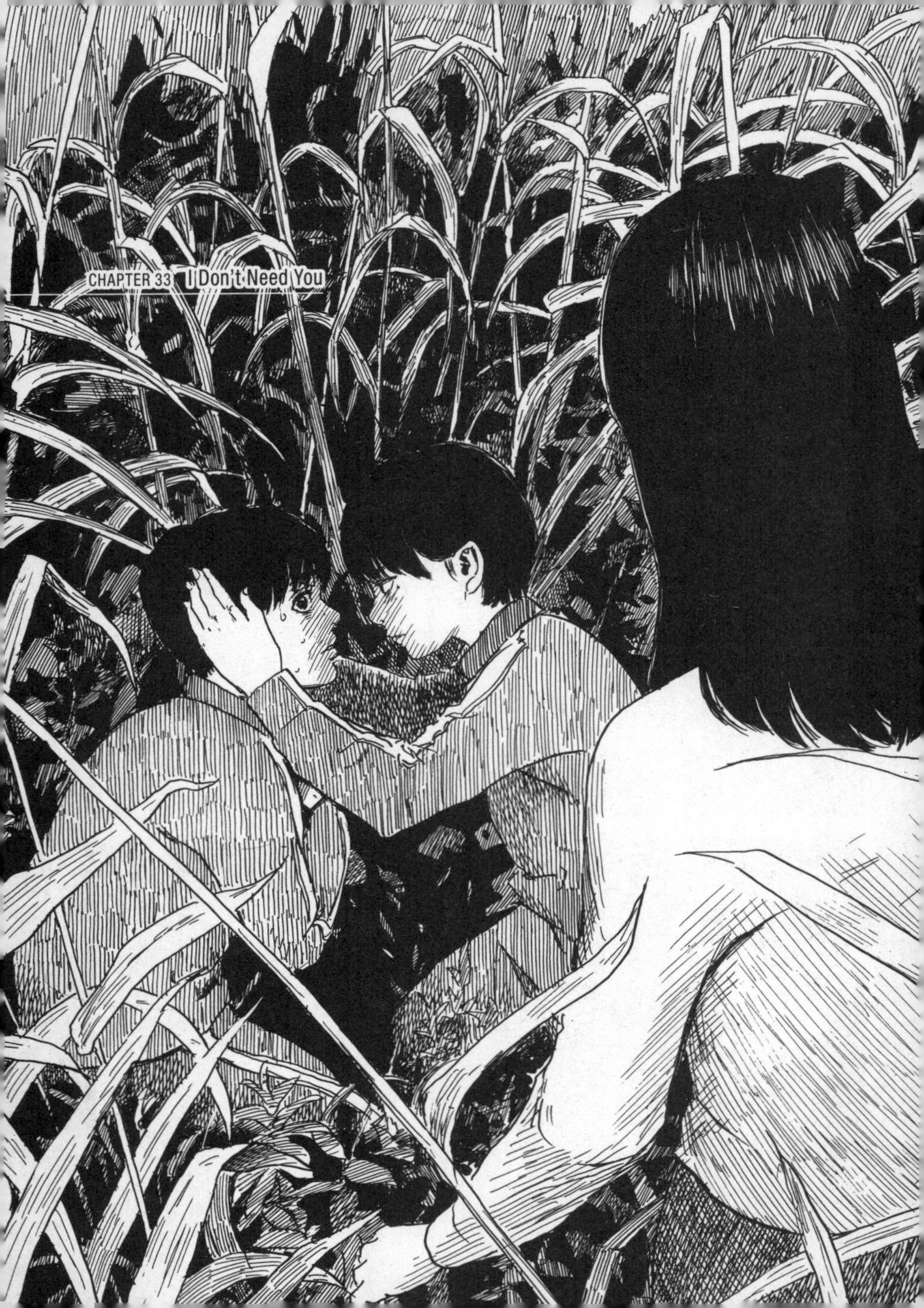
CHAPTER 33 I Don't Need You

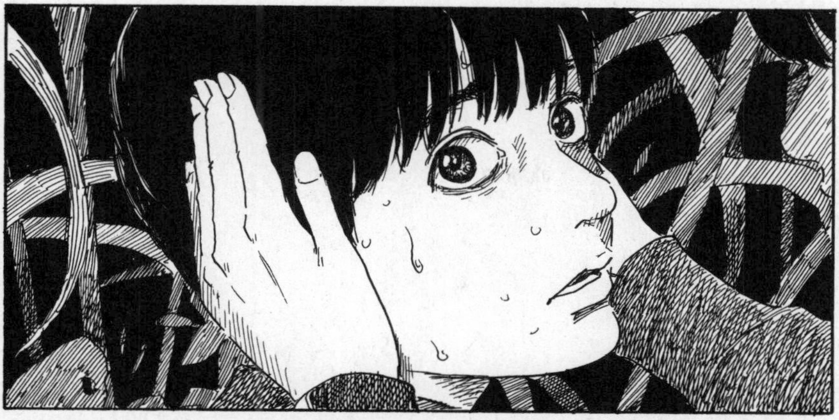
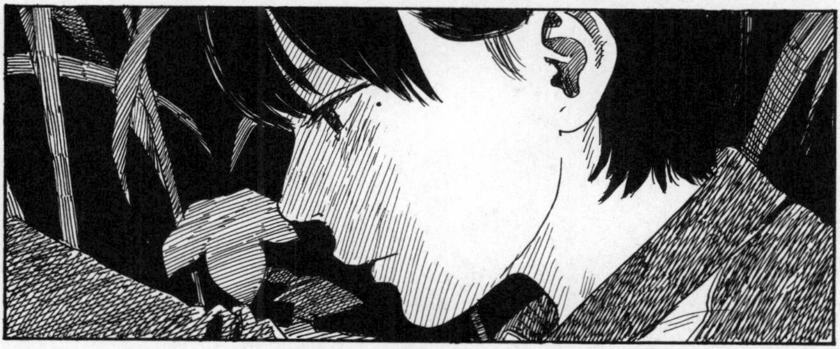
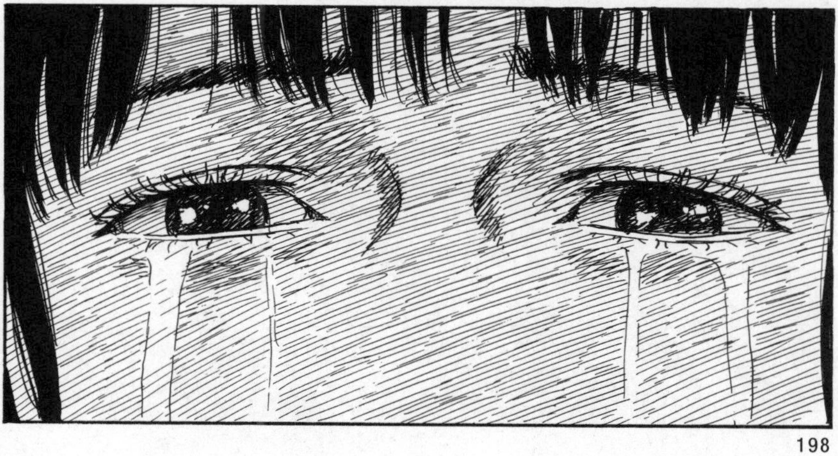

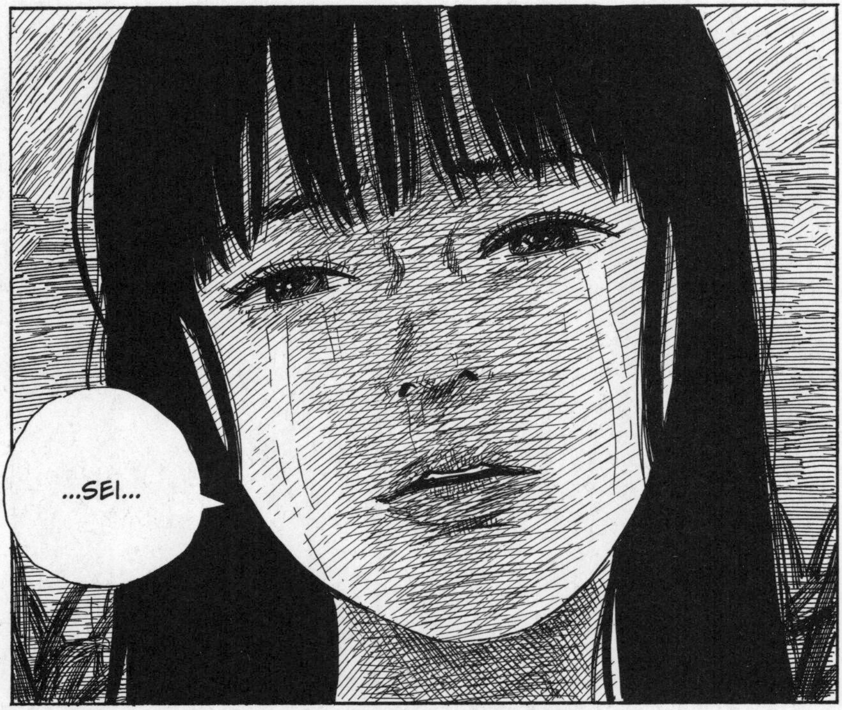
...SEI...
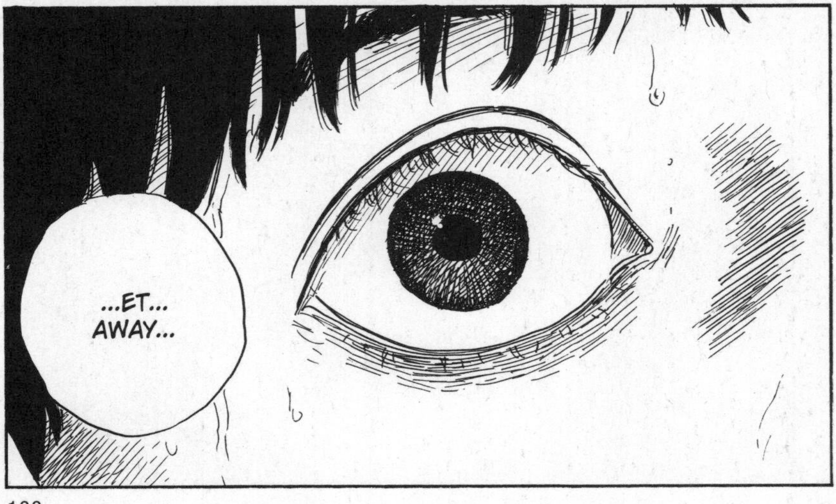
...ET... AWAY...

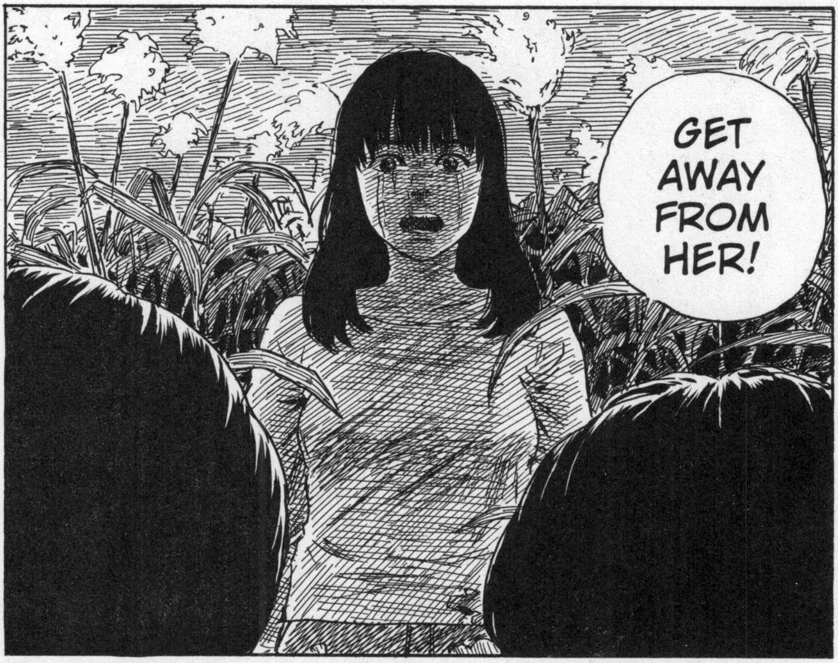
GET AWAY FROM HER!

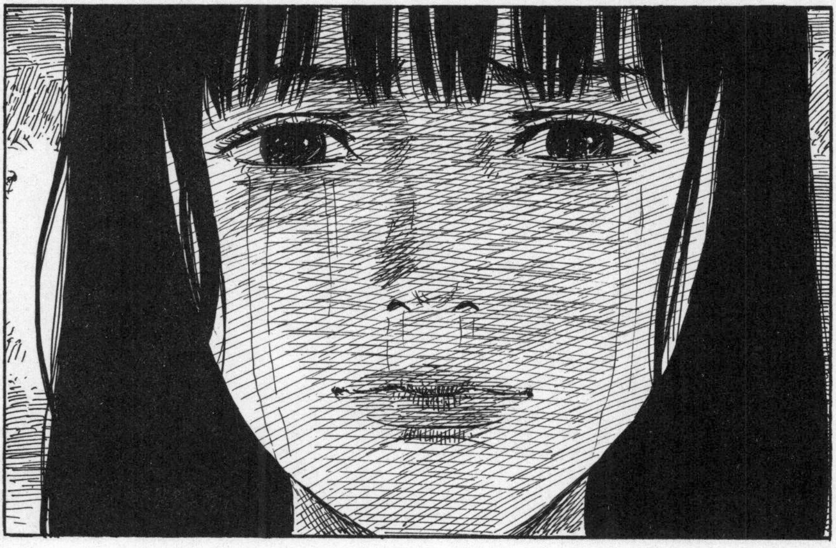

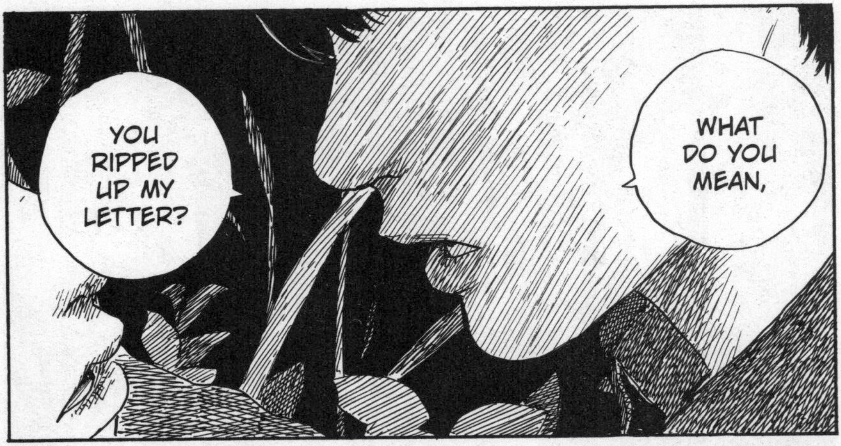
WHAT DO YOU MEAN,
YOU RIPPED UP MY LETTER?
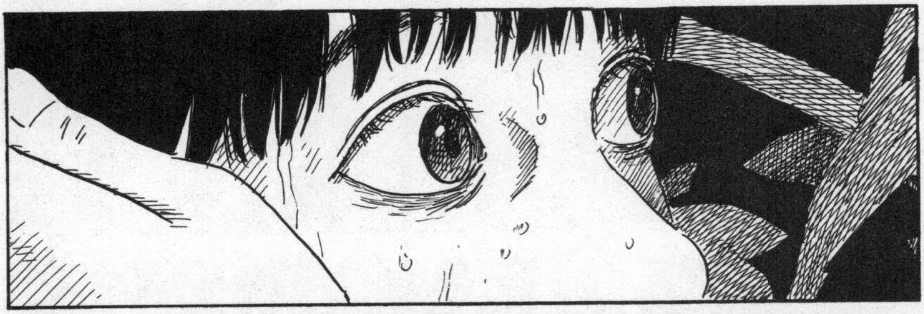
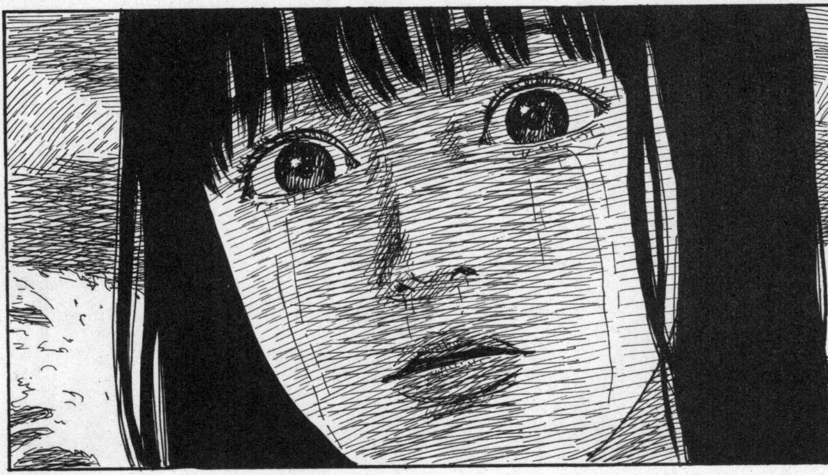

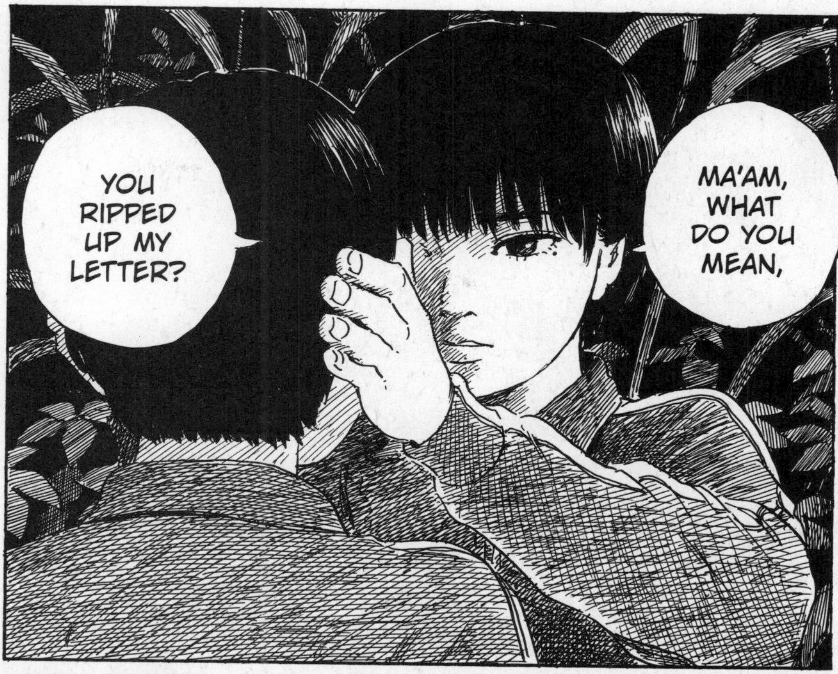
MA'AM, WHAT DO YOU MEAN,
YOU RIPPED UP MY LETTER?

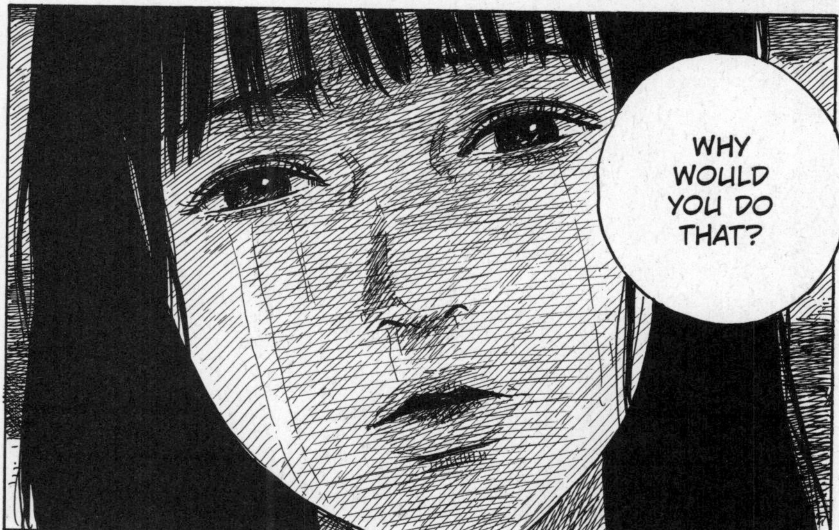
WHY WOULD YOU DO THAT?

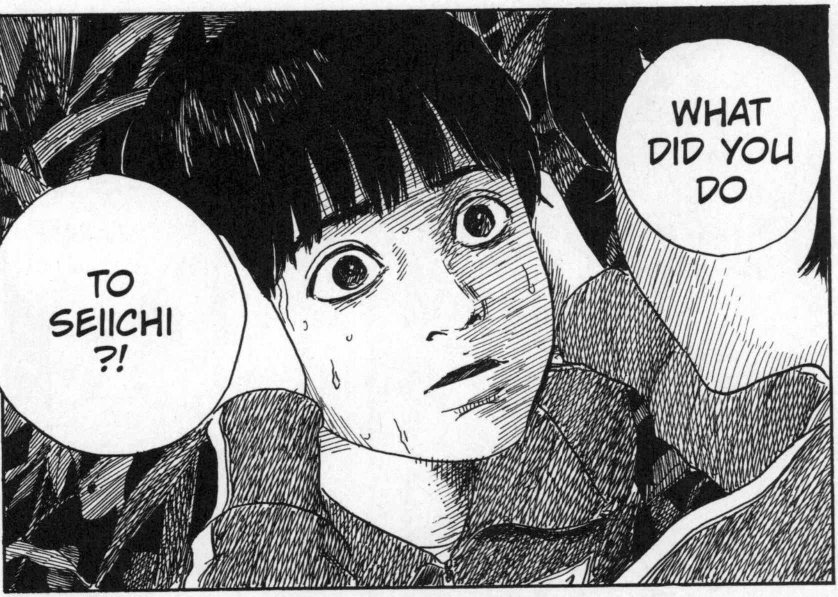
WHAT DID YOU DO
TO SEIICHI ?!
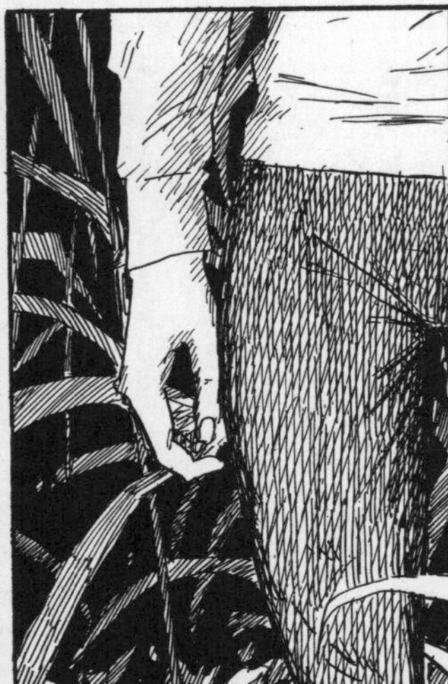
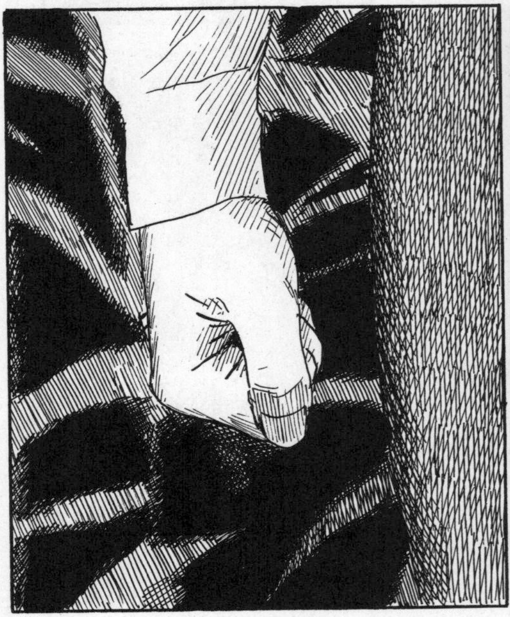

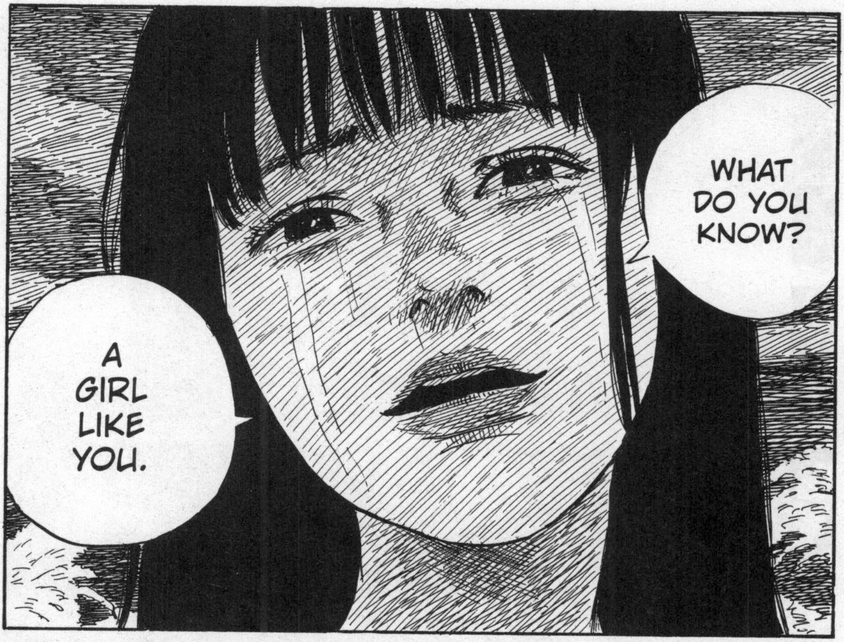
WHAT DO YOU KNOW?
A GIRL LIKE YOU.
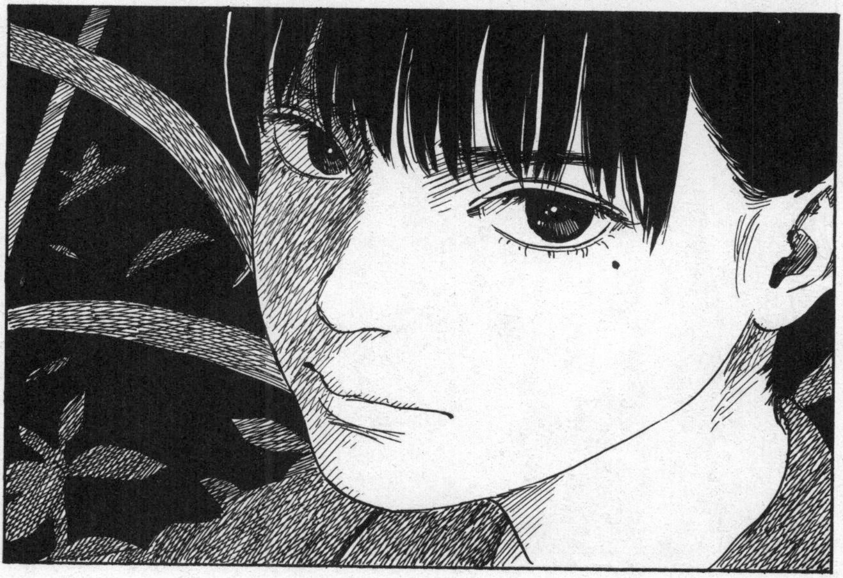

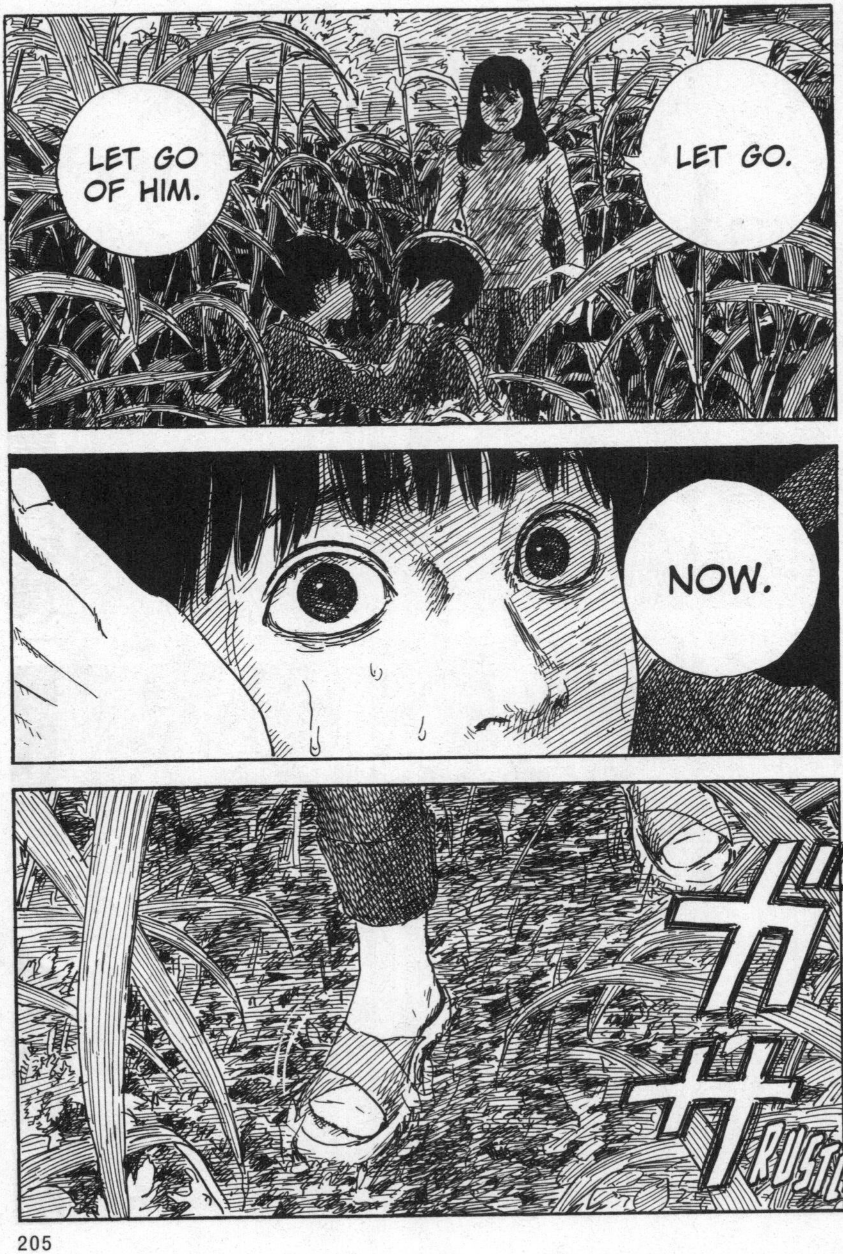
LET GO.
LET GO OF HIM.
NOW.
RUSTLE

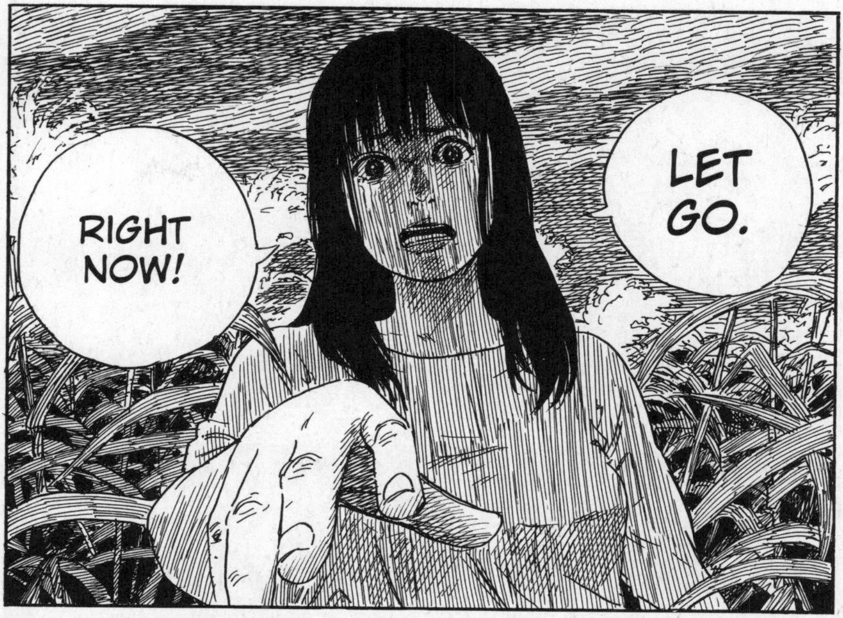
LET GO.
RIGHT NOW!

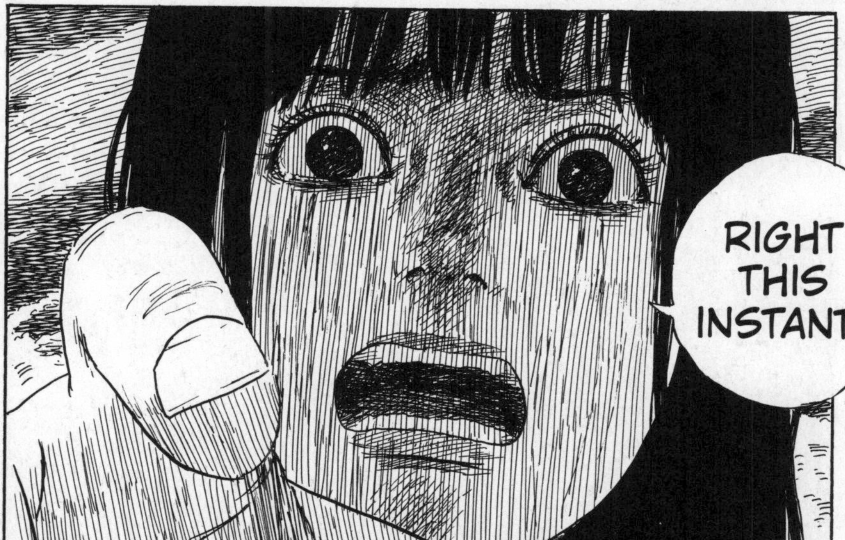
RIGHT THIS INSTANT!

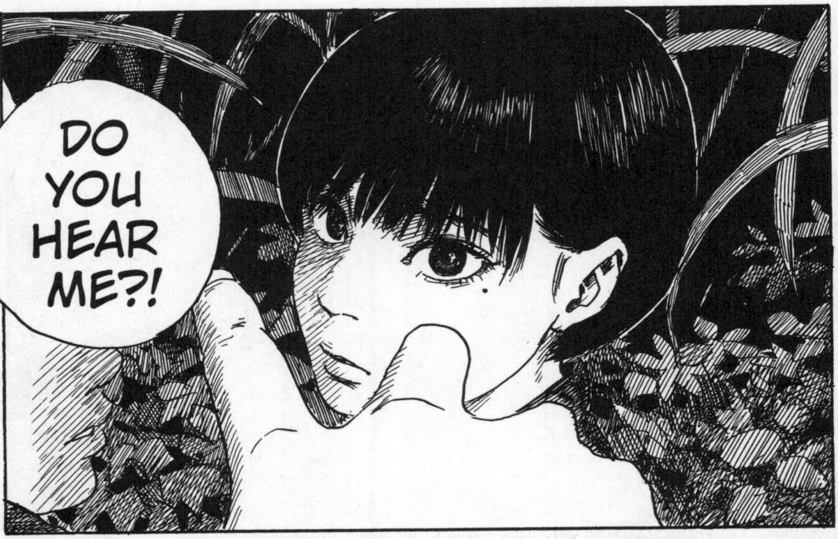
DO YOU HEAR ME?!
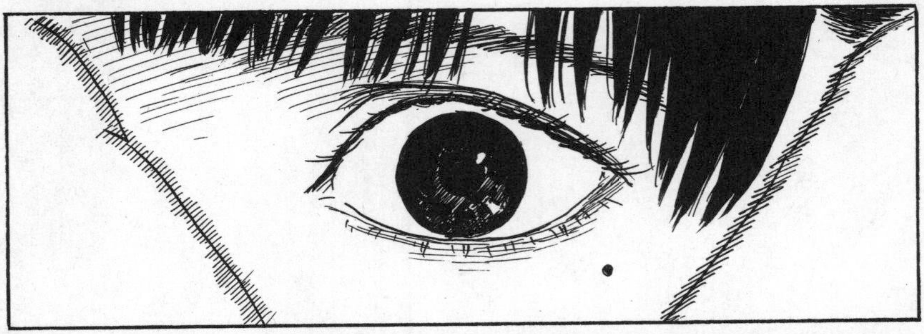
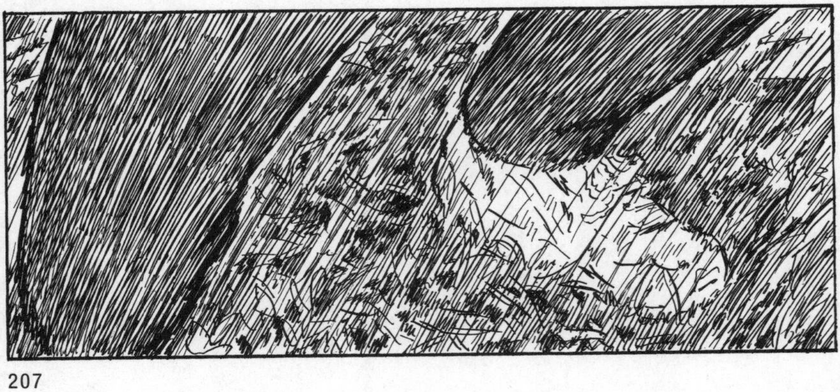

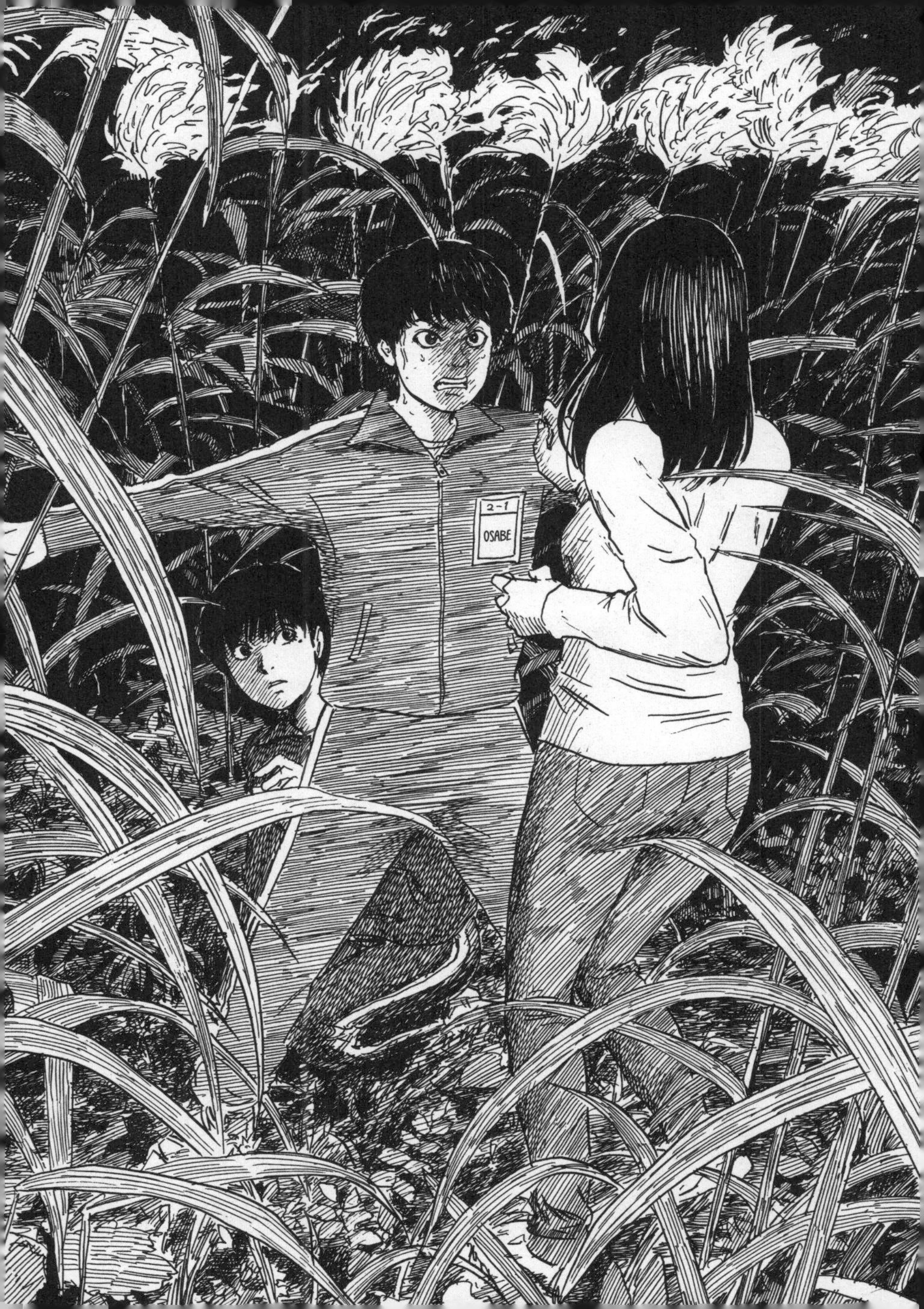
2-1
OSABE

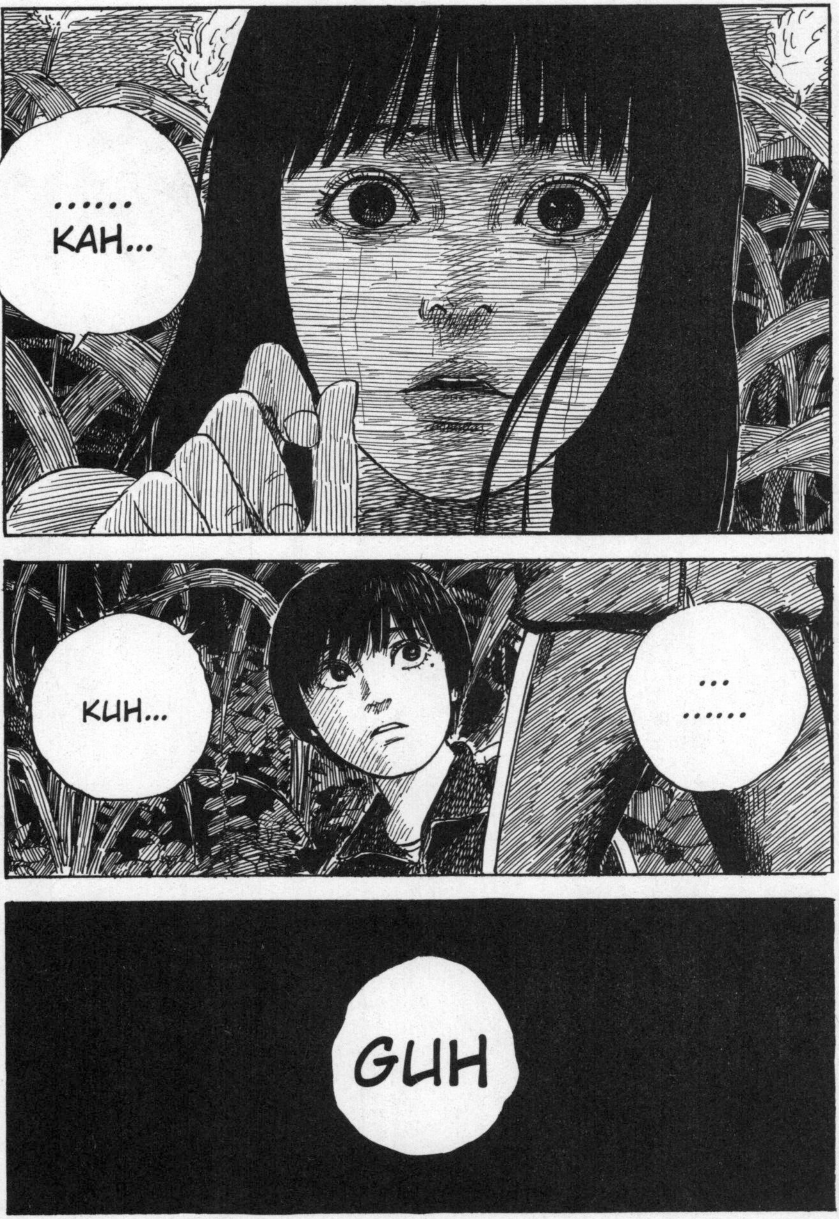

......
KAH...
...
......
KUH...
GUH

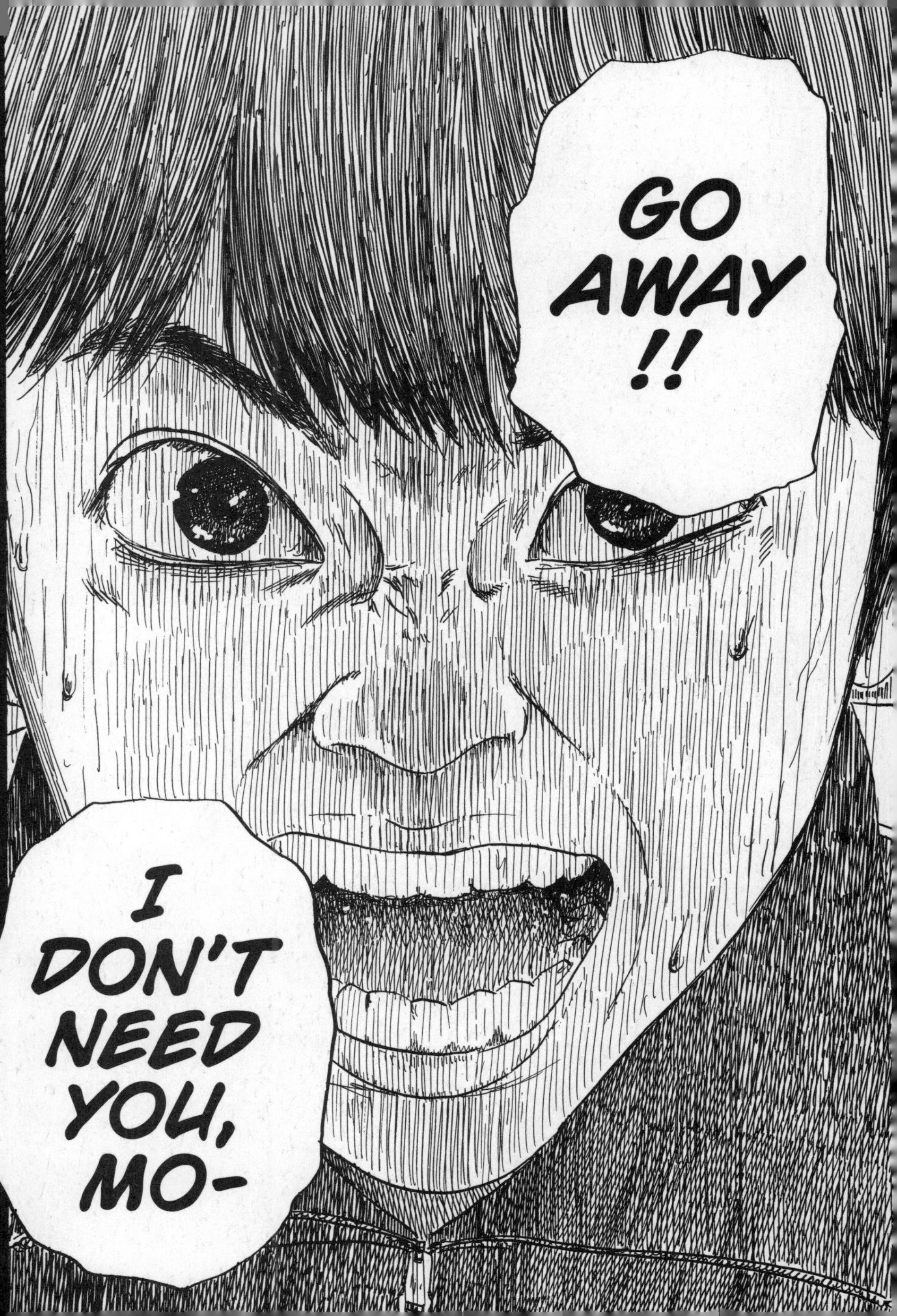
GO AWAY!!
I DON'T NEED YOU, MO-

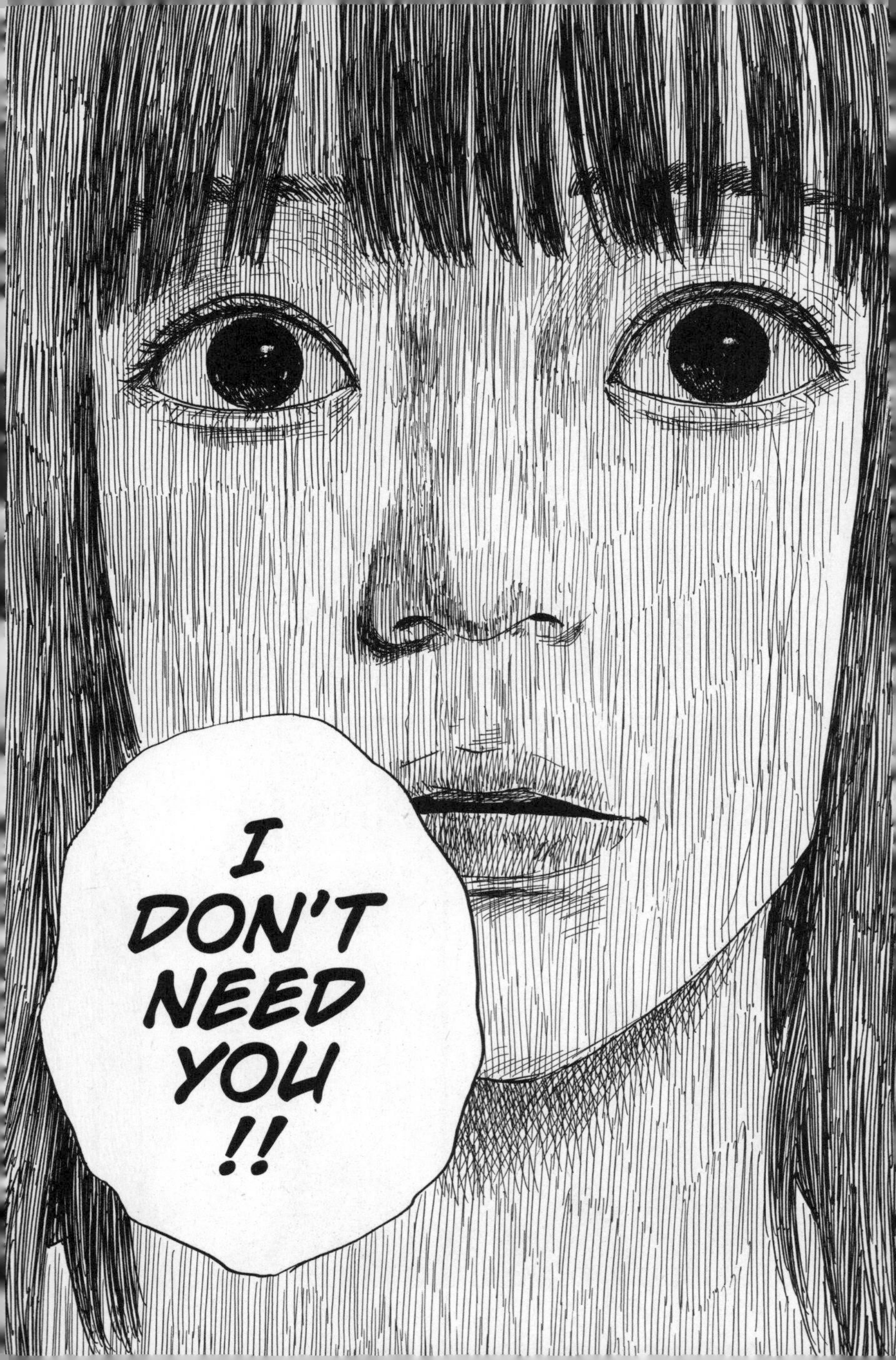
I DON'T NEED YOU!!

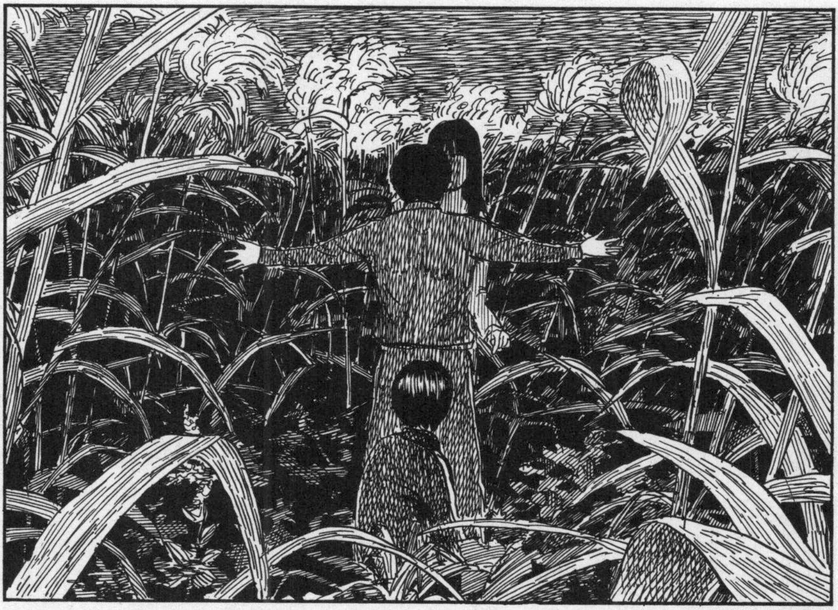

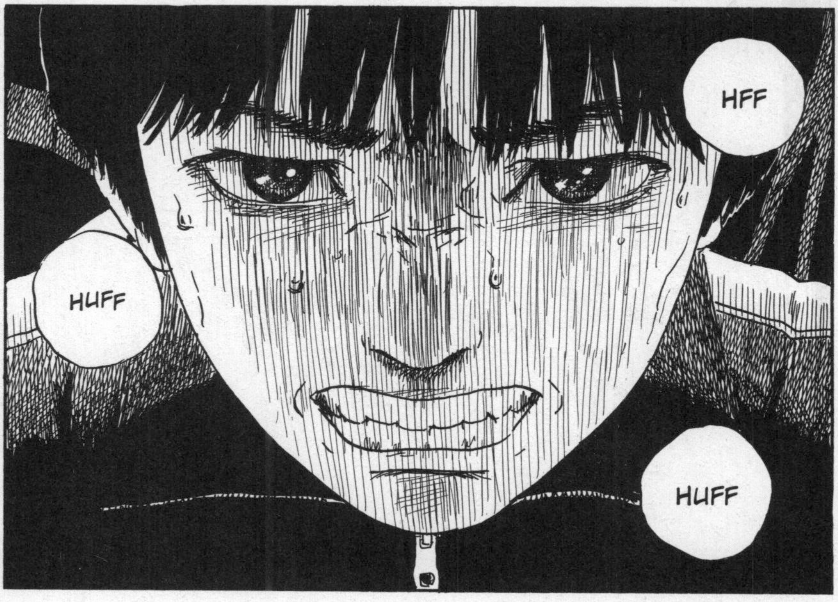
HFF
HUFF
HUFF

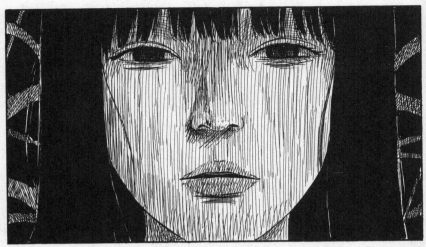

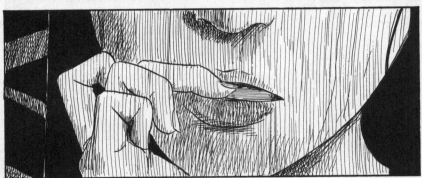

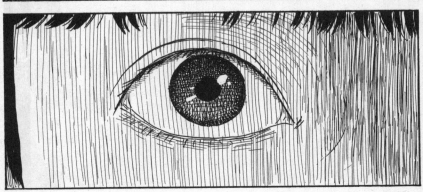

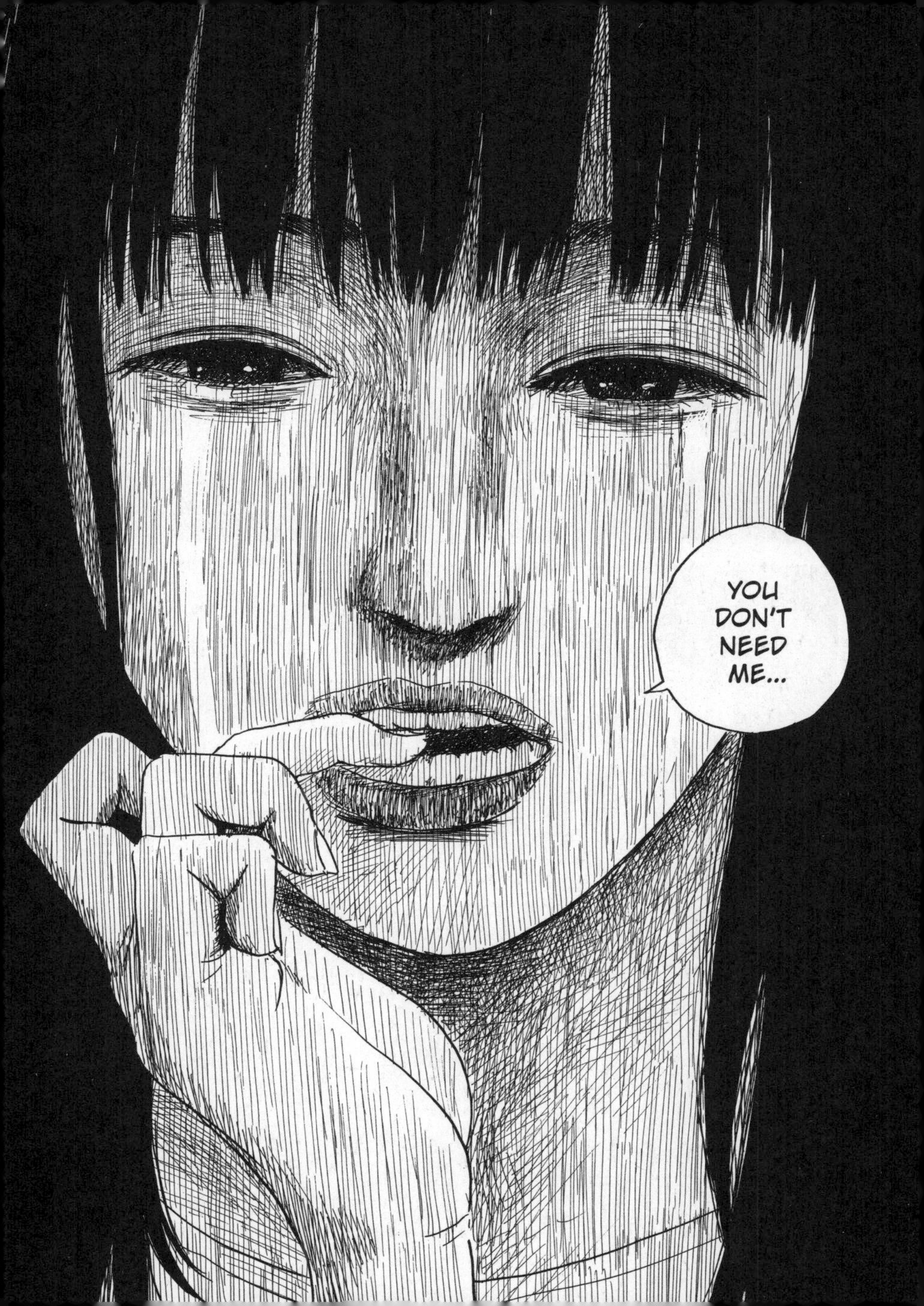
YOU DON'T NEED ME...

NO ONE NEEDS ME...
NO ONE EVER DID...
NO ONE...
E'ER... EE... E...

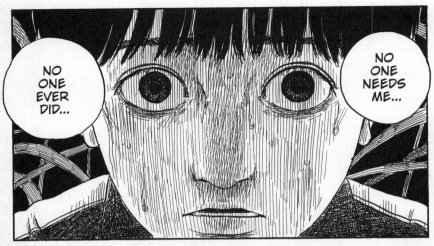

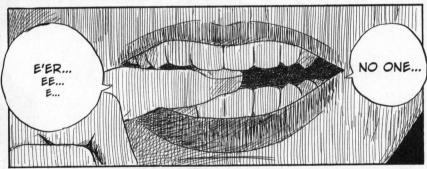

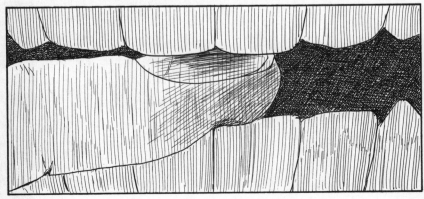

KRAK

パ°
キッ

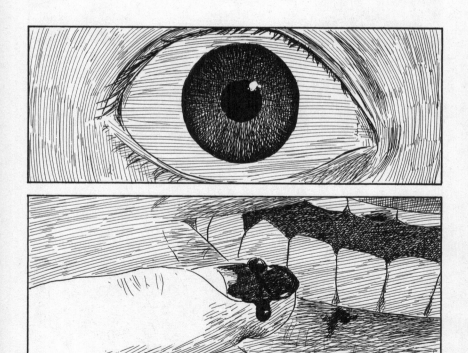

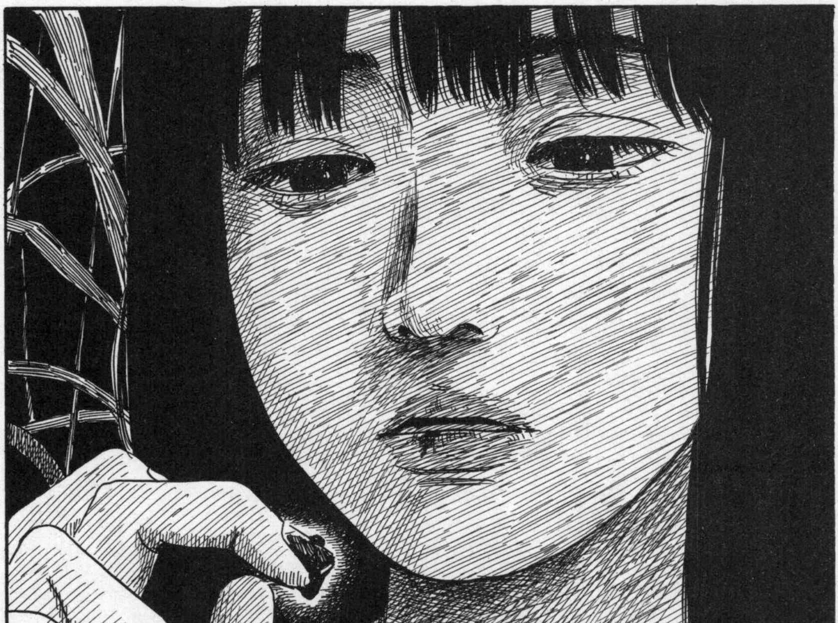

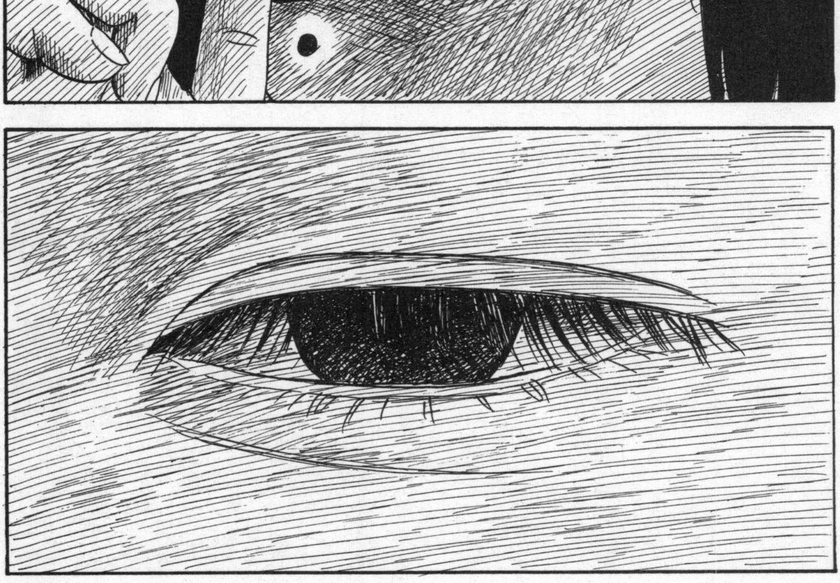

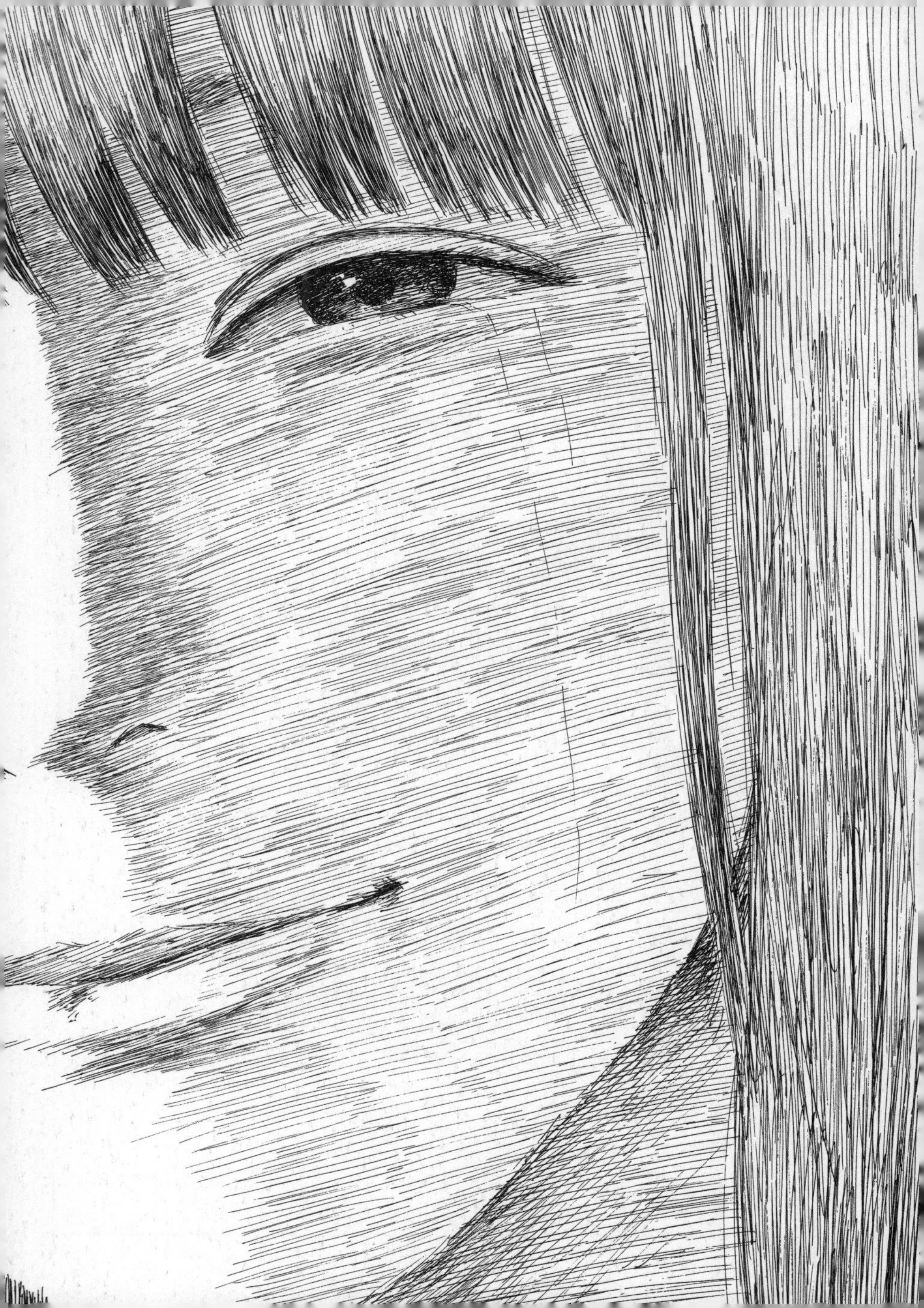

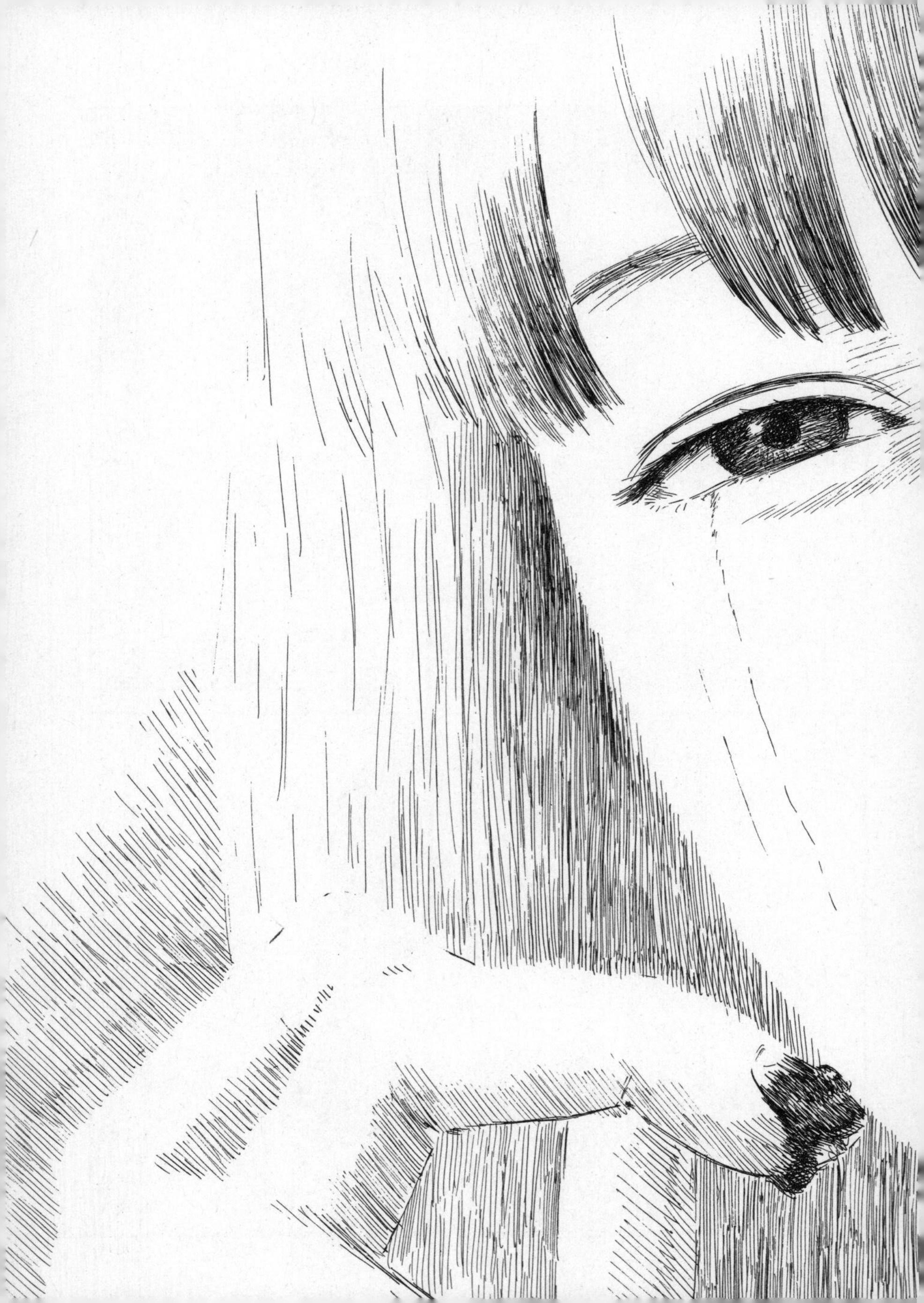

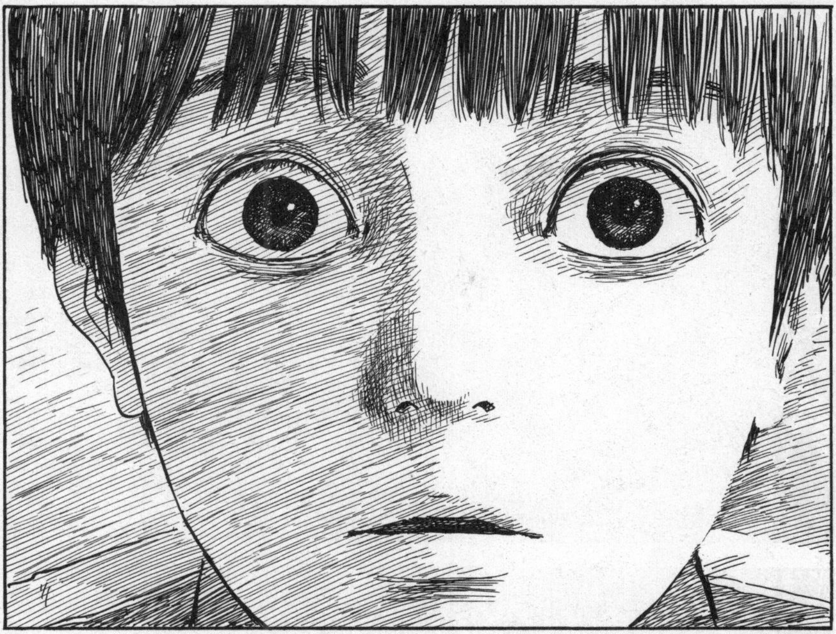
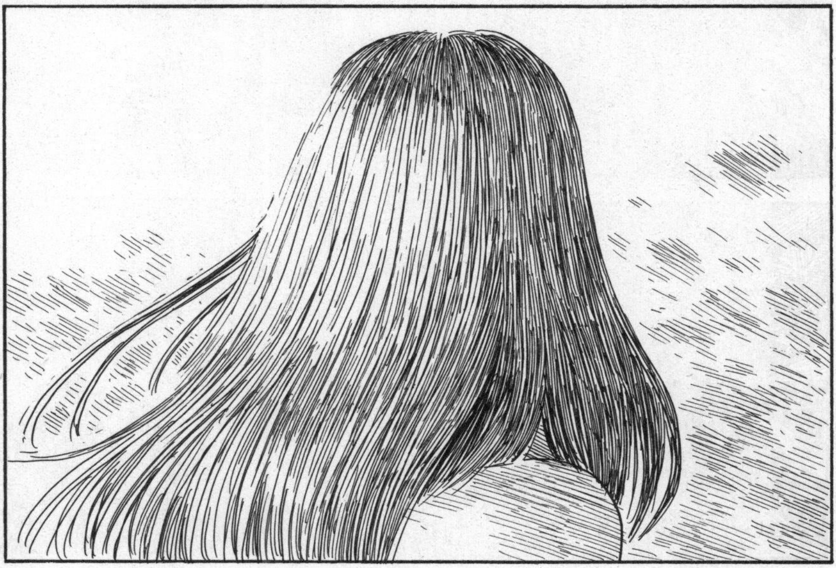

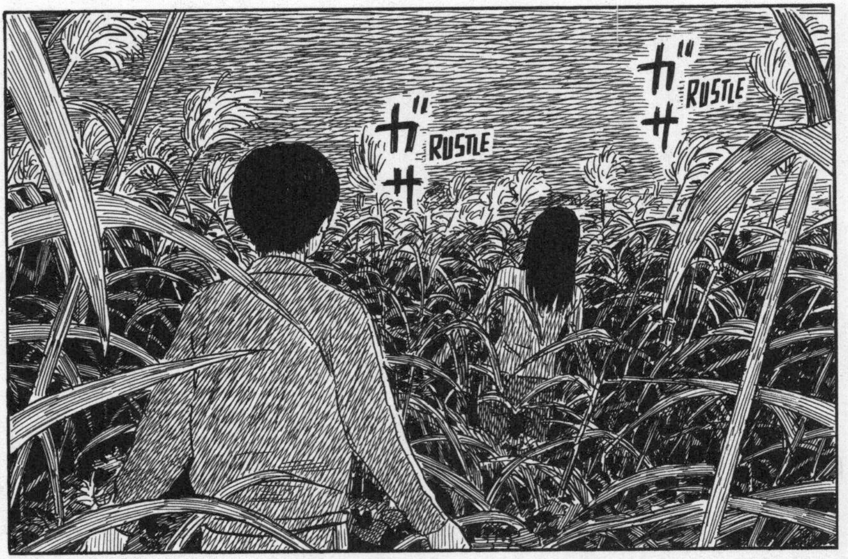
ガサ
RUSTLE
ガサ
RUSTLE

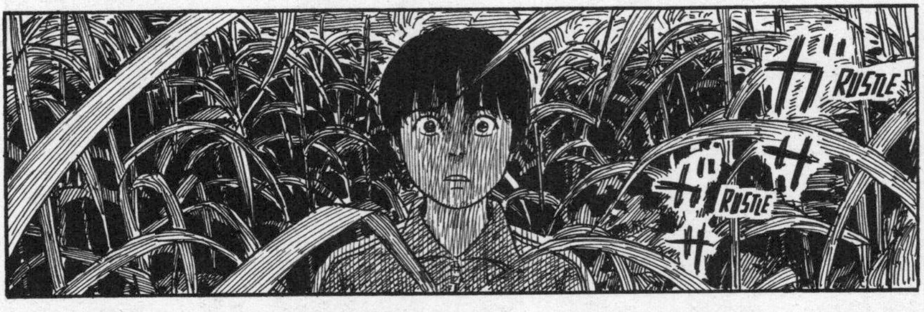
ガサ
RUSTLE
ガサ
RUSTLE

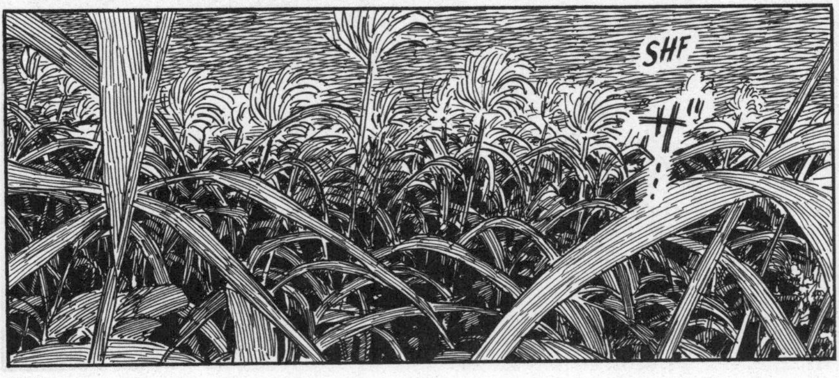
SHF
ザ

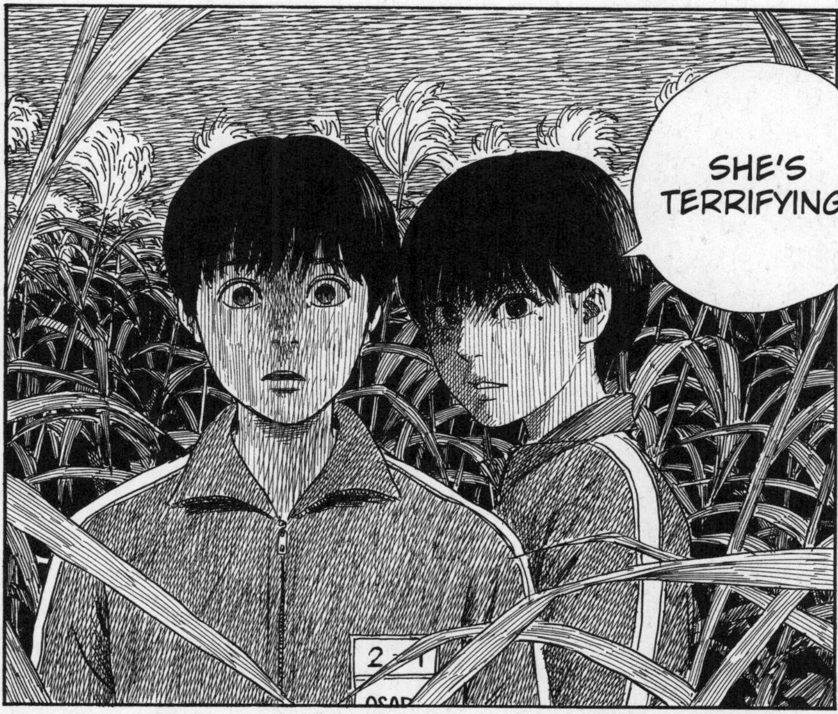
SHE'S TERRIFYING.
2-1

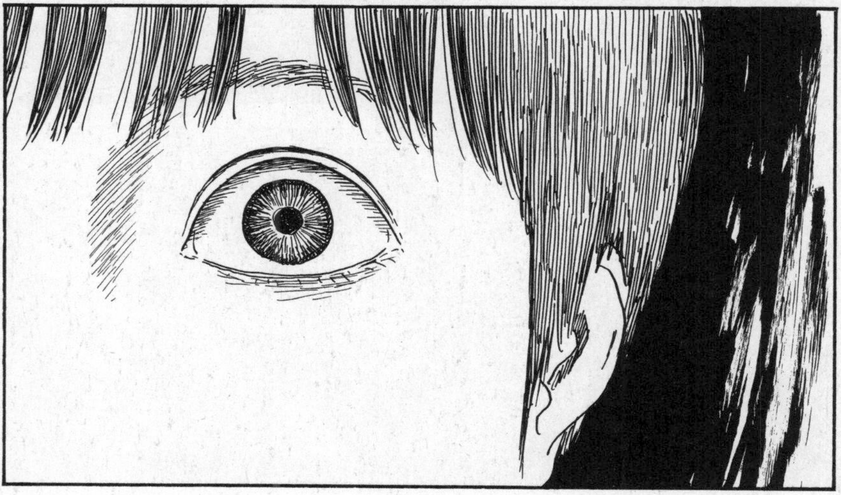

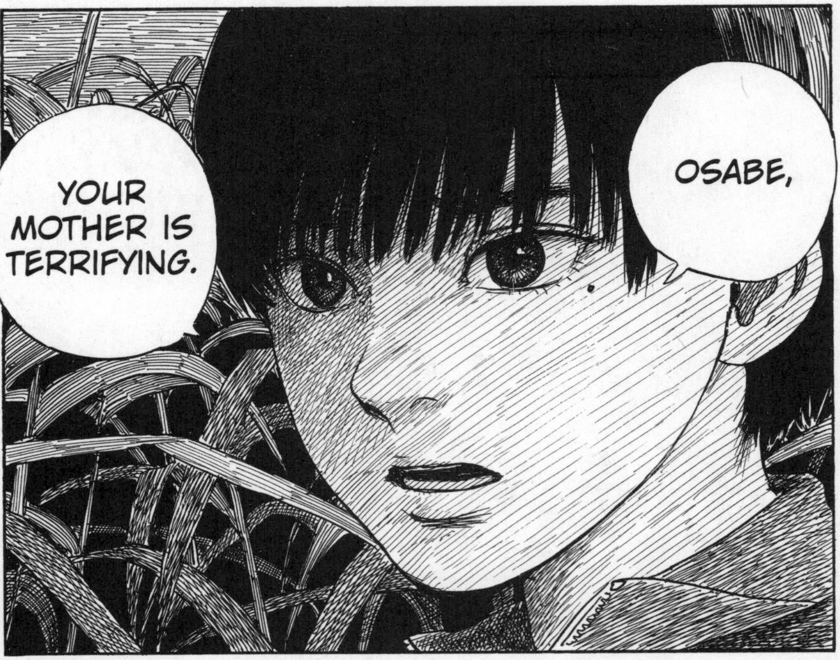
OSABE,
YOUR MOTHER IS TERRIFYING.

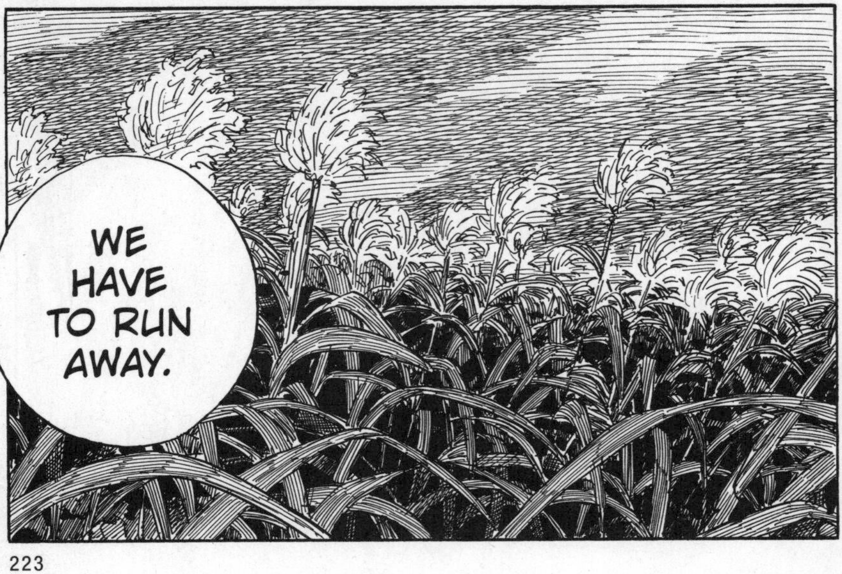
WE HAVE TO RUN AWAY.

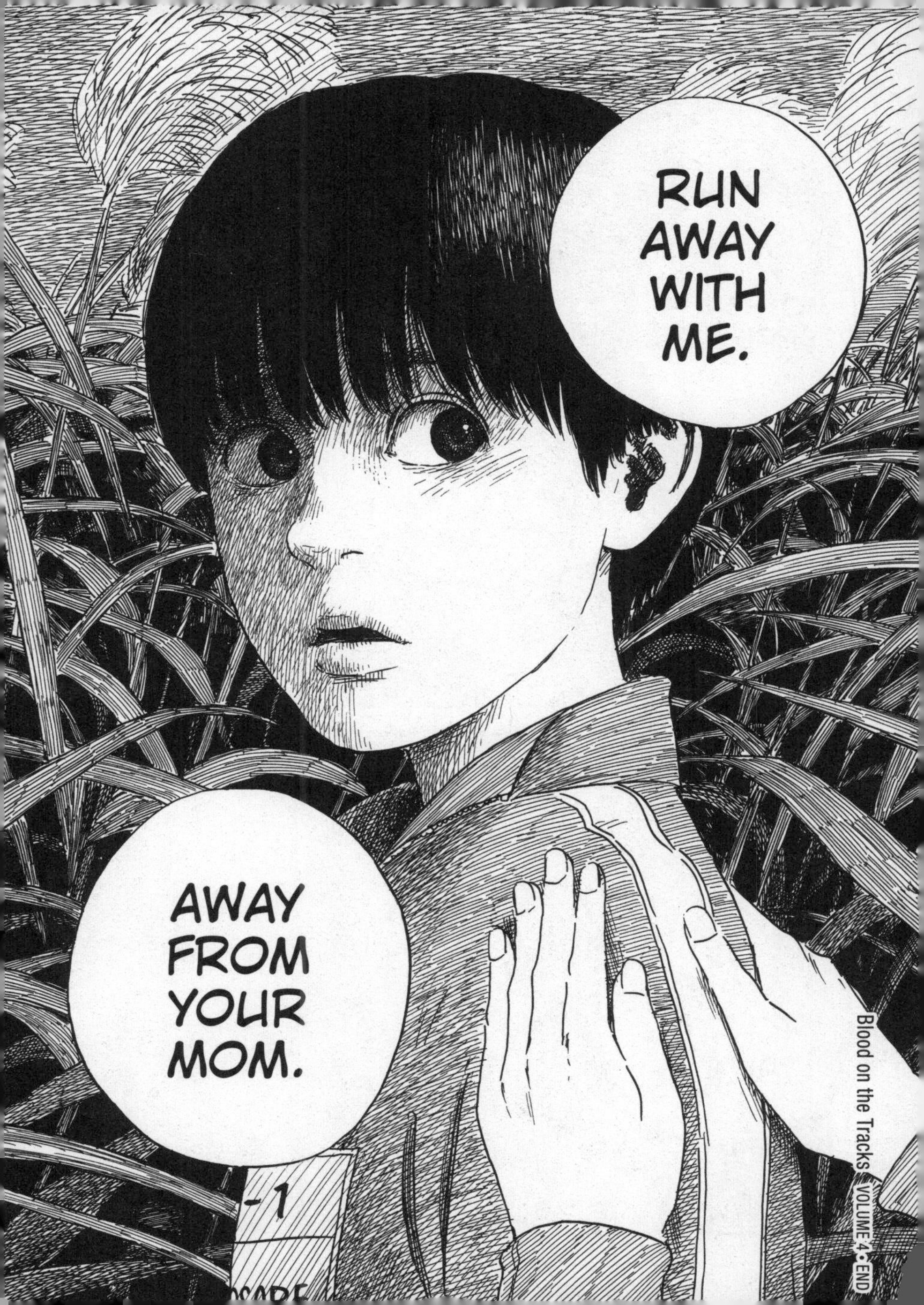
RUN AWAY WITH ME.
AWAY FROM YOUR MOM.
Blood on the Tracks VOLUME 4 • END

PHOTOGRAPHS

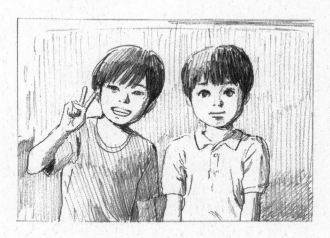

1986 /8/15 - 8/17
Family trip to the shore at Oarai

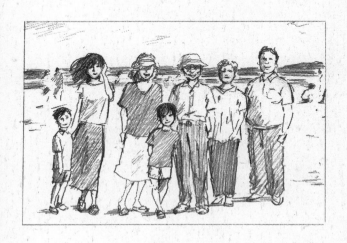

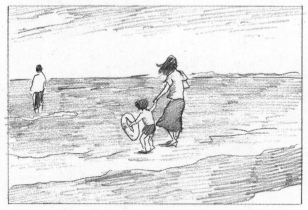

Sei's first time at the beach

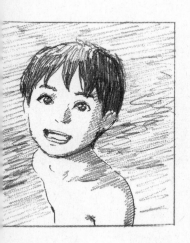

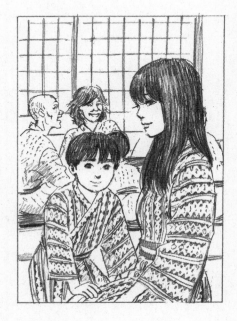

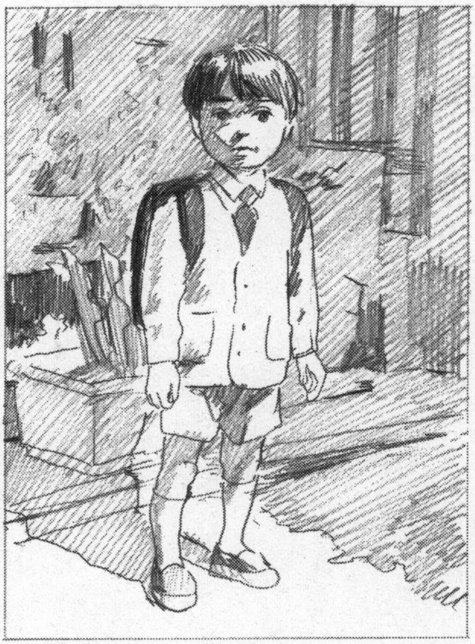

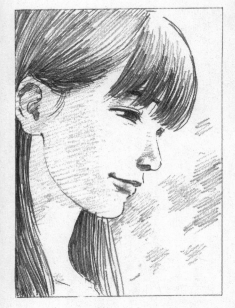

Elementary school entrance ceremony 1987/4/8

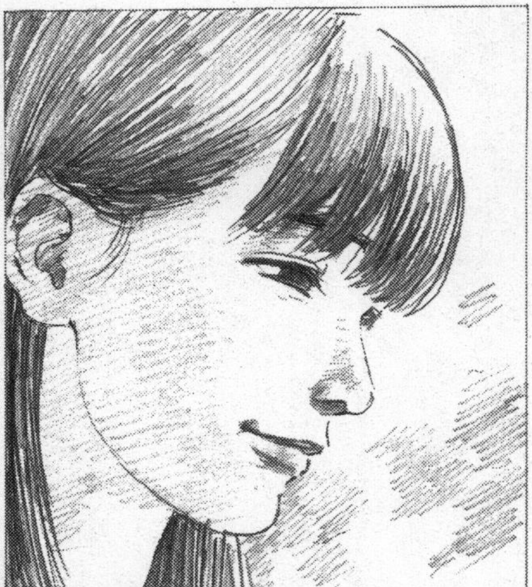

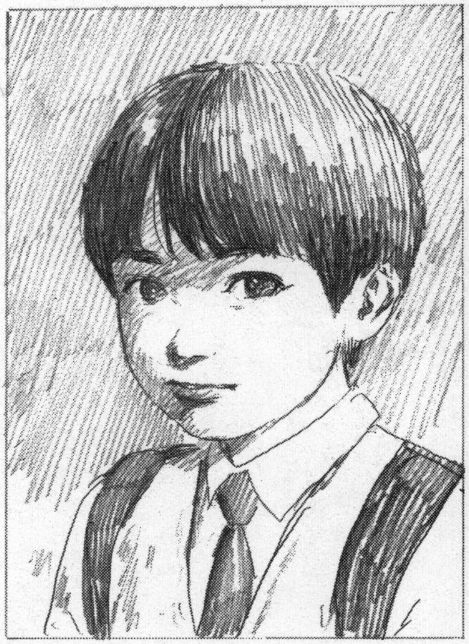

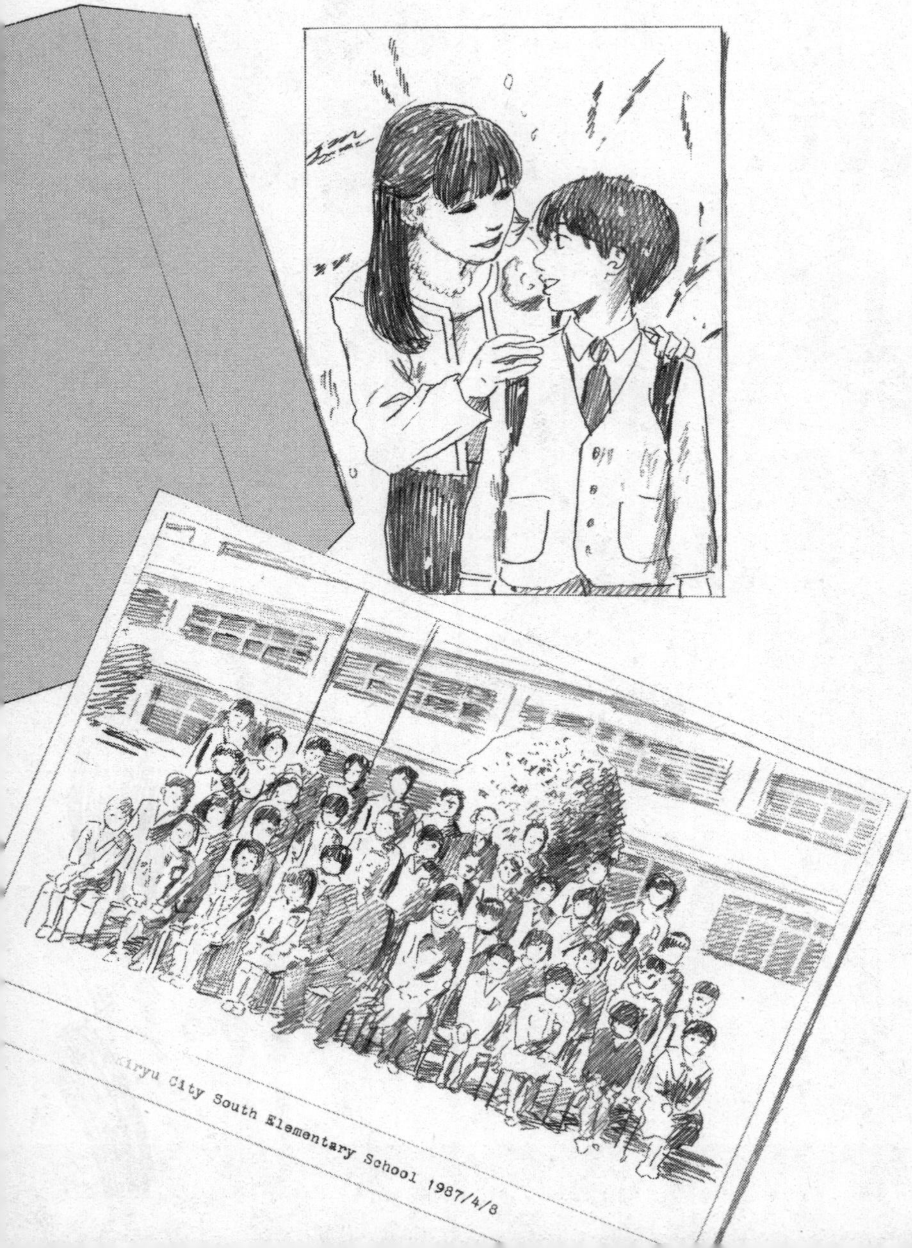
Kiryu City South Elementary School 1987/4/8

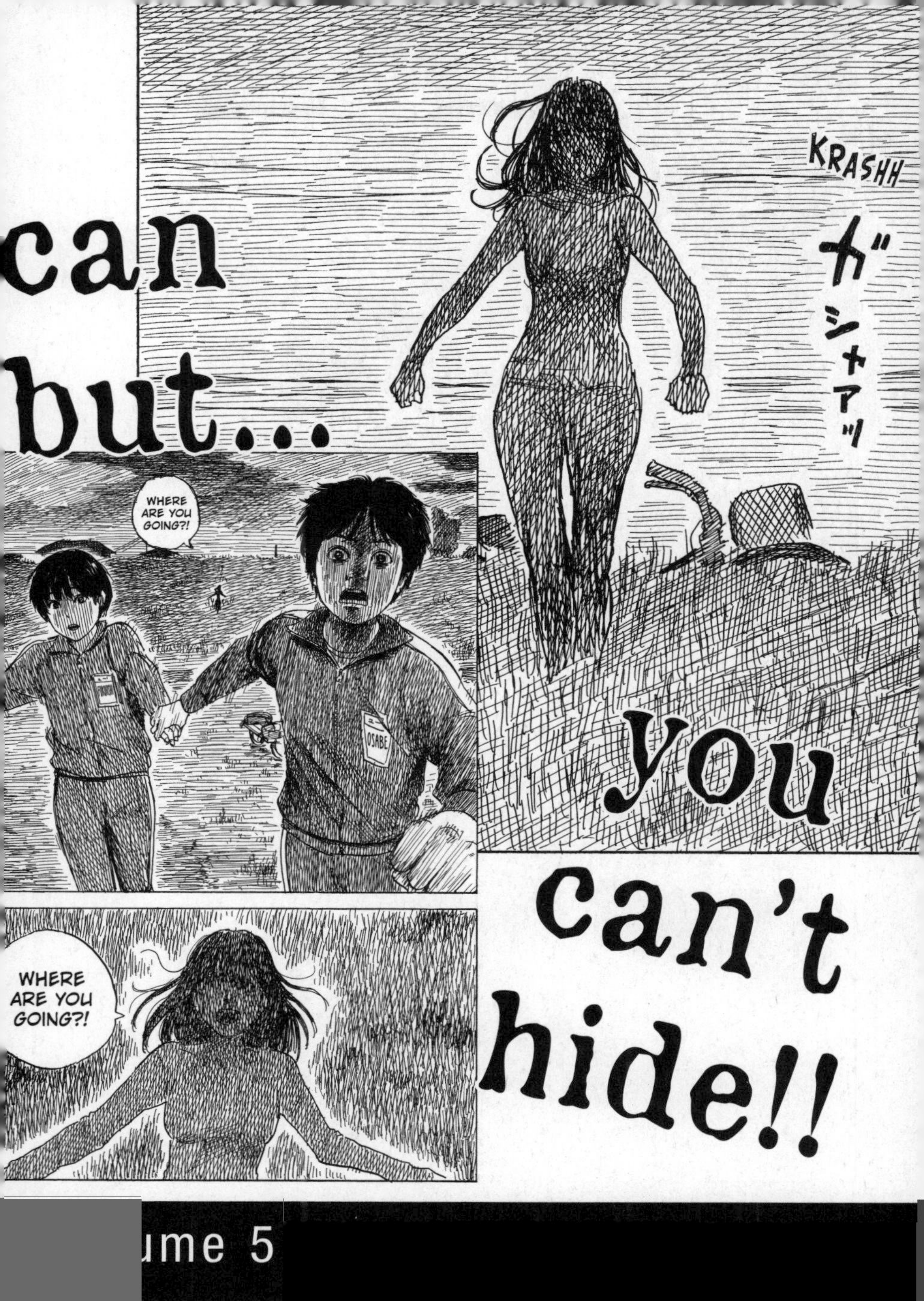
can
but...
KRASHH
ガシャアッ
WHERE ARE YOU GOING?!
WHERE ARE YOU GOING?!
you
can't
hide!!
ume 5

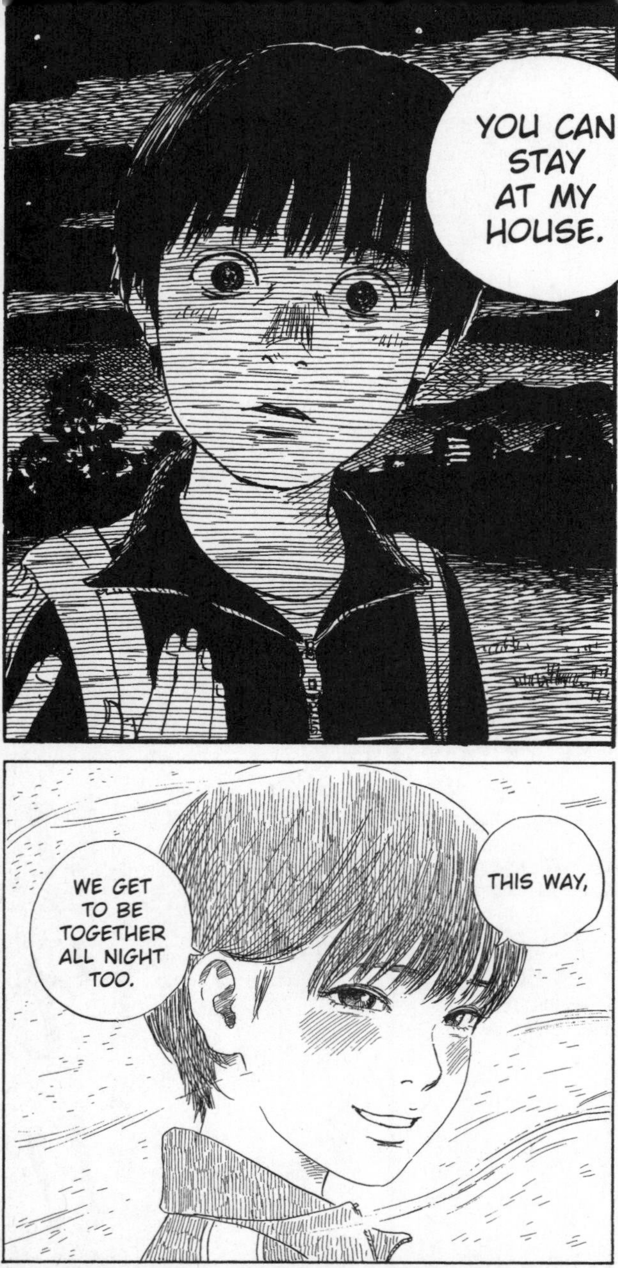
YOU CAN STAY AT MY HOUSE.
THIS WAY,
WE GET TO BE TOGETHER ALL NIGHT TOO.

You run

Blood on the Tracks 4
A Vertical Comics Edition

Editor: Daniel Joseph
Translation: Daniel Komen
Production: Risa Cho
                  Evan Hayden

CHI NO WADACHI 4
by Shuzo OSHIMI

© 2017 Shuzo OSHIMI
All rights reserved.
Original Japanese edition published by SHOGAKUKAN.
English translation rights in the United States of America and Canada
arranged with SHOGAKUKAN through Tuttle-Mori Agency, Inc.

Translation provided by Vertical Comics, 2021
Published by Vertical Comics, an imprint of Kodansha USA Publishing, LLC, New York

Originally published in Japanese as *Chi no Wadachi 4* by Shogakukan, 2018
Chi no Wadachi serialized in *Big Comic Superior*, Shogakukan, 2017-

This is a work of fiction.

ISBN: 978-1-949980-79-0

Manufactured in the United States of America

First Edition

Third Printing

Kodansha USA Publishing, LLC
451 Park Avenue South
7th Floor
New York, NY 10016
www.kodansha.us

Vertical books are distributed through Penguin-Random House Publisher Services.